Religion, Women of Color, and the Suffrage Movement

Feminist Studies and Sacred Texts Series

Series Editor: Susanne Scholz (sscholz@mail.smu.edu)

Advisory Board
Naomi Appleton, Tamara Cohn Eskenazi, Lynn Huber, Sa'diyya Shaikh, and Sharada Sugirtharajah

Feminist Studies and Sacred Texts makes available innovative and provocative research on the interface of feminist studies and sacred texts. Books in the series are grounded in religious studies perspectives, theories, and methodologies, while engaging with the wide spectrum of feminist studies, including women's studies, gender studies, sexuality studies, masculinity studies, and queer studies. They embrace intersectional discourses such as postcolonialism, ecology, disability, class, race, and ethnicity studies. Furthermore, they are inclusive of religious texts from both established and new religious traditions and movements, and they experiment with inter- and cross-religious perspectives. The series publishes monographs and edited collections that critically locate feminist studies and sacred texts within the historical, cultural, sociological, anthropological, comparative, political, and religious contexts in which they were produced, read, and continue to shape present practices and discourses.

Titles in Series

Religion, Women of Color, and the Suffrage Movement: The Journey to Holistic Freedom, Edited by SimonMary Asese A. Aihiokhai

Contested Masculinities: Polysemy and Gender in 1 Thessalonians, by Robert Stegmann

Minoritized Women Reading Race and Ethnicity: Intersectional Approaches and Early Christian (Con)Texts, Edited by Mitzi J. Smith and Jin Young Choi

Rape Culture and Religious Studies: Critical and Pedagogical Engagements, Edited by Rhiannon Graybill, Beatrice Lawrence, and Meredith Minister

Jewish Feminism: Framed and Reframed, by Esther Fuchs

Feminist Theory and the Bible: Interrogating the Sources, by Esther Fuchs

Unraveling and Reweaving Sacred Canon in Africana Womanhood, Edited by Rosetta E. Ross and Rose Mary Amenga-Etego

Religion, Women of Color, and the Suffrage Movement

The Journey to Holistic Freedom

Edited by
SimonMary Asese A. Aihiokhai

LEXINGTON BOOKS
Lanham • Boulder • New York • London

Published by Lexington Books
An imprint of The Rowman & Littlefield Publishing Group, Inc.
4501 Forbes Boulevard, Suite 200, Lanham, Maryland 20706
www.rowman.com

86-90 Paul Street, London EC2A 4NE

Copyright © 2022 by The Rowman & Littlefield Publishing Group, Inc.

All rights reserved. No part of this book may be reproduced in any form or by any electronic or mechanical means, including information storage and retrieval systems, without written permission from the publisher, except by a reviewer who may quote passages in a review.

British Library Cataloguing in Publication Information Available

Library of Congress Cataloging-in-Publication Data

Names: Aihiokhai, SimonMary Asese A., editor.
Title: Religion, women of color, and the suffrage movement : the journey to holistic freedom / edited by SimonMary Asese A. Aihiokhai.
Description: Lanham : Lexington Books, [2022] | Series: Feminist studies and sacred texts | Includes bibliographical references and index. | Summary: "This edited collection focuses on the uncelebrated insights and perspectives of women of color in a world where systemic discrimination persists. It articulates new strategies and paradigms for recognizing their contributions to the broader struggles for freedom and equity of women in our world"—Provided by publisher.
Identifiers: LCCN 2022026097 (print) | LCCN 2022026098 (ebook) | ISBN 9781793627698 (cloth) | ISBN 9781793627711 (paperback) | ISBN 9781793627704 (ebook)
Subjects: LCSH: Suffrage—Religious aspects—Christianity. | Minority women—Suffrage.
Classification: LCC BT738.15 .R45 2022 (print) | LCC BT738.15 (ebook) | DDC 261.7—dc23/eng/20220718
LC record available at https://lccn.loc.gov/2022026097
LC ebook record available at https://lccn.loc.gov/2022026098

Contents

Acknowledgments   vii

The Significance of the Nineteenth Amendment for Theology and Religion: An Introduction   ix
SimonMary Asese A. Aihiokhai

PART 1: STRUGGLES FOR FREEDOM FROM THE MARGINS   1

1. Black Women and Suffrage: A History of Political Freedom and Race in the United States   3
Christin Lee Hancock

2. National Association of Colored Women's Clubs and the Fight for Freedom   17
Anita R. Gooding

3. Struggles from the Margins, Advocacy at Intersections: Muslim Women's Advocacy in Europe, Canada, and the United States   33
Lara-Zuzan Golesorkhi

4. Oppression, Resistance, and Reform: Revisiting the Catholic Discussion on Women's Ordination   53
Carol J. Dempsey, OP

PART 2: UNDOING DUALISM: TOWARD AN ANTHROPOLOGY OF WHOLENESS   83

5. The Evolution of Male and Female Anthropology: Accommodation, Resistance, and Transformation   85
Christina Astorga

Contents

6 Does Christian Catechesis Have a Gender Problem?:
Toward a Catechesis of Wholeness   107
Valerie D. Lewis-Mosley

7 Gender, Race, God: A Case for a Pragmatic
Theological Anthropology   129
Anthonia Bolanle Ojo

8 Recovering an Ecologically Embodied Humanity:
Insights from Native American Women's Experiences   155
Lisa Ann Dellinger

PART 3: TOWARD A HERMENEUTIC OF LIBERATION   173

9 The Human Person as a Polyphonic Being: Giving Voice
to the Experiences of Black Women   175
SimonMary Asese A. Aihiokhai

10 Religion, African American Women, and the Suffrage
Movement: The Journey to Holistic Freedom   197
Kathleen Dorsey Bellow

11 Deep Down in My Soul: Black Women and the Spirituality of
Freedom: Reading the Signs of the Times   211
C. Vanessa White

12 A Theology of Women's Rights: Bridge-Building between
Individual Rights and Communal Rights—Insights from Africa   231
Okechukwu Camillus Njoku

PART 4: TOWARD PEDAGOGIES OF WHOLENESS   245

13 Toward the Flourishing of Women of Color through the
Lens of Intersectionality and Neuropsychology   247
Sarina Saturn

14 Defining the Contours of Pedagogies for Holistic Anthropologies   263
Dawn Michele Whitehead

15 Discursive Interventions toward Gender Justice:
The Academic Study of the Bible in the Neoliberal Age   279
Susanne Scholz

16 Slouching, together, after Pentecost: Toward a Post-traumatic
Pedagogy of (De)formation, Discomfort, and Difference   303
Brandy Daniels

Index   325

About the Contributors   327

Acknowledgments

It is truly a delight to celebrate this moment in our global history. In 2020, the United States of America celebrated the centenary of the passing of the Nineteenth Amendment to its Constitution. It was all about embracing the rainbow realities that define the country's social life. Though the country has not always lived by its ideals as stated in the opening lines of the Constitution—"We the people . . ."—some citizens have always stood up to call everyone prophetically to embrace the benefits of radical inclusivity. This embrace of the prophetic is what has shaped the vision of this anthology. In 2019, while having a conversation with my now-deceased father on the history behind the struggle for freedom and the right to vote by our Nigerian ancestors who fought for the end of British colonial rule in Nigeria, our conversation went beyond that and included the history of the civil rights movement in the United States. As is the wise approach of my father, he advised that I work on an anthology that celebrates the experiences of women, especially women of color in my adopted home, the United States. Though my father, Samson A. Aihiokhai, is not alive today to celebrate the vision that he gave birth in me, I dedicate and express my profound gratitude to him and my mother, Philomena T. Aihiokhai, for their radical embrace of inclusivity in all that they do and are. May this anthology immortalize Samson's memory and give credence to his and my mother's hard work for being agents of positive change in our world.

As the editor of this work, I am grateful to the contributors who worked diligently on the respective topics they explored in the chapters contained in it. Their insightfulness, creative thinking, prophetic witness, and love of knowledge are showcased in the pages of this anthology.

Gratitude also goes to Trevor F. Crowell and Jasper Mislak at Lexington Press for working closely with me on making sure that this work gets to the final stage. I cannot forget to express my gratitude to the many peer reviewers who diligently read the chapters and offered their insights to the contributors in order to make the final work what it is.

This work is possible because of all women in general, especially women of color, whose experiences have shaped and motivated the contributors to share their insights in their respective chapters. I cannot forget the exemplary witness to women's strength and talents in the life of my sister, Barrister Francisca O. Aihiokhai. You have and continue to teach me the radical truth that a world that does not celebrate the experiences of women is not one worth living in.

As you read this work, pause to acknowledge all the women in your lives who have helped form you to be the very best person you have become. A world without women at the table of life is a world that is defined by the trauma of death. May we all embrace the invitation to sit at the table of life where men, women, queer, nonbinary, and transpersons are accorded their rightful dignities.

SimonMary Asese A. Aihiokhai, PhD
April 24, 2022.

The Significance of the Nineteenth Amendment for Theology and Religion

An Introduction

SimonMary Asese A. Aihiokhai

Since the founding of the United States of America, one group after another has fought for their rights to be recognized by all. Beginning with African Americans, down to members of LGBTQIA+communities, the trauma of systemic discrimination continues to define the social psyche of the nation. It is already over one hundred years since the Nineteenth Amendment to the Constitution of the United States of America was adopted in 1920.[1] Though this amendment gave women the right to vote after a century-long political and grassroots struggle for it, one has to ask some critical questions, are all women in the country free? It took over four decades for Black women in America to be allowed to vote due to systemic discriminatory policies enacted and upheld by White-controlled political and governmental institutions. Even as the nation celebrates this historical moment in its history, one cannot ignore the fact that laws are being passed to disenfranchise minorities in the country. Issues of rights go beyond access to the electoral box. Today, the national conversation has to do with women's reproductive rights. Whether one is pro-life or pro-choice, the focus of the debate is reducible to the narrative on human dignity. How does the nation conceive of the dignity of its citizens? Are women accorded their rightful dignities as are men in the United States? Are women at the table of decision-making in all spheres of social, political, economic, and religious life in the country? Institutions of learning that ought to be exemplary communities for radical inclusivity are held captive by racial and gender biases that play out in the country. The same can be said of religious institutions.

Women are denied ordination into the ministerial priesthood in the Roman Catholic Church as well as in many, if not most, other religious institutions. One of the reasons for this exclusionary policy in the Roman Catholic tradition is that women are said to lack in their bodies what men have and that presumably makes them biologically and ontologically unable to represent the humanity of the incarnate Christ. This Roman Catholic position forces one to ask the question, what is the nature of this lack? Is it the fact that men, having a phallus, are ontologically oriented toward the humanity of the incarnate Christ? As I once asked a student of mine who thought it was a legitimate decision to exclude women from the priesthood, is soteriology dependent on having a phallus? Should the incarnate Christ be reduced to a phallus? Such paradoxes, and, at best, infantile biases against women go uncritiqued in the world and operate as though they are dogmatic truths to be embraced for all times. This anthology thus wrestles with these and related questions, some of them contextualized in Roman Catholic thought. Since some contributions to this anthology directly engage the Roman Catholic Church's tradition, it is proper to offer a brief critique on the male-only priesthood advocated by the Church's magisterium.

A CRITIQUE OF THE ROMAN CATHOLIC ARGUMENT ON MALE-ONLY PRIESTHOOD

Human imagination is always contextually conditioned. The images we have of ourselves are not abstract but come from our sociocultural locations. Even our language of the divine reveals something about our subconscious biases that are deeply rooted in the sociopolitical systems that form us. As noted by the theologian, Tina Beattie, "The idea of God as father figure modelled along the lines of patriarchal authority came to prominence in Christian theology after the conversion of Rome, when the social and sexual hierarchies of the ancient world began to pervade Christian ideas and institutions in a more thorough way than before."[2] These sexual and social hierarchies, especially in Roman society of antiquity, were radically oriented toward patriarchy. Quoting Jürgen Moltmann, who argues that "Romanisation of the image of God . . . involved transferring the Roman *patria potestas* to God," Beattie also states that "after the fourth century God becomes identified with a more domineering and authoritarian image of fatherhood."[3]

It is not surprising that Christian bias toward a particular form of social hierarchy within the context of family life where the man, as the father, is seen as the head of the family is still the norm. Before the argument is made that family is different from society, I posit the following, Christian anthropology has a bias toward family as the basic structure of social life. Thus, if the basic structure of social life is infused with a particular bias toward male hierarchy over a female, the logical conclusion is to prefer social systems in which men are at the center of power. The Roman Catholic Church's bias toward the exclusion of women in ministerial priesthood is couched in this type of social hierarchy. For instance, the following argument is made in the *Catechism of the Catholic Church*:

> The Lord Jesus chose men (*viri*) to form the college of the twelve apostles, and the apostles did the same when they chose collaborators to succeed them in their ministry. The college of bishops, with whom the priests are united in the priesthood, makes the college of the twelve an ever-present and ever-active reality until Christ's return. The Church recognizes herself to be bound by this choice made by the Lord himself. For this reason the ordination of women is not possible.[4]

The Roman Catholic Church's insistence on an exclusively male leadership model is obvious in this quote. However, the Church's argument is problematic for the following reasons, which do not directly address arguments related to the Nineteenth Amendment but contribute to the validity of the argument that women are, and ought to be, equal in all aspects of human society everywhere, including in the Roman Catholic Church.

First, the ministry of the ordained priesthood is linked to the new humanity in Christ that humanity has been gifted with through the meritorious actions of the God-human. Even the scholastic argument of a priest being an *altar Christus* (another Christ), who stands in the place of Christ and performs the ministerial duties in and through Christ (*in persona Christi*), that was appropriated by the Second Vatican Council in the conciliar document, *Presbyterorum Ordinis,* needs to be critiqued. If only men can participate fully in the ministerial priesthood of Christ, then Christ's salvific mission in reorienting our humanity toward that of the God-human is itself insufficient. The God-human reality is itself open to all of creation, and so women are not excluded from it. Priesthood ought thus to be understood as existing within the soteriological vision of Christ's humanity that all Christians participate in by virtue of their sacramental baptism. Consequently, soteriology must be understood as radically inclusive and not exclusive.

Second, Roman Catholic ministry does not originate solely from the social interactions of Jesus during his earthly life. Rather, ordination emerges from the mission received in the post-resurrection mandate. Who is sent? All are sent by the risen Christ to be witnesses to the Good News. However, in the New Testament, the first human to receive this mandate is a woman and not a man. The Gospels report that Mary of Magdala encountered the risen Christ and was sent by Christ to his followers to proclaim the resurrection message, a message that is at the heart of the priestly vocation, that Christ is risen and has overcome death (Jn. 20:11-19).[5] The exclusion of women from this ritual because of the argument of tradition ignores the fact that tradition is located within the boundaries of culture. One sees this dilemma play out in the Church of Corinth, according to 1 Corinthians 11:1-16. A culturally diverse faith community experienced the challenges of cultural differences. To help address the tensions, the community asks Paul to help them deal with these concerns. What did Paul do? He appealed to the cultural and religious biases against women.

The exclusion of women in social life is a problem not only in Christianity but also deeply rooted in culture. Often, culture is presented as a dogmatic tool for diminishing the rights of women in society. Peggy Levitt and Sally Engle Merry call attention to the enduring narrative of culture as sacrosanct, not to be diminished by an insistence on the rights of women in society. They explain:

> Many of the stories about the opposition of culture and rights have a gendered subtext. They typically zero in on women as the quintessential innocent victims of culture. Many of the examples where human rights challenge what are defined as oppressive cultural practices concern women . . . The response to critiques of these forms of injury is often that these are parts of culture and must be preserved, although such arguments are often made by political leaders or lineage heads rather than the women themselves. As passive and vulnerable persons, women need to be rescued by a muscular human rights or humanitarianism or even by a masculinist state.[6]

Culture is humanly constructed and embodies social biases present in a society. A critique of culture ought to allow for a new way of imagining human beings in their societal roles. This includes the experiences and roles of women in any given society.

A BRIEF CRITIQUE OF UNITED STATES OF AMERICA'S CULTURAL BIASES AGAINST WOMEN

Even the United States of America, which prides itself as the citadel of freedom in the world, is not free from the habits and practices of exclusion that define women solely as objects and not as persons to be appreciated for their innate dignities. The struggle for liberation of women in the United States of America, especially for women of color, is ongoing. In a society in which individualism is the mantra of social existence and marker of personal success, the liberation of women, and the affirmation of women's dignities cannot be done within a framework of individualism. Rather, a new way of seeing oneself as socially connected is crucial. Women, especially women of color, have always understood this fact of our collective humanity. It is no wonder then that in the late nineteenth century, Black women, in racially segregated America, formed the Black Women Club Movement serving as "a socioreligious movement against race-gender-class oppression. It was a social movement because through it black women created a milieu in which they were empowered to reinterpret the dominant racial, sexual, and class ideologies which oppressed them as women, while providing programs that addressed the oppression of black people."[7] This organization consisted of a progressive group of Black women who worked toward creating inclusive spaces for Black women in racially segregated American society.[8] A most important statement about this socioreligious movement of Black women appears in the vision statement of the organization. As stated in the motto of the National Association of Colored Women, Black women saw themselves as defined by the mandate of "Lifting as we Climb."[9] As noted by Marcia Riggs, this motto "reflected the black women's understanding of the interconnectedness and interrelatedness of Blacks as a group."[10] Yet the focus of this group was not limited to the advancement of Black women only but also included Black men. Thus, while race shaped the dominant narrative of women's liberation in the country, Black women saw the need to build a coalition that transcended divisive social structures. Riggs captures this strategic positionality of Black women when she elaborates on the goals of the Black Women Club Movement: "The women understood that in order to respond to their situation they needed to be flexible, holding in tension the specific aims of racial elevation, ameliorating gender and class oppression, and the comprehensive reform of society for the good of all citizens."[11] In other words, Black women have recognized for a long time that the needed literary approach must be grounded in female and male solidarity to fight political, cultural, and epistemic structures of women's oppression. The stance of Black women in the struggle for the collective liberation of all who are held down by structures of segregation is a prophetic witness to all women, especially White women in the United States, who do not always uphold this stance of radical solidarity as evidenced in the racialization of the Women Suffrage Movement of the early twentieth century.

Solidarity speaks to a particular way of embracing human social identities. It demands of all persons an intentional response to contribute to the flourishing of all persons without the unethical desire to take advantage of others. In the spirit of solidarity, Alexander Crummell offered his insightful speech in 1883 on the plight of Black women in the southern part of the United States. In a work titled, "The Black Woman of the South: Her Neglects and Her Needs, 1883," Crummell argued:

> If you want the civilization of a people to reach the very best elements of their being, and then, having reached them, there to abide as an indigenous principle, you must imbue the *womanhood* of that people with all its elements and qualities. Any movement which passes by the female sex is an ephemeral thing. Without them, no true nationality, patriotism, religion, cultivation, family life, or true social status is a possibility.[12]

Although this statement may sound essentializing to contemporary readers, Crummell recognized the cultural significance and political necessity of women's liberation in society and religion already in 1883.

WHY THIS ANTHOLOGY?

In today's United States of America, politicians are slowly chipping away at the rights of female and male citizens to vote. State legislators pass restrictive voting laws to give advantage to the governing party over the other party. In the spirit of solidarity, the struggles of women in the country that led to the passing of the Nineteenth Amendment ought to be centered in the national psyche and historical consciousness of the nation. This anthology contributes to this effort. Also, it is not enough to celebrate the right of women to vote in the United States. One also has to highlight the effort made by women of color in the struggle. In a racialized country like the United States, it is often the case to erase persons of color in the narratives of victory that speak to the progress of society. This anthology attempts to retrieve hidden memories of history to allow for the breadth of the contribution of women of color to the complex struggle for women's rights in society.

This anthology makes a deliberate effort to articulate a polyphonic narrative that sheds light on the tapestry of women's experiences even beyond the national borders of the United States. Hence, experiences of Muslim women migrants as they struggle for legal and social recognition in Europe and English-speaking parts of North America; African women and their struggles against patriarchy; the desires of members of LGBTQIA+communities to be accepted both in society and in religious communities; the psychological skills needed to empower and accompany BIPOC women in racialized societies; and the need for impactful pedagogies relevant for women of color's success are topics addressed squarely in this anthology.

Furthermore, this anthology makes an attempt to encourage dialogues of life that will help to dismantle structures of erasure that diminish the dignities of women in the world. To do this effectively, the contributors make a deliberate effort to deconstruct old systems of meaning and open up new horizons that allow for the birthing of healthy ways of fostering inclusive communities.

CONTENT OF THIS ANTHOLOGY

This anthology celebrates the tapestry of experiences that define the lives of women of all ethnic, religious, and cultural backgrounds and identities. It also celebrates the contributions of women of color to the Woman Suffrage Movement that led to the eventual passing of the Nineteenth Amendment. The anthology is divided into four parts. Part One, entitled "Struggles for Freedom from the Margins," sheds light on the struggles for freedom from the margins by women of color in their effort to gain political and social recognition in the United States. Four chapters appear under the first part of the anthology.

In chapter 1, Christin Hancock provides a historical analysis of the struggle for the right to vote by Black, Indigenous, and other women of color in the United States. Entitled "Black Women and Suffrage: A History of Political Freedom and Race in the United States," the essay centers on the roles, stories, and strategies of Black women in the struggle for women's rights to vote in the United States of America. Hancock uses her own agency as a White woman historian to amplify the voices of Black women, including both historians and civil rights activists, to feature Black women as agents in their social and political forms of resistance against structural systems of oppression.

In chapter 2, entitled "National Association of Colored Women Clubs and the Fight for Freedom," Anita Gooding examines the contributions of African American Club women to the sociopolitical advancement of the Black community in the late nineteenth and early twentieth century. Gooding explains how Black women constructed a sociopolitical identity to help articulate participatory agency in America's political life, how relationships with other Black women provided healing and hope, and how they envisioned freedom for African American women in America's public life.

In chapter 3, entitled "Struggles from the Margins, Advocacy at Intersections: Muslim Women's Advocacy in Europe, Canada, and the United States," Lara-Zuzan Golesorkhi explores various forms and spaces of Muslim women's advocacy in Europe, Canada, and the United States. Through the analysis of case studies, Golesorkhi examines how Muslim women mobilize, organize, and communicate their advocacy in pursuit of freedom. She stresses how these advocacy strategies and methods reflect struggles from the margins that are inherently intersectional.

In chapter 4, entitled "Oppression, Resistance, and Reform: Revisiting the Catholic Discussion on Women's Ordination," Carol J. Dempsey, OP critiques four documents that the Roman Catholic Church uses to argue against women's ordination to the priesthood. Dempsey not only examines how Church documents weaponize the Bible but also sheds light on four strategies with which Church officials keep women from participating in ecclesial ministries reserved currently for ordained men only. The chapter calls for gender equity and an end to the embrace of male hegemonic power that marginalizes Roman Catholic women. The chapter also showcases two prominent examples of resistance to give hope, support, and a challenge to women desiring priestly ordination in the Roman Catholic Church.

Part Two, entitled "Undoing Dualism: Toward an Anthropology of Wholeness," articulates holistic anthropology that removes exclusionary labels speaking of the human person to diminish the surplus ways human identities play out in the world. All four chapters in this part of the anthology articulate inclusive anthropologies delegitimizing patriarchy, whether found in cultures, epistemologies, philosophies, religious traditions, or sociopolitical systems.

In chapter 5, entitled "The Evolution of Male and Female Anthropology Accommodation, Resistance, and Transformation," Christina Astorga sheds light on the evolution of male and female anthropology, particularly from the perspective of the Western cultural and intellectual tradition. The chapter shows that the dualistic view of female and male has shaped Western cultural and religious practices. The essay questions how the gender binary was instituted in Hellenistic culture in the first century CE, how early Christianity attempted to disrupt it, and how contemporary feminist theology resists this binary in various ways. Astorga proposes a new anthropological model that is premised on gender fluidity, offering to transform gender relationships for both male and female.

In chapter 6, entitled "Does Christian Catechesis Have a Gender Problem? Toward A Catechesis of Wholeness," Valerie Lewis-Mosley probes deeply into the theology inherent in Christian catechesis to showcase vestiges of religious patriarchy and systemic erasure of Black experiences, especially those of Black women. The theological principle of *lex credendi lex vivendi* (the law of believing is the law of living) explores critically what Christian theology teaches and embraces in its liturgical praxis. The chapter makes a case for Black existential experience to be a necessary aspect of doing catechesis in the ecclesial tradition of the Roman Catholic Church.

In chapter 7, entitled "Gender, Race, God: A Case for a Pragmatic Theological Anthropology," Anthonia Bolanle Ojo, SSMA, appropriates the theological insight that humans are created in the image and likeness of God to argue for an inclusive anthropology. The essay focuses on the sociocultural experiences of women, most especially in Africa, and the dynamics and effects of racism on society. Offering ideas for the articulation of a pragmatic anthropology of dependence and relationality, the essay also provides the necessary orientation for an inclusive theological discourse.

In chapter 8, entitled "Recovering an Ecologically Embodied Humanity: Insights from Native American Women's Experiences," Lisa Dellinger asks an important question that society cannot ignore any longer: How do dualistic anthropologies perpetuate ecological violence? To address this question, Dellinger turns to insights from Native American thought, especially insights from Native American women. The chapter unpacks the scarcity of imagination that White colonizing intellectualism represents, having led to past and present exploitation of resources and people. A turn to ecology as the place for birthing-forth an anthropology of surplus offers an escape from exploitative cultures currently doing harm in the world. Dellinger maintains that this turn can best be achieved by engaging honestly with the intellectual traditions and existential memories of Indigenous Peoples and Cultures.

Part Three of this anthology, entitled "Toward a Hermeneutic of Liberation," explains the content and implications of a hermeneutic of liberation that speaks to the experiences of women, especially women of color. The works under this section of the anthology shed light on the paradoxes and contradictions inherent in the so-called "traditional" models of liberation that often serve as tools for erasing women's voices, especially those of women of color, from the broader discourses of society. Four essays appear in this part of the anthology.

In chapter 9, entitled "The Human Person as a Polyphonic Being: Giving Voice to the Experiences of Black Women," SimonMary Asese A. Aihiokhai argues for the relevance of polyphonic identities when we speak of realities shaping the experiences and a sense of self by women of color, especially African and African American women. Appropriating insights from different religious traditions, such as Christianity or African Religion, along with existentialist philosophical thoughts within Western and African intellectual traditions and cultures, Aihiokhai articulates the contours of an inclusive anthropology that affirms and celebrates the dignities of African and African American women in today's world.

As the United States of America celebrates the centenary of women's suffrage, this is the time to reflect on the future. In chapter 10, entitled "Religion, African American Women, and the Suffrage Movement: The Journey to Holistic Freedom," Kathleen Dorsey Bellow observes that "true truth" of the Woman-Suffrage Movement in the United States confirms the durability of White supremacy in the nation's ongoing struggle to live up to its reputation as a democratic country. Bellow focuses on the untold commitment of nineteenth and twentieth-century African American suffragists who persevered, despite antiblack racism, the betrayal by the White leaders of the Movement, and the constant disappointments in every fight for social change. Relying on their religious heritage, Black women and voting-rights activists fought for universal enfranchisement as a right and responsibility of every citizen. Their courageous relentlessness inspires today's generations of Black women suffragists and many others in the struggle for fair and equal election rights for every citizen of the United States.

In chapter 11, entitled "Deep Down in My Soul: Black Women and the Spirituality of Freedom: Reading the Signs of the Times," C. Vanessa White looks at characteristics of Black women's spirituality of freedom that have sustained Black women and provided hope to the community from the time of enslavement through the suffragette and civil-rights movements to today's Black-Lives-Matter Movement, shaped and led by Black women. What has been characteristic of their spiritual strivings and strength? What biblical texts have provided a source of hope? What insights can be gained from two central New Testament female characters, first, Mary, the strong mother of Jesus and a woman of color, and second, Mary Magdalene, a woman maligned over the centuries. How do they compare to strong Black women today, as they strive to say "yes" to their stories in the midst of oppression and struggle? What spiritual stories of Black women suffragettes, such as Hallie Quinn Brown, Ida B. Wells, Nanie Helen Burroughs, Sojourner Truth, Anna Julia Cooper, and Helen Quinn Brown, serve as models for women of color striving for freedom nowadays?

In chapter 12, entitled "Theology of Women's Rights: Bridge-Building between Individual Rights and Communal Rights—Insights from Africa," Okechukwu Camillus Njoku articulates a theology of women's rights to build bridges between individual and communal rights. In order to accomplish this task, he rethinks the Western Enlightenment construction of personhood. While appreciating the Enlightenment achievements that repositioned the individual as a subject of autonomy and rights, the essay also highlights how the Enlightenment mindset has long pitted claims of individuality against the claims of the community. Drawing on Trinitarian theology and Igbo African religious anthropological worldview, Njoku uses the category of relationality to articulate a theology of rights that keeps the seemingly paradoxical claims of individuality and community in creative tension.

Part Four of this anthology, "Toward Pedagogies of Wholeness," sheds light on those pedagogies that affirm holistic experiences of women, especially women of color. This essay upholds the claim that a singular pedagogical approach is insufficient to address the experiences of women. Pedagogies, showcased in this part of the anthology, open up new horizons for inquiry into social systems of erasure used to oppress women. Four essays fall under this part of the anthology.

In chapter 13, entitled "Toward the Flourishing of Women of Color through the Lens of Intersectionality and Neuropsychology," Sarina R. Saturn addresses the intersectionality of gender, class, spirituality, and mental health. She explains that an analysis of these connections supports women of color in the United States. Since women who experience multiple marginalities professionally and personally benefit from guidance and advocacy, this essay also describes effective and ineffective ways to offer beneficial mentorship.

The teaching of anthropology that is holistic in content and purpose demands strategic approaches. In chapter 14, entitled "Defining the Contours of Pedagogies for Holistic Anthropologies," Dawn Michele Whitehead asks how teaching ought to be done in a globalized classroom. Defining the contours of the pedagogies that are relevant to today's globalized classrooms, the essay also raises related questions about the roles of teachers and how their teaching will lead to a deep and impactful self-understanding within learners to help students formulate visions for shaping society. Whitehead maintains that this kind of radical and inclusive pedagogy is necessary for women to be accorded their rightful places in society.

With the rise of the Second Feminist Movement around the world, a considerable number of Bible scholars have read the Hebrew Bible and the New Testament with gender-hermeneutical concerns in mind since the 1970s. At the same time, neoliberal principles have come to permeate Western-capitalist societies. In chapter 15, entitled "Discursive Interventions toward Gender Justice: The Academic Study of the Bible in the Neoliberal Age," Susanne Scholz critically engages the following questions: Do feminist, womanist, and queer biblical readings represent only the latest assimilation of intellectual discourse into the political, economic, and social conditions of the neoliberal agenda or do gendered biblical approaches envision viable intellectual-exegetical alternatives to contemporary structures of domination? How shall we read the Bible in an era in which neoliberal principles morph increasingly into authoritarian practices, while economic-social precarity is shifting intellectual discourse, including in biblical studies, to the political right?

In chapter 16, entitled "Slouching, Together, after Pentecost. Toward a Post-traumatic Pedagogy of (De)formation, Discomfort, and Difference," Brandy Daniels uses Carmela Soprano's question as a starting point. The essay turns to William Butler Yeats' poem as both an interlocutor and a navigational guide, a compass, to explore the teaching of theology and religious studies and/at the intersections of gender, race, and sexuality (among other sites and forms of difference). Daniels maintains that discomfort and (de)formation are imperative for liberative pedagogies addressing and affirming differences in the contemporary sociopolitical context of the United States, resembling Yeats' early twentieth-century Irish milieu. Daniels asserts that this pedagogical approach ought to be practiced especially by teachers of religious studies and/or theology.

CONCLUDING COMMENTS

In the sixteen essays that offer a wide array of interdisciplinary perspectives, assessments, and visions about the experiences, insights, gifts, and aspirations of women, especially women of color within the global North and the global South, this anthology intends to restart a much-needed dialogue on the relevance of radical inclusivity of all persons and within all areas of society. Exclusion of women from this dialogue inhibits the opportunity of embracing a new horizon of life that ought to open up when all persons are valued and acknowledged for their inherent dignities. The fact that this anthology is intentionally interdisciplinary in nature allows for the celebration of women as persons who have diverse gifts and insights. To speak of woman is to give credence to a polyphony of life. Without this polyphonic reality, all of humanity will be conditioned by an anemia of imagination. It is time all the members of the human race heal themselves of this life-negating sickness.

In the contemporary United States and many parts of the world, including the continent of Africa, it is important that the rights of women in society are not reduced to moments of disruption where patriarchy still reigns supreme. History shows that in precolonial Africa, "matrilineal institutions united Africans and were more important than superficial differences. ... Women were the agriculturalists, and men were hunters. What made this system unique was the sanctity of the mother and her ultimate authority."[13] Unfortunately, for many Africans, the retrieval of this history has become difficult due to the traumas of colonialism. Colonialism has shaped and promoted an exclusionary narrative that presents women as persons who were historically never active in African societies. Although the centenary of the Nineteenth Amendment is about the right of women to vote in the United States, societies in Africa and beyond can benefit from this historical moment in the United States. Postcolonial African societies ought to retrieve their rich cultural heritage that allowed women to have leadership roles in religious and secular spaces.

The dignity of women cannot end only with women's constitutional right to vote. Women ought to be centered in leadership roles as well. Postcolonial Africa has a scarce imagination that prevents many societies from electing women as leaders. Only nine African women have served as presidents of their countries.[14] It is even worse in the United States. No woman has ever been elected president of the country. Why is this the case? What can be done to upend the current status quo of male-only presidents? It took over two hundred years for the United States to elect a female vice president in the person of Kamala Harris; thanks to the political astuteness of African American women, who, during the presidential campaign, rallied behind Joe Biden, and who, in turn, reciprocated the gesture of support by embracing Harris as his running-mate. Also, it has taken the political astuteness of African American women to help encourage President Joe Biden to nominate the first African American woman to the Supreme Court of the United States of America in the person of Justice Ketanji Brown Jackson. The demand for inclusivity in the political institutions of the nation has led

President Joe Biden to appoint the first African American person who also is the first openly LGBQIA+ individual as the White House press secretary in the person of Katrine Jean-Pierre. These steps toward building an inclusive nation cannot stop with these gestures. All aspects of national life ought to be radically inclusive.

I conclude the introduction to this anthology by stating the following; our world would have entered the much-needed space of progress when the news of a woman being a president of a nation; the head of the Roman Catholic Church; the head of the United Nations; and the head of major global and national institutions are received as the norm and a way of being in the world. Until that time arrives, all of humanity has some work to do. May this anthology be part of that much-needed work.

NOTES

1. "19th Amendment to the U.S. Constitution: Women's Right to Vote (1920)," *National Archives*, https://www.archives.gov/milestone-documents/19th-amendment.

2. Tina Beattie, *Woman* (London and New York: Continuum, 2003), 158.

3. Ibid.

4. *Catechism of the Catholic Church. Second Edition* (Vatican City: Libreria Editrice Vaticana, 1997), 394.

5. Biblical passages are taken from *The New American Bible. School and Church Edition* (Wichita, KS: Fireside Bible Publishers, 1998).

6. Peggy Levitt and Sally Engle Merry, "Making Women's Human Rights in the Vernacular: Navigating the Culture/Rights Divide," in *Gender and Culture at the Limit of Rights*, ed. Dorothy L. Hodgson (Philadelphia: University of Pennsylvania Press, 2011), 81–82.

7. Marcia Riggs, "What Do Nineteenth-Century Reformers Have to Say to Twentieth-Century Liberationists?," in *Womanist Theological Ethics: A Reader*, ed. Katie Geneva Cannon, Emilie M. Townes, and Angela D. Sims (Louisville, KY: Westminster John Knox Press, 2011), 23.

8. "Black Women's Club Movement," *Encyclopedia.com*, https://www.encyclopedia.com/history/encyclopedias-almanacs-transcripts-and-maps/black-womens-club-movement.

9. In 1896, the National Federation of Afro-American Women and the National League of Colored Women joined together to form the National Association of Colored Women to help address racial segregation. See "National Association of Colored Women," *Encyclopedia.com*, May 18, 2018, https://www.encyclopedia.com/history/biographies/korean-history-biographies/national-association-colored-women.

10. Riggs, "What Do Nineteenth-Century Reformers Have to Say to Twentieth-Century Liberationists?," 24.

11. Ibid., 25.

12. Alexander Crummell, "The Black Woman of the South: Her Neglects and Her Needs, 1883," in *The Modern African American Political Thought: Reader. From David Walker to Barack Obama*, ed. Angela Jones (New York and London: Routledge, 2013), 83.

13. Ifi Amadiume, *Reinventing Africa. Matriarchy, Religion and Culture* (London and New York: Zed Books Ltd, 1997), 161. It ought to be stated that even with this freedom of women in precolonial Africa, vestiges of patriarchy are found in that era because of how women were mainly defined by their societal roles as mothers.

14. Peter Pedroncelli, "9 Times A Female President Took Charge of An African Country," *The Moguldom Nation*, November 13, 2019, https://moguldom.com/239138/9-times-a-female-president-took-charge-of-an-african-country/#:~:text=These%20include%20Ellen%20Johnson%20Sirleaf%20of%20Liberia%2C%20who,an%20interim%20capacity%20at%20a%20time%20of%20need.

REFERENCES

"19th Amendment to the U.S. Constitution: Women's Right to Vote (1920)." *National Archives*. https://www.archives.gov/milestone-documents/19th-amendment.

Amadiume, Ifi. *Reinventing Africa: Matriarchy, Religion and Culture*. London and New York: Zed Books Ltd, 1997.

Beattie, Tina. *Woman*. London and New York: Continuum, 2003.

"Black Women's Club Movement." *Encyclopedia.com*. https://www.encyclopedia.com/history/encyclopedias-almanacs-transcripts-and-maps/black-womens-club-movement.

Catechism of the Catholic Church (2nd ed.). Vatican City: Libreria Editrice Vaticana, 1997.

Crummell, Alexander. "The Black Woman of the South: Her Neglects and Her Needs, 1883." In *The Modern African American Political Thought: Reader From David Walker to Barack Obama*, edited by Angela Jones, 73–86. New York and London: Routledge, 2013.

Levitt, Peggy, and Sally Engle Merry. "Making Women's Human Rights in the Vernacular: Navigating the Culture/Rights Divide." In *Gender and Culture at the Limit of Rights*, edited by Dorothy L. Hodgson, 81–100. Philadelphia: University of Pennsylvania Press, 2011.

"National Association of Colored Women." *Encyclopedia.com*, May 18, 2018. https://www.encyclopedia.com/history/biographies/korean-history-biographies/national-association-colored-women.

Pedroncelli, Peter. "9 Times a Female President Took Charge of an African Country." *The Moguldom Nation*, November 13, 2019. https://moguldom.com/239138/9-times-a-female-president-took-charge-of-an-african-country/#:~:text=These%20include%20Ellen%20Johnson%20Sirleaf%20of%20Liberia%2C%20who,an%20interim%20capacity%20at%20a%20time%20of%20need.

Riggs, Marcia. "What Do Nineteenth-Century Reformers Have to Say to Twentieth-Century Liberationists?" In *Womanist Theological Ethics: A Reader*, edited by Katie Geneva Cannon, Emilie M. Townes, and Angela D. Sims, 22–34. Louisville, Kentucky: Westminster John Knox Press, 2011.

The New American Bible: School and Church Edition. Wichita, Kansas: Fireside Bible Publishers, 1998.

Part 1

STRUGGLES FOR FREEDOM FROM THE MARGINS

Chapter 1

Black Women and Suffrage

A History of Political Freedom and Race in the United States

Christin Lee Hancock

On August 26, 2020, the United States celebrated the 100-year anniversary of the ratification of the Nineteenth Amendment to the Constitution of the United States of America ensuring women's suffrage. And yet this widely heralded amendment failed to provide access to suffrage for the majority of Black, Indigenous, and all women of color living in the United States in 1920. Thus, whether and how we should commemorate this event depends significantly upon our understanding of the historical narrative that shaped this movement for women's political freedom. Owing in large part to the construction of the narrative by white suffragists including Elizabeth Cady Stanton and Susan B. Anthony, the predominant history of the women's suffrage movement has focused its beginning point on the Seneca Falls Convention of 1848 and highlighted white women's political activism at both the expense and erasure of the history of women of color.[1] But as women historians have demonstrated, Black women, Indigenous women, and all women of color played essential historical roles in struggles for "political freedom." In the process, they helped to redefine its meaning. From Black women's abolitionist and civil rights work to Native women's struggles for sovereignty rights and Latina women's efforts at both labor and immigration reform, decentering white women's history leads to a broader understanding of the suffrage narrative in the United States. As the horrifying 2020 police killing of Breonna Taylor as well as recent violence against Native women and Asian American women continue to demonstrate, political freedom for women of color demands first and foremost the basic right to survive.[2]

Whereas the traditional narrative of women's suffrage has limited the meaning of "political" to the act of voting, for communities of color "political" has always expanded far beyond the scope of civic engagement to encompass the terms of one's personal life and living conditions.[3] Despite the fact that second-wave white feminist women did not openly stake their claim to the phrase "the personal is political" until the late 1960s and early 1970s, historically the activism of women of color has always been framed by this recognition of the ways that racialized thinking and racism have impacted every facet of their lives such that their personal experiences have always been political. Although broadly speaking, race and racism have impacted all women of color in their struggles for political freedom, that impact has occurred differently based on the specific histories of each distinct group of women. Recognizing these unique historical contexts, in this chapter, I will focus on the history of Black women in particular. As Rosalyn Terborg-Penn has noted, the movement for women's suffrage began during a period in which the overwhelming majority of Black women living in the United States were enslaved.[4] Thus their history, which encompasses a trajectory from racialized enslavement to "freedom," is uniquely important to the story of woman suffrage. As a white woman historian exploring inequalities of power between and among women of different races, I am committed to listening to and amplifying the voices of the many Black women historians from our present and more recent past who have worked tirelessly over several decades to uncover and make visible the previously erased history of Black women activists.[5] In this chapter then, I hope to provide an overview of their work. In so doing, the leading actors of this narrative become not only the historical Black women committed to suffrage and civil rights, but also Black women historians who have written their stories. Their thorough and painstaking historical recovery combined with incisive historical and political analysis not only makes this history visible, but also contributes to the most recent chapter in the ongoing struggle toward true political freedom. In the process, their research challenges the boundaries of "suffrage," enlarging and enriching our understanding of both politics and "political freedom." In honor of that vital work, this chapter foregrounds these historians' voices, synthesizing the work they have done to reshape our collective understanding of the American past by putting Black women at the center of the story of the struggle for political freedom.

POLITICAL RIGHTS AND CITIZENSHIP

First, I will begin with an overview of the ways that political rights, which have historically been tied to citizenship, have been racialized and gendered.

The Naturalization Act of 1790, which established the first set of requirements regarding who could access citizenship limited that access to "free white persons," signaling the founders' insistence on the racialization of citizenship. Not until the post–Civil War ratification of the fourteenth amendment in 1868 did the Constitution explicitly extend citizenship to all people (men and women) who were born in the United States, thus confirming citizenship for newly freed peoples and thereby offering political rights to Black Americans. In practice, however, this constitutional protection, important as it was, failed to properly protect and fully include Black women (and men) in the body politic. Indeed, in the aftermath of Reconstruction, a violent backlash against Black civil rights created a period of entrenched racism, Jim Crow segregation, and systemic violence and hostility that resulted in brutal lynchings. In the meantime, citizenship continued to be shaped by racialized ideas and assumptions, first with the legalized exclusion of Asian immigrants beginning in the late nineteenth century, and then with increasingly more restrictive and racially exclusive immigration laws in 1921 and 1924. The latter law, the Johnson-Reed Act of 1924, introduced racial quotas, banned Asian immigration, and began the process of constructing Mexican immigration as "illegal."[6] Prominent immigration scholar Mae Ngai has written extensively about the ways that immigration restrictions of the 1920s led to what she calls the "ethnoracial remapping of America."[7] And as MacArthur Genius Award winner Natalia Molina has noted, the 1924 law continued the process begun in 1848 during the U.S. war with Mexico of making Mexicans "legally white but racially other," a process that "codified their position as unequal citizens…"[8] Although the Snyder Act of 1924 granted Native American women and men citizenship for the first time, several states nonetheless continued to limit Native American suffrage. Race and racism continued to gatekeep the doors of American citizenship until legislation passed in 1952 and 1965 finally removed racial restrictions from immigration and naturalization. Also in 1965, the landmark Voting Rights Act sought to remove long-standing racial barriers to voting by holding states accountable for establishing fair and nondiscriminatory access to suffrage.

Secondly, while the original limitations on citizenship as outlined in 1790 did not specifically exclude women, allowing for the naturalization of all "free white *persons*," local practices quickly established women's exclusion, with the original states passing laws denying women the right of suffrage in the new nation; in addition, state laws restricted women's property, divorce, and custodial rights making clear that women's citizenship differed significantly from that of men. Additionally, women's citizenship itself was framed in the context of marriage. Federal and state laws operated on the assumption that women's political interests in suffrage were covered by that of their husbands.[9] With the nuclear heterosexual family situated as the primary social institution, the law perceived women as merely adjacent to men. These assumptions became highly visible with the passage of the Expatriation Act of 1907, which mandated that an American-born woman lose her citizenship if she married a noncitizen man. Although the Cable Act of 1922 reversed this decision for women who married men eligible for naturalization, it nonetheless continued the practice of racial exclusion by continuing to strip citizenship from women who married Asian-born men. By contrast, a man's marriage to a noncitizen woman made her immediately eligible for citizenship.[10] The laws clearly established the gendered and racialized limitations of access to citizenship and the political rights that it conferred.

BLACK WOMEN REDEFINING "POLITICAL FREEDOM"

It is within this broader historical context that Black women's struggle for political freedom emerges. As historian Martha S. Jones has recently noted, Black women were consistently the "Vanguard" of this political movement.[11] In the context of a post–Civil War racial backlash so intense that surviving racial violence shaped women's everyday lives, merely enduring and resisting that hostility represented the first and most primary struggle for political freedom, and yet Black women still played a leading role in the suffrage struggle. But as Jones explains, "Black women never limited their work to a single issue..." rather suffrage was perceived as a "companion to securing civil rights, prison reform, juvenile justice, and international human rights."[12] Thus, tracing Black women's political struggles requires that we explore not only their participation in the political arena, but also the ways that Black women fundamentally redefined "political." Jones' use of the term "vanguard" serves both to illuminate and also reshape our collective understanding of suffrage; after all, as Jones argues, the term "suffragist" is far too limiting to capture the totality of Black women's leadership and struggle.[13] As Jones writes, Black women fought for "political power that was redemptive, transformative, and a means toward realizing the equality and the dignity of all persons."[14] Rather than fighting for themselves alone, Black women sought universal political freedom.

Black women shaped the meaning of political freedom through their consistent articulation of the interconnectedness of race and gender.[15] In Zora Neale Hurston's classic 1937 novel *Their Eyes Were Watching God*, Nanny, grandmother of the main character Janie, tells her granddaughter that Black women are the mules of the earth, reflecting the lived experience of this double oppression.[16] Building upon historian Nell Irvin Painter's concept of "embodied rhetoric," Gender and Africana Studies scholar Brittney Cooper argues that from Sojourner Truth to Anna Julia Cooper, nineteenth-century

Black women deployed their own embodied experiences to theorize the consequences of these interconnections.[17] From 1851 when Truth proclaimed her womanness at the Women's Rights Convention in Akron, Ohio with her famous "A'n't I a Woman Speech" through the publication of Anna Julia Cooper's *A Voice from the South* in 1892 wherein she wrote her famous words, "Only the Black Woman can say 'when and where I enter," Brittney Cooper argues that collectively these words make up an "embodied discourse."[18] As such, Brittney Cooper further notes, "Embodied rhetoric, then, is one strategy in a range of embodied discursive strategies through which black women understand, locate, and theorize their bodies in order to disrupt gender-exclusive definitions of race and racially exclusive definitions of gender."[19] Throughout the late nineteenth and early twentieth centuries, Black women insisted upon recognizing the unique space they occupied; centering this intertwined gender and racial oppression redefines the beginning point for any struggle toward freedom.

One of the clearest examples of Black women using their physical bodies to resist oppression occurred repeatedly in what Jones refers to as "ladies car activism."[20] Long before Rosa Parks refused to give up her seat on a Montgomery bus in 1955, Black women regularly resisted being denied access to "ladies cars" on public transportation. Recalling Frances Ellen Watkins Harper's 1866 speech at the American Equal Rights Association, Jones notes that rather than discussing suffrage, she focused her attention on streetcar discrimination. Jones quotes Watkins' incisive analysis when she said "You white women speak of rights. I speak of wrongs."[21] Jones has meticulously traced the history of Black women standing up against racial segregation, and she places this activism front and center in terms of our understanding of political freedom.

Black women fought against racial injustice in tandem with their women's rights work. This twinned approach to justice is deeply evident in the life and work of anti-lynching activist Ida B. Wells. In the aftermath of the Civil War, white southerners worked to maintain the pre-war racial hierarchy in multiple ways, including violence and intimidation. More than 2500 Black men and women were lynched in the United States between the years 1884 and 1900.[22] In 1892, responding to the lynching of her dear friend Thomas Moss and two of his business associates, Ida B. Wells spoke out against this brutal and inhumane practice.[23] Writing in her newspaper, the *Memphis Free Speech*, she exposed the systemic racism that undergirded lynching. Defending Black men who were brutalized and killed by white mobs who frequently made false accusations of rape in order to justify these horrific acts, Wells wrote,

> Nobody in this section of the country believes the old threadbare lie that Negro men rape white women. If Southern white men are not careful, they will

overreach themselves and public sentiment will have a reaction; a conclusion will then be reached which will be very damaging to the moral reputation of their women.[24]

Interrupting nineteenth-century racialized gender ideology, Wells daringly suggested that white women *chose* Black men. The white community of Memphis responded to this perceived insult by destroying Wells' office and publicly threatening her life. Although forced to flee, this pivotal moment launched Wells' anti-lynching work. In earnest she began gathering lynching data from white newspapers, persuasively writing these stories into a series of anti-lynching pamphlets, the first of which, *Southern Horrors: Lynch Law in all its Phases*, was published in 1892. She followed this with a second pamphlet, *A Red Record*, published in 1895, and a third and final pamphlet, *Mob Rule in New Orleans* in 1900.[25] Wells traveled to Great Britain in order to press the case of American racism and its violence to a global audience. As historian Gail Bederman has argued, Wells effectively subverted western notions of "manhood and civilization," in order to lay bare the racist violence perpetrated against Black Americans on a daily basis.[26]

During the decades of her anti-lynching work, Wells also fought for women's suffrage, but she never agreed to privilege her womanness over her Blackness nor vice versa. Like both Truth and Cooper, Wells' writing and activism committed itself to centering a distinctive Black woman's experience. Wells fought to keep race at the forefront of the issue of suffrage as well, critiquing white activists like Frances Willard, president of the popular nineteenth-century temperance organization, the Woman's Christian Temperance Union (WCTU), and the mainstream White women's suffrage organizations when they neglected and excluded Black women.

BLACK WOMEN AND SUFFRAGE

Several women historians have called into question the prevailing women's suffrage timeline, which typically begins in 1848. As Jones has demonstrated, if we broaden our idea of what constitutes "women's rights" to include the many issues of civil rights that were central to Black women's lives, then abolitionism, church, organizing, and streetcar activism present just a few examples of important and in some cases earlier starting points.[27] Historian Lisa Tetrault notes the arbitrary nature of marking Seneca Falls as the beginning, arguing that white women suffragists Elizabeth Cady Stanton and Susan B. Anthony self-consciously created this "origin" story in an effort to shape and lay claim to this political history.[28] In the process, as Terborg-Penn has argued, Stanton and Anthony willfully left out Black women, whose voices they didn't see as meaningfully contributing to the particular narrative they hoped to convey. In fact, Terborg-Penn notes that the first edition of their suffrage chronicle failed to include even one Black suffragist.[29] Their curation of the suffrage story erased Black women in particular and women of color more broadly. Indeed, as Terborg-Penn observed, white women suffragists traded on their whiteness in order to make an exclusionary argument for their own enfranchisement at the expense of others.[30] The Declaration of Sentiments, written and signed at the 1848 Convention, illustrated and foreshadowed this strategy in its claim that Man "has withheld from her rights which are given to the most ignorant and degraded men- both natives and foreigners."[31] From the moment of the convention itself, white women advanced this idea that race trumped gender in accessing the vote, deploying fear about the consequences of allowing non-white men to vote instead of white women. As Terborg-Penn points out, white women's suffrage organizations aggressively advanced this strategy, advocating for "educated suffrage," a goal that intentionally privileged white middle-class women's access to the vote over both men and women of color.[32]

Rosalyn Terborg-Penn first began challenging the dominant suffrage narrative in the late 1970s and 1980s. Her research corrected the mistaken notion that "Black women had been uninterested in feminist politics," and instead she argued that Black women "had remained in the woman suffrage movement throughout the struggle, fighting both racism and sexism simultaneously."[33] Terborg-Penn was among the first Black women historians to recover the voices and stories of Black women suffragists from the 1850s through and beyond ratification of the Nineteenth Amendment. She noted that with the beginnings of women's rights so closely intertwined with abolitionism, Black women were certainly present in the movement, even if their words had not been considered worthy of inclusion by the white recorders.[34] Terborg-Penn's meticulous work brought students of history the names of three generational waves of Black women suffragists.[35] Spanning multiple generations and diverse political outlooks, these women helped advance the movement for women's political rights. And though they differed with regard to how to frame the struggle, they all lived their lives as *both* women *and* African Americans, unwilling to separate out their multiple and interlocking identities.

By the 1890s Black women fought for suffrage through their participation in social reform organizations, women's clubs, church groups, and suffrage organizations. Although the WCTU, which was the largest women's social reforming organization of the nineteenth century, racially segregated women, Black women nonetheless participated in the WCTU because they believed temperance to be important for community survival.[36] Like their white counterparts, Black women also created numerous women's clubs both local and national in scope; these clubs, which focused on both race and gender, created a public space for Black women to assert their authority in the realm of social reform. In 1896, Black women founded the National Association of Colored Women (NACW) an organizational feat that historian Paula Giddings calls a "watershed," because of its Black woman-centeredness both in leadership and participation.[37] With the motto "Lifting as We Climb," NACW members including Mary Church Terrell who served as President of the organization, clearly articulated goals that included reform and change for the poorest and most destitute community members in the nation.[38] The NACW included a "suffrage department," as part of its structure.[39] In turn, members of the NACW helped to find the National Association for the Advancement of Colored People (NAACP) in 1909, the enduring organizational entity dedicated to Black civil rights in the United States. Thus, even as Black women such as Victoria Earle Matthews founded Black suffrage organizations, arguing in favor of women's suffrage, they simultaneously invested in civil rights, seeing the two as fully interconnected.[40]

Black women's political activism was also deeply rooted in religious tradition and community religious practice. Evelyn Brooks Higginbotham has argued that "the public dimension of the black church" provided the foundation for all Black women's social reforming efforts.[41] Noting the distinctive significance of the Black Church, and specifically the National Baptist Convention, Higginbotham claims that "In the closed society of Jim Crow, the church afforded African Americans an interstitial space in which to critique and contest white America's racial domination."[42] Black women, she further notes, played a major role in creating and shaping the Black church, even despite the gendered division of labor within the Church, which provided this important public space from which women's activism blossomed.[43] According to Jones, Black women not only honed their organizing and political skills within their church communities, but they also "unsettled these spaces with debates over what sorts of power women could exercise . . ."[44] According to Higginbotham, the Black women's club movement was itself dependent upon the organizing strategies learned by Black Baptist women over decades, highlighting the connections that Black women made especially in the 1890s between racial justice and the desire for "temperance, educational opportunity, suffrage, and a variety of gender-related issues."[45] As historian Darlene Hine Clark has similarly argued,

> For free black women the line between involvement in religious institutions and in the women's suffrage movement was a permeable one. Because their religious orientation was toward spiritual liberation and personal autonomy, suffrage for black women became the political expression of their persistent yearnings to be free.[46]

Black women historians have made visible the ways that Black women's search for political freedom demanded a simultaneous acknowledgment of gender and racial oppression. And because political freedom always started with survival in a white-dominated world, Black religious institutions, which created the physical space for resistance, became the centerpiece of this struggle.

In the aftermath of the ratification of the nineteenth amendment in 1920, the majority of Black women continued to be barred from suffrage. The movement for suffrage continued up through the 1964 Civil Rights Act and the 1965 Voting Rights Act, which finally protected and increased voting access for Black women. Higginbotham has demonstrated that Black women activists continued their work for political freedom in the 1920s and beyond through club work in particular.[47] From Pauli Murray to Rosa Parks to Fannie Lou Hamer, Septima Clark, Ella Baker, and many more lesser-known names, Black women figured centrally in the ongoing movement for civil rights and universal suffrage from the 1930s through the 1960s. As Martha Prescod Norman, a civil rights activist and field secretary for the Student Nonviolent Coordinating Committee (SNCC) wrote about Black women in the 1950s and 1960s, "A lifetime of daily struggle against the harshest forms of racism had prepared them for a political struggle to change such conditions."[48] Though they may not have held named leadership positions, Black women literally put their lives on the line by organizing, resisting, and registering to vote in the south, inviting both harassment and beatings.[49] Their role in securing full civil rights cannot be overstated. Returning to Rosalyn Terborg-Penn's historical work, in their long-enduring fight for political freedom, Black women sought "universal suffrage," and as such, their struggle continued until citizenship and practical access to the vote were secured for all.[50]

CONCLUSION

In the aftermath of the successful passage of the 1965 Voting Rights Act, which effectively opened voting access to Black Americans long denied this full citizenship, Black women's struggle for freedom has continued in the form of civil rights activism aimed at demanding true equity in public education, housing, health care, and the criminal justice system. In the aftermath of the 2013 Shelby v. Holder Supreme Court decision, which stripped away the accountability clause of the 1965 Voting Rights Act, many state legislatures have again moved to restrict access to the vote, disproportionately disenfranchising communities of color. These renewed attacks on equal access to the vote combined with the reality of continued police violence against Black men and women suggest that although the struggle for political freedom has changed shape over time, it is nonetheless ongoing. When organizers Alicia Garza, Opal Tometi, and Patrice Kahn-Cullors co-founded the hashtag and then movement #BlackLivesMatter in 2013 as a response to the murder of Trayvon Martin, these Black women activists continued a long historical tradition of Black women's organizing for political freedom. As Jones points out, Black women are still the "Vanguard," leading both in their daily survival against persistent and systemic forms of racism, and also by continually directing our attention to a more expanded understanding of political freedom itself.[51]

NOTES

1. Rosalyn Terborg-Penn *African American Women in the Struggle for the Vote, 1850-1920* (Bloomington: Indiana University Press, 1998), 15; Lisa Tetrault, *The Myth of Seneca Falls: Memory and the Women's Suffrage Movement, 1848-1898* (Chapel Hill: The University of North Carolina Press, 2014), 1–17.

2. Richard A. Oppel Jr. and Derrick Bryson Taylor, "What to Know about Breonna Taylor's Death," *New York Times*, July 6, 2020, https://www.nytimes.com/article/breonna-taylor-police.html%20accessed%20on%20July%207; Will Wright, Nicholas Bogel-Burroughs, and John Eligon, "Breonna Taylor Grand Jury Audio Reveals Conflicting Accounts of Fatal Raid," *New York Times*, October 2, 2020, https://www.nytimes.com/2020/10/02/us/breonna-taylor-grand-jury-audio-recording.html; Maya Salam, "Native American Women are Facing a Crisis," *New York Times*, April 12, 2019, https://www.nytimes.com/2019/04/12/us/native-american-women-violence.html; Richard Fausset and Neil Vigdor, "8 People killed in Atlanta-Area Shootings at Massage Parlors," *New York Times*, March 16, 2021. https://www.nytimes.com/2021/03/16/us/atlanta-shootings-massage-parlor.html.

3. Elsa Barkley Brown notes that "our notion of politics is severely circumscribed." See Elsa Barkley Brown, "To Catch the Vision of Freedom: Reconstructing Southern Black Women's Political History, 1865-1880," in *African American Women and the Vote, 1837-1965*, ed. Ann D. Gordon (Amherst: University of Massachusetts Press, 1997), 86.

4. Terborg-Penn, *African American Women in the Struggle for the Vote*, 7.

5. Some of these historians include Paula Giddings, Darlene Clark Hine, Martha S. Jones, Elsa Barkley Brown, Evelyn Higginbotham, Nell Irvin Painter, Rosalyn Terborg-Penn, and Tera Hunter.

6. See Mae Ngai, *Impossible Subjects: Illegal Aliens and the Making of Modern America* (Princeton: Princeton University Press, 2014), and Natalia Molina, *How Race is Made in America: Immigration, Citizenship, and the Historical Power of Racial Scripts* (Berkeley: University of California Press, 2014), 35.

7. Mae Ngai, "Nationalism, Immigration Control, and the Ethnoracial Remapping of America," *OAH Magazine of History*, vol. 21, no. 3 (July 2007).

8. Molina, *How Race is Made in America*, 40.

9. Linda Kerber explains "*coverture*" as an "elaborate system" premised on the idea "that married women's civil identity was 'covered' by her husband's." See Linda

Kerber, "The Meanings of Citizenship," *The Journal of American History*, vol. 84, no. 3 (December 1997), 838.

10. Molina, *How Race is Made in America*, 74.

11. Martha S. Jones, *Vanguard: How Black Women Broker Barriers, Won the Vote, and Insisted on Equality for All* (New York: Basic Books, 2020), 11.

12. Ibid., 9.

13. Ibid., 11, 14.

14. Ibid., 11.

15. In 1989 Black legal scholar Kimberlé Crenshaw first named this concept "intersectionality" in a legal paper. See Kimberlé Crenshaw, "Demarginalizing the Intersection of Race and Sex: A Black Feminist Critique of Antidiscrimination Doctrine, Feminist Theory and Antiracist Politics," *University of Chicago Legal Forum*, vol. 1989, article 8, http://chicagounbound.uchicago.edu/uclf/vol1989/iss1/8.

16. Zora Neale Hurston, *Their Eyes Were Watching God* (New York: Harper Collins, 1937, 1965), 17.

17. Brittney Cooper, "A'n't I a Lady?: Race Women, Michelle Obama, and the Ever-Expanding Democratic Imagination, *Melus*, vol. 35, no. 4 (Winter 2010): 40–41.

18. Ibid., 39; Martha S. Jones notes that Sojourner Truth did not actually say the words "Ain't I a Woman," Rather she points out that it was a White woman, Frances Dana Gage, who first attributed these words to Truth in print over a decade after the speech was given. See Jones, *Vanguard*, 82. Referring to the speech in print, different scholars have variously spelled the words "Ain't," "A'nt," and A'n't." I have used the spelling used by the scholar I am referencing.

19. Cooper, "A'n't I a Lady?" 40–41.

20. Martha S. Jones, "What if Black Women have always been the Vanguard of Women's Suffrage," Keynote Speech, Western Association of Women Historians 50th Anniversary Conference, Portland, Oregon, April 26, 2019.

21. Frances Ellen Watkins Harper as quoted in Jones, *Vanguard*, 95.

22. Evelyn Brooks Higginbotham, *Righteous Discontent: The Women's Movement in the Black Baptist Church, 1880-1920* (Cambridge: Harvard University Press, 1993), 4.

23. Ida B. Wells, *Southern Horrors and other Writings: the anti-lynching campaign of Ida B. Wells, 1892-1900*, edited with an introduction by Jacqueline Jones Royster (Boston: Bedford/St. Martins, 2016).

24. Ibid., 52.

25. Ibid., 210.

26. Gail Bederman, "Civilization, the Decline of Middle-Class Manliness, and Ida B. Wells's Anti-Lynching Campaign, 1892-1894," in *Gender and American History Since 1890*, ed. Barbara Melosh (New York: Routledge, 1993), 208.

27. Jones, *Vanguard*, 15–120.

28. Tetrault, *The Myth of Seneca Falls,* 1–17.

29. Terborg-Penn, *African American Women in the Struggle*, 15.

30. Ibid., 9–10.

31. Declaration of Sentiments, 1848, https://www.nps.gov/wori/learn/historyculture/declaration-of-sentiments.htm.
32. Terborg-Penn, *African American Women in the Struggle*, 10, 109–112.
33. Ibid., 3–4.
34. Ibid., 14–15.
35. See Ibid., 15–73.
36. Ibid., 85–86; Paula Giddings, *When and Where I Enter: The Impact of Black Women on Race and Sex in America* (New York: Amistad, 1984), 91.
37. Giddings, *When and Where I Enter*, 95.
38. Ibid., 98–99.
39. Terborg-Penn, *African American Women in the Struggle*, 92.
40. Ibid., 81–106.
41. Higginbotham, *Righteous Discontent*, 9.
42. Ibid.,10.
43. Ibid., 1–18.
44. Jones, *Vanguard*, 9, 15–42.
45. Higginbotham, *Righteous Discontent*, 13.
46. Darlene Hine Clark, *Hine Sight: Black Women and the Re-Construction of American History* (Bloomington: Indiana University Press, 1994), 9.
47. Evelyn Brooks Higginbotham, "Clubwomen and Electoral Politics," in *African American Women and the Vote, 1837-1965*, ed. Ann D. Gordon (Amherst, MA: University of Massachusetts Press, 1997), 134–155.
48. Martha Prescod Norman, "Shining in the Dark: Black women and the Struggle for the Vote, 1955-1965," in *African American Women and the Vote, 1837-1965*, 180.
49. Ibid., 173, 176, 178, 180.
50. Terborg-Penn, *African American Women in the Struggle*, 9, 24–35.
51. Jones, *Vanugard*, 268.

FURTHER READINGS

Bay, Mia, Farah J. Griffith, Martha S. Jones, and Barbara Savage, eds. *Toward an Intellectual History of Black Women*. Chapel Hill, NC: University of North Carolina Press, 2015.

Berry, Daina Ramey, and Kali Nicole Gross. *A Black Women's History of the United States*. Revisioning History Book 5. Boston: Beacon Press, 2020.

Giddings, Paula. *Ida: A Sword Among Lions: Ida B. Wells and the Campaign Against Lynching*. New York: Amistad, 2008.

Harley, Sharon, and Rosalyn Terborg-Penn, eds. *The Afro-American Woman: Struggles and Images*. Baltimore, MD: Black Classic Press, 2013.

Higginbotham, Evelyn Brooks. "African American Women's History and the Metalanguage of Race." *Signs: Journal of Women in Culture and Society* 17, no. 2 (1992): 251–274.

Hine Clark, Darlene, and Kathleen Thompson. *A Shining Thread of Hope: The History of Black Women in America*. New York: Broadway Books, 1999.

Jones, Martha S. *All Bound Up Together: The Woman Question in African American Public Culture, 1830–1900*. Chapel Hill, NC: The University of North Carolina Press, 2007.

REFERENCES

Bederman, Gail. "Civilization, the Decline of Middle-Class Manliness, and Ida B. Wells's Anti-Lynching Campaign, 1892–1894." In *Gender and American History Since 1890*, edited by Barbara Melosh, 207–239. New York City: Routledge, 1999.

Brown, Elsa Barkley. "To Catch the Vision of Freedom: Reconstructing Southern Black Women's Political History, 1865–1880." In *African American Women and the Vote, 1837–1965*, edited by Ann D. Gordon, 66–99. Amherst: University of Massachusetts Press, 1997.

Clark, Darlene Hine. *Hine Sight: Black Women and the Re-Construction of American History*. Bloomington: Indiana University Press, 1994.

Cooper, Brittney. "A'n't I a Lady?: Race Women, Michelle Obama, and the Ever-Expanding Democratic Imagination." *Melus* 35, no. 4 (Winter 2010): 39–57.

Crenshaw, Kimberlé. "Demarginalizing the Intersection of Race and Sex: A Black Feminist Critique of Antidiscrimination Doctrine, Feminist Theory and Antiracist Politics." *University of Chicago Legal Forum* 1989, Article 8. http://chicagounbound.uchicago.edu/uclf/vol1989/iss1/8.

Declaration of Sentiments. 1848. https://www.nps.gov/wori/learn/historyculture/declaration-of-sentiments.htm.

Fausset, Richard, and Neil Vigdor. "8 People Killed in Atlanta-Area Shootings at Massage Parlors." *New York Times*, March 16, 2021. https://www.nytimes.com/2021/03/16/us/atlanta-shootings-massage-parlor.html.

Giddings, Paula. *When and Where I Enter: The Impact of Black Women on Race and Sex in America*. New York: Amistad, 1984.

Higginbotham, Evelyn Brooks. "Clubwomen and Electoral Politics." In *African American Women and the Vote, 1837–1965*, edited by Ann D. Gordon, 134–155. Amherst: University of Massachusetts Press, 1997.

———. *Righteous Discontent: The Women's Movement in the Black Baptist Church, 1880–1920*. Cambridge: Harvard University Press, 1993.

Hurston, Zora Neale. *Their Eyes Were Watching God*. New York: HarperCollins 1937, 1965.

Jones, Martha S. *Vanguard: How Black Women Broke Barriers, Won the Vote, and Insisted on Equality for All*. New York: Basic Books, 2020.

———. "What If Black Women Have Always Been the Vanguard of Women's Suffrage." *Keynote Speech*. Western Association of Women Historians 50th Anniversary Conference. Portland, Oregon, April 26, 2019.

Kerber, Linda. "The Meanings of Citizenship." *The Journal of American History* 84, no. 3 (December 1997): 833–854.

Molina, Natalia. *How Race is Made in America: Immigration, Citizenship, and the Historical Power of Racial Scripts*. Berkeley: University of California Press, 2014.

Ngai, Mae. *Impossible Subjects: Illegal Aliens and the Making of Modern America*. Princeton: Princeton University Press, 2014.

———. "Nationalism, Immigration Control, and the Ethnoracial Remapping of America." *OAH Magazine of History* 21, no. 3 (July 2007): 11–15.

Norman, Martha Prescod. "Shining in the Dark: Black Women and the Struggle for the Vote, 1955–1965." In *African American Women and the Vote, 1837–1965*, edited by Ann D. Gordon, 172–199. Amherst: University of Massachusetts Press, 1997.

Oppel, Richard A., Jr., and Derrick Bryson Taylor. "What to Know About Breonna Taylor's Death." *New York Times*, July 6, 2020. https://www.nytimes.com/article/breonna-taylor-police.html%20accessed%20on%20July%207.

Salam, Maya. "Native American Women Are Facing a Crisis." New York Times, April 12, 2019. https://www.nytimes.com/2019/04/12/us/native-american-women-violence.html.

Terborg-Penn, Rosalyn. *African American Women in the Struggle for the Vote, 1850–1920*. Bloomington: Indiana University Press, 1998.

Tetrault, Lisa. *The Myth of Seneca Falls: Memory and the Women's Suffrage Movement 1848–1898*. Chapel Hill: University of North Carolina, 2014.

Wells, Ida B. *Southern Horrors and Other Writings: The Anti-Lynching Campaign of Ida B. Wells, 1892–1900*. Edited With an Introduction by Jacqueline Jones Royster. Boston: Bedford/St. Martins, 2016.

Wright, Will, Nicholas Bogel-Burroughs, and John Eligon. "Breonna Taylor Grand Jury Audio Reveals Conflicting Accounts of Fatal Raid." *New York Times*, October 2, 2020. https://www.nytimes.com/2020/10/02/us/breonna-taylor-grand-jury-audio-recording.html.

Chapter 2

National Association of Colored Women's Clubs and the Fight for Freedom

Anita R. Gooding

From the early 1800s through the beginning of the twentieth century, the National Association of Colored Women (NACW) clubs were at the core of sociopolitical advancements made by the Black community. Using their relationships with each other as mechanisms of action, club women specialized in the "wholly impossible"[1]—they developed social services, social networks, literary societies, and engaged in suffragist actions to meet the needs of the African American community at the time. While the club women's influence is not always mentioned in traditional historical accounts of social work history, their fight for freedom was significant and necessitated a deep faith. This chapter explores the social context which gave rise to the African American club women[2], including as it relates to social welfare history, and how faith—faith in each other, faith in their God, and faith that racial uplift and gender parity were possible—advanced the sociopolitical lives of the Black community.

CLUB WOMEN'S SOCIOPOLITICAL ENGAGEMENT

The reconstruction period (1865–1880) saw the first-time social services were formally provided to African Americans. The Freedmen Bureau was created by the United States Congress after the Civil War to provide assistance to poor people of all races[3] and was the first federally funded welfare system in the United States to serve Black people[4]. The Bureau participated in legal proceedings to mitigate discriminatory practices, formalized marriages, helped with employment contracts, and offered medical treatment[5]. Though the Bureau's services were open to everyone, segregation in the south meant their facilities were not integrated. Therefore, the Bureau's offices soon became spaces where Blacks could commune safely to support educational and community development.

In addition to the Bureau, the reconstruction period also saw Black mutual aid societies developed and led by some of the first Black social workers as sites for activism, training, education, recreation, and more [6]—"within these organizations, African American social workers functioned to mobilize the community towards participatory action. As such, they represent early constructs of community development."[7] Settlement houses not only provided services, but radically departed from prior understandings of social welfare and service provision.[8] It understood that welfare benefited both the individual and the community because educated youth returned to instruct the next generation of students.[9] In essence, settlement houses created oppositional consciousness where African Americans could commune and use their shared identity to reject subordination and oppressive rule.[10] These houses were invaluable, and continued long after the dissolution of the Freedmen Bureau.

In 1896, the NACW was formed to promote the upward mobility of all African American peoples, and to actively counter racist oppression. Its founders included Ida B. Wells-Barnett, famed anti-lynching activist; abolitionist Harriet Tubman; and suffragist and civil rights activist Mary Church Terrell. In their first biennial meeting, where NACW clubs from around the country were represented, Mary Church Terrell was elected president.[11] With the motto "Lifting as We Climb," they established a radical agenda that included childcare, employment training, and wage equity for the Black community. The women of the NACW made it clear that their intention was racial pride and advocating for women's rights. The term racial uplift was used in place of equal rights because the women wanted to avoid open confrontation with Whites on the issue, and equal rights was not a part of the lexicon at the time.[12]

Club women, who were registered members of NACW clubs around the United States, were socially and politically engaged reformers who envisioned healing and hope for a Black community dealing with the effects of slavery, and the subsequent restrictions which arose to curtail their education, financial growth, housing options, employment, and the like; the NACW was extremely active in meeting these unmet needs. In North Carolina, for example, they used taxes accrued from annual membership fees to create the Tent Sisters Old Folks' Home. In addition to their money, club members also volunteered their time to the daily operations of the home and caretaking of its residents.[13]

In Chicago, Ida B. Wells-Barnett created a settlement house named the Negro Fellowship League and Reading Room which offered parenting classes, employment options, health care, literacy programs, and voting access.¹⁴ Meanwhile in Florida, Mary McLeod Bethune opened the Daytona Educational and Industrial Training School for Negro Girls in 1904 to help meet the unmet educational needs of African American women at the time. The school eventually merged with the Cookman Institute and became a co-ed institution. It is now known as Bethune-Cookman University and is one of the oldest historically Black colleges and universities in the nation.

In addition to creating social services, club women were also very involved in political issues of the time. They were anti-lynching advocates and fought against segregation and discrimination in transportation, education, employment, and public space. Club women used print medium to confront political issues facing the African American community. For instance, in Atlanta, the city refused to provide adequate educational opportunities for Black children. Club women in the area developed a petition and used the power of writing to persuade local officials about public schooling. Their campaign ended with an increase in teacher salaries and the development of a school in south Atlanta.¹⁵

In addition, reformers created literary clubs where African American women could gather to think critically about the issues of the day, and read and engage in literature, politics, and philosophy. Literary clubs created a "distinctly feminized sphere, in which they encouraged one another to articulate new ideas, support their interpretations, write their own words, and critique one another."¹⁶ The publication, *The Women's Era,* was the first paper in the United States written by and for African American women, and the official paper of the NACW.¹⁷ The paper offered one medium where club women could engage in social action and critical thought.

Clubs around the country were very much involved in politics, specifically around women's suffrage and elections. They believed that civic engagement, including through voting, was a necessary weapon in order to advance the rights of African Americans. When club women in Chicago were granted the right to vote in local and state elections in 1913, they immediately engaged in get out the vote efforts, educating community members on how to use voting machines, and teaching community members about race issues and the ballot. In 1914 they were central to the nomination of Oscar de Priest as the first African American alderman for Chicago's Second Ward.¹⁸

THE INTERSECTIONS OF GENDER, RACE, AND CLASS

In her infamous piece on intersectionality, Kimberlé Crenshaw argues violence against African American women lies at the juncture of racism and sexism, and cannot be understood independently. Therefore, Crenshaw posits that when examining domestic violence in Black communities, it is vital to name the ways race, gender, and class intersect to inform the issue. She explains:

> Although racism and sexism readily intersect in the lives of real people, they seldom do in feminist and antiracist practices. And so, when the practices expound identity as woman or person of color as an either/or proposition, they relegate the identity of women of color to a location that resists telling. My objective in this article is to advance the telling of that location by exploring the race and gender dimensions of violence against women of color. Contemporary feminist and antiracist discourses have failed to be represented within the discourses of either feminism or antiracism. Because of their intersectional identity as both women and of color within discourses that are shaped to respond to one or the other, women of color are marginalized within both. [19]

The notion of intersectionality is pertinent to conversations about club women, specifically the ways race, class, and gender influenced their work. A key reason they attempted to counteract the effects of racism on the Black community was that despite the privileges they could access as middle- and upper-class women, their race meant they still faced discrimination. They understood that regardless of their class status, they would always be read as African American, thus subject to the same issues facing poor Black women such as political disenfranchisement and verbal and sexual assault.[20]

Many club women wanted to challenge the racist view that Black women were promiscuous and immoral. Instead, they insisted that African American women were key to the future of the race, especially because of their role as mothers. As a result, they spoke of "other mothering":

> the club women articulated their own vision—rooted in the community mores of "other mothering" a deep-seated Christianity and an admixture of Du Boisian and Washingtonian tenets. Respectability, tucked within the prevailing concerns of race advancement and progress, assumed gendered and classed forms as club women constructed various layers of sisterhood and allegiances to poorer women while also maintaining class distinctions. Such positions were not contradictory. Rather, they pointed to a resilience in the club women's rhetoric, demonstrated by adapting their language to the multiple audiences of African American men, White club women, and poorer African American women.[21]

Women who participated in the club movement understood that due to slavery they were not free to express and define motherhood in culturally specific ways; in fact, they were never confined to a home life of submissive domesticity like their White counterparts. Therefore, the core of their social welfare programs was this "other mothering," their own version of domestic life that allowed for taking charge of the home and raising children who could further advance the race.[22] Their understanding of the role of culture in mothering informed their development of homes for children and youth and orphanages for young working girls.

FAITH AS A TOOL OF RESISTANCE TO DISENFRANCHISEMENT

For African American women during this era, social responsibility was tied to a womanist orientation, which embraced the power of God's will as well as a commitment to community survival, freedom, and liberation.[23] Alice Walker notes that "womanist is to feminist as purple to lavender."[24] Meaning that though all women deal with issues of gender and sexism, Black femininity is also shrouded in racism due to the inherent nature of American social institutions. In this way, it is distinct from White feminism and "offers a vocabulary for addressing gender issues within African American communities . . . and appears to provide an avenue to foster stronger relationships between Black men and women."[25] Furthermore, womanism highlights Black motherhood as a leadership role to create, sustain, and advance Black culture and community; this idea is clearly reflected in the way club women spoke of the need for "other mothering."[26]

African American club women engaged the church in their social welfare programs and at their peak, "outperformed the Black churches,"[27] which had traditionally met the welfare needs of the Black community. Their theology understood that the direct services they provided—such as their creation of homes for older adults, children, and working women—would lead to greater emotional, physical, psychological, and spiritual health for the African American community.[28] The women also used their relationships with each other as both a site for spiritual healing and a reprieve from an oppressive world, and their womanist orientation allowed them to, "recognize the political nature of sexism long before their White counterparts . . . these pioneers faced the fact that sexual exploitation and violence were perpetuated by both African American and white men. Politicizing sexual exploitation and harassment for African American women placed it squarely within the context of race."[29] Thus, spirituality became a tool of empowerment—it posited that all life, including Black life, was created by God and inherently valuable.

African American club women were also keenly aware that racism affected African American men and women similarly. Because their goals dovetailed regarding racial uplift, club women "tended to vote along racial lines, just as their men did. And like most women, they benefited from the political process by being able to highlight issues relevant to the lives of families and communities,"[30] which included such issues as voting access, the creation of schools, and food provision. While African American men established institutions like the National Association for the Advancement of Colored People (NAACP) and National Business League to address race-based discrimination, women created the economic, social, educational, and religious institutions which emphasized self-improvement alongside racial advancement.[31]

Through their involvement in politics, club women showed a keen understanding of institutional racism and its connections to disenfranchisement in the African American community. They understood the need to provide access to economic, social, and political power in order to resist oppressive societal conditions.[32] In their work, club women showed faith—faith in each other, faith in their God, and faith that racial uplift was possible.

First, club women could not have created homes, economic institutions, and health services without faith in each other. Their connections with each other opened a path to social change. While the African American community has traditionally enlisted voluntary associations to work through internal problems, club women were unique in that they were able to nationally mobilize through the NACW and were the nation's leading race organization for a decade and a half before the NAACP was founded.[33]

The relationship club women had with each other was further strengthened by the fact that they were from different churches, neighborhoods, and families, but with similar traditions and values. The inherent diversity amongst their ranks generated the creation of the NACW in order to "perpetuate the historical traditions of self-help, community development, and racial uplift."[34] The faith the club women had in each other made their work possible.

Second, club women remained faithful to their God. Though some of their homes were bombed and their livelihoods threatened, they persisted with the belief that their work was connected to a being higher than themselves and advanced the greater good; their womanist embracement of community survival merged with a belief that God's plan included a path to freedom and liberation for the African American community. They were also very aware of the role of Christianity in Black life. Club chapters enlisted the support of churches to house families, feed community members, and nurture spiritual growth. In this way, their shared faith in God became a place for club women to integrate their aims with those of the Church. Even more, club women's faith in God allowed them to merge African American spirituality and religiosity, to social welfare and social well-being.

Finally, African American club women had faith that racial uplift was possible. They witnessed the increased risk African Americans faced in a blatantly racist society and knew that their wealth would not shield them from its wrath. Their understanding relates to what is now called Critical Race Theory, which was developed by legal scholars Derrick Bell and Alan Freeman in the 1970s to explain the ways laws have traditionally upheld racist artifacts, and the need for a radical shift. CRT holds that because racism benefits Whites materially and psychically, a large portion of society has no incentive to extinguish it.[35] As racism advances the interests of Whites, in order for meaningful social change to occur, the interests of historically marginalized groups and Whites must converge.[36] Club women were able to find Black and White benefactors who similarly championed racial uplift and used this point of interest convergence to fund social welfare programs. Without their faith that fighting for voting rights, suffrage, and political representation would lead to social change, it would have been difficult to sustain the urgency at which they worked.

CRT also states that race organizes society and to rebuild, the insights and experiences of historically marginalized racial groups must be incorporated into social and political life. Based on their varying histories, and personal experiences with race and racism, racial minority groups have unique insights.[37] Club women illustrated such insights when they fought for suffrage because they knew that legal representation would afford them direct involvement in the policies and programs which impacted life in their neighborhoods. Furthermore, they understood that creating a powerful sociopolitical organization like the NACW would afford them access to each other, and the ability to incorporate their own worldview into programs and services. In her 1898 address to the National American Women Suffrage Association, Club activist Mary Church Terrell proclaimed:

> With tireless energy and eager zeal, colored women have, since their emancipation, been continuously prosecuting the work of educating and elevating their race, as though upon themselves alone devolved the accomplishment of this great task . . . By banding themselves together in the interest of education and morality, by adopting the most practical and useful means to this end, colored women have in thirty short years become a great power for good. Through the National Association of Colored Women...much good has been done in the past, and more will be accomplished in the future, we hope. Believing that it is only through the home that a people can become really good and truly great, the National Association of Colored Women has entered that sacred domain.[38]

CLUB WOMEN'S WORLDVIEW

It is worth mentioning that while the Afrocentric worldview was formalized in the 1990s, long after the peak of the club movement, I believe that club women's values aligned seamlessly with the Africana worldview. As a paradigm, the Africana perspective is rooted in traditional African and contemporary African American philosophy, with origins in precolonial Africa.[39] Jerome H. Schiele, a social work scholar who has written extensively on the Afrocentric perspective in social work explains that this framework has three main assumptions. The first assumption is that individual identity is collective identity; individual identity is important, but the spiritual connectedness between humans means that we are interdependent, therefore, there is no separation between individuals and others.[40]

The second assumption of the Afrocentric worldview is that spirituality is just as important as materiality. Here, spirituality is defined as "that invisible universal substance that connects all human beings to each other and to the creator."[41] Through spiritual development, humans are reminded of their interconnectedness. In the Eurocentric view, "spirituality, collectivity, mutual aid, and cooperation are de-emphasized and underdeveloped"[42] whereas within the Africana worldview, spiritual development and growth are forefronted. Within social work specifically, the Africana worldview offers a lens through which to address the oppression and spiritual isolation faced by the communities they serve.

The final assumption of the Africana perspective is that affective responses are a way of knowing, and are epistemologically valid:

> Afrocentric social work acknowledges the linear, materialist understanding of reality, but it draws heavily on an affective and holistic means of knowing and understanding the world. Indeed, the Afrocentric paradigm regards affect (i.e., feeling) as a means to offset the excessive emphasis on rationality found in the Eurocentric perspective.[43]

Club women's worldview aligns with the Afrocentric perspective, and is clearly rooted in traditional African and contemporary African American understandings of community. They too believed that the individual could not be understood on their own, but as part of a collective society. Club women formed a national coalition, the NACW, whose work addressed local, state, and national issues pertaining to African Americans at the time. Furthermore, they knew that when they helped others, especially other Black women, they also benefitted.

Another way club women reflected an Africana perspective is that they understood that humans are spiritually connected, and so they engaged members of the community to aid their cause—including low-income women, white benefactors, leaders, and the like:

> Whether in the form of poor rural women who stole a little time when possible to come together for mutual support or more formally identified through the church or on the society pages of African American newspapers, women's and men's mutual benefit societies and their beneficence in general have been an obvious and steadfast part of the community's civic engagement.[44]

Club women's utilization of religious spaces is also indicative of their spiritual investment in the Black community; they recognized the African

American church not only as a site for spiritual development, but also as one site where sociopolitical activism could occur.

In addition, club women's relationships with each other were a place where they built spiritual and emotional connections with other African American women. At their national conferences, literary society meetings, and other gatherings, club women were able to form bonds with other like-minded women and use those spiritual, emotional, and psychological bonds as a launching pad for sociopolitical action. In this way, members of the NACW recognized that ". . . race pride, in sum, was a way of guarding the Black spirit."[45]

Finally, the Africana perspective can be seen in club women's acceptance of affect as an epistemologically valid way of knowing and therefore a valid way of engaging in social service provision. Club women felt that African American women must be given a chance to mother in ways that were culturally appropriate and focused much of their effort on childcare, education, parenting classes, housing, and other programs to aid Black mothers and children. They were also passionate and driven in their vision for the African American community which included uplift and race pride. Club women's holistic understanding was not about materialism, but about valuing social and human rights, many of which were historically denied to African Americans.

RESPECTABILITY AND THE CLUB WOMEN MOVEMENT

In addition to concerns about race and gender, Club women wanted to show to the world that African American women deserved the same respect and opportunities provided to White women. In this way, club women were entrenched in respectability politics, where there was the assumption that they needed to step in to uplift the "bad" traits of poorer Blacks;[46] an assumption that ignores the structural, political, economic, and social practices which have sustained racism in the United States. Club membership was also not accessible to many lower-class women. Within the Illinois Federation of Colored Women's Clubs (IFCWC), there was a five-dollar fee just to join, with additional yearly fees. Members also need to have the time to be able to participate in social and benevolent activities which further restricted access for poorer African Americans.[47]

Club women's respectability politics around showing the world they were "good" women, can be seen clearly in their work to teach poor and working-class women lessons in morality in the hopes that they would pass that morality on to family members. As part of their programming, club officials developed:

Committees on hygiene, temperance, and civic responsibility were set up to teach women about the necessity of cleanliness, abstention from alcoholic beverages, and the importance of self-help. The mothers' department instructed Black women about child rearing and other domestic duties associated with the family. To be sure, the dissemination of these middle-class Victorian values reflected an attempt by the club women to direct, and to a degree control, people's lives, and suggests that they believed that it was their job to be the moral caretakers and uplifters of the masses.[48]

Knupher (1996) notes that the motto, "Lifting as We Climb" exemplifies the class differences that existed between middle- and upper-class club women and their beneficiaries;[49] club women "saw their social welfare crusade as improving both their own lives and the lives of those around them. Equally devoted to uplifting the community and to aiding themselves, they found that participation in the club movement offered them a rare opportunity to associate with like-minded individuals who were also seeking collective advancement"[50] for the Black community; thus, allowing the women to work toward racial uplift, yet maintain class distinctions. This point is illustrated in an excerpt from a speech by Josephine St. Pierre Ruffin, convener of the First National Conference on Colored Women of America as well as editor and publisher of *The Woman's Era*:

> for the sake of the fine cultured women who have carried off the honors in school here and often abroad, for the sake of our own dignity, the dignity of our race, and the future good name of our children, it is "meet, right, and our bounden duty" to stand forth and declare ourselves and principles, to teach an ignorant and suspicious world that our aims and interests are identical with those of all good aspiring women.[51]

It is important to name NACW's respectability politics as it relates to the time period because this too informed their perspectives and their work. Given the historical context in which these women were imbued, it is unclear if they were aware of the ways they replicated white supremacist ideals amongst the poor women they worked with. Yet their class positionalities made it so they still assumed other African Americans could reach middle- and upper-class status if they behaved in a certain way—which contradicts a structural analysis of race and racism.

CONCLUSION

The NACW clubs' achievements, passion, drive, and commitment greatly advanced community reforms, so much so that by the 1930s the need for club women's services declined. However, NACW is still active today with clubs in every region of the United States. There are also college and youth chapters of the organization and their mission remains to uplift:

> women, children, families, the home and the community through service, community education, scholarship assistance and the promotion of racial harmony among all people, so that those we serve are better able to take their proper and rightful place in society as citizens, community leaders, parents and family members.[52]

Club women developed social support services specifically catered to the Black community, pushed for suffrage and civic engagement, and saw Black women as a powerful force for change and social good. The legacy of the NACW is one of advocacy, intervention and civic engagement, and faith. They used their sociopolitical identity as Black middle- and upper-class women to create powerful connections with each other, and to articulate faith in what was possible for the Black community then, and in the future.

NOTES

1. Tricia Bent-Goodley, Cudore L. Snell and Iris Carlton-LaNey, "Black perspectives and Social Work Practice," *Journal of Human Behavior in the Social Environment*, vol. 27 (2017): 31.

2. National Association of Colored Women's Clubs and African American Club women are used interchangeably to refer to the group of women involved in this work. Furthermore, these terms are consistent with those used by other scholars to talk about the NACW.

3. John H. Franklin, "Public Welfare in the South during the Reconstruction Era, 1865-1880," *Social Science Review*, vol. 44 (1970): 382.

4. Stephanie Howard, "Social Work in the Black Community: A Collective Response to Contemporary Unrest," *Journal of Sociology & Social Welfare*, vol. 44 (2017): 84.

5. Ibid., 85.
6. Ibid., 81.
7. Ibid., 87.
8. Ibid., 84.
9. Ibid., 86.

10. Charles Hounmenou, "Black Settlement Houses and Oppositional Consciousness," *Journal of Black Studies*, vol. 43, no. 6 (2012): 662.

11. Wanda A. Hendricks, *Gender, Race and Politics in the Midwest: Black Club Women in Illinois* (Indiana: Indiana University Press, 1998), xi–xii.

12. Hounmenou, "Black Settlement Houses and Oppositional Consciousness," 653.

13. Iris Carlton-LaNey, "African American Social Work Pioneers' Response to Need," *Social Work*, vol. 44 (1999): 317.

14. Bent-Goodley, Snell, and Carlton-LaNey, "Black perspectives and Social Work Practice," 29.

15. Anne Ruggles Gere and Sarah R. Robbins, "Gendered Literacy in Black and White: Turn-of-the-Century African-American and European-American Club Women's Printed Texts," *Signs: Journal of Women in Culture and Society*, vol. 21 (1996): 667.

16. Anne M. Knupfer, "Toward a Tenderer Humanity and a Nobler Womanhood: African American Woman's Clubs in Chicago, 1890 to 1920," *Journal of Women's History*, vol. 7 (1995): 64.

17. Carlton-LaNey, "African American Social Work Pioneers' Response to Need," 312.

18. Anne M. Knupfer, *Toward a Tenderer Humanity and Nobler Womanhood: African American Women's Clubs in Turn-of-the-century Chicago* (New York: New York University Press, 1996), 136.

19. Kimberlé Crenshaw, "Mapping the margins: Intersectionality, Identity Politics, and Violence Against Women of Color," *Stanford Law Review*, vol. 43 (1991): 1242–1243.

20. Knupfer, "Toward a Tenderer Humanity and a Nobler Womanhood: African American Woman's Clubs in Chicago, 1890 to 1920," 64.

21. Knupfer, *Toward a Tenderer Humanity and Nobler Womanhood*, 7.

22. Ibid.

23. Kelly Brown, "Womanist Theology," *Black Women in America*, 1276, quoted in Iris Carlton-LaNey, "Doing the Lord's Work: African American Elders Civic Engagement," *Generations*, vol. 30 (2006): 48.

24. Alice Walker, *In Search of Our Mother's Gardens* (New York: Harcourt, 1983), xii, quoted in Patricia Hill Collins, "What's in a Name? Womanism, Black Feminism and Beyond," *The Black Scholar*, vol. 26 (1996): 10.

25. Collins, "What's in a Name? Womanism, Black Feminism and Beyond," 11.

26. Nah Dove, "African Womanism: An Afrocentric Theory" *Journal of Black Studies*, vol. 28, no. 5 (1998), 535.

27. Elmer P. Martin and Joanne M. Martin, *Spirituality and the Black Helping Tradition in Social Work* (Washington, DC: NASW Press, 2002), 138.

28. Carlton-LaNey, "Doing the Lord's Work: African American Elders Civic Engagement," 48.

29. Carlton-LaNey, "African American Social Work Pioneers' Response to Need," 318.

30. Hendricks, *Gender, Race and Politics in the Midwest*, 131.

31. Carlton-LaNey, "African American Social Work Pioneers' Response to Need," 316.

32. Bent-Goodley, Snell, and Carlton-LaNey, "Black Perspectives and Social Work Practice," 29.

33. Stephanie J. Shaw, "Black Club Women and the Creation of the National Association of Colored Women." *Journal of Women's History* 3 (1991): 19.

34. Ibid.

35. Monique Constance-Huggins, "Critical Race Theory in Social Work Education: A Framework for Addressing Racial Disparities," *Critical Social Work*, vol. 13 (2012): 8.

36. Narda Razack and Donna Jeffery, "Critical Race Discourse and Tenets for Social Work," *Canadian Social Work Review/Revue Canadienne de Service Social*, vol. 19 (2002): 264.

37. Derrick A. Bell, "Who's Afraid of Critical Race Theory?" *University of Illinois Law Review* (1995): 899.

38. Mary Church Terrell, "Beyond Rosa Parks: The Progress of Colored Women," *Teaching Tolerance* (2017), https://www.learningforjustice.org/sites/default/files/general/96_TT_Beyond_Rosa_Parks_MChurchTerrell.pdf.

39. Jerome H. Schiele, "Afrocentricity: An Emerging Paradigm in Social Work Practice," *Social Work*, vol. 41, no. 3 (1996): 285.

40. Jerome H. Schiele, "The Contour and Meaning of Afrocentric Social Work," *Journal of Black Studies*, vol. 27, no. 6 (1997): 805.

41. Ibid.

42. Ibid., 808.

43. Ibid., 807.

44. Carlton-LaNey, "Doing the Lord's Work: African American Elders Civic Engagement," 49.

45. Bent-Goodley, Snell, and Carlton-LaNey, "Black perspectives and Social Work Practice," 28.

46. Frederick C. Harris, "The Rise of the Respectability Politics" *Dissent*, vol. 61 (2014): 33.

47. Hendricks, *Gender, Race and Politics in the Midwest*, 26.

48. Ibid., 27.

49. Knupfer, "Toward a Tenderer Humanity and a Nobler Womanhood: African American Woman's Clubs in Chicago, 1890 to 1920," 59.

50. Hendricks, *Gender, Race and Politics in the Midwest*, 38.

51. Eileen Boris, "The Power of Motherhood: Black and White Activist Women Redefine the Political," *Yale Journal of Law and Feminism*, vol. 2 (1989): 32.

52. National Association of Colored Women's Clubs, "Our Mission," *Mission Statement*, 2019, https://www.nacwc.com/mission.

FURTHER READINGS

Bent-Goodley, Tricia, Colita N. Fairfax, and Iris Carlton-LaNey. "The Significance of African-Centered Social Work for Social Work Practice." *Journal of Human Behavior in the Social Environment* 27 (2017): 1–6.

Berman-Rossi, Toby, and Irving Miller. "African-Americans and the Settlements During the Late Nineteenth and Early Twentieth Centuries." *Social Work With Groups* 17 (1994): 77–95.

Diner, Steven J. "Chicago Social Workers and Blacks in the Progressive Era." *Social Science Review* 44 (1970): 393–410.

Gatwiri, Kathomi. "Afrocentric Ways of 'Doing' Social Work." In *Disrupting Whiteness in Social Work*, edited by Sonia Tascón and Jim Ife, 58–73. New York: Routledge, 2020.

hooks, bell. *Yearning: Race, Gender, and Cultural Politics*. London: Turnaround, 1991.

Kolivoski, Karen M., Addie Weaver, and Monique Constance-Huggins. "Critical Race Theory: Opportunities for Application in Social Work Practice and Policy." *Families in Society: The Journal of Contemporary Social Services* 95 (2014): 269–276.

Lewis, Gail. "Situated Voices." *Feminist Review* 53 (1996): 24–56.

REFERENCES

Bell, Derrick A. "Who's Afraid of Critical Race Theory." *University of Illinois Law Review* (1995): 893–910.

Bent-Goodley, Tricia, Snell, Cudore L. Snell, and Iris Carlton-LaNey. "Black Perspectives and Social Work Practice." *Journal of Human Behavior in the Social Environment* 27, nos. 1–2 (2017): 27–35. https://doi.org/10.1080/10911359.2016.1252604.

Boris, Eileen. 1989. "The Power of Motherhood: Black and White Activist Women Redefine the Political." *Yale Journal of Law and Feminism* 34 (1989): 25–49.

Brown, Kelly. "Womanist Theology." In *Black Women in America*, edited by Darlene Clark Hine, Elsa B. Brown, and Rosalyn Terborg-Penn, 1276–1277. Indiana: Indiana University Press, 1993.

Carlton-LaNey, Iris. "African American Social Work Pioneers' Response to Need." *Social Work* 44 (1999): 311–321.

———. "Doing the Lord's Work: African American Elders Civic Engagement." *Generations* 30, no. 4 (2006–2007): 47–50.

Collins, Patricia Hill. "What's in a Name? Womanism, Black Feminism and Beyond." *The Black Scholar* 26 (1996): 9–17.

Constance-Huggins, Monique. "Critical Race Theory in Social Work Education: A Framework for Addressing Racial Disparities." *Critical Social Work* 13, no. 2 (2012): 1–16.

Crenshaw, Kimberle. "Mapping the Margins: Intersectionality, Identity Politics, and Violence Against Women of Color." *Stanford Law Review* 43, no. 6 (1991): 1241–1299.

Dove, Nah. "African Womanism: An Afrocentric Theory." *Journal of Black Studies* 28, no. 5 (1998): 515–539.

Franklin, John H. "Public Welfare in the South During the Reconstruction Era, 1865–1880." *Social Science Review* 44 (1970): 379–392.

Gere, Anne Ruggles, and Sarah R. Robbins. "Gendered Literacy in Black and White: Turn-of-the-Century African-American and European-American Club Women's Printed Texts." *Signs: Journal of Women in Culture and Society* 21, no. 3 (1996): 643–678.

Harris, Frederick C. "The Rise of the Respectability Politics." *Dissent*. 2014. https://www.dissentmagazine.org/article/the-rise-of-respectability-politics.

Hendricks, Wanda A. *Gender, Race, and Politics in the Midwest: Black Club Women in Illinois*. Indiana: Indiana University Press, 1998.

Hounmenou, Charles. "Black Settlement Houses and Oppositional Consciousness." *Journal of Black Studies* 43, no. 6 (2012): 646–666.

Howard, Stephanie. "Social Work in the Black Community: A Collective Response to Contemporary Unrest." *Journal of Sociology & Social Welfare* 44 (2017): 81–97.

Knupfer, Anne M. "Toward a Tenderer Humanity and a Nobler Womanhood: African-American Women's Clubs in Chicago, 1890 to 1920." *Journal of Women's History* 7, no. 3 (1995): 58–76. https://doi.org/10.1353/jowh.2010.0419.

———. *Toward a Tenderer Humanity and a Nobler Womanhood: African American Women's Clubs in Turn-of-the-Century Chicago*. New York: New York University Press, 1996.

Martin, Elmer P., and Joanne M. Martin. *Spirituality and the Black Helping Tradition in Social Work*. Washington, DC: NASW Press, 2002.

National Association of Colored Women's Clubs. "Our Mission." 2019. https://www.nacwc.com/mission.

Razack, Narda, and Donna Jeffery. "Critical Race Discourse and Tenets for Social Work." *Canadian Social Work Review/Revue canadienne de service social* (2002): 257–271.

Schiele, Jerome H. "Afrocentricity: An Emerging Paradigm in Social Work Practice." *Social Work* 41, no. 3 (1996): 284–294.

———. "The Contour and Meaning of Afrocentric Social Work." *Journal of Black Studies* 27, no. 6 (1997): 800–819.

Shaw, Stephanie J. "Black Club Women and the Creation of the National Association of Colored Women." *Journal of Women's History* 3, no. 2 (1991): 11–25.

Terrell, Mary Church. "The Progress of Colored Women." *Teaching Tolerance*. 2017. https://www.learningforjustice.org/sites/default/files/general/96_TT_Beyond_Rosa_Parks_MChurchTerrell.pdf.

Walker, Alice. *In Search of Our Mother's Gardens*. New York: Harcourt, 1983.

Chapter 3

Struggles from the Margins, Advocacy at Intersections

Muslim Women's Advocacy in Europe, Canada, and the United States

Lara-Zuzan Golesorkhi

In 2017, the European Court of Justice (ECJ) issued a decision on religious garb in private employment. The ECJ held that restrictions on Islamic garb are lawful if they are part of general religious garb policies.[1] The Court's decision heightened already contentious discourse and politics regarding Muslims and Islam at a time when migration from Muslim majority countries reached new levels. The decision also occurred in the context of increasingly restrictive policies on Islamic garb throughout Europe. According to a 2018 report by the Open Society Foundation, one-third of all European Union (EU) countries have national and/or local restrictions on Islamic garb in private and/or public employment. The Open Society Foundation identified five common justifications for these restrictions: the imperative to provide security and counter terrorism, the drive for equality between men and women, the desire for homogeneity, the need for integration and assimilation, as well as the pursuit of neutrality and secularity.[2]

Muslim women in Québec Canada face similar challenges. Bill 21, a Canadian province bill passed in 2019 and upheld by the Québec Superior Court in 2021, restricts some public sector employees (i.e., teachers, judges, and police officers) from wearing religious garb.[3] These restrictions have received support across the country and have deepened debates about Muslims, Islam, women's rights, and migration. Meanwhile, in the United States, Ilhan Omar became the first Muslim Congresswoman to wear Islamic garb in 2018. In the United States, a Congressional hat ban, which has been in place since the 1830s, prohibits the wearing of headgear as part of broader provisions on the dress code for members of Congress. With her election, Omar, a Somali refugee, put the Congressional hat ban to the test by invoking protections under the U.S. Constitution.[4]

In response to these developments in Europe, Canada, and the United States, Muslim women, many of whom are first- or second-generation migrants, have advocated for their rights: #MuslimWomenBan is a collective of activists in Europe that have mobilized around the 2017 ECJ decision; "Hands Off My Hijab" is a global initiative that has rallied against Canada's Bill 21; and, "I stand with Ilhan Omar" has become a solidarity tagline for Congresswoman Omar. While these examples of collective action demonstrate different advocacy strategies and methods, all have embraced intersectionality as an approach in their struggles from the margins.

In this chapter, I explore various forms and spaces of Muslim women's advocacy that speak to struggles from the margins as it pertains to gender, migration, and religion. By drawing on case studies from Europe, Canada, and the United States, I examine how Muslim women mobilize, organize, and communicate their advocacy. Based on my analysis of these advocacy strategies and methods, I argue that struggles from the margins are an inherently intersectional endeavor in that they challenge the presumed uniformity of the center. Indeed, I propose that struggles from the margins and advocacy at intersections in the context of the topics discussed in this edited book volume raise important questions about feminism, agency, and identity. In regard to Muslim women's advocacy in Europe, Canada, and the United States, this means going beyond conventional inquiries about whether Muslim women have rights and rather interrogating the structures that frame Muslim women's advocacy, hereby shifting the starting point of discussion around gender, migration, and religion.

I suggest that at this gender-migration-religion advocacy nexus, there exists what I refer to as a "double binarism of absolutes:" within gender discourse and politics, these absolutes manifest in the conceptual binarism of oppressed Muslim women versus liberated "Western" women; within migration discourse and politics, these absolutes manifest in the conceptual binarism of Muslim men as terrorists and security threats on the one hand, and Muslim women as disempowered and in need of integration on the other hand. This double binarism of absolutes points to an antagonism between advocating for women's rights *or* advocating for minority rights—in this case, religious rights and migrant rights. It is this antagonism of advocating for either/or that then posits struggles from the margins as an inherently intersectional endeavor as it pertains to Muslim women. As a scholar-activist who situates her work at this gender-migration-religion advocacy nexus, I share my own experiences in the #MuslimWomenBan campaign toward the end of this chapter as a means of demonstrating the significant implications that this antagonism poses to collective action.

SITUATING STRUGGLES FROM THE MARGINS AND ADVOCACY AT INTERSECTIONS

In situating struggles from the margins in Europe, Canada, and the United States as it pertains to Muslim women's advocacy, histories and legacies at the gender-migration-religion advocacy nexus provide an important framework for my analysis. In the United States, for instance, religion has historically played an important role in collective action around migrant rights. As Pierette Hondagneu-Sotelo observes, migrant rights advocacy informed by religion can take various forms: religion can serve as a social movement language; religion can offer explanations for injustices; religion can establish frameworks for moral claims; religion can provide resources; and, religion can share ritual and cultural practices.[5] Examining civil rights struggles by Muslims in the United States, Hondagneu-Sotelo notes that religion is "the central basis for discrimination and is a primary means of mobilization."[6] However, religion does not serve as a rationale for making claims to assert civil liberties. This assertion of a "deliberately non-disruptive, institutional, and non-pious public identity" in advocacy efforts points to the largely secular modes of political participation which have been adopted in Muslim collective action in the United States.[7]

These modes of political participation and advocacy carry gender dynamics as Katherine Bullock discusses in the book *Muslim Women Activists in North America*. Bullock finds that in the contemporary moment, "if a Muslim woman takes to the podium, it is not usually to teach others as an authority on the Islamic sciences," but rather to lecture about Muslim women's rights, often with a focus on the right to education.[8] For Bullock, this focus on Muslim women's rights to education can be conceived of as a decline in the status and role of Muslim women in their communities. This becomes noticeable when one sheds light on the historical contribution of female scholars to the Islamic intellectual traditions, Bullock argues.

An example that highlights the widespread focus on Muslim women's rights in collective action at the intersection of migration, gender, and religion is the "Shariah Debate" in Ontario, Canada. The Shariah Debate arose between 2003 and 2005 when the Canadian Society of Muslims proposed the establishment of Darul-Qada, or a Muslim arbitration board (Islamic Institute of Civil Justice—IICJ), to provide mediation and arbitration services on family matters (i.e., spousal and child support, custody, and access or division of property). The IICJ was to offer Muslims in Ontario the option to resolve personal law matters according to religious values and beliefs while remaining within the framework of the Ontario judicial system.[9] The debates around the establishment of the IICJ led to tensions between various Muslim organizations, such as the Canadian Islamic Congress (CIC) and the Muslim

Canadian Congress (MCC). In examining these tensions, Meena Sharify-Funk asserts that these disputes between Muslim organizations had a distinct gender dimension in that they posited the question of "who will protect Muslim women" at the center of the debate.[10]

The framing of who "will protect Muslim women," and by extension Muslim women's rights, has become a prominent rallying point for collective action at the intersection of migration, gender, and religion. As Elénor Lépinard stresses, the Canadian feminist movement engaged in the Shariah Debate in the name of gender equality and in the name of protecting "vulnerable" women.[11] Several women's rights organizations joined together under the umbrella of a "No Religious Arbitration" coalition that mobilized against what they considered a "dangerous excess legitimated in the name of multiculturalism."[12] For Lépinard, the formation of such a coalition showcases the lack of intersectionality (gender, migration, and religion) in feminist mobilization in that advocates had not yet elaborated legal rationales on how to protect migrant or religious women—they only had elaborated legal rationales on how to protect women.

In Europe, debates about Muslim women's rights have similarly been contentious and have informed collective action at the intersection of migration, gender, and religion in important ways. As Armando Salvatore points out, much of the research on Muslims and Islam in Europe has emphasized the production of a specific "Euro-Islam" that is deemed "fit" to be integrated into preexisting structures.[13] For Salvatore, collective action on these matters challenges legal and political aspects of European institutions (particularly regarding secularism), but comes with important limitations, including restricted access to spaces of power, divergent representation (internal diversity of Muslim communities), and a lack of official legal recognition of many Muslim organizations.[14] These limitations carry important gender dynamics.

Cassandra Balchin asserts that Muslim women's advocacy in Western Europe, North America, Australia, and New Zealand (WENAAZ) is still emerging while it has been firmly established for more than two decades in Muslim majority and minority contexts outside of these diasporic areas.[15] The state of Muslim women's advocacy in WENAAZ thus presents a contrast to a vibrant transnational activism elsewhere. For instance, Balchin holds that Muslim women in Britain have historically not engaged in transnational feminist advocacy due to a lack of collective consciousness.[16] The events of September 11, 2001, however, changed this significantly as Muslim women's advocacy groups began to address patriarchal domination in their own communities and in politics more broadly.[17]

Although histories and legacies of Muslim women's advocacy have emerged and developed differently in Europe, Canada, and the United States, they all raise important conceptual questions about feminism, identity, and agency. Indeed, matters of autonomy, collective consciousness, access to spaces of power, as well as representation frame how Muslim women mobilize, organize, and communicate their advocacy as I discuss below.

CONCEPTUALIZING STRUGGLES FROM THE MARGINS AND ADVOCACY AT INTERSECTIONS

In her work, "The Active Social Life of Muslim Women's Rights," Lila Abu-Lughod prompts us to move away from arguing about whether Muslim women do or do not have rights, to instead examine conceptualizations and practices of Muslim women's rights in contemporary spaces. Abu-Lughod suggests that the kinds of questions that guide this refined inquiry should shift the gaze from "Do Muslim women have rights?" (or "Do Muslim women need saving?") to insights on the mediations and transformations of Muslim women's rights across the world. Questions of inquiry then become: In what debates and institutions do Muslim women's rights partake? What infrastructures support them? And how do they manifest in various places, for various kinds of women?[18] Abu-Lughod further reminds us to treat Muslim women's rights as a social fact rather than a rallying cry.[19] In doing so, we can begin to better understand the complex structures that frame struggles from the margins and advocacy at intersections as it pertains to Muslim women's advocacy.

In light of Abu-Lughod's prompt, I argue that these structures are informed by particular conceptualizations of feminism, identity, and agency that have postulated the "(veiled) Muslim woman" as the ultimate signifier of otherness that is at odds with feminist trajectories, that embodies a contested identity, and that inherently lacks agency. As Sirma Bilge observes, discourse and politics on Muslim women in the "West" (Europe, Canada, and the United States) are framed around two main readings of Islamic garb: Islamic garb as a symbol of women's subordination to men or Islamic garb as an act of resistance to Western hegemony.[20] These readings of Islamic garb have been omnipresent in contemporary debates over migration and migrant/Muslim integration and find their roots in colonial and imperial projects.

In "Algeria Unveiled," Frantz Fanon, for instance, asserts that the unveiling (forcibly removing of Islamic garb) of Algerian women by the French can be seen as an act of "para-neurotic brutality and sadism."[21] The veiled Algerian woman represented a "site" that was to be occupied by colonial forces in order to take control over Algerian society.[22] These conceptions of Muslim women's oppression and hereby the lack of agency assigned to Muslim women continue to be used to underline a sense of inferiority that exhibits itself in the paradoxical portrayal of Muslim women as passive victims of their oppressive patriarchal religion and male kin, and an active threat to "Western" modernity and freedoms.[23]

This "binarism of absolutes", in its varied forms, as characterized by Fauzia Erfan Ahmed, is heightened of discourse and politics on gender and migration, and results in what I conceive of as "double binarism of absolutes:"[24] within gender discourse and politics, these absolutes manifest in the conceptual binarism of oppressed Muslim women versus liberated "Western" women; within migration discourse and politics, these absolutes manifest in the conceptual binarism of Muslim men as terrorists and security threats on the one hand, and Muslim women as disempowered and in need of integration on the other hand. The question then of whether "veiled" Muslim women should be "tolerated" or "outlawed" through Islamic garb policies becomes a showcase of the antagonism between advocating for women's rights *or* advocating for minority rights; in the case of my analysis, religious rights and migrant rights.

The prevalence of this antagonism has reinforced a presumed lack of agency of Muslim women which frames contentions between different strands of feminism and speaks to conceptualizations of identity (constructed by self and others).[25] Since women (at intersections) have historically been perceived as non-agentic subjects, agency has become foundational for Muslim women's advocacy.[26] Agency of Muslim women has been a focal point for the "submission frame"—Islamic garb as oppressive—which corresponds with liberal/universalist feminist accounts, and the "resistance frame"—Islamic garb as resistance—which corresponds with postcolonial feminist accounts.[27]

Navigating around these contending feminist strands and situating agency within them has led to ascribed identity formations of Muslim women into what Jasmine Zine and Sunaina Maira have discussed as "good" versus "bad" Muslim feminists.[28] These identity formations are heavily gendered and Orientalized, and have (in many ways) created a divide between secular and faith-centered Muslim feminists. While secular feminists have built transnational alliances connected to global gender equality movements, they remain ideologically at odds with faith-centered Muslim women who root their resistance within religious reform.[29] This has posed challenges in developing strategic solidarities in Muslim women's advocacy, particularly in the context within which ascribed conceptions of "good" Muslim feminists and "bad" Muslim feminists have been situated: the "good" Muslim feminist places the locus of their struggles strictly in religious paradigms and repression by other Muslims while the "bad" Muslim feminist interrogates the root causes behind the rise of fundamentalism, global conflicts, and terror.[30] More concretely, the "good" Muslim feminist declares Islamic fundamentalism as the primary culprit for the oppression of women; the "bad" Muslim feminist, on the other hand, is vilified for their anti-imperialist political stance.[31] These ascribed conceptions have been materialized around "culture talk", the dehistoricization of identities through which religious experiences become political categories, that is entrenched in globalized processes of domination (Mamdani, 2004). [32]

In many ways then, Muslim women's advocacy is shaped by a diverse feminist consciousness within Muslim communities *and* by external culture talk and binarism of absolutes of varied forms. These complex structures that frame Muslim women's advocacy have informed specific strategies and methods used to converge often opposing conceptualizations of feminism, identity, and agency, and are evidenced in the ways in which Muslim women mobilize, organize and communicate around their struggles in Europe, Canada, and the United States as I explore below.

PRACTICING STRUGGLES FROM THE MARGINS, ADVOCACY AT INTERSECTIONS

Muslim women's advocacy, whether faith-centered, secular, or otherwise, has taken various forms across space and time. Hodan A. Mohamed's ethnographic research in "The Triple Consciousness of Black Muslim Women" demonstrates this clearly. Based on interviews with Somali women in Canada, Mohamed explores the nature of "triple consciousness" of being Black, Muslim, and a woman, and discusses how this shapes the lived experiences and identity formation among Somali women. Mohamed interrogates narratives of Blackness, which often exclude the experiences of Muslim migrant women; Mohamed also interrogates prevailing discussions around Islamophobia which often erase the experiences of Black migrant women. Mohamad finds that Somali Muslim women challenge the conventional sociological definition of Blackness as a nondivergent and monolithic identity by self-identifying as Black *and* Somali *and* Muslim.[33]

This triple consciousness significantly informs advocacy strategies and methods as Somali Muslim women reconcile multiple identities and hereby multiple spheres of agency: they fight against anti-Blackness, Islamophobia, and anti-migrant racism at the same time. Mohamed situates this intersectional advocacy within discussions on Somalinimo, the essence of being a Somali, which includes Islam as an integral part of such identity.[34] Being Muslim then is perceived as a category that contains multiple meanings, including religion and race. Two interview excerpts speak to this explicitly:[35]

Burco: I guess being a Black activist entails for you to be a Christian, so if you are a Muslim, you seem to be the other even within the Black community. So, it's very challenging for me to identify as Black activist because I just don't feel I am being accepted enough, right now.

Kismayo: Not only do Black lives matter for us, but our womanhood matters to us, so does us being Muslims matter. Some of us don't have the luxury to separate ourselves and just call ourselves Muslims.

Mohamed finds that a common pattern amongst all of the first-generation Somali women interviewed concerned the women's focus on "creating the space, thought process, and intellectual discourse" in recognizing and challenging the pervasiveness of anti-Blackness, Islamophobia, and anti-migrant racism in Canada.[36]

Another important intersecting experience to highlight in this context is that of Muslim youth. In their examination of Muslim youth engagement in Toronto, Canada, Katherine Bullock and Paul Nesbitt-Larking explore conceptions of political participation, self-identification as political actors, formal, informal, and civic political involvement, as well as the relationship between religious identities and Canadian identities. Despite the negative public discourse around Muslims and Islam, and lived experiences of racism, faith was central in the youth's advocacy strategies and methods. Bullock and Nesbitt-Larking write:

> The 20 Muslim youths interviewed for this study have been able to transcend feelings of being negatively perceived by others. They have all arrived mostly at positions of deep affection and attachment to Canada, if a fragile sense of being welcomed and included, and this is in spite of an overriding sense that they and their faith are misunderstood by the wider Canadian society and having experienced some societal or institutional Islamophobia.[37]

This transcending commitment to collective action carries gender dynamics as Bullock and Nesbitt-Larking's analysis revealed that all in the "most highly politically engaged" category were young Muslim women. In talking about navigating intersecting identities in collective action, including wearing Islamic garb, an excerpt from an interview with one of the young Muslim women is telling:

> Yes, I would consider [myself a political person] ... try to keep myself aware of what's going on, I—I look at different parties that are in the Canadian system, at the electoral system .... I haven't voted yet but because I wasn't much in politics before but now that I'm like I'm becoming interested and when the time comes I'll probably vote as well.[38]

This pattern of high civic engagement by Muslim women, albeit not necessarily in formalized political spaces, resonates with Daood Hamdani's

2006 report "Engaging Muslim Women: Issues and Needs," published by the Canadian Council of Muslim Women, an organization established in 1982 and dedicated to the empowerment, equality, and equity of all Muslim women in Canada. In this report, Hamdani finds that while voter turnout is generally low amongst Muslim women, they were more likely to engage in informal political engagement such as petition writing.[39]

These multifaceted experiences, strategies, and methods of Muslim women's advocacy exemplified in Canada are also manifested in the United States. In their book, *Muslim Women in America,* Yvonne Haddad et al. discuss the public roles of Muslim women and how these roles have shaped "the process of defining, and redefining, the meaning of American Islam."[40] Haddad et al. find that the presence of Muslim women in varied professions (including political ones) and the publicly "giving voice" to Muslim communities, has led Muslim women to change the face of Islam in the United States in that these efforts have challenged "perennial images of Islamic women as oppressed and forced into seclusion."[41]

Haddad et al. outline different spaces within which Muslim women's advocacy has taken place (i.e., Muslim organizations and mosques) and explore corresponding advocacy strategies and methods. For instance, Muslim women have served as chaplains in various kinds of institutions, including prisons, universities, as well as hospitals. Additionally, Muslim women made up around three-quarters of the teaching staff in full-time Islamic schools and charter schools.[42] These developments in Muslim women's representation across different spaces, and in advocacy efforts more broadly, can be explained through what Fauzia Erfan Ahmed has identified as distinct types of leadership models held by Muslim women in the United States.

Ahmed differentiates between different types of leadership models in Muslim women's advocacy that are tied to specific historical migration patterns. According to Ahmed, the "Scholar-Activist Model of Leadership" emerged in the context of migration policy changes in 1965 which transformed the ethnoscape of Muslims in the United States.[43] During this time, female Muslim migrants came from diverse ethnic, religious, and national backgrounds, and were highly educated. Upon arrival in the United States, the women were confronted with racialized dynamics in feminist movements on the one hand, and patriarchal structures within Muslim communities on the other hand. Advocacy was thus organized around the leadership of educated female Muslim migrants who had fought Western imperialism, rejected traditional gender stereotypes, and participated in the public sphere in their countries of origin.[44] The women often became a focal point in their migrant communities in the United States: as scholars, they focused on feminist interpretations of Islamic texts to actively defy stereotypes; as activists, they challenged Western feminism through advocacy.

Moving along the historical timeline, Ahmed notes that with changes in migration policy post–9/11, the "Intersectional Leadership Model" emerged. Migration from Muslim majority countries became increasingly securitized and Muslim (migrant) communities were increasingly surveilled.[45] To Ahmed, this new leadership model is hence based on intersectional agency defined as "the ability to not only simultaneously lead different coalitions, but to effectively enable their intersections on a number of political projects relevant to the followership."[46] In this model, Muslim women's advocacy reaches beyond Muslim communities and navigates around globalized practices of collective action that address self-definition, coalition-building, and youth-leadership development.

An interesting case study to examine in this context is *Muslimah Watch* (MMW), a blog site by and for Muslim women. Founded in 2007 as a personal blog by Fatemeh Fakhraie, a Muslim-American woman of Iranian descent in the Bay Area, MMW is now a team of 21 female bloggers of various nationalities, some of whom self-identify as Muslim feminists. The site describes its mission as one of locating and critiquing misogyny, sexism, patriarchy, Islamophobia, racism, and xenophobia.[47] In analyzing MMW as a case study for Muslim collective action, Nabil Echchaibi finds that blogging, as an advocacy tool, reveals itself as a form of resistance. For Echchaibi, blogging "renders legible and actualizes the political" and has hereby become "a prime discursive and performative space where young Muslims debate and contest what it means to be modern in transnational settings."[48]

By connecting Muslim women's advocacy across the Atlantic, Caroline Nagel and Lynn Staheli explore how religious identities function amongst Muslim Arab activists in the United States and the UK.[49] They conclude that Muslim activists are far from unified in their views on religion as a basis for political action and mobilization.[50] While some interviewed activists were keen to "place Islam squarely in mainstream political spaces," most of the interviewees insisted that Islam should remain a private (identity) matter whereas advocacy should take place under the aegis of "Arabness" or other "secular" identities.[51] For instance, Muslim activists who expressed commitments to move Islam away from the margins of public life engaged in outreach efforts by distributing reading material on Islam in public libraries, holding "open house" events at mosques, participating in interfaith networks and events, and creating advertising material (i.e., billboards) that project a positive image of Muslims, particularly regarding Muslim women and Islamic garb.[52] On the other hand, Muslim activists who expressed commitments to decenter Islam as the basis of political claims or political mobilization, advocated within and beyond their communities around domestic political issues such as civil and migrant rights, domestic surveillance, mass deportations, and airport profiling (see Ahmed's Intersectional Leadership Model).[53]

Speaking to these intersectional dimensions in advocacy efforts, Aleksandra Lewicki and Therese O'Toole's study on the political engagement of Muslim women in Bristol, UK reveals important insights. Lewicki and O'Toole's study focused on advocacy strategies and methods used to mobilize against violence against women and to renegotiate terms of participation in religious spaces such as mosques. Lewicki and O'Toole found that with regard to both of these issues, advocacy was not confined to the local community or national level, but was rather supported by and embedded in related transnational struggles.[54] Advocacy strategies and methods used to make mosques more inclusive demonstrate this transnational connection in interesting ways.

Historically, mosques in Bristol have been mainly located in confined properties, such as terraces or warehouses, and have not provided spaces for women's worship. While some mosques have moved to larger facilities and enabled women's attendance, others only invite women to larger functions or do not offer suitable prayer spaces for women. The governing boards of the seventeen Bristol-based mosques where decisions about these matters have been made are exclusively male. In response, Muslim women expressed concerns about "unsuitable or even undignified arrangements for women's prayer in mosques," including relegation to a narrow kitchen space or behind curtains at the back of the room.[55] Indeed, Lewicki and O'Toole point out that the women viewed the provision of women's prayer spaces and inclusion on mosque committees as "peripheral to a more radical vision of women's inclusion."[56] This more radical vision expressed by the women was based on transnational advocacy methods and strategies, notably from the United States. Lewicki and O'Toole elaborate:

> Their [Muslim women] inspiration was, among others, the US based Islamic scholar Amina Wadud, who has provided theological justifications for women's ritual leadership, and was among the organizers of events during which she led audiences of women and men in prayer . . . —an act regarded as controversial by many. Activists who supported the ideas behind Wadud's activism reasoned that current local mosque leaderships were so unresponsive to women's concerns that the only way to bring about social change was to hold separate events for those who agreed on more inclusive procedures.[57]

In efforts of pursuing this more radical vision of women's inclusion, Muslim women in Bristol connected with like-minded individuals (including Amina Wadud), the Muslim Women's Network UK (MWNUK) in Birmingham, and the Inclusive Mosque Initiative (IMI) in London through social media (Facebook and Twitter). These connections provided theological expertise, extended community support, and offered role model resources for Muslim women and their advocacy.[58]

Relatedly, in her analysis of Muslim women's political participation in Italy, Alessia Belli finds that the visibility and active engagement of Muslim women "not only works as a litmus test of the status quo but also as a sensor of the complex social dynamics under way" in matters of gender, migration, and religion in Europe.[59] Belli interviewed Muslim women who were appointed or nominated for political positions across institutional levels (local, state, and federal) and shows that "acting for the general interest" (Muslim women, migrant women, and Muslim migrant women) was a shared commitment among all of the interviewees.[60] For instance, one woman described the right to vote as "the first step to become a full citizen and to feel a legitimate and active part of the wider society"; while another woman stressed the significance of "giving voice" to the second generation (of migrants) and to young people more broadly: "I really hoped to be elected because I have so many ideas; I wanted to represent the youth, the young person that could be multicultural, Italian, religiously different, differently able: different in all the existing meanings. I wanted to be an example."[61]

Analyzing these varied experiences and conceptions of Muslim women's advocacy in Italy, Belli notes that "the fact that women stand for election makes a huge impact in that it introduces a female presence into a traditionally male bastion," yet, questions about whether the presence of women will make gender equality more relevant in a political setting that is not exactly renowned for its gender-sensitive orientation, remain.[62] These findings from Italy and the UK provide an important framework for my discussion of the #MuslimWomenBan campaign in which an intentional focus was placed on intersectional approaches in Muslim women's advocacy.

THE CASE OF #MUSLIMWOMENBAN

The #MuslimWomenBan campaign emerged in the context of the 2017 decision by the ECJ concerning Islamic garb in private employment. The ECJ held that restrictions on Islamic garb are lawful if they are part of general religious garb policies. The decision was based on the cases of Samira Achbita, an employee at G4S Secure Solutions in Belgium and Asma Bougnaoui, an employee at Micropole SA in France. While the ECJ itself did not rule on these individual cases, the Court's interpretations of EU law are binding on the national courts that requested the preliminary inquiry (Belgium and France) as well as on national courts of EU member states before which a similar issue is raised.[63]

The potential range and impact of this decision informed the organizing and mobilizing around #MuslimWomenBan across Europe as an inherently transnational and intersectional endeavor. Organizing began in anticipation of the decision and involved press releases on the potential impacts of the unknown outcome. In a coalition meeting with civil society organizations from across Europe one day after the decision, refined strategies and methods on how to respond to the decision were discussed based on the details of case law. The objective of #MuslimWomenBan was—from the get go—to first and foremost center those affected by the decision, namely Muslim women in Europe wearing a headscarf. This included providing information and creating an awareness campaign in which Muslim women posted a selfie on social media with a poster #MuslimWomenBan and shared their experiences of discrimination in the labor market. An accompanying Facebook page, which outlined the purpose and goal of this collective action, was also created.

While those affected by the ECJ's decision were front and center of the #MuslimWomenBan awareness campaign, the collective action also involved transnational outreach to civil society organizations within and outside of Muslim communities, especially feminist and human rights organizations. The aim of this expanded outreach was to mobilize around an intersectional common cause, namely antidiscrimination in the labor market. This intersectional common cause was addressed through strategic messaging to employers as well as showcasing of inclusive working environments. The focus on employers rather than lawmakers was intentional: since the ECJ itself did not rule on the cases, the individual cases were referred back to national courts. With each country having its own policies on Islamic garb, #MuslimWomenBan coalition members across Europe were tasked to take the lead in communicating the campaign's message within their own countries, targeting stakeholders on social media, particularly on Twitter.

The invitation for my involvement in the #MuslimWomenBan coalition emerged based on my role as the Executive Director and Founder of WoW—WithorWithout at the time.[64] WoW is a community-based, nonprofit, NGO that promotes equality and diversity in the German labor market. WoW's focus is on women who experience intersectional discrimination in the labor market by addressing four main stakeholders: employees, employers, society, and politics. For employees (women), WoW offers leadership workshops, antidiscrimination, and "Know Your Rights (KYR)" courses, as well as individual mentoring to prepare for the labor market. WoW reaches employers through diversity trainings and annual Diversity Day activities. Through the "With or Without Campaign," WoW raises awareness about intersectional discrimination in the labor market. For example, in 2016/2017, WoW developed two ongoing campaigns: bags and postcards with the organization's motto "What matters in the job market is what's in the head, not on it," as well as a card game on "Muslims and Islam in Germany." WoW's political work includes research as well as advocacy across institutional levels, including at the United Nations, the European Commission, and the European Parliament.

I established WoW as one of ten winners of the 2015 Global Diversity Contest hosted by the United Nations Academic Impact. My work as a scholar-activist has since developed and has found a new home in the Center for Migration, Gender, and Justice (CMGJ) where I am the Founder, Executive Director, and Advocacy Director. CMGJ is a nonprofit NGO that addresses human rights at the intersection of migration and gender.[65] At CMGJ, we believe in gender justice beyond borders. Our focus is on shrinking spaces, figuratively and literally, between migrant communities and governing bodies. It is through my experiences of doing community-based work as part of WoW and globally engaged research, advocacy, and education at CMGJ, that I have come to deeply understand the complexities of navigating contested spaces of feminism, identity, and agency in advocacy efforts at intersections.

CONCLUSION

In what debates and institutions do Muslim women's rights partake? What infrastructures support them? And how do they manifest in various places, for various kinds of women? I reiterate Abu-Lughod's prompting questions as an opener to my conclusion with the hopes that they will guide future research on struggles from the margins and advocacy at intersections. It is these and other probing inquiries explored in this article that address the pervasive antagonism between advocating for women's rights *or* advocating for minority rights (i.e., religious rights and migrant rights). This antagonism of either/or in advocacy efforts reinforces various conceptual binarisms of absolutes and posits struggles from the margins as an inherently intersectional endeavor.

Indeed, struggles from the margins don't operate in a vacuum, they operate at intersections. At these intersections, questions about identity and agency are raised and contested by those advocating *for themselves and their communities*, and by those advocating *for others*. Advocacy at the intersection of gender, migration, and religion is complex as a collective consciousness at this nexus remains to be formed. The absence of a collective consciousness is, in many ways, what keeps certain struggles at the margins, while others perpetuate the center, as is evidenced in my analysis of Muslim women's advocacy in Europe, Canada, and the United States.

Since I began doing community-based work and global research that aligns with advocacy and education, I have met hundreds of inspiring activists. They have taught me how to be a guide, a resource, a learner, and a listener at the same time. Many of their experiences resonate with mine—Experiences of discrimination; experiences of being talked about and not talked with; and experiences of a lack of representation. Other experiences, I can at-best relate to, at worst I contribute to. It is my hope that by understanding struggles at intersections, rather than as isolated realities, advocacy in the twenty-first century can move beyond *one* woman's struggle being *another* woman's detached rallying cry.

NOTES

1. "C-157/15 – G4S Secure Solutions," InfoCuria, The Court of Justice of the European Union, https://curia.europa.eu/juris/liste.jsf?num=C-157/15; "C-188/15 – Bougnaoui and ADDH," InfoCuria, The Court of Justice of the European Union, https://curia.europa.eu/juris/liste.jsf?language=en&jur=C,T,F&num=C-188/15&td=ALL.
2. "Restrictions on Muslim Women's Dress in the 28 EU Member States," Open Society Foundation, https://www.opensocietyfoundations.org/sites/default/files/restrictions-on-womens-dress-in-28-eu- member-states-20180709.pdf.
3. "Canada: New Bill Prohibits Religious Symbols for Public-Sector Workers in Quebec," Library of Congress, updated August 6, 2019, https://www.loc.gov/law/foreign-news/article/canada-new-bill-prohibits-religious-symbols-for-public-sector-workers-in-quebec/.
4. Mythili Sampathkumar, "House Democrats Push to End Floor Ban on Hijab and Other Religious Headwear as First Muslim Women Enter Congress," *The Independent*, November 20, 2018, https://www.independent.co.uk/news/world/americas/us-politics/hijab-ban-house-congress-religious-headwear-democrats-floor-muslim-omar-tlaib-a8643151.html.
5. Pierrette Hondagneu-Sotelo, *God's Heart Has No Borders: How Religious Activists are Working for Immigrant Rights* (Berkeley, CA: University of California Press, 2008), 19.
6. Ibid., 30.
7. Ibid., 70.
8. Katherine Bullock, *Muslim Women Activists in North America: Speaking for Ourselves* (Austin, TX: University of Texas Press, 2008), xiii.
9. Meena Sharify-Funk, "Representing Canadian Muslims: Media, Muslim Advocacy Organizations, and Gender in the Ontario Shari'ah Debate," *Global Media Journal*, vol. 2, no. 2 (2009): 80; see also, Natasha Bakht, "Religious Arbitration in Canada: Protecting Women by Protecting Them From Religion," *Canadian Journal of Women and the Law*, vol. 19, no. 1 (2007): 119–144.
10. Ibid., 79.
11. Eléonore Lépinard, "In the Name of Equality? The Missing Intersection in Canadian Feminists' Legal Mobilization Against Multiculturalism," *American Behavioral Scientist*, vol. 53, no. 12 (2010): 1764.
12. Ibid., 1765.

13. Armando Salvatore, "Making Public Space: Opportunities and Limits of Collective Action Among Muslims in Europe," *Journal of Ethnic and Migration Studies*, vol. 30, no. 5 (2004): 1014.

14. Ibid., 1028–1029.

15. Cassandra Balchin, "Emergence of a Transnational Muslim Feminist Consciousness Among Women in the WENAAZ (Western Europe, North America, Australia and New Zealand) Context," in *Muslim Diaspora in the West: Negotiating Gender, Home and Belonging*, eds. Haideh Moghissi and Halleh Ghorashi (London: Taylor & Francis: 2010), 39.

16. Ibid., 44.

17. Ibid., 74.

18. Lila Abu-Lughod, "The Active Social Life of 'Muslim Women's Rights': A Plea for Ethnography, Not Polemic, with Cases from Egypt and Palestine," *Journal of Middle East Women's Studies*, vol. 6, no. 1 (Winter 2010): 1–2.

19. Ibid., 34.

20. Sirma Bilge, "Beyond Subordination vs. Resistance: An Intersectional Approach to the Agency of Veiled Muslim Women," *Journal of Intercultural Studies*, vol. 31, no. 1 (2010): 9.

21. Frantz Fanon, *A Dying Colonialism* (New York: Grove Press, 1965), 45–46.

22. Ibid., 30.

23. Annelies Moors, "Colonial Traces? Islamic Dress, Gender, and the Public Presence of Islam," in *Colonial and Post-Colonial Governance of Islam: Continuities and Ruptures*, eds. Marcel Maussen, Annelies Moors, Veit-Michael Bader (Amsterdam: Amsterdam University Press, 2011), 144.

24. Fauzia Erfan Ahmed, "Globalization and Women's Leadership in the Muslim Diaspora," in *Muslim Diaspora in the West: Negotiating Gender, Home and Belonging*, eds. Haideh Moghissi and Halleh Ghorashi (London: Taylor & Francis, 2010), 30.

25. See also Liz Fekete, "Enlightened Fundamentalism? Immigration, Feminism and the Right," *Race and Class*, vol. 48, no. 2 (2006): 1–22.

26. See Bronwyn Davies, *A Body of Writing 1990-1999* (Walnut Creek, CA: Altamira Press, 2000).

27. Bilge, "Beyond Subordination vs. Resistance: An Intersectional Approach to the Agency of Veiled Muslim Women," 14.

28. Jasmine Zine, "Between Orientalism and Fundamentalism: The Politics of Muslim Women's Feminist Engagement." *Muslim World Journal of Human Rights*, vol. 3, no 1 (2006): 1. See also Sunaina Maira, ""Good" and "Bad" Muslim Citizens: Feminists, Terrorists, and U. S. Orientalisms," *Feminist Studies*, vol. 35, no. 3 (2009): 631–656.

29. Jasmine Zine, "Between Orientalism and Fundamentalism: The Politics of Muslim Women's Feminist Engagement," 2.

30. Ibid., 12.

31. Ibid.

32. See Mahmoud Mamdani, *Good Muslim, Bad Muslim* (New York: Pantheon Press, 2004).

33. Hodan A. Mohamed, "The Triple Consciousness of Black Muslim Women: The Experiences of First Generation Somali-Canadian Women Activists," *Journal of Somali Studies*, 4, no. 1–2 (2017), 18.

34. Ibid., 19.

35. Ibid., 29.

36. Ibid., 26.

37. Katherine Bullock and Paul Nesbitt-Larking, "Becoming 'Holistically Indigenous': Young Muslims and Political Participation in Canada," *Journal of Muslim Minority Affairs*, vol. 33, no. 2 (2013): 201.

38. Ibid., 191.

39. Daood Hamdani, *Engaging Muslim Women: Issues and Needs*, Toronto: Canadian Council of Muslim Women, 2006), https://www.ccmw.com/publications/2019/1/22/engaging-muslim-women-issues-and-needs.

40. Yvonne Haddad, Jane I. Smith, and Kathleen M. Moore. *Muslim Women in America: The Challenge of Islamic Identity Today* (New York: Oxford University Press, 2011), 122.

41. Ibid.

42. Ibid., 129.

43. Ahmed, "Globalization and Women's Leadership," 129.

44. Ibid., 131.

45. Ibid., 134.

46. Ibid.

47. Nabil Echchaibi, "'Muslimah Media Watch': Media Activism and Muslim Choreographies of Social Change," *Journalism*, vol. 14, no. 7 (2003): 852.

48. Ibid.

49. Caroline R. Nagel and Lynn A. Staheli, "Muslim Political Activism or Political Activism by Muslims? Secular and Religious Identities Amongst Muslim Arab Activists in the United States and United Kingdom," *Identities: Global Studies in Culture and Power*, vol. 18 (2011): 437.

50. Ibid.

51. Ibid.

52. Ibid., 448.

53. Ibid., 451.

54. Aleksandra Lewicki and Therese O'Toole, "Acts and Practices of Citizenship: Muslim Women's Activism in the UK," *Ethnic and Racial Studies*, vol. 40, no, 1 (2017): 152.

55. Ibid., 163.

56. Ibid.

57. Ibid.

58. Ibid.

59. Alessia Belli, "Limits and Potentialities of the Italian and British Political Systems Through the Lens of Muslim Women in Politics," in *Muslim Political Participation in Europe,* ed. Jørgen Nielson (Edinburgh: Edinburgh University Press, 2013), 163.

60. Ibid., 178.

61. Ibid.
62. Ibid.
63. "C-157/15 – G4S Secure Solutions," InfoCuria, The Court of Justice of the European Union.
64. "English," *With or Without: WOW*, http://www.wow-withorwithout.com/english.
65. "Meet the Center for Migration, Gender, and Justice, https://www.migrationgenderjustice.com/.

FURTHER READINGS

Bullock, Katherine. "The Gaze and Colonial Plans for the Unveiling of Muslim Women." *Studies in Contemporary Islam* 2, no. 2 (2000): 1–20.

Golesorkhi, Lara-Zuzan. "Islamic Garb in Public Employment in Europe and the US: From Integration to Accommodation to Anti-Discrimination." *Journal of Muslim Minority Affairs* 39, no. 4 (2019): 551–568.

Kahf, Mohja. *Western Representations of the Muslim Woman*. Austin, Texas: University of Texas Press, 1999.

Mahmood, Saba. *Politics of Piety: The Islamic Revival and the Feminist Subject*. Princeton, NJ: Princeton University Press, 2005.

Manji, Irshad. *The Trouble With Islam*. Toronto: Random House Canada, 2003.

Shaikh, Sa'diyyah. "Transforming Feminism: Islam, Women and Gender Justice." In *Progressive Muslims*, edited by Omid Safi, 147–162. Oxford: Oneworld Press, 2003.

Zine, Jasmine. "Creating a Critical Faith-Centered Space for Antiracist Feminism: Reflections of a Muslim Scholar-Activist." *Journal of Feminist Studies in Religion* 20, no. 2 (2004): 167–187.

REFERENCES

Abu-Lughod, Lila. "The Active Social Life of 'Muslim Women's Rights': A Plea for Ethnography, Not Polemic, With Cases From Egypt and Palestine." *Journal of Middle East Women's Studies* 6, no. 1 (Winter 2010): 1–45.

Ahmed, Fauzia Erfan. "Globalization and Women's Leadership in the Muslim Diaspora." In *Muslim Diaspora in the West: Negotiating Gender, Home and Belonging*, edited by Haideh Moghissi and Halleh Ghorashi, 23–38. London: Taylor & Francis, 2010.

Bakht, Natasha. "Religious Arbitration in Canada: Protecting Women by Protecting Them From Religion." *Canadian Journal of Women and the Law* 19, no. 1 (2007): 119–144.

Balchin, Cassandra. "Emergence of a Transnational Muslim Feminist Consciousness Among Women in the WENAAZ (Western Europe, North America, Australia and New Zealand) Context." In *Muslim Diaspora in the West: Negotiating Gender,*

Home and Belonging, edited by Haideh Moghissi and Halleh Ghorashi, 39–52. London: Taylor & Francis, 2010.

Belli, Alessia. "Limits and Potentialities of the Italian and British Political Systems Through the Lens of Muslim Women in Politics." In *Muslim Political Participation in Europe*, edited by Jørgen Nielson, 163–189. Edinburgh: Edinburgh University Press, 2013.

Bilge, Sirma. "Beyond Subordination Vs. Resistance: An Intersectional Approach to the Agency of Veiled Muslim Women." *Journal of Intercultural Studies* 31, no. 1 (2010): 9-28.

Bullock, Katherine. *Muslim Women Activists in North America: Speaking for Ourselves.* Austin, Texas: University of Texas Press, 2008.

Bullock, Katherine, and Paul Nesbitt-Larking. "Becoming 'Holistically Indigenous': Young Muslims and Political Participation in Canada." *Journal of Muslim Minority Affairs* 33, no. 2 (2013): 185–207.

"C-157/15 – G4S Secure Solutions." *InfoCuria.* The Court of Justice of the European Union. https://curia.europa.eu/juris/liste.jsf?num=C-157/15.

"C-188/15 – Bougnaoui and ADDH." *InfoCuria.* The Court of Justice of the European Union. https://curia.europa.eu/juris/liste.jsf?language=en&jur=C,T,F&num=C-188/15&td=ALL.

"Canada: New Bill Prohibits Religious Symbols for Public-Sector Workers in Quebec." *Library of Congress.* Updated August 6, 2019. https://www.loc.gov/law/foreign-news/article/canada-new-bill-prohibits-religious-symbols-for-public-sector-workers-in-quebec/.

Center for Migration, Gender, and Justice. "Meet the Center for Migration, Gender, and Justice." https://www.migrationgenderjustice.com/.

Davies, Bronwyn. *A Body of Writing 1990–1999.* Walnut Creek, CA: Altamira Press, 2000.

Echchaibi, Nabil. "'Muslimah Media Watch': Media Activism and Muslim Choreographies of Social Change." *Journalism* 14, no. 7 (2013): 852–867.

"English." *With or Without: WOW.* http://www.wow-withorwithout.com/english.

Fanon, Frantz. *A Dying Colonialism.* New York: Grove Press, 1965.

Fekete, Liz. "Enlightened Fundamentalism? Immigration, Feminism and the Right." *Race and Class* 48, no. 2 (2006): 1–22.

Haddad, Yvonne, Jane I. Smith, and Kathleen M. Moore. *Muslim Women in America: The Challenge of Islamic Identity Today.* New York: Oxford University Press, 2011.

Hamdani, Daood. *Engaging Muslim Women: Issues and Needs.* Toronto: Canadian Council of Muslim Women, 2006. https://www.ccmw.com/publications/2019/1/22/engaging-muslim-women-issues-and-needs.

Hondagneu-Sotelo, Pierrette. *God's Heart Has No Borders: How Religious Activists Are Working for Immigrant Rights.* Berkeley, CA: University of California Press, 2008.

Lépinard, Eléonore. "In the Name of Equality? The Missing Intersection in Canadian Feminists' Legal Mobilization Against Multiculturalism." *American Behavioral Scientist* 53, no. 12 (2010): 1763–1787.

Lewicki, Aleksandra, and Therese O'Toole. "Acts and Practices of Citizenship: Muslim Women's Activism in the UK." *Ethnic and Racial Studies* 40, no. 1 (2017): 152–171.

Maira, Sunaina. "'Good' and 'Bad' Muslim Citizens: Feminists, Terrorists, and U. S. Orientalisms." *Feminist Studies* 35, no. 3 (2009): 631–656.

Mamdani, Mahmoud. *Good Muslim, Bad Muslim*. New York: Pantheon Press, 2004.

Mohamed, Hodan A. "The Triple Consciousness of Black Muslim Women: The Experiences of First Generation Somali-Canadian Women Activists." *Journal of Somali Studies* 4, nos. 1–2 (2017): 9–42.

Moors, Annelies. "Colonial Traces? Islamic Dress, Gender, and the Public Presence of Islam." In *Colonial and Post-Colonial Governance of Islam: Continuities and Ruptures*, edited by Marcel Maussen, Annelies Moors, and Veit-Michael Bader, 135–155. Amsterdam: Amsterdam University Press, 2011.

Nagel Caroline R., and Lynn A. Staheli. "Muslim Political Activism or Political Activism by Muslims? Secular and Religious Identities Amongst Muslim Arab Activists in the United States and United Kingdom." *Identities: Global Studies in Culture and Power* 18 (2011): 437–458.

"Restrictions on Muslim Women's Dress in the 28 EU Member States." *Open Society Foundation*. https://www.opensocietyfoundations.org/sites/default/files/restrictions-on-womens-dress-in-28-eu- member-states-20180709.pdf.

Salvatore, Armando. "Making Public Space: Opportunities and Limits of Collective Action Among Muslims in Europe." *Journal of Ethnic and Migration Studies* 30, no. 5 (2004): 1013–1031.

Sampathkumar, Mythili. "House Democrats Push to End Floor Ban on Hijab and Other Religious Headwear as First Muslim Women Enter Congress." *The Independent*, November 20, 2018. https://www.independent.co.uk/news/world/americas/us-politics/hijab-ban-house-congress-religious-headwear-democrats-floor-muslim-omar-tlaib-a8643151.html.

Sharify-Funk, Meena. "Representing Canadian Muslims: Media, Muslim Advocacy Organizations, and Gender in the Ontario Shari'ah Debate." *Global Media Journal* 2, no. 2 (2009): 73–89.

Zine, Jasmine. "Between Orientalism and Fundamentalism: The Politics of Muslim Women's Feminist Engagement." *Muslim World Journal of Human Rights* 3, no. 1 (2006): 1–24.

Chapter 4

Oppression, Resistance, and Reform

Revisiting the Catholic Discussion on Women's Ordination

Carol J. Dempsey, OP

Pope Francis enlarged the institutional tent of the historically male-led Roman Catholic Church when he appointed women to key Vatican positions. In 2021, French Sister Nathalie Becquart became undersecretary of the General Secretariat of the Synod of Bishops, the second-highest-ranking person in the Synod of Bishops. This position requires her to organize meetings of world bishops. Another woman, Italian magistrate Catia Summaria, is the first woman prosecutor in the Vatican's Court of Appeals.[1] Spanish Old Testament biblical scholar, Sr. Nuria Calduch-Benages, was appointed as the secretary of the Pontifical Biblical Commission. She joins Benedicte Lemmelijn from Belgium, Maria Armida Nicolaci and Bruna Costacurta from Italy, and Mary Healy from the United States. For the first time in history, five women have thus become part of the twenty-member biblical commission. Pope Francis also modified church law to allow women to take a greater liturgical role during Mass.[2] They are now readers at liturgies, altar servers, and distributors of communion. Previously, such roles were officially reserved for men. With this modification now official, conservative bishops can no longer block women in their dioceses from those roles. To support his decision, the Pope also revised a clause of Canon Law from "lay men" to "lay persons,"[3] thus enabling women and men to perform "the ministries of lector and acolyte" in Catholic services. The Pope appointed yet another woman to a key Vatican position, Francesca Di Giovanni, who coordinates the Church's relationships with multilateral organizations, such as the United Nations. These appointments recognize the important contributions that women have been making to the Church.

While Pope Francis's appointments of women to high-ranking positions in the Vatican are helpful, the question is whether the appointments will change positively women's authority status in the church. This question is relevant because other papal decisions exclude women from the highest offices of ecclesial leadership reserved only for males ordained to the priesthood. For example, in 2020, the Amazon Synod recommended that women be ordained deacons, but Pope Francis rejected the synod's recommendation. Instead, he organized for a second time a commission to study the question. His decision frustrated some Roman Catholics who had hoped for more revolutionary reform during his pontificate. The Pope also reiterated that only ordained priests are allowed to preside at a Roman Catholic Mass. He sees the priestly role and function as particular and principal to the priesthood; it cannot be delegated. Thus, for Francis, only males can serve as ordained priests. Furthermore, to date, Pope Francis joins a host of other Church officials, including other popes, cardinals, archbishops, and bishops relying on the doctrinal paradigm to argue against women's ordination. Since the paradigm conceives authority and truth claims of the biblical text for the Christian faith and the Church in ahistorical and dogmatic terms, this doctrinal paradigm understands the Bible as the literal "word of God." Defining the Bible as divinely inspired, divinely revealed, authoritative, and binding to Christians, this doctrinal paradigm enables Church officials to "speak with authority" against the ordination of women.

This essay examines four Church documents that Roman Catholic Church officials use to reject the ordination of women in the Roman Catholic Church. The documents are the "Declaration *Inter Insigniores*: On the Question of Admission of Women to the Ministerial Priesthood" issued by the Sacred Congregation for the Doctrine of Faith (1976);[4] "Apostolic Letter *Ordinatio Sacerdotalis* of John Paul II to the Bishops of the Catholic Church on Reserving Priestly Ordination to Men Alone" by Pope John Paul II (1994);[5] "Ten Frequently Asked Questions about the Reservation of Priestly Ordination to Men," A Pastoral Response by the Committee on Doctrine of the National Conference of Catholic Bishops (CDNCCB; 1998);[6] and "Book VI" of the new revised Code of Canon Law by Pope Francis (2021).[7] The four documents illustrate particularly well four strategies that Church officials use to exclude women from the ordained priesthood in the Roman Catholic Church. Any Bible scholar will immediately recognize the rather limited exegetical value of these ecclesial interpretations, as their executive power in the ongoing assertions of exclusively male hegemonic authority is particularly forceful. The critical analysis of the Church documents demonstrates that they lack any use of contemporary biblical hermeneutics that would open wide the door for gender justice in the Church. It is about time that academically credentialed Bible scholars take on the task of critically studying these documents, perhaps even encouraging sophisticated and justice-oriented interpretations by future Church officials. Finally, the essay's purpose is to expose Church officials' use of hegemonic power to block women's ordination to the priesthood.

Four sections structure the essay. The first section explores the hermeneutical strategy of prooftexting. The second section considers the strategy of essentializing the male gender of Jesus and of the twelve apostles with which Church officials assert exclusively male ordination and apostolic succession. The third section exposes, from Pope Paul VI to Pope Francis, the Vatican's overall strategic plan, which consists of one pope building on and reinforcing another pope's documents to prohibit women from priestly ordination. The fourth section examines Pope Francis's new revision to the Code of Canon Law. This new revision specifically excludes Roman Catholic women from ordination. The conclusion summarizes the discourse on the four strategies, situates Roman Catholic feminists in the context of Buddhist feminists also working toward their priestly ordination with Buddhism, and showcases two prominent examples of resistance that offer hope and support to Roman Catholic women called to serve as Catholic priests in the Church.

STRATEGY 1: PROOFTEXTING THE BIBLE

The first strategy that Church officials use to block women from priestly ordination is prooftexting. It uses biblical texts to prove or justify particular arguments or theological positions without regard for the context of the cited passages. Using this strategy, ecclesial officials appeal to various biblical texts to explain why women cannot be ordained to the priesthood. One reason for an all-male priesthood is that Jesus, inspired by God, chose twelve male apostles, and so the Church is to follow in Jesus's footsteps by ordaining men apostles only. Texts cited to support this argument are Mk 3:13, Lk 6:12-13, and Jn 15:16. Another reason for not ordaining women to the priesthood is that, like Jesus, the apostles chose male fellow workers only. 1 Tim 3:1-13, 2 Tim 1:6, and Tit 1:5-9 are foundational for this argument. Yet another reason to prohibit women from being ordained priests refers to the story of the "Last Supper," which Church officials interpret as a meal shared between Jesus and his twelve male apostles only. Texts cited to support this interpretation include Matt 26:17-30, Mk 14:12-31, Lk 22:14-23, and Jn 13:1-30. To give further authority to their reasons, Church officials link the biblical phrase, "Do this in remembrance of me" (Lk 22:19 and 1 Cor 11:24-25) to sacramental ordination. By establishing this link, Church officials affirm an all-male priesthood, justifying Holy Orders as a sacrament to be conferred on males only. These two biblical passages, together with the link to sacramental ordination—"Holy Orders"—foreground yet another argument that priestly ordination is directly tied to apostolic succession, the uninterrupted line of continuity from the Apostles of Jesus Christ, available to men only.

The strategy of prooftexting not only provides material for the formulation of reasons against women's priestly ordination but also lends authority to official church documents that address priestly ordination as a sacrament for males only. To accomplish this task, Church officials imbed certain biblical texts into their documents, their "teachings" against women's ordination. A good and first example of this hermeneutical strategy is Pope John Paul II's Apostolic Letter *"Ordinatio Sacerdotalis"* (1994). John Paul II imbeds into this letter biblical passages such as Matt 10:1, 7-8; 16:14-15; 28:16-20, Mk 3:13-16, Lk 6:12, Jn 6:70, Acts 1:2, and Rev 21:14. The Pope refers to these biblical texts to argue four points: first, Christ called and chose freely only men as Apostles; second, Christ made this call in accordance with God's divine plan and in union with God through the Holy Spirit after spending the night in prayer; third, Christ made these twelve men the foundation of his Church; and fourth, the twelve men were intimately associated with the mission of Christ himself. Having argued for an all-male priesthood with citations taken from the Bible, John Paul II adds a final linchpin to his argument. He cites Lk 22:32 to make the case that the Church has no authority to confer priestly ordination on women. This statement, indicating the parameters of Church authority, appears at the end of a letter that intends to stop the debate about women's ordination and to silence any further dialogue on the issue.

A second church document arguing for an all-male priesthood is "Ten Frequently Asked Questions about the Reservation of Priestly Ordination to Men." This document that the CDNCCB (later called the United States Conference of Catholic Bishops/USCCB 2001) composed in 1998[8] is a response to *"Ordinatio Sacerdotalis."* In this document, the bishops imbed Matt 9:37-38 and Lk 10:2 to maintain that no one can become a "laborer in the vineyard" unless sent by Christ. The bishops also reference Mk 3:13 and Lk 6:12 to stress that Jesus not only chose the twelve apostles but also sent them as laborers and that the twelve apostles were all males. The bishops assert that only males can fulfill the tasks of the twelve apostles, as Christ himself selected them. The bishops explain that the Church has always understood that Jesus's prayer for laborers, which the bishops equate with "workers," "has in part been answered in Christ's sending of the Apostles and their successors as laborers to continue the work in the harvest of salvation."[9] The bishops maintain that "we see an essential part of God's splendid answer to our prayers for workers in this harvest."[10] In other words, the bishops understand apostolic succession as the transmission of spiritual authority from the male apostles to successive male popes and male bishops, and thus the related sacrament of Holy Orders instructs that spiritual authority is open to males only. Additionally, by writing this pastoral response, the bishops exercise ecclesial power to assert that only men are capable of being divinely chosen. Since the bishops are part of the Magisterium and their pastoral response cites biblical texts, this second document on "Ten Frequently Asked Questions about the Reservation of Priestly Ordination to Men" becomes "authoritative" as part of the official teaching of the Roman Catholic Church. Ironically, the characterization of this document as a "pastoral response" is a misnomer. The document is an edict that solidifies, particularly for U.S. Roman Catholics, the Vatican's case against women's ordination to the priesthood.

The prooftexting strategy that Church officials use to formulate their arguments against the ordination of women elicits critical responses from New Testament Catholic Bible scholars, in particular, Michael F. Patella, O.S.B. and Elisabeth Schüssler Fiorenza. With respect to Lk 10:1-16 and Lk 10:2 in particular, Patella raises several questions about the constitution of the seventy-two laborers. He wonders whether the Twelve are part of the seventy-two; perhaps they are not. As Patella speculates that perhaps women are involved standing in the lineage of Deborah, Hulda, Esther, Miriam, or Ruth, he also observes that no definitive answer exists about the gender and identity of those whom Jesus chose. Could it not be that among the laborers were also women? In Patella's view, whether the mission is restricted to men thus remains uncertain.[11]

Another critique refers to the implied doctrinal paradigm of Catholic bishops, as they argue for Jesus choosing male disciples only. Schüssler Fiorenza shows that this paradigm is pervasive when Roman Catholic Church officials make "authoritative" statements to maintain power and control of the institutional church. Schüssler Fiorenza asserts that "in controversial theological questions, the Bible functions as proof text or first principle. The biblical books become a source of proof texts that are often taken out of context to legitimate predetermined dogmas, principles, or institutions of the Church."[12] She also observes that the bishops use the Bible authoritatively, as they argue that the Bible reveals "eternal truth" and "timeless principles." The bishops thus use biblical passages to justify "the moral, doctrinal, or institutional interests of the church."[13] Schüssler Fiorenza's observations illustrate that the use of the doctrinal paradigm and the prooftexting strategy are conscious choices of the bishops serving the institutional agendas of the male Roman Catholic Church hierarchy. Said differently, Church officials want to see only male priests, and so they read men into the Bible. In short, Roman Catholic Bible scholars challenge the prooftexting hermeneutics of Church officials to justify the exclusion of women from the ranks of the ordained clergy.

In sum, the bishops maintain that the Bible is the divinely inspired and revealed "Word of God" and thus has to be read literally. They select verses to fit the ecclesiological agenda of prohibiting women's ordination. As

Church officials use the doctrinal paradigm, they create "authoritative" official documents to weaponize the Bible for political-institutional purposes. The resulting documents make the "maleness" of those called, chosen, and sent sacrosanct, enabling Church officials to preserve and sustain a male hierarchical, patriarchal institution of the ordained priesthood and the Church. The weaponization of the Bible in official church documents is thus a strategy to prohibit women from the priesthood and to deny women access to ordained leadership in the Church. Even more egregious, Church officials violate the personhood of women by accentuating in the church documents the "maleness" of those chosen, called, and sent. Church leaders tell Roman Catholic women that because they are women, they are not worthy of being called, chosen, and sent by Christ or God. This sexist and misogynist attitude, masked by the inordinate use of the Bible, leads to the second strategy that Church officials use to exclude women from priestly ordination. This strategy essentializes the gender of the twelve apostles.

STRATEGY 2: ESSENTIALIZING GENDER

The second strategy that Church officials use to block women from priestly ordination is essentializing gender. The Vatican's Sacred Congregation for the Doctrine of the Faith (CDF) employs this strategy in the document "*Inter Insigniores*: Declaration on the Question of Admission of Women to the Ministerial Priesthood." Four sub-strategies develop this strategy that enables the CDF to argue for an exclusively male priesthood. The four elements focus on the Catholic theological and ecclesial tradition, the person of Jesus, the attitude of Jesus, and the practice of the Apostles. Both biblical references and ecclesial-doctrinal sources support the gender-essentializing arguments.

The first sub-strategy that assumes an essentializing notion about gender is based on the maleness of Christ, *in persona Christi*. The CDF maintains that "the priest is a sign, the supernatural effectiveness of which comes from the ordination received, but a sign that must be perceptible and which the faithful must be able to recognize with ease."[14] This claim is followed by a sentence from the writings of Thomas Aquinas who argues that a "natural resemblance" must exist between Christ and "his" minister because God incarnates through a man and not through a woman. Thus, the CDF believes the faithful would find it difficult to see the image of Christ in the person of a female priest. Several biblical passages aim to support this claim. Relying on the heteronormative metaphor in which Christ is the bridegroom and the Church is the bride, the CDF contends that the priest must be male. Like Christ, the priest is the head of the Church. He exercises Christ's ministry of salvation, culminating in the celebration of the Eucharist. As a result, a woman cannot serve as a priest.

This theological assertion has not remained without criticism. Theologian Sonya A. Quitslund rejects the CDF's sexist assumption inherent in the translation of *in persona Christi* (2 Cor 2:10).[15] Quitslund maintains that Christ's presence in the priest should be based on the mystical and not the biological. Because the CDF's claim focuses on biology, the implication is: "If woman cannot image Christ . . . then being a man is clearly more desirable than being a human being."[16] Quitslund incorporates into her critique the thought of a group of Berkeley Catholic theologians who reject the notion that only a man can act *in persona Christi*. According to these theologians, both women and men, as priests, demonstrate to the faithful that all Christians, regardless of gender, embody Christ. To the Berkeley theologians, the prohibition of women from priestly ordination is a symbol of sexual discrimination within the Catholic Church. Furthermore, they see the alignment of the ordained priesthood with masculinity as indicative of a regressive vision of the Church.[17]

The second sub-strategy highlights the "attitude of Christ." Vatican officials maintain that Jesus Christ "did not call any women to become part of the Twelve. If he acted in this way, it was not in order to conform to the customs of his time, for his attitude towards women was quite different from that of his milieu, and he deliberately and courageously broke with it."[18] To support this claim, the CDF prooftexts several gospel verses (e.g., Jn 4:27, Matt 9:20; Lk 7:37). Furthermore, the CDF also believes that Christ did not entrust the apostolic charge to women.[19] The CDF's interpretation of the Bible suggests that Jesus could have chosen women to be part of the Twelve, but he did not. In other words, the CDF affirms a male-centric view of Christ's attitude that excludes women from ordained ministry in the Catholic Church.

A powerful critique comes from Catholic feminist theologian and Bible scholar, Elisabeth Schüssler Fiorenza. She unpacks the claim that Jesus does not call any woman to be a member of the Twelve. She interrogates the assertion that the Twelve had to be and were all males, pointing out that "the Declaration assumes that the male character of the Twelve is essential for their function and mission"[20] and that therefore "we must ask... whether the Twelve's mission and function necessitates that they are males."[21] Unsurprisingly, Schüssler Fiorenza states that "the Declaration's argument that the Church, in faithfulness to the example of Jesus who did not choose women as members of the Twelve, cannot ordain women has no basis in the NT,"[22] and that "the Church can entrust the apostolic ministry and power to whomever it chooses without maintaining any historical-lineal connection with the Twelve."[23] Schüssler Fiorenza's comments underscore the fallacies and their misguided reasoning of the CDF's claims against the ordination of women.

The second sub-strategy also includes another CDF comment on the "attitude of Christ." The CDF characterizes Mary, the mother of Jesus, as a model woman to contend that Jesus made no allowance for even his mother to be part of his apostolic ministry and thus Church officials allow also do not allow women to be part of any apostolic ministry associated with apostolic succession. In support of this conviction, the CDF quotes Pope Innocent III: "Although the Blessed Mary surpassed in dignity and in excellence all the Apostles, nevertheless it was not to her but to them that the Lord entrusted the keys of the Kingdom of Heaven."[24] Mary is the best woman around Jesus, but even she only serves Jesus and does not lead with or instead of him after his death. As the CDF highlights Jesus's exclusive appointment of men, the CDF also appeals uncritically to biblical texts, patristic writers, and the writings of one pope. The CDF excludes female personhood because, in the CDF's mind, Jesus preferred male over female leadership, without ever considering the work of contemporary feminist theologians and Bible scholars, such as Elisabeth Schüssler Fiorenza. By highlighting Christ's attitude toward women, then, Church officials assume to know Christ's mind, an assumption based on prooftexting and the uncritical interpretation of select Bible passages which become the impetus to exclude women from apostolic succession and Christ's apostolic charge.

The third sub-strategy centers on the practices of the apostles. Here, the CDF refers to two biblical events to endorse male ordination only. The first biblical event appears in the report on the gathering in the Upper Room (Acts 1:14, 23); and the second event is about Pentecost. The CDF explains that the Twelve choose Mathias in the Upper Room to replace Judas, but the Twelve do not choose Mary despite her privileged place. Citing Acts 1:14, 23, the CDF also emphasizes that the Holy Spirit comes to both women and men on Pentecost, but only Peter and the Eleven proclaim the fulfillment of the prophecies in Jesus (Acts 1:14; 2:1,14). The CDF mentions that the Apostles break away from Mosaic practices to preach the Gospel just as Jesus breaks away from the religious customs of his day. Thus, to the CDF, the Apostles, like Christ, reject the ordination of women. In other words, Church officials emphasize that the Apostles follow what they perceive as their faithful duty to Jesus. Thus, none of them ordain women. Accordingly, the CDF concludes: "[A]t no time was there a question of conferring ordination on these women."[25]

After focusing on two events involving the Twelve Apostles, the CDF draws attention to the apostle Paul. By appealing to the Pauline letters, the CDF embellishes its position against women's ordination, contending that Paul used the title "my fellow workers" (Rom 16:3; Phil 4:2-3) for men and women but reserved the title "God's fellow workers" (1 Cor 3-9; 1 Thess 3:2) for three men: Apollos, Timothy, and himself because "they are directly set apart for the apostolic ministry and the preaching of the Word of God."[26] The CDF's comments historicize Paul to the point of claiming to know his thoughts, reasoning, and choices. Hence, according to the CDF, Paul understood the official and public proclamation of the message as belonging exclusively to apostolic succession.

The fourth sub-strategy emphasizes the ecclesial tradition. Its aim is to reject women's ordination to the priesthood by showing that the Church Fathers and the canonical documents of the Antiochan and Egyptian traditions support fully this position. The CDF notes that the writings of the patristic era condemn various sects that ordained women. Accordingly, the Church Fathers considered ordained female priests theologically unacceptable. Quoting the theological positions of the Church Fathers in *Inter Insigniores,* the CDF endorses this tradition. Similarly, the CDF refers to canonical documents from the Antiochan and Egyptian traditions to assert that the Church should ordain only men to the priesthood, thus maintaining an unbroken tradition throughout ecclesial history, "universal in the East and West, and alert to repress abuses immediately."[27] The CDF also contends that this standard is based on Christ's example, and an all-male priesthood conforms to "God's plan for his Church."[28] Claims to patristic theology, presumably authorized by Christ, reinscribes the male gender into the priesthood and makes male biology the sole requirement for the ordained priesthood in the Roman Catholic Church. The male gender is essentialized as the sole biological criterion for the ordained priesthood.

In sum, the CDF documents essentialize gender by stressing Christ's maleness, his and the Apostles' exclusionary practice toward women, and the patristic rejection of female ordination in early Christian communities. Although the CDF documents emphasize Mary, the mother of Jesus, as the most perfect woman, even she does not qualify for the ordained priesthood. The fixation on the biological gender of Jesus excludes women from ordained leadership. Like Mary, women are valued only as mothers and wives. Although the CDF gives even "male" Apostles less dignity and excellence than Mary, they are adequate to be ordained priests but not the women. Thus, according to the CDF, the male gender in Jesus and the Apostles is the most significant factor for the male-ordained priesthood in the Roman Catholic Church. Consequently, women cannot be priests.

This position is an intellectual and spiritual assault on women because it reduces the *imago Dei* to biology. As a rebuttal to the CDF's fixation on the male gender of Jesus, Canadian woman priest Monika Kilburn-Smith states that "women are the face of the Divine, too."[29] The implication that women cannot represent Christ in ministry, which the CDF defines as culminating in the celebration of the Eucharist, violates the intrinsic equality of women and men. Unsurprisingly, this theological stance forces women to the ecclesiastical margins in a Church dominated by sexism. In other words, a gender essentializing hermeneutic is part and parcel of the CDF's justification for the exclusion of women from the ordained priesthood in the Roman Catholic Church.

STRATEGY 3: REINFORCING HEGEMONIC RHETORIC FROM POPE TO POPE

The third strategy that Church officials use to block women from priestly ordination is to write documents that reinforce hegemonic rhetoric from pope to pope. Three examples of the papal documents are, first, the "Declaration *Inter Insigniores*: On the Question of Admission of Women to the Ministerial Priesthood" (1976); second, the "Apostolic Letter *Ordinatio Sacerdotalis* of John Paul II to the Bishops of the Catholic Church on Reserving Priestly Ordination to Men Alone" (1994); and third, "Ten Frequently Asked Questions about the Reservation of Priestly Ordination to Men" (1998). The documents contain four elements that demonstrate how various popes and other Church officials support one another's rhetoric, with the goals of keeping women from becoming ordained priests in the Roman Catholic Church, and preserving the patriarchal church structure with male clerical leaders only in power. The four elements include the use of papal quotes and references to past popes, statements about women, a phallocentric emphasis on the maleness of Christ, and the repeated assertion that the Church has no authority to admit Roman Catholic women to priestly ordination. The four elements accomplish the patriarchal clergy rule. Hence, the rhetoric of these three documents.

The first element, pertaining to the use of papal quotes and references to past popes, features prominently in all three documents. In *Inter Insigniores,* written by the CDF and in dialogue with Pope Paul VI who approved, confirmed, and ordered the published document, the CDF quotes four popes, John XXIII, Paul VI, Pius XII, and Innocent III. The CDF uses these quotes to lend authority to the views presented in the document on the topic of women's priestly ordination. A quote from Pius XII strengthens arguments for male priests who, like Christ, dispense the sacraments, particularly the Eucharist. By employing a quote from Pope John XXIII and Pope VI, the CDF affirms the contributions of women in society and the Church. Yet with another quote from Paul VI, along with one from Innocent III, his predecessor, the CDF negates the possibility of women being ordained in the Roman Catholic Church.

In the apostolic letter *Ordinatio Sacerdotalis* written by Pope John Paul II, the Pope opens the document by quoting the remarks of his predecessor,

Pope Paul VI, who wrote the following comments in a letter to F.D. Coggan, Anglican archbishop of Canterbury:

> She [the Church] holds that it is not admissible to ordain women to the priesthood, for the very fundamental reasons. These reasons include: the example recorded in the sacred Scriptures of Christ choosing his Apostles only from among men; the constant practice of the Church, which has imitated Christ in choosing only men and her living teaching authority which has consistently held that the exclusion of women from the priesthood is in accordance with God's plan for his Church.[30]

In the context of the Anglican Church's discernment of whether to ordain women to the priesthood, Pope Paul VI was reminding Archbishop Coggan of the Roman Catholic Church's steadfast position on the matter. Pope John Paul II mentions Pope Paul VI a second time in *Inter Insigniores* to affirm Paul VI's directive to the CDF. The directive instructed the CDF to formulate *Inter Insigniores* to expound on the Church's teaching on women's priestly ordination. John Paul II then states that the "Supreme Pontiff" (Pope Paul VI) approved *Inter Insigniores* and ordered its publication. This statement and other references to Paul VI sent a strong message, specifically, that he, John Paul II, is aligned with Paul VI's rhetoric concerning women's ordination. John Paul II argues against women's ordination throughout *Ordinatio Sacerdotalis*. To add further weight to his arguments, John Paul II even refers to *Inter Insigniores* in *Ordinatio Sacerdotalis*. He quotes Paul VI who explained in that document why women cannot be ordained. John Paul II, increasing strength to his arguments against women's priestly ordination, quotes his apostolic letter *Mulieris Dignitatem*. In this letter, John Paul II argues that Christ's actions sanction the Church's decision not to ordain women.

In "Ten Frequently Asked Questions about the Reservation of Priestly Ordination to Men," written by the U.S. Committee on Doctrine of the National Conference of Catholic Bishops (CDNCCB), the bishops refer to *Ordinatio Sacerdotalis*, the thought of John Paul II, and the work of the CDF. These references provide the CDNCCB with the needed support for its document that simply reiterates the Vatican's adverse position on women's ordination. The reiteration indicates that the CDNCCB embraces the mindset and position of its patriarchal, hierarchical leaders and their hegemonic rhetoric.

The second element found in the three papal documents are statements about women. In *Inter Insigniores*, the CDF, under the direction of Paul VI, writes statements that recognize the role of women in public life. To support the statements, the CDF quotes Pope John XXIII from his encyclical *Pacem in Terris*, drawing on the Second Vatican Council's Pastoral Constitution *Gaudium et Spes*. That document stresses that the Church views discrimination, especially "discrimination based upon sex,"[31] as contrary to God's plan.

The CDF then advocates for the elimination of discrimination. To further support women and their achievements, the CDF notes the significant roles that three women, namely Clare of Assisi, Theresa of Avila, and Catherine of Siena, played in the Church during the Middle Ages. Next, the CDF cites the Decree *Apostolicam Actuositatem*[32] from the Second Vatican Council. This document emphasizes the activity of women in society to concur with other Church leaders that "it is very important that [women] participate more widely in the various sectors of the Church's apostolate."[33] The papal document *Inter Insigniores* contains encouraging rhetoric for Roman Catholic women, but it also presents the CDF's case bluntly. It claims that Roman Catholic women cannot become ordained priests because Christ didn't choose women, not even Mary, his own mother, for this apostolic charge and ministry. The CDF's quote from Pope Innocent III permits the Committee to give indisputable support to the papal argument that prohibits women's ordination.

In *Ordinatio Sacerdotalis*, Pope John Paul II also makes statements about women in his message to the Catholic Church's bishops. He praises women, defining them as essential to the life and mission of the Church but not important enough to be ordained. John Paul II expresses even stronger sentiments in the same vein as his predecessors in *Inter Insigniores*. He affirms that women are true disciples of the Church, witnesses to Christ in the family and in society, and persons in total consecration to the service of God and of the Gospel. To reinforce the Church's acceptance of women, John Paul II quotes *Inter Insigniores*: "The Church desires that Christian women should become fully aware of the greatness of their mission: today their role is of capital importance both for the renewal and humanization of society and for the rediscovery by believers of the true face of the Church."[34] Yet after affirming women, John Paul II focuses on Mary, calling her the "Mother of God" and the "Mother of the Church," as he reiterates Pope Paul VI and the CDF position in *Inter Insigniores*. Thus, to Pope John Paul II, too, Mary "received neither the mission proper to the Apostles nor the ministerial priesthood."[35] Having made Mary an example to argue against women's ordination in the Roman Catholic Church, John Paul II adds another point: Mary's inability to participate in both the specific mission of the Apostles and the ministerial priesthood does not mean women are of lesser dignity, nor is the Church discriminating against women. To John Paul II, women are absolutely necessary and irreplaceable, but their presence and roles in the Church do not include the ordained priesthood. John Paul II embellishes on the thought of Paul VI and the CDF, all of whom argue that only men can be ordained priests.

In "Ten Frequently Asked Questions about the Reservation of Priestly Ordination to Men," the bishops make statements about women. This document contains a sexist argumentation about women's ordination. On the one hand, the CDNCCB affirms women in the Church by stressing that the Church upholds the equality of both men and women. On the other hand, the CDNCCB follows the argument of Pope Paul VI, the CDF, and Pope John Paul II, asserting that women and men have different roles in the Church. Like the other two Church documents, the CDNCCB document also mentions Mary, the mother of Jesus, to emphasize that she is not part of the twelve male apostles and that even though she does not have a designated place in Jesus's mission and ministry, women still have to follow her example. The document, reinforcing the arguments made by Pope Paul VI, the CDF, and Pope John Paul II in *Inter Insigniores* and *Ordinatio Sacerdotalis*, emphasizes that women are not called to be among the Twelve. Unlike the other two documents, however, the CDNCCB document expands this point even further when the bishops state: "The Church cannot consider the claim of a woman that God has called her to ordained ministry because the very possibility of priestly ordination arises only within the framework of a divine plan and order in which participation in Christ's role as head of the Church is reserved to men."[36] Thus, in the CDNCCB document, the bishops allege that women cannot be ordained to the Roman Catholic priesthood even if they were called by God. Importantly, in the view of the bishops, the person and work of the male Christ supersede a woman's divine call from God to the ordained ministry.

The third element found in all three documents is a phallocentric emphasis on the maleness of Christ. In *Inter Insigniores*, the CDF focuses on both the biological maleness of Jesus and the male priest as a sign and symbol of Jesus. The CDF contends that the Church, by calling only men to priestly ordination and ministry in its true sense, remains faithful to the ordained ministry as willed by Christ and maintained by the Apostles. *Ordinatio Sacerdotalis* features the same logic also appearing in *Inter Insigniores*. In *Ordinatio Sacerdotalis*, John Paul II makes four claims. First, Christ chooses twelve men and makes them the foundation of the Church. Second, the Apostles receive a function that could only be carried out by them and their successors. Third, the Apostles are intimately and specifically associated with the mission of Jesus himself; and fourth, the Apostles choose "fellow workers" to represent Christ and to carry on the mission. Both the CDF in *Inter Insigniores* and John Paul II in *Ordinatio Sacerdotalis* interpret "fellow workers" as a reference to men validating apostolic succession. In the CDNCCB document, the bishops reinscribe into the CDNCCB document the metaphor used by the CDF in *Inter Insigniores*, namely, that Christ is the Church's male bridegroom. They believe that the Church embodies this metaphor. Accordingly, Jesus chooses only men for apostolic and priestly office because they represent Christ as the bridegroom and as the head of the Church. The bishops uphold the CDF's argument made in *Inter Insigniores* that Christ's male gender is needed as a sacramental sign for the celebration of the Eucharist. The CDNCCB document thus reinforces the teachings of *Inter Insigniores* and *Ordinatio Sacerdotalis*, according to which the sacrament of the Holy Orders is reserved for men only in fidelity to Christ's example and apostolic practice.

The fourth element that appears in all three documents asserts repeatedly that the Church has no authority to admit Roman Catholic women to the ordained priesthood. Relying on papal authority, the CDF makes the following statement in *Inter Insigniores*:

> For these reasons, in execution of a mandate received from the Holy Father and echoing the declaration which he himself made in his letter of 30 November 1975, the Sacred Congregation for the Doctrine of the Faith judges it necessary to recall that the Church, in fidelity to the example of Christ the Lord, does not consider herself authorized to admit women to priestly ordination.[37]

Although the CDF is one of the highest ecclesial theological authorities, its document declines theological authority to give access to women's ordination. Similarly, in *Ordinatio Sacerdotalis*, Pope John Paul II affirms the claim made by Pope Paul VI and the CDF when he also does not recognize the Church to have this theological authority. He maintains:

> Wherefore, in order that all doubt may be removed regarding a matter of great importance, a matter which pertains to the Church's divine constitution itself, in virtue of my ministry of confirming the brethren (cf. Lk 22:32) I declare that the Church has no authority whatsoever to confer priestly ordination on women and that this judgment is to be definitively held by all the Church's faithful.[38]

Pope John Paul II not only reiterates the position of Pope Paul VI and the CDF but also strengthens it by casting an emphatic tone to statements that already discriminate, marginalize, and keep women from becoming ordained priests in the Roman Catholic Church.

Endorsing the fourth element and lending even greater authority to the final statement of John Paul II's apostolic letter is the *Responsum ad dubium* issued October 28, 1995, by Cardinal Joseph Ratzinger, head of the CDF who later became Pope Benedict XVI. The *Responsum ad dubium*, enables Church leaders to decline theological authority to give women the right to the ordained priesthood. The *dubium* affirms the Pope's teaching that the Church has no authority whatsoever to confer priestly ordination on women, and that this teaching is to be held definitively and must be understood as belonging to the deposit of faith. The *dubium* declares emphatically that "this teaching requires definitive assent, since, founded on the written Word of God, and from the beginning constantly preserved and applied in the Tradition of the Church, it has been set forth infallibly by the ordinary and universal

Magiterium."[39] Pope John Paul II, with the assistance of Cardinal Ratzinger and the CDF, concurs. The inter-papal agreement on the lack of theological authority in the case of women's ordination illustrates the power-play that situates the Magisterium as the primary articulator of Church teaching when, in fact, this role falls to the entire college of bishops, as outlined in the Vatican II document, *Lumen Gentium* #25.[40] In current Roman Catholic ecclesiology, the Roman Curia and the CDF play only auxiliary roles in assisting the bishops in exercising power and authority to teach the faith. Thus, from the Vatican's perspective, no further conversation about women's ordination or any similar movement can be tolerated.

Finally, in "Ten Frequently Asked Questions about the Reservation of Priestly Ordination to Men," in the last of the three documents containing the fourth element, the bishops continue to support the claim that the Church has no authority to ordain women to the ministerial priesthood. On this point, they refer to the teachings of Pope Paul VI, John Paul II, and *Ordinatio Sacerdotalis*. According to the bishops, John Paul II's teaching in *Ordinatio Sacerdotalis* on the matter of church authority and women's ordination is to be held definitively by the faithful as belonging to the deposit of faith. The bishops affirm the CDF's statements that the Church's teaching on this matter is founded on the Bible as the written "Word of God," constantly preserved and applied in the Tradition of the Church, and that this teaching has been set forth as infallible by the universal ordinary magisterium. Hence, the bishops give full assent to Cardinal Ratzinger's declarations in *Responsum ad dubium*.

In sum, the three documents, "Declaration *Inter Insigniores*: On the Question of Admission of Women to the Ministerial Priesthood," the "Apostolic Letter *Ordinatio Sacerdotalis* of John Paul II to the Bishops of the Catholic Church on Reserving Priestly Ordination to Men Alone," and the "Ten Frequently Asked Questions about the Reservation of Priestly Ordination to Men," reiterate, reinforce, and advance the hegemonic rhetoric set forth from pope to pope and from doctrine committee to doctrine committee, arguing against women's priestly ordination in the Roman Catholic Church and limiting women's roles to motherhood and marriage. The documents provide Church officials a smokescreen to exert male hegemonic power over women and to hide deeply misogynist and sexist attitudes and practices among Church leaders. Taken together, the ecclesial documents strangle women's spirit-filled call to priestly ordination, including the administration of the sacraments and preaching. Importantly, these documents prohibit women from participating fully and on all levels of the ordained ministry in the institutional governance of the Roman Catholic Church. Thus, women are sidelined in the ecclesial hierarchy because of papal claims and authority. In 2013, Pope Francis establishes that the "door is closed" on women's ordination.

His new revision of Canon Law, published in 2021, turns the prohibition of women's ordination into Church law.

STRATEGY 4: TURNING A PROHIBITION INTO LAW

The fourth strategy that Church officials use to block women from priestly ordination revises Pope John Paul II's 1983 Code of Canon Law; Pope Francis made a revision in 2021. Before his revision of the 1983 Code, Francis issues the Apostolic Letter *"Spiritus Domini"* in January 2021 to modify canon 230 no.1 of the 1983 Code.[41] According to this letter, women can serve as lectors and acolytes but not as ordained priests. Then, in December 2021, Pope Francis affirms the views of previous popes on women's ordination by revising the 1983 Code of Canon Law to prohibit women's ordination within the Roman Catholic Church. The previous version of Canon 1024 of the 1983 Code of Canon Law states: "A baptized male alone receives sacred ordination validly."[42] This law only affirms male ordination to the priesthood while it does not address explicitly the status of women. Yet the revision of the 1983 law makes explicit what the earlier version states implicitly: only men, and not women, can be ordained. Accordingly, in Pope Francis's 2021 revision, Canon 1024 becomes Canon 1379 no. 3, affirming: "Both a person who attempts to confer a sacred order on a woman, and the woman who attempts to receive the sacred order, incur *latae sententiae* excommunication reserved to the Apostolic See; a cleric, moreover, may be punished by dismissal from the clerical state."[43] The revised law is much longer and it also states explicitly that women are excluded from ordained priesthood *and* dismissed from the Church if they seek to become ordained. Unlike previous papal laws, then, Pope Francis's revision is aggressively and explicitly denying women any path to the ordained priesthood.

The placement of Canon 1379 no. 3 indicates how serious Pope Francis is with regard to making the quest for women's ordination even harder, if not impossible, than what appeared in canon 230 no.1 in the 1983 Code of Canon Law. Canon 1379 no. 3 appears under the title, "Offences against the Sacraments" in a new Book VI entitled, "Penal Sanctions in the Church" that Pope Francis added to his revised Code of Canon Law. For the first time in the history of Code Canon Law revisions, the statement on priestly ordination contains a *specific* reference to women, including specific penalties. No previous canon ever mandated that a baptized woman seeking ordination must be penalized with dismissal from her bishop. Also, no canon ever prescribed that any bishop ordaining a woman would be dismissed. Only Francis's 2021 revision prohibits explicitly women's ordination in an ecclesiastical law, essentially stopping any discussion on the matter.

Furthermore, his revision codifies the penalties for ordaining women clearly and succinctly. The revision escalates the prohibition of women's ordination at a time when Catholic clergy, including a former Cardinal, have been legally exposed for abusing, assaulting, and raping girls, boys, women, men, and even sisters of religious communities. The inclusion of Canon 1379 no. 3 in Book VI ensures that the penalties are listed for "Christ's faithful who commit offences." The question is what would motivate Pope Francis to include the specific canon on women's ordination that punishes not only women but also male clergy. The harshness of his revision and the highly problematic placement among the canons of penal sanctions are so noticeable that Pope Francis's reasons for the drastic changes must be considered.

Three reasons may have motivated Pope Francis to add Canon 1379 no. 3 to Book VI. They pertain, first, to the increase of the women's ordination movement around the world, second, to the pressure the Pope experiences in his midst, and three, to the enormous burden of sexual abuse and violent criminality among male Catholic clergy. First, the burgeoning alternative international movement known as "Roman Catholic Women Priests (RCWP)" has gained tremendous momentum in Canada, Europe, South and Central America, South Africa, the Philippines, Taiwan, and the United States. This movement began with the priestly ordination of seven Catholic women on the Danube River in 2002. The women were from Germany, Austria, and the United States. Canonical male bishops ordained the women, two of whom were also ordained as bishops. Both women bishops then ordained other women as priests and bishops to ensure apostolic succession into the future. As a reaction to the 2002 ordinations at the Danube River, the CDF (under the direction of Cardinal Joseph Ratzinger) issued the "Decree on the Attempted Ordination of Some Catholic Women" that excommunicated the "Danube Seven." The Decree aimed to make null and void any ordination that already did or would take place thereafter.[44] In the United States, the 2007 ordination of two women by a woman bishop from South Africa, who herself had been ordained a bishop in 2005, sparked a sharp response from Cardinal Burke, who at the time was Archbishop of Missouri. He stated: "[B]y the commission of the most grave delict of schism, all three of the guilty parties have lost membership in, good standing in, and full communion with the Roman Catholic Church, which bond each and every baptized Catholic is obliged to maintain."[45] His statement keeps with the CDF's "Decree on the Attempted Ordination of Some Catholic Women." Accordingly, the magisterium of the Roman Catholic Church considered the ordained women in full communion with the Roman Catholic Church since the women were not in compliance with Church teaching on ordination. The Vatican excommunicated them swiftly. In 2007, the CDF issued another decree, signed by Cardinal Prefect, Cardinal William Levada, the former Archbishop of the Archdiocese of San Francisco, CA, and former Archbishop of the Archdiocese of Portland, OR. The 2007 decree stated:

> [B]oth the one who attempts to confer a sacred order on a woman, and the woman who attempts to receive a sacred order, incur an excommunication *latae sententiae* reserved to the Apostolic See. If, in fact, the one who attempts to confer a sacred order on a woman, or the woman who attempts to receive a sacred order, is one of Christ's faithful subject to the *Code of Canons of the Eastern Churches*, that person, without prejudice to the prescript of can. 1443 of the same Code, is to be punished with a major excommunication, the remission of which is also reserved to the Apostolic See.[46]

The decree, signed by Cardinal Levada, foregrounds Pope Francis's revision of canon 1024 in the newest version of Canon Law (2021).[47] Pope Francis's revised canon law resembles closely the statement made by Cardinal Levada and the Congregation for the Doctrine of Faith in the "General Decree Regarding the Delict of Attempted Sacred Ordination of a Woman." The similarities suggest that Pope Francis used the CDF's document when he revised the 1981 version of canon 1024 to the current 2021 version, which is currently canon 1379 no. 3.

Second, another possible reason for Pope Francis's harsh revision of the prohibition of women's ordination in Canon Law 1379 no. 3 weighs even more heavily. It is likely that Francis has experienced extensive pressure from within the Vatican which might have pushed him to "sacrifice" women seeking ordination to solidify his own papal authority in the Vatican. Cardinal Burke opposes vehemently RCWP and the two ordained U.S. women. He is also a strong opponent of some of Francis's teachings. Burke publicly supported Archbishop Viganò's denunciation of the Pope and even endorsed Viganò's call for the Pope's resignation.[48] Together with three other Cardinals, Burke and his colleagues issued a letter containing a *dubia*[49] to Pope Francis. The letter requested that the Pope answer five yes-or-no questions. With these questions,[50] the Cardinals attempted to mount a heresy case against the Pope. The Cardinals allege that in his apostolic exhortation *"Amoris Laetitia,"* Francis has opened the door to give the sacrament of Holy Communion to divorced and remarried Catholics. Pope Francis thus experiences growing and fierce pressure from some Cardinals who are only one hierarchical level below the papal office. Adding Canon 1379 no. 3 to Book VI, Pope Francis may have attempted not only to save his papacy but also to address the growing movement and ordination of women priests that evoked the ire of Cardinals Burke and Levada. Perhaps the Pope tried to appease his most outspoken critics by prohibiting explicitly women's ordination, unlike any previous pope.

Third, another serious development may have provoked Pope Francis to revise Canon Law Code 1379 no. 3 in the harshly exclusionary fashion. Perhaps he attempted to obfuscate the legal reality of the sexual abuse cases by making women's ordination the problem. Unexpectedly, Francis's revision of Canon Law posits that the ordination of women to the Roman Catholic priesthood is as big a problem as clerical sexual abuse and violence. The fact that the Pope chooses to place a statement about ordination specifically into the section that outlines penal codes for sex crimes among other offenses exposes not only his alliance with past popes but also his inconsistent stance toward women. After all, many women have also been rape victim survivors of Catholic male clergy. A statement, published by the Women's Ordination Conference, captures the gravity of the male sex abuse suffered by many women: "If the church is to heal from its wounds of abuse, we know that canonical punishments alone will not suffice, particularly if the Vatican prioritizes excommunicating women above all else. The continued exclusion of women from holy orders contributes to the very culture of abuse that has failed and harmed so many."[51] Yet Pope Francis's revised code does not mention the abuse women have suffered especially sexual abuse from male clergy within the Church. This omission illustrates that Francis ignores the physical, emotional, psychological, and sexual suffering of women within the Church, as he attempts to uphold exclusively male power in the institutional Church that perpetuates sexism and discrimination. By prioritizing women's ordination as the main issue to be punished by excommunication, Pope Francis revises the canon law to deflect from the sexual violence perpetrated by male clergy.

In sum, an earlier vague prohibition of female ordination turns into a code of Canon Law in 2021 that includes statements of severe punishment for women and their male or female supporters. They are threatened with excommunication if they seek ordination to the Roman Catholic priesthood. One can only speculate on the reasons for the Pope's addition of Canon 1379 no. 3 to Book VI. Perhaps he wants to counteract the growing strength of the Roman Catholic Women Priest movement detested by the CDF and two Cardinals. Perhaps he tries to appease Vatican officials, who oppose him, in the effort of finding alliance with his predecessors. Perhaps he tries to obfuscate ongoing legal battles over the rape and pedophilia crimes of male clergy members by placing a new prohibition of women's ordination among the penal sanctions for sexual abuse. No matter what his reasons are, the new law "is a painful reminder of the Vatican's patriarchal machinery, and its far-reaching attempts to subordinate women."[52] As long as Roman Catholic women and men approve of ecclesial documents and revised Codes of Canon Law, such as Canon 1379 no. 3, without offering a public critique, the Roman

Catholic Church and its male leadership exert androcentric theological and doctrinal authority causing violence against boys and girls, women and men, as well as the faithful.

SAYING "NO" TO CLAIMS OF ECCLESIAL AUTHORITY: CONCLUDING COMMENTS

Fearing the demasculinization of their personal and professional status and terrified by the prospect of losing power, Roman Catholic male Church officials produce copious documents. They explain why women should not be ordained to the priesthood. To support their position, male Church officials use four hermeneutical strategies to garner their theo-doctrinal position with ecclesial authority. They prooftext the Bible, essentialize gender, reinforce hegemonic rhetoric from pope to pope, and revise canon laws. Prooftexting, dismissing the critical hermeneutical study of the Bible, weaponizes biblical verses for political and ecclesial purposes. Essentializing gender historicizes Jesus by privileging his maleness over all other human qualities, reducing ordained priesthood to biology, and denying women access to ordained leadership in the Roman Catholic Church. The documents produced by Vatican officials reinforce the hegemonic rhetoric and practices of the Church, preserve the Church's male power structure, and solidify papal opposition to women's ordination. The 2021 revision to Canon Law turns women into scapegoats for male clerical sexual abuses and violence by explicitly threatening them and their supporters with excommunication if they seek ordination to the priesthood. All four strategies, discriminating against, marginalizing, and suppressing Roman Catholic women, expose the deep-seated gender injustice existing within the Roman Catholic Church. Changing age-old religious structures to allow for gender equity and the abolishment of sinful discrimination thus is a challenging task. However, Roman Catholic women are not alone in their efforts for gender justice in church structures.

Another group of women addressing discrimination related to priestly ordination is in the Buddhist Tibetan and Theravada traditions. In the edited volume, entitled *Dignity and Discipline: Reviving Full Ordination for Buddhist Nuns*, Thea Mohr and Jampa Tsedroen feature prominent Buddhist feminist women's voices who focus on the status of women in Buddhism, the controversy over and implications of full ordination for women in Buddhism, and the potential for restructuring Buddhism for gender equity.[53] The contributions to this volume arose as a response to the Dalai Lama's request for the revival of the precepts of fully ordained nuns. The Dalai Lama suggests: "Were the Buddha to come to the twenty-first century and see the situation in the world now, he might well modify the rules."[54] Thus, Buddhist feminist women, like many Roman Catholic women theologians and Bible scholars, challenge religious structures on the topic of women's ordination, writing books, journals, and essays on women's ordination.

Roman Catholic feminists, however, have taken specific steps to resist their ongoing secondary status in the Roman Catholic Church. One prominent example of resistance is Christine Vladimiroff, OSB, former prioress of the Benedictine Sisters of Erie, Pennsylvania. In 2001, Vladimiroff refused to comply with the Vatican's request to forbid Benedictine sister Joan Chittister from speaking at the International Women's Ordination Worldwide Conference in June 2001. With the support of her congregation, Vladimiroff issued a powerful statement to Vatican officials. Her statement acknowledges:

> For the past three months I have been in deliberations with Vatican officials regarding Sister Joan Chittister's participation in the Women's Ordination Worldwide Conference, June 29 to 31, Dublin, Ireland. The Vatican believed her participation to be in opposition to its decree (Ordinatio Sacerdotalis) that priestly ordination will never be conferred on women in the Roman Catholic Church and must therefore not be discussed. The Vatican ordered me to prohibit Sister Joan from attending the conference where she is a main speaker. I spent many hours discussing the issue with Sister Joan and traveled to Rome to dialogue about it with Vatican officials. I sought the advice of bishops, religious leaders, canonists, other prioresses, and most importantly with my religious community, the Benedictine Sisters of Erie. I spent many hours in communal and personal prayer on this matter.
>
> After much deliberation and prayer, I concluded that I would decline the request of the Vatican. It is out of the Benedictine, or monastic, tradition of obedience that informed my decision. There is a fundamental difference in the understanding of obedience in the monastic tradition and that which is being used by the Vatican to exert power and control and prompt a false sense of unity inspired by fear. Benedictine authority and obedience are achieved through dialogue between a community member and her prioress in a spirit of co-responsibility. The role of the prioress in a Benedictine community is to be a guide in the seeking of God. While lived in community, it is the individual member who does the seeking.
>
> Sister Joan Chittister, who has lived the monastic life with faith and fidelity for fifty years, must make her own decision based on her sense of Church, her monastic profession and her own personal integrity. I cannot be used by the Vatican to deliver an order of silencing.
>
> I do not see her participation in this conference as a "source of scandal to the faithful" as the Vatican alleges. I think the faithful can be scandalized when honest attempts to discuss questions of import to the church are forbidden.
>
> I presented my decision to the community and read the letter that I was sending to the Vatican. 127 members of the 128 eligible members of the Benedictine Sisters of Erie freely supported this decision by signing her name to that letter.

> Sister Joan addressed the Dublin conference with the blessing of the Benedictine Sisters of Erie.
>
> My decision should in no way indicate a lack of communion with the Church. I am trying to remain faithful to the role of the 1500-year-old monastic tradition within the larger Church. We trace our tradition to the early Desert Fathers and Mothers of the 4th century who lived on the margin of society in order to be a prayerful and questioning presence to both church and society. Benedictine communities of men and women were never intended to be part of the hierarchical or clerical status of the Church, but to stand apart from this structure and offer a different voice. Only if we do this can we live the gift that we are for the Church. Only in this way can we be faithful to the gift that women have within the Church.[55]

Vladimiroff's statement to the Vatican not only is courageous but also demonstrates the work of religious congregations called not to be conformists but to be prophetic voices and instruments of change.

Another example of resistance is the growing numbers of ordained women in the international RCWP movement which offers a new model of apostolic succession within the Roman Catholic Church. Members see their ministry as part of the renewal and transformation of the Catholic Church. They challenge Canon Law as a document written by an all-male clergy, and they resist the canons that forbid the priestly ordination of women. In the global struggle for diversity, equity, and inclusion, RCWP work for justice not only in the world but also in their own church structure. Unlike many men and women who have left the Roman Catholic Church because of horrific injustices done to men and women alike by the institution, RCWP members, even though excommunicated by the Vatican, remain faithful to their baptismal vocation as Catholics and their calling as priests. In keeping with Vatican II, they claim that the church is not limited to its clerical leaders. The church is composed of the whole people of God. Thus, as RCWP members, they affirm their God-given authority. They resist the institutional Church's efforts to suppress their power as women who embody the Divine and the hegemonic oppression of the Church's male leadership.[56]

In conclusion, if change is to come to discriminatory religious structures, then feminist people must challenge and resist oppressive leaders, while taking risks to create new structures. In the case of Roman Catholicism, such efforts will, undoubtedly as recent history bears out, cause courageous women and men to be excommunicated by male Church officials. Unfortunately, the ordination of women to the Roman Catholic priesthood is at an impasse because of the current Church's male hegemonic power and rigidity. The work of gender justice, however, is prophetic work, done by people who live on the margins and speak truth to power. Regardless, the struggle to work for gender justice must continue within the Roman Catholic Church even as new alternative structures that affirm women's priestly ordination take root on the margins. The time has come to resist oppressive clerical male hegemony so that just and lasting reform can finally begin.[57]

NOTES

1. With Francis's efforts, the Vatican's criminal justice system is more active with major prosecutions of financial crimes involving the Holy See.

2. See Canon 230 § 1 of the 2021 *Code of Canon Law*; see also Francis, "Apostolic Letter Spiritus Domini in the form of a 'Motu proprio' on the amendment of canon 230 § 1 of the *Code of Canon Law* on the access of female persons to the instituted ministries of Lector and Acolyte." 11.01.2021, https://press.vatican.va/content/salastampa/en/bollettino/pubblico/2021/01/11/210111a.html.

3. Ibid.

4. See Sacred Congregation for the Doctrine of the Faith, "Declaration *Inter Insigniores*: On the Question of Admission of Women to the Ministerial Priesthood," October 15, 1976, https://www.vatican.va/roman_curia/congregations/cfaith/documents/rc_con_cfaith_doc_19761015_inter-insigniores_en.html. I wish to note that after I completed the draft of this essay, Pope Francis issued a new apostolic constitution on the Roman Curia, *Praedicate evangelium* (Preach the Gospel) which replaces *Pastor Bonus* (1988). Under the new constitution, all the Vatican's main departments are now called "dicasteries." The powerful Vatican Congregation for the Doctrine of the Faith (CDF) will now be called the "Dicastery for the Doctrine of the Faith." See Francis, "Apostolic Constitution '*Praedicate Evangelium*' on the Roman Curia and its service to the Church and to the World, 19.03.2022" (Vatican City, March 19, 2022), https://press.vatican.va/content/salastampa/en/bollettino/pubblico/2022/03/19/220319b.html.

5. See John Paul II, "Apostolic Letter *Ordinatio Sacerdotalis* to the Bishops of the Catholic Church on Reserving Priestly Ordination to Men Alone," May 22, 1994, https://www.vatican.va/content/john-paul-ii/en/apost_letters/1994/documents/hf_jp-ii_apl_19940522_ordinatio-sacerdotalis.html.

6. See Committee on Doctrine of the National Conference of Catholic Bishops, "Ten Frequently Asked Questions about the Reservation of Priestly Ordination to Men," 1998, https://www.usccb.org/beliefs-and-teachings/vocations/priesthood/ten-frequently-asked-questions-about-the-reservation-of-priestly-ordination-to-men.

7. See Francis, "Book VI," *Code of Canon Law*, https://www.vatican.va/archive/cod-iuris-canonici/cic_index_en.html.

8. See "Ten Frequently Asked Questions about the Reservation of Priestly Ordination to Men."

9. Ibid.

10. Ibid., "Introduction."

11. See Michael F. Patella, O.S.B., "The Gospel according to Luke," in *New Collegeville Bible Commentary*; ed. Daniel Durken, O.S.B. (Collegeville, MN: Liturgical Press, 2017), 1131.

12. See Elisabeth Schüssler Fiorenza, *Bread Not Stone: The Challenge of Feminist Biblical Interpretation* (Boston, MA: Beacon Press, 1984), 26.

13. Ibid.

14. *"Inter Insignores,"* sec. 5: "The Ministerial Priesthood in the Light of The Mystery of Christ."

15. Sonya A. Quitslund, "In the Image of Christ," in *Women Priest: A Catholic Commentary on the Vatican Declaration*, ed. Leonard Swidler and Arlene Swidler (New York: Paulist Press, 1997), 263–264.

16. Ibid., 263.

17. See *Commonweal* (April 1, 1977), 205 as cited by Quitslund in note 10.

18. See *"Inter Insigniores,"* sec. 2: "The Attitude of Christ."

19. Ibid. On this point, the CDF acknowledges the argument of New Testament scholars that the Twelve represent the twelve tribes of Israel. Yet the CDF also insists that "the essential meaning of the choice of the Twelve should rather be sought in the totality of their mission." Unfortunately, the CDF's argument is circular. Its understanding of the choice of the Twelve is based on the CDF's interpretation which the CDF then deems as the "essential meaning." See note 10 of *"Inter Insigniores."*

20. See Elisabeth Schüssler Fiorenza, "The Twelve," in *Women Priest: A Catholic Commentary on the Vatican Declaration*, ed. Leonard Swidler and Arlene Swidler (New York: Paulist Press, 1997), 114–122.

21. Ibid., 115.

22. Ibid., 120.

23. Ibid.

24. See *"Inter Insigniores,"* sec. 2: "The Attitude of Christ"; see also specifically note. 11 that cites the following reference: Pope Innocent III, *Epist* (December 11, 1210) to the Bishops of Palencia and Burgos, included in *Corpus Iuris*, Decret. Lib. 5. Tit. 38 *De Paenit.*, ch. 10 *Nova*: ed. Emil Albert Friedberg and Aemil Richter, vol. 2, col. 886–887 (Leipzig: Tauchnitz, 1879–1881).

25. See *"Inter Insigniores,"* sec. 3: "The Practice of the Apostles," par. 3.

26. Ibid., par. 4.

27. Ibid., sec. 4: "Permanent Value of the Attitude of Jesus and the Apostles."

28. Ibid.

29. As quoted in Jill Peterfeso, *Womanpriest: Tradition and Transgression in the Contemporary Roman Catholic Church* (New York: Fordham University Press, 2020), 148.

30. See *"Ordinatio Sacerdotalis,"* sec. 1; see also Paul VI, Response to the Letter of His Grace the Most Reverend Dr. F.D. Coggan, Archbishop of Canterbury, concerning the Ordination of Women to the Priesthood" (November 30, 1975): in *Acta Apostolicae Sedis*, vol. 68 (1976), 599.

31. See, *"Inter Insigniores,"* "Introduction: The Role of Women in Modern Society and the Church"; see also Second Vatican Council, *Pastoral Constitution on the Church in the Modern World: Gaudium et Spes*, December 7, 1965, no. 29, https://www.vatican.va/archive/hist_councils/ii_vatican_council/documents/vat-ii_const_19651207_gaudium-et-spes_en.html; *Acta Apostolicae Sedis*, vol. 58 (1966), 1048–1049.

32. Ibid.; see also Second Vatican Council, *Decree on the Apostolate of the Laity: Apostolicam Actuositatem*, November 18, 1965, no. 9, https://www.vatican.va/archive/hist_councils/ii_vatican_council/documents/vat-ii_decree_19651118_apostolicam-actuositatem_en.html: *Acta Apostolicae Sedis*, vol. 58 (1966), 846.

33. See "*Inter Insigniores*," Introduction: "The Role of Women in Modern Society and the Church."

34. See John Paul II, *Apostolic Letter: Ordinatio Sacerdotalis* May 22, 1994, no. 3; https://www.vatican.va/content/john-paul-ii/en/apost_letters/1994/documents/hf_jp-ii_apl_19940522_ordinatio-sacerdotalis.html; see also "*Inter Insigniores*," sec. 6: "The Ministerial Priesthood Illustrated by the Mystery of the Church."

35. See "*Ordinatio Sacerdotalis*," no. 3.

36. See "Ten Frequently Asked Questions about the Reservation of Priestly Ordination to Men," ques. 9.

37. See "Introduction: The Role of Women in Modern Society and the Church," in "*Inter Insigniores*."

38. See *Ordinatio Sacerdotalis*, no. 4.

39. Congregation for the Doctrine of the Faith, *Responsum ad Propositum Dubium. Concerning The Teaching Contained in 'Ordinatio Sacerdotalis,'* October 28, 1995, https://www.vatican.va/roman_curia/congregations/cfaith/documents/rc_con_cfaith_doc_19951028_dubium-ordinatio-sac_en.html.

40. See Austin Flannery, O.P., ed. *Vatican Council II: The Conciliar and Post Conciliar Documents* (Northport, NY: Costello Publishing Company, 1975), 379–381.

41. See Pope Francis, *Apostolic letter. Issued 'Motu Proprio' Spiritus Domini*, January 15, 2021, https://www.vatican.va/content/francesco/en/motu_proprio/documents/papa-francesco-motu-proprio-20210110_spiritus-domini.html.

42. See *Code of Canon Law* (Vatican City, 1983), https://www.vatican.va/archive/cod-iuris-canonici/eng/documents/cic_lib4-cann998-1165_en.html#THOSE_TO_BE_ORDAINED; see also the 1917 edition of Canon Law (1917 Pio-Benedictine Code of Canon Law by Edward N. Peters, curator [San Francisco: Ignatius Press, 2001]) where canons 232–293 state the stipulations and process for males only seeking ordination.

43. See "Book VI: Penal Sanctions in the Church," *Code of Canon Law*.

44. See Congregation for the Doctrine of the Faith, "Decree on the Attempted Ordination of Some Catholic Women," December 21, 2002, https://www.vatican.va/roman_curia/congregations/cfaith/documents/rc_con_cfaith_doc_20021221_scomunica-donne_en.html.

45. See "St. Louis Archbishop Excommunicates Three for Attempted Women's Ordination," *Catholic News Agency*, March 15, 2008, https://www.catholicnewsagency.com/news/12081/st-louis-archbishop-excommunicates-three-for-attempted-womens-ordination.

46. See Congregation for the Doctrine of the Faith, "General Decree Regarding the Delict of Attempted Sacred Ordination of a Woman," https://www.vatican.va/roman_curia/congregations/cfaith/documents/rc_con_cfaith_doc_20071219_attentata-ord-donna_en.html.

47. See "New Book VI: Penal Sanctions in the Church," of the *Code of Canon Law*.

48. See Gerald O'Connell, "Cardinal Burke: It Is 'licit' to call for the resignation of Pope Francis," *America* (August 29, 2018); https://www.americamagazine.org/faith/2018/08/29/cardinal-burke-it-licit-call-resignation-pope-francis.

49. *Dubia* is the Latin plural for *dubium,* translated as *"doubts."* In the Roman Catholic Church, *Dubia* refers to a set of doctrinal questions asked by Church officials. The questions require responses in the form of *Responsa*.

50. For the specific questions asked, see Edward Pentin, "Full Text and Explanatory Notes of Cardinals' Questions on 'Amoris Laetitia,'" *National Catholic Register* (November 14, 2016), https://www.ncregister.com/blog/full-text-and-explanatory-notes-of-cardinals-questions-on-amoris-laetitia.

51. See Kate McElwee, "Updates to Canon Law Fail to Correct the 'Crime' of Women's Ordination," *Women's Ordination Conference* (June 1, 2021), https://www.womensordination.org/2021/06/updates-to-canon-law-fail-to-correct-the-crime-of-womens-ordination/.

52. Ibid.

53. Thea Mohr and Jampa Tsedroen, eds., *Dignity & Discipline: Reviving Full Ordination for Buddhist Nuns* (Boston, MA: Wisdom Publications, 2010).

54. Ibid., ix.

55. See the statement by Christine Vladimiroff, OSB on the Women's Ordination Worldwide website: Christine Vladimiroff, OSB, "Statement of Christine Vladimiroff," *Women's Ordination Worldwide* (June 2001), http://womensordinationcampaign.org/dublin-2001/2014/2/2/statement-of-benedictine-prioress-sr-christine-vladimiroff. Christine Vladimiroff was also President of the Leadership Conference of Women Religious (2004-2005) and President and CEO of Second Harvest National Food Bank Network (1991-1998). She was a personal friend and passed away September 25, 2014.

56. For a full discussion on womenpriests, see Peterfeso, *Womanpriest: Tradition and Transgression in the Contemporary Roman Catholic Church*.

57. Under Pope Francis's new constitution of the Roman Curia, the laity, including women, will be able to lead the different dicasteries of the Roman Curia. See Francis, "Apostolic Constitution *'Praedicate Evangelium'* on the Roman Curia and its service to the Church and to the World, 19.03.2022." See also Phillip Pullella, "Pope Rules Baptised Catholics, Including Women, Can Lead Vatican Departments," *Reuters*, March 19, 2022, https://www.reuters.com/world/europe/pope-rules-any-baptized-lay-catholic-including-women-can-head-vatican-2022-03-19/.

* Finding my thought and voice as a Roman Catholic woman in a colonizing church structure that has educated me to be compliant is no easy task. This essay is the fruit of that struggle. To my astute Bible colleague, Susanne Scholz, PhD, I owe an immense debt of gratitude for helping to free my once passive voice and compliant thought. Susanne's clear thinking brought clarity to my own, and her meticulous behind-the-scenes editing of many drafts helped turn my muddled essay into an organized analysis. To SimonMary Asese A. Aihiokhai, PhD, my delightful department colleague and editor of this volume, I owe great thanks for the invitation to contribute and for the helpful suggestions, encouragement, and patience afforded me to bring this essay to completion.

FURTHER READINGS

Clifford, Anne M. *Introducing Feminist Theology*. Maryknoll, NY: Orbis Books, 2001.
Helman, Ivy A. *Women and the Vatican: An Exploration of Official Documents*. Maryknoll, NY: Orbis Books, 2012.
Madigan, Kevin and Carolyn Osiek, eds. *Ordained Women in the Early Church*. Baltimore, MD: The Johns Hopkins University Press, 2005.
Mohr, Thea and Jampa Tsedroen, eds. *Dignity and Discipline: Reviving Full Ordination for Buddhist Nuns*. Boston, MA: Wisdom Publications, 2010.
Rue, Victoria. "Crossroads: Women Priests in the Roman Catholic Church." *Feminist Theology* 17, no. 1 (2008): 11–20.
Scholz, Susanne. *Introducing the Women's Hebrew Bible*. New York: Bloomsbury T&T Clark, 2017.
Schüssler Fiorenza, Elisabeth. *Discipleship of Equals*. New York: Crossroad Publishing Company, 1993.

REFERENCES

Committee on Doctrine of the National Conference of Catholic Bishops. "Ten Frequently Asked Questions About the Reservation of Priestly Ordination to Men." 1998. https://www.usccb.org/beliefs-and-teachings/vocations/priesthood/ten-frequently-asked-questions-about-the-reservation-of-priestly-ordination-to-men.
Congregation for the Doctrine of the Faith. "Decree on the Attempted Ordination of Some Catholic Women." December 21, 2002. https://www.vatican.va/roman_curia/congregations/cfaith/documents/rc_con_cfaith_doc_20021221_scomunica-donne_en.html.
———. "General Decree Regarding the Delict of Attempted Sacred Ordination of a Woman." https://www.vatican.va/roman_curia/congregations/cfaith/documents/rc_con_cfaith_doc_20071219_attentata-ord-donna_en.html.
———. *Responsum ad Propositum Dubium: Concerning The Teaching Contained in 'Ordinatio Sacerdotalis.'* October 28, 1995. https://www.vatican.va/roman_curia/congregations/cfaith/documents/rc_con_cfaith_doc_19951028_dubium-ordinatio-sac_en.html.
Flannery, O. P., Austin, ed. *Vatican Council II: The Conciliar and Post Conciliar Documents*. Northport, NY: Costello Publishing Company, 1975.
Francis. "Apostolic Constitution *'Praedicate Evangelium'* on the Roman Curia and Its Service to the Church and to the World, 19.03.2022." *Vatican City*, March 19, 2022. https://press.vatican.va/content/salastampa/en/bollettino/pubblico/2022/03/19/220319b.html.

———. "Apostolic Letter Spiritus Domini in the Form of a 'Motu Proprio' on the Amendment of Canon 230 § 1 of the *Code of Canon Law* on the Access of Female Persons to the Instituted Ministries of Lector and Acolyte. 11.01.2021." January 10, 2021. https://press.vatican.va/content/salastampa/en/bollettino/pubblico/2021/01/11/210111a.html.

———. "Book VI." *Code of Canon Law*, December 8, 2021. https://www.vatican.va/archive/cod-iuris-canonici/eng/documents/cic_lib6_en.pdf.

Friedberg, Emil Albert and Aemil Richter, eds. *Corpus Iuris*, Decret. Lib. 5. Tit. 38 *De Paenit*., Chapter 10. *Nova*: volume 2. Column 886–887. Leipzig: Tauchnitz, 1879–1881.

John Paul II. "Apostolic Letter *Ordinatio Sacerdotalis* to the Bishops of the Catholic Church on Reserving Priestly Ordination to Men Alone." May 22, 1994. https://www.vatican.va/content/john-paul-ii/en/apost_letters/1994/documents/hf_jp-ii_apl_19940522_ordinatio-sacerdotalis.html.

———. "Code of Canon Law." *Vatican City*, 1983. https://www.vatican.va/archive/cod-iuris-canonici/eng/documents/cic_lib4-cann998-1165_en.html#THOSE_TO_BE_ORDAINED.

McElwee, Kate. "Updates to Canon Law Fail to Correct the 'Crime' of Women's Ordination." *Women's Ordination Conference*, June 1, 2021. https://www.womensordination.org/2021/06/updates-to-canon-law-fail-to-correct-the-crime-of-womens-ordination/.

Mohr, Thea and Jampa Tsedroen, eds. *Dignity & Discipline: Reviving Full Ordination for Buddhist Nuns*. Boston: Wisdom Publications, 2010.

O'Connell, Gerald. "Cardinal Burke: It Is 'Licit' to Call for the Resignation of Pope Francis." *America*, August 29, 2018. https://www.americamagazine.org/faith/2018/08/29/cardinal-burke-it-licit-call-resignation-pope-francis.

Patella, O. S. B., Michael F. "The Gospel According to Luke." In *New Collegeville Bible Commentary*, edited by Daniel Durken, O. S. B., 1108–1162. Collegeville, MN: Liturgical Press, 2017.

Paul VI. "Response to the Letter of His Grace the Most Reverend Dr. F.D. Coggan, Archbishop of Canterbury, Concerning the Ordination of Women to the Priesthood." November 30, 1975. In *Acta Apostolicae Sanctae* 68 (1976).

Pentin, Edward. "Full Text and Explanatory Notes of Cardinals' Questions on 'Amoris Laetitia.'" *National Catholic Register*, November 14, 2016. https://www.ncregister.com/blog/full-text-and-explanatory-notes-of-cardinals-questions-on-amoris-laetitia.

Peterfeso, Jill. *Womanpriest: Tradition and Transgression in the Contemporary Roman Catholic Church*. New York: Fordham University Press, 2020.

Peters, Edward N. *1917 Pio-Benedictine Code of Canon Law*. San Francisco: Ignatius Press, 2001.

Pullella, Phillip. "Pope Rules Baptised Catholics, Including Women, Can Lead Vatican Departments." *Reuters*, March 19, 2022. https://www.reuters.com/world/europe/pope-rules-any-baptized-lay-catholic-including-women-can-head-vatican-2022-03-19/.

Quitslund, Sonya A. "In the Image of Christ." In *Women Priest: A Catholic Commentary on the Vatican Declaration*, edited by Leonard Swidler and Arlene Swidler, 260–269. New York: Paulist Press, 1977.

Sacred Congregation for the Doctrine of the Faith. "Declaration *Inter Insigniores*: On the Question of Admission of Women to the Ministerial Priesthood." October 15, 1976. https://www.vatican.va/roman_curia/congregations/cfaith/documents/rc_con_cfaith_doc_19761015_inter-insigniores_en.html.

Schüssler Fiorenza, Elisabeth. *Bread Not Stone: The Challenge of Feminist Biblical Interpretation*. Boston: Beacon Press, 1984.

———. "The Twelve." In *Women Priest: A Catholic Commentary on the Vatican Declaration*, edited by Leonard Swidler and Arlene Swidler, 114–121. New York: Paulist Press, 1997.

Second Vatican Council. "Decree on the Apostolate of the Laity: Apostolicam Actuositatem." November 18, 1965. https://www.vatican.va/archive/hist_councils/ii_vatican_council/documents/vat-ii_decree_19651118_apostolicam-actuositatem_en.html: Acta Apostolicae Sedis, 58 (1966).

———. "Pastoral Constitution on the Church in the Modern World: Gaudium et Spes." December 7, 1965. https://www.vatican.va/archive/hist_councils/ii_vatican_council/documents/vat-ii_const_19651207_gaudium-et-spes_en.html. *Acta Apostolicae Sedis* 58 (1966).

"St. Louis Archbishop Excommunicates Three for Attempted Women's Ordination." *Catholic News Agency*, March 15, 2008. https://www.catholicnewsagency.com/news/12081/st-louis-archbishop-excommunicates-three-for-attempted-womens-ordination.

Vladimiroff, Christine, OSB., Christine. "Statement of Vladimiroff." *Women's Ordination Worldwide*, June 2001. http://womensordinationcampaign.org/dublin-2001/2014/2/2/statement-of-benedictine-prioress-sr-christine-vladimiroff.

Part 2

UNDOING DUALISM

TOWARD AN ANTHROPOLOGY OF WHOLENESS

Chapter 5

The Evolution of Male and Female Anthropology

Accommodation, Resistance, and Transformation

Christina Astorga

In her article, "Is Female to Male as Nature is to Culture?" Sherry Ortner calls attention to the universal devaluation of the female based on biases of the dominion of culture (the sphere of human control) over nature (spontaneous processes beyond human control). The female is seen as "closer to nature" while the male is seen as belonging to the sphere of culture. This assumption is due to the female's biological role in reproducing the species, seen as confining her to child nurture and domestic labor. Her social roles are regarded as inferior to those of males, falling lower on the nature–culture hierarchy.[1]

Pursuing Ostner's postulation, Rosemary Radford Ruether writes that the development of the male consciousness toward the female is influenced by the male puberty rite that releases the male from the female context of early socialization and identifies the pubescent male with the male community and its roles and functions.[2] This release happens in patriarchal societies as well as in matrilineal-matrifocal societies.[3] The sexes, segregated in female and male roles, are clearly defined. The mother's world is confined to the settled domestic circle of childbearing, lactation, early child nurture, transformation of the raw into the cooked, and creation of domestic implements. The social mobility of females, confined to this world, is viewed as restricted. They work in groups gathering food, hunting small animals, and transforming them into food, clothes, and artifacts for the entire society. But is this not the work of culture, as the natural raw products are transformed? Why is this work of women considered "closer to nature" and thus is inferior to male's work?[4]

As the lawmakers, ritualists, and cultural bearers of the society, the males are the ones who define the nature of the work of the females. Brought into the sphere of his father's world, the male child devalues and repudiates the world of his mother, from which he is released. Unlike the female child who is initiated into the mother's world in her growth to adulthood, the male child becomes an adult through a forcible uprooting from the world of the mother, which is termed a psychocultural revolution. According to Ruether, this forced release explains in part the violent character of the male puberty rites compared to the female puberty rites. Included in the male puberty rites are the mythical tales of how females once controlled the instruments of culture, but were defeated by the males. Now in full control of the symbols of culture power (sacred flutes or holy bundles), the males absolutely prohibit the females from touching them under the pain of retribution. The young male is taught to regard the male sphere as superior to the female sphere, the place of lower self, that he has now "transcended."[5]

Males as definers of culture have the privilege of a leisure class with relatively little to do but to decorate themselves, sharpen their weapons, and prepare for occasional excursions of hunting and war, while females are left with the burden of the tedious day-to-day grind of domestic work and economic production. The work of females viewed as inferior to that of males is premised on the aforementioned distinction of culture and nature. Furthermore, the female's body and her reproductive processes are owned by men and are defined from a male point of view. The reproductive roles of women and their domestic production of food and clothes for men are regarded by males as beneath them, but in need of their control and domination.[6]

Continuing her line of thought, Ruether writes that when the definition of culture is dominated by men, women are reduced to objects rather than addressed as subjects. Both male and female spheres are defined from the male hierarchical point of view, making the male superior and female inferior. More highly valued cultural activities are reserved for males. These often do with ritual and leisure functions rather than with ordinary and daily needs. The females make ordinary clothes; while the males do the festival clothes. The females cook the daily food while the males do the food for festivals. As males belong to the realm of freedom and females to the realm of necessity, males see females as a threatening lower power that seeks to drag down their freedom to necessity. Male transcendence means flight from the maternal sphere, and from the realm of body and nature, all that limits and confines male control.[7]

Ruether asks: "Is dominated woman/dominated nature always culturally correlated?"[8] Sherry Ortner believes that the earliest social patterns lay at the root of this universal cultural correlation. However, she points out the ambiguity in the cultural symbol of the female. While the female is devaluated by being seen as closer to nature, by virtue of her bodily and reproductive functions, she is one of the crucial agents of culture with reference to the socialization of children, in a sense in the conversion of nature into culture. She writes that "feminine symbolism, far more often than masculine symbolism, manifests this propensity toward polarized ambiguity—sometimes utterly exalted, sometimes utterly debased, rarely within the normal range of human possibilities."[9] The feminine symbols of witches, evil eye, menstrual pollution, and castrating mothers are as captivating as the feminine symbols of mother, goddess, and dispenser of justice.[10] What Ortner fails to notice, as Ruether points out, is that the symbol of nature is also ambivalent. While nonhuman is viewed as beneath the human, that which is to be controlled and dominated, it is also seen as the cosmos, infused by the divine, in which gods and humans have their being.[11]

This chapter inquires on how this dualistic view of male and female was passed on through the ages and how early Christianity attempted to disrupt it, but with limits, and how contemporary feminist theology continues to resist this view, in varying ways. It presents an evolution of the male and female anthropology, first, as it was codified in the Graeco-Roman tradition, second, as it was shaped in the Judeo-Christian tradition, and third, as it is deconstructed and reconstructed by contemporary feminist theology.

In tracing the evolution of the male and female anthropology, the chapter is only focused on the Western Christian tradition. In its study of the male and female anthropology in early Christianity, it does not go beyond the context of the New Testament period, and thus it does not include the Patristic period, in particular, where dualistic and misogynistic views on women by some of the Fathers like Tertullian were shaped by their own cultural and historical contexts. The New Testament literature shows that early Christianity negotiated between accommodation and resistance, as it was shaped by its Jewish roots, within the context of Graeco-Roman influence. While it accommodated these dualistic views, to survive in the cultures and societies in which it was situated, it also resisted and disrupted these views and offered a vision of men and women, promoted by its ethos of inclusion and hospitality, especially those who were cast at the margins of society. Contemporary feminist theology continues to resist and disrupt these dualistic views, in varying ways, with its new anthropological constructs. This work contributes to the ongoing discussion on male and female anthropology that shapes aspects of contemporary feminist theology. It seeks to bring new light to the female and male relationship, which impacts all aspects of human life, and can either enrich or diminish our common humanity.

MALE AND FEMALE IN THE GREEK CULTURE

Many scholars have commented on the association of the female with the body in ancient Greece.[12] Corporeality defines the condition of the female, as she is cast as responsible for looking after the bodies of others, like giving birth, feeding the young, caring for the sick, and burying the dead.[13] She appears to be essentialized as body in the Greek culture. But this association with the body extends beyond physiology. The female bears the signs of fragility of the body—sickness, vulnerability, and infirmity.

The relation between the female and the body is found in the association of the female body with pain. The experiences of pain and suffering are typically encoded as female. By merely having her body, the female is imaged as afflicted by illness and suffering.[14] If pain is the natural state of the female body, then it tends toward the state of dissolution. Pain obliterates and diminishes. The model of the female body as prone to dissolution is viewed across genres of literature, medicine, science, and philosophy.[15] The idea of female flesh in the Greek culture entails a notion of dissolution within the Hippocratic model of female flesh. For example, the female body is wet, soft, and spongy, lacking the more solid form of the male body.[16] It is believed that a girl will result from a weak seed while a boy from a strong seed.[17] The female fetus is considered inferior to the male fetus.[18] And if the pregnant woman has a poor complexion, it will be a girl (*Aphorisms* 5.42).[19]

The female body, however, is paradoxical. As both foundational and marginal to classical culture, the signification of woman as body is complicated. The female body is considered to be foundational by virtue of the production of sons and daughters who are important for the perpetuation of the polis. However, while the female body plays this important role, the woman herself holds a marginal place in society. Her status and place in the polis are low, as she is regarded as unruly and wild, closer to "nature," a potential that the male must control and contain. While woman is cast at the margin of culture, man is at the center.[20]

If the female is defined by her body, what is the male in relation to the body? Controlled, detached, and disciplined, the male body is a cultural icon as it is buffed and paraded in the gymnasium and *palaestra*; it is also the male's chief weapon in war and a rhetorical instrument in the democratic polls.[21] Raised as the proof of *andreai* (manliness, manly courage), the male is believed to achieve transcendence, accomplished paradoxically through the body. *Kleos*, which means glory, a kind of everlasting fame, is achieved through the paradox of risking and giving up the male body.[22] In this light, the Iliadic hero experiences a complex relationship with his body, for his body serves as his instrument to attain *kleos*, but in order to attain this, he must deny the demands and longings of his body for eros, survival, and sustenance. This paradox describes the touchstone of a tragic hero's fraught experience with his body.[23]

A further contrast to the female relationship with the body is the view that the male is less invested in the body, unlike the female who has a natural intimacy with the body, primarily in the experience of childbirth and caring for the bodies of children and other family members. This is because his male body is positioned as a public icon, the male experiences a public–private tension.[24] "The uses of this male body are therefore public and are opposed to its physical satisfactions or desires in the private sphere."[25] It is said that classical Athenian men who appear to be permitted to indulge in the pleasure of the body far more freely and openly than women become vulnerable to a libidinal attachment to the male body, threatening the potential sacrifice demanded by the state.[26] Citing Plato's, Laws 944 e, Elizabeth Spellman writes how men are diminished to the level of women in their indulgence of the body: "To have more concern for your body than your soul is to act just like a woman; hence, the most proper penalty for a soldier who surrenders to save his body, when he should be willing to die out of the courage of his soul, is for the soldier to be turned into a woman."[27] A warrior, thus, who tries to save his body by his capitulation to the enemy, endangering the good of the state, receives a fitting punishment of being turned into a woman. What is shown here is "the opposition between the desires of the body and the private sphere, encoded female, and the desires of the state, the public sphere, coded male and the subsequent dilemma faced by the male who has to choose between the two."[28]

This diminishment of the female is also shown in the view of the female in the practice of pederasty in the Greek culture, which is a passage rite from the femininity of youth to the masculinity of the older male body. The young male who plays the passive partner is an "impersonator of the female."[29] The young will eventually be the penetrating older male, the opposite of the penetrated "womanish" man. The problem with physical love between men is that men are acting like women. Furthermore, an adult male who allows himself to be penetrated violates the norm of the ideal adult male body as impervious and impenetrable. He is no different from women and slaves, both endlessly penetrable.[30] The binary of male and female regards the male, penetrator as active, while the female, penetrated, as passive.

The ideal man must preclude pathos from his dealings with others, particularly in war. "Empathy or pity, a most important emotion in the Greek culture does appear at times to be a disallowed emotion for a man."[31] The ideal man, a master of himself, is one who demonstrates restraint and control of his emotions and his cravings. A balance, however, is sought here. A man, for instance, must permit at times, the touch of others, one for instance of a supplicant.[32] The practice of supplication demonstrates the dilemma that the human touch holds for the male. Touching another provokes a crisis of boundaries, which one must reckon with. The ancient Greeks upheld the crucial importance of boundaries, both personal and extra-personal to guarantee social order.[33] The touch of a supplicant brings the vulnerability of body into the space of the male, reminding him of his own vulnerability, thus creating a predicament for himself.[34] The character of Odysseus in Sophocles' *Ajax*

(121-6) expresses this sentiment poignantly. "I pity him in his utter distress, though he's an enemy, yoked as he is to catastrophic fate. And here I see myself as much as him. I know that we are nothing more in all our life than feeble image or fragile shades."[35] Expressing what vulnerability does to the male, Don Fowler likens images of fallen warriors to the images of girls being deflowered.[36] J.-P. Vernant writes: "Marriage is for the girl what war is for the boy . . . a girl who refuses marriage, renounces her 'femininity' . . . becomes the equivalent of a warrior."[37]

Continuing the line of thought regarding the relation between suffering and maleness, tragedy feminizes the hard body of the hero. "The hard hero's body becomes soft, mollified by suffering, the feminizing process of tragedy."[38] Sophocles' *Ajax*, who is compared with a sword, and who possesses an unyielding mind, a hard body, and speech as strong as iron, is cast as the traditional male hero. Pity, however, renders him vulnerable, making him "womanish."[39] Ajax moans: "For even I, erst so wondrous firm,—yea, as iron hardened in the dipping,—felt the keen edge of my temper softened by yon woman's words; and I feel the pity of leaving her a widow with my foes, and the boy an orphan."[40] The ideal warrior's body should remain impenetrable, and he should be impervious to emotions of pity and compassion that feminize them. But it is the wounding in the heat of the battle that makes him masculine. His wounds are marks of *andreia*, the quality of manhood. "With an open gash in his body, he is destined to be seen for what he is, a great hero."[41] Both the victim and the perpetrator are masculinized. "In this sense, the discourse of wounds might therefore serve as a subtle qualification or resolution to the problem of the penetrated male body, perhaps existing to protect the male from the stain of becoming female through the opening of his body in the process of being wounded."[42] Wounds masculinize a man; wounding a man's body marks him a male. Matthew Leigh argues that this "valorisation of wounds in antiquity" takes on a signification in ancient Greece.[43] A wound to the front is received while facing one's enemy; a wound to the back is received whilst running away from one's opponent, which is a mark of capitulation, a mark of disgrace, which renders a man "womanish."[44]

The theme of the female transmitting suffering to the male is exemplified in the figure of Helen in tragedy. Helen is often cast as facilitating the induction of men into the complexities of "tragic consciousness."[45] She is likened to a "catalyst which propels men into the condition of corporeality and mortality."[46] Helen is the classical "bearer of the tragic" in the Greek tradition. As the carrier of suffering, the female is believed to displace the pain onto men and make them female.[47] This theme of female transmitting suffering to the male is demonstrated in the tragic characterization of Clytaemnestra in Aeschylus' Agamemnon. "She fatally slashes Agamemnon's body with an axe while he is vulnerable, naked in the bath, and turns him into a woman in a sense by robbing him of kleos."[48] This same theme of men being transformed into women is found in Plato's Timaeus (90e-91a), where "all those creatures generated as men who proved themselves cowardly and spent their lives in wrong doing were transformed, at the second incarnation, to women."[49] Here weak and debauched men are born again as women, and those who fail to exhibit *andreia*, are demoted from the ranks of the brave and manly to the ranks of women."[50]

In summary, the male and female anthropology of the Greek culture is fundamentally dualistic and misogynistic. It essentializes female in its state of dissolution. The female bears the sign of the fragility of the body—weakness, vulnerability, and infirmity. Thus, not only is the female associated with body, she is associated with pain and suffering. What is the male in relation to body and to pain? The male has a complex and fraught relationship with the body. While the male body is raised as proof of *andreai* (manliness, manly courage), it is by taking flight from the body's cravings and eros, through control and detachment, and by the body being wounded in battle and ultimately sacrificed for the state, does the male reach the epitome of his maleness. Because the female is associated with pain, when a man succumbs to pain, even out of empathy for another, he is diminished as a woman. Anything that is associated with the female is what disgraces the male. The ultimate punishment of a male is to be incarnated as a female.

In the subsequent presentation of the Christian tradition, what is shown is that the hierarchy of male and female, with the male as superior and the female as inferior, at the base of the anthropology of the Greek culture is also what determines the social status of male and female around the Jewish purity laws and the patriarchal families. Early Christians, however, both accommodated and resisted the practices of their day. They were forced to accommodate in order to survive, but in their resistance, they attempted to transform the patriarchal-structured families and communities, even as they fell short of eradicating them completely. The work of transformation continues till today, as contemporary feminist theologians are proposing ways of being male and female, that uphold gender equality and justice. This will be presented in the anthropological models proposed by Elizabeth Johnson and Sara Butler.

MALE AND FEMALE IN THE JUDEO-CHRISTIAN TRADITION

Research into the social history of Palestine in Jesus's day, and of his followers in the next two generations, shows evidence of Jesus in the Gospels responding and challenging highly stratified relationships. These relationships are supported by a religious ideology that determines social status around purity laws and by a gender hierarchy determined by patriarchy. Early Christianity does not reject purity observance as such, but it rejects the ethos of exclusion and dislodges power elitism.[51]

Purity societies are organized around the binary of pure and impure, clean and unclean, which determines a person's status. This binary applies to both individuals and to groups. Purity is determined by what passes in and out of bodily orifices.[52] The intake of food and emission of fluids, especially those related to waste products and sex constitutes the key axes of purity laws. Purity and impurity are determined by "birth (caste), behavior (eating, sex, washing, etc.), social position (including occupation), and physical condition (wholeness and health or disfigurement and diseases, as well as sexual and reproductive functions."[53] "Social boundaries are established on gradations of purity, from the most pure, to temporary purity, to the socially marginal, to the outcast."[54] In purity societies, women are classified under the impure category since sexual contact with women is stigmatized as impure for men, and women are considered to be in impure state when they menstruate and give birth.[55]

As a natural symbol, the body expresses the mode of relationships between and among persons. Presenting the front rather than the back of one's body expresses respect; intimacy is expressed through physical closeness; and casting-off of physical waste products (urinating and spitting) violates the norms of social decency.[56] Bodily expressions and their cultural meanings are tied to the social order. Certain patterns of social behavior are reflected in embodied relations. Mary Douglas writes that the "physical experience of the body, always modified by the social categories through which is known, sustains a particular view of society."[57] As a symbol of societal relations, the body can represent society's "powers and dangers."[58] Douglas advances the hypothesis that "bodily control is an expression of social control."[59]

In the Jewish context, the purity laws were developed and systematized in ancient Judaism during the exile in which a people who had lost their patrimony struggled to reestablish their identity over and against the foreign cultures and cults alien to them.[60] The purity laws were seen as a resistance of a people to domination, as they lived their way of life in the midst of cults and practices that defied theirs. The Jewish purity laws are understood as a way of making sacred the entirety of ordinary life by dedicating it to God, so that everything that was unclean was separated from the clean.[61] While the original function of the purity laws was premised on this understanding of holiness, it later evolved into an ethos of exclusion by the elites who defined who and what is impure. It also determined who possesses greater or lesser social status, and who controls social and political resources.[62]

The moral ethos of early Christianity was shaped in the context of the Jewish purity practices.[63] There is no evidence that Jesus, as a Jew, rejected all observance of purity laws, as constituting the traditional form of holiness. But he disrupted some of these laws in the way he dealt with men and women.[64] John Dominic Crossan cites Jesus's iconoclastic table fellowship and healing of the diseased as a repudiation of the exclusion and discrimination of certain classes of people perpetuated by the purity system. Table fellowship is "a map of economic discrimination, social hierarchy, and political differentiation."[65] Jesus ate with social outcasts, including tax collectors, sinners, and whores, whom elites in society found beneath their dignity. The parables were iconoclastic of the purity system's distinctions.[66] Jesus, however, did not only engage in renunciation; he opened a new way of life—a life of invitation and inclusion.

He manifested his new way of life not only through table fellowship, but also through the practices of itinerancy, healing, the raising of Lazarus, and exorcisms. In Jesus's world, disease often meant ritual impurity and social ostracism. Healing meant integration back into the community, and repudiation of the boundaries set by the gatekeepers meant to exclude those who are regarded as unclean.[67] The woman who had a "flow of blood" for 12 years (Mark 5: 25-34) was regarded as ritually impure, thus compounding the gender alienation she suffered from the stigmatization of physical illness.[68]

The moral challenge for the first Christians was to reckon with the practices that threatened the quality of their communal life. They lived in a social context where women's sexual and reproductive capacities, as well as those of men, were stratified, organized, and controlled for the ends of patriarchy.[69] "Resistance was a challenge which the early Christianity did not always meet successfully. But neither, on the whole, did they fail."[70] Lisa Sowle Cahill argues that the New Testament instructions on sex and gender challenged and resisted the social hierarchy contained in the Jewish and Graeco-Roman traditions. While it is true that in certain cases, early Christianity accommodated the context in which it was situated, in general, it offered an alternative vision by which it sought to live.

Hierarchy and authority were important to the ancient Israelite family, structured around male prerogative and the favored male son. A woman's religious and social identity was anchored to her relations with male family members and was acquired through marriage and the birth of sons. Women, like unmarried daughters, divorcees, or widows outside of the male support system were left at the social margins, at a serious disadvantage. While a liberating hermeneutics of Gen. 1–3 can pose as a critical norm against the subordinate status of women in ancient Israel, recent scholarship, however, argues that women may have had higher status historically, than is usually told.[71]

In the first-century CE, Christians reenvisioned their Jewish heritage, in the context of the Greco-Roman culture and the growth of churches in Hellenistic cities like Corinth. Judaic and Graeco-Roman cultures are patriarchal at their core.[72] Early Christianity offered an alternative view as "Christian communities emphasized solidarity and sharing across the traditional status boundaries, such as sex (male/female), class (slave-free), and culture (Jew-Greeks)."[73] In the new communities of discipleship, one was called to live the new life of hospitality and inclusion, particularly of the outcasts and the poor—a new life that was a sign of contradiction to the culture of discrimination and dominion. It was a new life mediated by sharing of property, table fellowships, and inclusion of slaves and women in the community, beyond the demarcations and exclusions of the Jewish society.[74] Viewed as a distinctive contribution of Christianity, virginity was an ideal sexual state. It was lived out not as a negative rejection of sex but rather as resistance to patriarchy. It was not only a path to celibate lifestyle in one's pursuit of religious excellence; it was an escape route from patriarchy and its imposed duty to procreate, contrary to a more inclusive love and solidarity for others.[75] Sexual sins, which Paul condemned, represented power relationships. With reference to divorce in particular, Matthew 19 shows Jesus's teaching about the "one flesh" unity of men and women in marriage. The Matthean texts accused men of committing adultery if they divorce and remarry, or marry a divorced woman. If a woman divorced by her husband remarries, this adultery is the man's responsibility (Matt. 5:32). Early Christian teaching against divorce is also seen as protecting women from the Jewish man's unilateral right to dismiss his wife, and also from the Roman man's utilitarian use of his wife and female relatives in the economic and political game. It also protected family members, especially children from problems caused by the transiency and instability of the Roman nuclear family.[76] The teaching against divorce was one among the acts of resistance of early Christianity against the practices of its day.

While it resisted, it also accommodated. A perplexing problem for feminists about sex and gender in the New Testament is the *haustafeln* or "household codes" which command the submission to the *paterfamilias* by women, slaves, and children. Scholars theorize that Christian churches were forced to accommodate or to conform to social pressures in order to survive.[77] Cahill writes that "What the *haustafeln* illustrate is that early Christians were neither morally perfect nor socially sectarian. They engaged their religious experience with their social reality—in this case the patriarchal family commandeered by political claims and transformed it with varying degrees of success."[78] Their attempt, however, was to transform the patriarchal status-structured family and community, even as early Christians were not able to completely eradicate it. One example is the leadership roles women assumed in the Christian community. These included Prisca, leader of a local church

(1 Cor. 16; Rom. 16:2; Acts 18:18, and 18:25). Phoebe, a deacon (Rom., 16:1 – 2); Junia, called an apostle by Paul (Rom. 16:7) and Mary Magdalene, whom the gospels attest to as one of the first, if not the first witness to the resurrection.[79]

CONTEMPORARY CONSTRUCTIONS OF MALE–FEMALE RELATIONSHIPS

The transformation of the relationship between men and women continues to be the task of contemporary feminists. Butler and Johnson, two eminent feminist theologians, are brought into dialogue about what they envision as transformed male and female relationships. Both affirm the equality of men and women but they differ in how sexual differences determine social roles. Butler, who posits what she calls an anthropology of complementarity, argues that women and men play pregiven roles based on the differences in their sexual identities, while Johnson, who holds to what she calls an egalitarian anthropology of partnership, argues that men and women play roles that are proper to their unique gifts. For Butler, gender is a given that determines which roles are reserved specifically for women and men, while for Johnson, gender is a construct shaped by the givens of the changing historical contexts. With reference to the two anthropological models, there is a need to distinguish between sex and gender. Human beings, although biologically sexed as female or male, act according to socially constructed roles and expectations, which is called gender. Beyond the fixed inscription of body or the predetermined outcome of one's biological sex, gender is a malleable construct as it is culturally negotiated.[80]

A proponent of the "Equal and Complementary" model, Butler rejects the hierarchical relations of power or a polar opposition between the sexes. She employs John Paul II's theology of sex complementarity that maintains equality as well as difference.[81] Using the Trinitarian analogy of the one divine nature, fully possessed by the Father, Son, and Holy Spirit, distinct but not identical, persons in relations, Butler explains that both man and woman possess the entirety of the human substance, but they are not identical; they are two different persons in relations. Human nature, thus, is not parceled out, one half to men, the other half to women, but is possessed in its entirety by men and women, and yet as male and female, they remain distinct persons. The two sexes are "two ways of being," two incarnations of human nature.[82]

Though of the same nature, man and woman are not the same. Like two hands, the left and the right, they are created to work together in a mutual and reciprocal way. Neither two, nature nor unisex, they are complementary.[83] This understanding is in line with the biblical teaching that "God created humankind in his image . . . male and female he created them. (Gen. 1:27). "Being a person in the image and likeness of God," writes Pope John Paul, "involves existing in a relationship."[84] The nuptial meaning of the body refers to the capacity of persons, as males and females, for intimacy and self-donation, in the generation of new life. The primary complementarity between the two sexes is found in marriage, whereby through their male body and female body, they make a "sincere gift of self" to one another that fully realizes the meaning of different yet complementary sexuality.[85]

Butler holds that bodily sex is a "constituent part of the person" defining his or her identity. More than racial or ethnic differences, one's sexual identity constitutes one's personhood, and it is that which impacts society in a critically necessary way, as it is indispensable for the continuation of the species. Sexual differences which determine one's capacity to love and give life have profound relevance for personal identity and for the social order. The gifts and contributions of men and women to each other and to the community are specific to their being members of their respective sex. These distinctive gifts and contributions come from feminine and masculine in mutually inclusive ways, which enrich human coexistence in the family and in society.[86]

Johnson proposes replacing the theory of complementarity with a multipolar anthropological model. On the one hand, she avoids the unisex model, and on the other hand, she eliminates the central focus on sexual difference. The anthropology she proposes features "one human nature, celebrated in an interdependence of multiple differences." Along with sex, race, social condition, nationality, age, state of health, sexual preference, and cultural location, are "anthropological constants" that constitute a person's identity and humanity. This anthropology does not hold the primacy of sex in defining a person's identity.[87] Butler, however, contends against the notion that when sexual difference is given primacy, women suffer from stereotypes, and are made victims of gender injustice. On the contrary, she believes that taking the personal meaning of sex seriously—for both women and men—is precisely what is necessary for defending their equal dignity.[88]

Johnson, however, asserts that we have inherited a tradition of theology that has diminished the core teaching of Genesis that women and men together, equally, relationally, as human beings, are created in the image and likeness of God.[89] In her words, "Not one more than the other, not one over the other, but together as human race."[90] This core teaching of Genesis is diminished when men are privileged over women as images of God, as they are believed to belong to the realm of spirit, while women belong to the realm of matter. Belonging to the realm of spirit, men are "nearer to the divine, endowed with soul, rationality, power to take initiative, power to act while women by nature are oriented to the body, irrational and uncontrollable emotions, passivity and receptivity."[91]

This dualistic tradition has played into a real and lasting ambiguity about whether women were truly created in the image and likeness of God. Words spoken by influential teachers in the Church cast long dark shadow on women through the centuries. For example, Tertullian infamously interpreted Gen. 3 as a story of sexual temptation and cast all women in the role of Eve:

> Do you not realize that you are each an Eve? The curse of God on this sex of your lives on even in our times. Guilty, you must bear its hardships. You are the gateway of the devil; you desecrated the fatal tree, you first betrayed the law of God; you softened up with your cajoling words the one against whom the devil could not prevail by force. All too easily you destroyed the great image of God, Adam. You are the one who deserved death, and because of you the Son had to die.[92]

Augustine, while affirming that woman is equal to man in her soul, her body, and her concomitant social role, denies her of the fullness of God's image:

> The woman with her husband is the image of God in such a way that the whole of that substance is one image, but when she is assigned her function of being a helper, which is her concern alone, she is not the image of God, whereas in what concerns the man alone he is the image of God, as fully and completely as when the woman is joined to him in one whole (she needs the male head for rationality and control).[93]

Thomas Aquinas's definition of woman as a "defective male," "a misbegotten male," in *Summa Theologiae*, 1,q. 92, a.1, gravely diminished women. This prejudice against women shaped public consciousness, and women have internalized what has been passed on from time to time, from age to age.[94]

In our day, official Roman Catholic teaching has taken a vigorous stand against any teaching that denies the core belief that women and men are equally made in God's own image. In 1988, Pope John Paul II, in his encyclical, *Mulieris Dignitatem* (On the Dignity and Vocation of Women), wrote that both man and woman are human beings to an equal degree, as both are created in God's image.[95] Many, however, raised the question, why he did not speak of equality in all ministries of church and governance. Johnson points out that John Paul II is still using the traditional dualistic view that men and women embody human nature in two contrasting ways, which means that possessing special characteristics, they play distinct social roles. This papal thinking, however, is an advance from previous thinkers who use this dualistic theology, as John Paul II declares that the two sides of the divide are of equal value and are mutually related. That woman and man are separate but equal and related is the core principle of John Paul II's anthropology.[96]

Holding up Mary's motherhood as a woman's true vocation, John Paul II calls women to live their vocation of physical or spiritual motherhood. Johnson criticizes this papal feminism as romanticizing feminism, as women are held up to an ideal, that "they are too good to get involved in the messiness of the public realm."[97] Responding to this image of women, a young woman remarked that she would not want to be elevated; she would rather be equal, while a young man responded and said: "Saying that women are more fitted to love means that they are better able to follow Jesus's teaching to love God and your neighbor with all your heart. Where does that leave me? Second best?"[98] Johnson critically reflects that by "boxing women's and men's identities into innate differences, based on traditional gender stereotypes, a dualistic anthropology inevitably compromises the human and spiritual potential of both."[99]

Johnson holds that a holistic egalitarian anthropology of partnership is more consonant with reality and experience. She describes this anthropology in the following:

> A persons' characteristic and vocation are not predetermined by sex, vital though. This is as a component of personal identity. Rather, human aptitudes exist across a wide spectrum for women and men. Women can be rational and great at leadership; men can be loving and nurturing. And rational and nurturing men can form beautiful mutual relationships. In fact, the range of differences among women themselves ends up being just as great or even greater than the differences between some women and some men Accordingly, social roles are not to be preassigned according to gender, but engaged in according to person's gifts, callings, and education.[100]

This anthropology admits the multiplicity and plurality of qualities that span across male and female humanity. No specific quality is assigned to either sex by virtue of maleness and femaleness, as all humans are capable of possessing qualities, for weal or woe. This anthropological construct reflects more the reality of women and men in their beauty, complexity, and ambiguity.

CONCLUDING STATEMENT

Even in societies and cultures, where the female, identified with body, is demeaned, and the male, identified with spirit, is elevated, there is a strain of ambiguity and ambivalence, as the female holds the power of life and perpetuation of life. Thus, while she is held at the lower strand of the hierarchy of culture and nature, spirit and body, she creates a dissonance and disruption. This dissonance and disruption are continued in early Christianity, even as it accommodates for survival in the Jewish and Graeco-Roman cultures in which it was situated. The same accommodation and resistance are seen in contemporary feminist theology as it wrestles with its inherited traditions, in its pursuit of new social anthropological constructs that liberate women from the shackles of the past.

The anthropology proposed by Butler, while it claims to be premised on gender equality, its complementarity model contradicts it. It is the model used against gender justice in the Catholic church as women are denied the sacrament of ordination, because they are women. And their positions of leadership are limited as well. The complementarity model premised on biological sex differences of male and female perpetuates gender inequality not only in the church, but in families and homes, in places of work, and in society at large, as it denies women of certain roles and positions, because they are women.

Gender complementary is also not a truthful account of being male and female—of being human. While biological sex clearly distinguishes male from female, it is not what predetermines social gender roles. Our being human is not limited to genital difference. Many other factors and variables come to play across a wide spectrum—age, race, culture, ethnicity, education, gifts and talents, and others. For this reason, women can be pilots and astronauts, while men can be nurses and cooks. Women can be rational and great at leadership, while men can be emotional and nurturing.

The model of egalitarian anthropology of partnership of Elizabeth Johnson premised on gender fluidity is much more in consonance with our experience of being male and female, and of being human. It equalizes the power dynamics between male and female, as gender roles are not determined by biological sex. For instance, it dislodges the ground on which stands the century-old teaching of the church on male priesthood—"the natural resemblance" of male priests to the maleness of Christ. It is the *humanum* in Jesus and not his male sex that is the locus of God's salvific revelation. Thus, it is the humanity of the one who exercises priesthood, not his maleness, that bears the "natural resemblance" of Christ.

The discourse on male and female anthropology is not just an abstract intellectual exercise. When men view women as inferior to them, they treat women as such. Gender violence is rooted in gender inequity. Women are most vulnerable to male violence in cultures where they are reduced and diminished in their worth and value as persons and as women. There is a need for radical deconstruction of age-long male and female anthropologies which are dualistic and misogynistic, and build new anthropologies that are truly liberating and redemptive not only of women, but of both men and women. For when men diminish women, they too are diminished.

NOTES

1. See Sherry B. Ortner, "Is Female to Male as Nature is to Culture?" in *Woman, Culture, and Society,* eds. Michael Zimbalist Rosaldo and Louise Lamphere (Stanford, CA: Stanford University Press, 1974), 71–83.
2. Rosemary Radford Ruether, *Sexism and God Talk: Toward a Feminist Theology* (Boston, MA: Beacon Press, 1993), 73.
3. See Yolanda Murphy and Robert F. Murphy, *Woman of the Forest* (New York: Columbia University Press, 1974), 78–110.
4. Ruether, *Sexism and God-Talk*, 73–74.
5. Ibid. 74.
6. Ibid., 74–75.
7. Ibid.
8. Ibid., 75.
9. Ortner, "Is Female to Male as Nature is to Culture," 86.
10. Ibid.
11. Ibid., 75–76.
12. See Elizabeth V. Spelman, "Woman as Body: Ancient and Contemporary Views," *Feminist Studies,* vol. 8, no 1 (Spring 1982): 109–131.
13. Froma I. Zeitlin, *Playing the Other: Gender and Society in Classical Literature* (Chicago: University of Chicago Press, 1996), 351–352.
14. Ruth Padel, "Women: Model for Possession by Greek Daemons," in *Images of Women Antiquity*, eds. Averil Cameron and A. Amélie (London: Croom Helm, 1983), 16. See also Nicole Loraux, *The Experiences of Tiresias: The Feminine and the Greek Man,* trans. Paula Wissing (Princeton, NJ: Princeton University Press, 1995), 12.
15. The theme of dissolution and the female body is perhaps implicit in Anne Carson, "Putting Her in Her Place: Women, Dirt, and Desire," in *Before Sexuality: The Construction of the Erotic Experience in the Ancient Greek World,* eds. David M. Halpern, John J. Winkler, and Froma I. Zeitlin (Princeton, NJ: Princeton University Press, 1990), 135–169.
16. Helen King, *Hippocrates' Woman: Reading the Female Body in Ancient Greece* (New York: Routledge, 1998), 39.
17. Ibid., 8.
18. Ann Ellis Hanson, "Conception, Gestation, and the Origin of Female Nature in the 'Corpus Hippocraticum,'" *Helios*, vol. 19, no. 1–2 (1992): 32.
19. King, *Hippocrates' Woman: Reading the Female Body in Ancient Greece*, 31.
20. Katrina Cawthorn, *Becoming Female: The Male Body in Greek Tragedy* (London: Bloomsbury, 2008), 49.
21. Ibid., 60.
22. Ibid., 60–61.
23. Ibid., 62.
24. Zeitlin, *Playing the Other: Gender and Society in Classical Greek Literature*, 211.
25. Ibid.

26. Cawthorn, *Becoming Female: The Male Body in Greek Tragedy*, 63.
27. Spelman, "Woman as Body: Ancient and Contemporary Views," 115.
28. Cawthorn, *Becoming Female: The Male Body in Greek Tragedy*, 63.
29. Spelman, "Woman as Body: Ancient and Contemporary Views," 116.
30. John Winkler, "Laying Down the Law: The Oversight of Men's Sexual Behavior in Classical Athens," in Halpern, Winkler, and Zeitlin, *Before Sexuality*, 179.
31. Cawthorn, *Becoming Female: The Male Body in Greek Tragedy*, 65.
32. Ibid.
33. Carson, "Putting Her in Her Place: Women, Dirt, and Desire," 134.
34. Cawthorn, *Becoming Female: The Male Body in Greek Tragedy*, 65.
35. See line 1338. W. B. Stanford, *Greek Tragedy and the Emotions: An Introductory Study* (London: Routledge and Kegan Paul, 1983), 27.
36. Don Fowler, "Vergil on Killing Virgins," in *Homo Viator: Classical Essays*, eds. M. Whitby and P. Harder (Bristol: Bristol Classical Press, 1987), 185–198, passim.
37. J.-P. Vernant, *Myth and Society in Ancient Greece*, trans. Janet Lloyd (New York: Zone Books, 1990), 34.
38. Cawthorn, *Being Female: The Male Body in Greek Tragedy*, 66–67.
39. Zeitlin, *Playing the Other: Gender and Society in Classical Literature*, 350.
40. *The Tragedies of Sophocles*, trans. Richard C. Jebb (Cambridge: At the University Press, 1928), 196.
41. Loraux, *The Experiences of Tiresias: The Feminine and the Greek Man*, 95.
42. Cawthorn, *Being Female: The Male Body in Greek Tragedy*, 68.
43. Matthew Leigh, "Wounding and the Popular Rhetoric at Rome," *Bulletin of Institute of Classical Studies*, vol. 40, no. 1 (1995): 196–197.
44. Ibid., 196.
45. See Zeitlin's general comments on woman as the model for "tragic consciousness" in *Playing the Other: Gender and Society in Classical Greek Literature*, 239–240.
46. Cawthorn, *Being Female in the Male Body in Greek Tragedy*, 70.
47. Ibid., 71.
48. Ibid.
49. Ibid., 64.
50. Winkler, "Laying Down the Law: The Oversight of Men's Sexual Behavior in Classical Athens," 178.
51. Lisa Sowle Cahill, *Sex, Gender, and Ethics* (Cambridge: Cambridge University Press, 1996), 123.
52. Ibid.,129.
53. Ibid.).
54. Ibid. See also Marcus J.Borg, *Conflict, Holiness, and Politics in the Teachings of Jesus* (New York and Toronto: Edwin Mellen Press, 1984), 54.
55. Ibid.,130).
56. Ibid.
57. Mary Douglas, Natural Symbols: Explorations in Cosmology (Barrie & Rockliff: The Cresset Press, 1970), 65.

58. Mary Douglas, *Purity and Danger: An Analysis of Concepts of Pollution and Taboo* (New York and Washington D.C.: Frederick A. Praeger Publishers, 1966), 115.

59. Douglas, *Natural Symbols*, 70.

60. See Daniel L. Smith, *Religion of the Landless: The Social Context of the Babylonian Exile* (New York: Meyer Stone Books, 1989), 80–84.

61. Jacob Neusner, *Purity in Rabbinic Judaism: A Systematic Account, The Sources, Media, Effects, and Removal of Uncleanness* (Atlanta: Scholars Press,1994), 48–49. See also Judith Plaskow, "Embodiment and Ambivalence: A Jewish Feminist Perspective," in *Embodiment, Medicine, and Morality*, eds. Lisa Sowle Cahill and Margaret Farley (Dordrecht and New York: Kluwer Publishers, 1995), 23–26.

62. Martin Goodman, *The Ruling Class of Judaea: The Origins of the Jewish Revolt Against Rome A. D. 66–70* (Cambridge: Cambridge University Press, 1987), 119.

63. Not all Christian interpreters would hold that there was an abrupt rupture between Judaism and Christianity. See Anthony J. Saldarini, *Matthew's Jewish-Christian Community* (Chicago and London: The University of Chicago Press, 1994), 19, 134, 162.

64. Cahill, *Sex, Gender, and Early Christianity*, 134.

65. John Dominic Crossan, *Jesus: A Revolutionary Biography* (New York: HarperCollins Publishers, 1992), 68.

66. Ibid., 69.

67. Ibid., 82.

68. Cahill, *Sex, Gender, and Early Christianity*, 135.

69. Ibid., 141.

70. Ibid.

71. See Phyllis Trible, *God and the Rhetoric of Sexuality* (Philadelphia: Fortress Press, 1978); and her *Texts of Terror: Literary-Feminist Readings of Biblical Narratives* (Philadelphia: Fortress, 1984). See also Cheryl Exum, *Fragmented Women: (Sub) Versions of Biblical Narratives* (Valley Forge: PA: Trinity Press International, 1993), 1–9.

72. W. K. Lacey, *The Family in Classical Greece* (Ithaca, NY: Cornell University Press, 1968), 21.

73. Cahill, *Sex, Gender, and Christian Ethics*, 150.

74. Ibid.

75. Ibid., 152–153.

76. Ibid., 155–156.

77. Ibid., 160.

78. Ibid., 161

79. Ibid.

80. Aloysius Lopez Cartagenas, "Provoking the 'Resident Evil': Feminist and Gender Provocations to Clericalism in the Philippine Context," in *Feminist Catholic Theological Ethics: Conversations in the World Church*, eds. Linda Hogan and A. E. Orobator (Maryknoll, New York: Orbis Books, 2014), 92.

81. Sara Butler, "Embodiment: Women and Men, Equal and Complementary," in *The Church Women Want: Catholic Women in Dialogue*, ed. Elizabeth A. Johnson (New York: Crossroad, 2002), 36.
82. Ibid., 38.
83. Ibid., 39.
84. John Paul II, "On the Dignity and Vocation of Women," *Origins*, vol. 18, no. 17 (October 6, 1988): art. 7.
85. See John S. Grabowski, "Mutual Submission and Trinitarian Self-Giving," *Angelicum*, vol. 74, no. 4 (1997): 489–512.
86. Butler, "Embodiment," 40–41.
87. Ibid., 37.
88. Ibid.
89. Elizabeth A. Johnson, "Imaging God, Embodying Christ: Women as Signs of The Times," in *The Church Women Want*, 49.
90. Ibid., 48.
91. Ibid., 49.
92. Tertullian, *On the Dress of Women* 1.1 (CSEL 70.59), cited in Elizabeth Clark, *Women in the Early Church* (Collegeville, Minn.: Liturgical Press, 1983), 39.
93. Augustine, *The Trinity* 12.7.10, trans. Edmund Hill (Brooklyn, N.Y.: New City Press, 1991), 328. See Kim Power, *Veiled Desire: Augustine on Women* (New York: Continuum, 1996), 131–157.
94. Johnson, "Imaging God, Embodying Christ," 50.
95. John Paul II, "On the Dignity and Vocation of Women," art. 6.
96. Johnson, "Imaging God, Embodying Christ," 52–53.
97. Ibid., 54.
98. Ibid.
99. Ibid.
100. Ibid., 54–55.

FURTHER READINGS

Brown, Anne. *No Longer Be Silent: First Century Jewish Portraits of Biblical Women.* Louisville: Westminster/John Knox, 1992.

Clark, Elizabeth. *Women in the Early Church.* Collegeville, MN: Liturgical Press, 1983.

Douglas, Mary. *Purity and Danger: An Analysis of Concepts of Pollution and Taboo.* London and Henley: Routledge and Kegan Paul, 1966.

Fantham, Elaine, Helene Peet Foley, Natalie Boymel Kampen, Sarah B. Pomeroy, and Harvey Alan Shapiro. *Women in the Classical World Image and Text.* New York and Oxford: Oxford University Press, 1991.

Kraemer, Rose Shepard. *Her Share of the Blessings: Women's Religions Among Pagans, Jews, and Christians in the Greco-Roman World.* Oxford/New York/Toronto: Oxford University Press, 1992.

Peter Brown, *The Body and Society: Men, Women, and Sexual Renunciation in Early Christianity*. New York: Columbia University Press, 1988.

Power, Kim. *Veiled Desire: Augustine on Women*. New York: Continuum, 1996.

REFERENCES

Augustine. *The Trinity 12.7.10*, translated by Edmund Hill. Brooklyn, NY: New City Press, 1991.

Borg, Marcus J. *Conflict, Holiness, and Politics in the Teachings of Jesus*. New York and Toronto: Edwin Mellen Press, 1984.

Butler, Sara. "Embodiment: Women and Men, Equal and Complementary." In *The Church Women Want: Catholic Women in Dialogue*, edited by Elizabeth A. Johnson, 35–44. New York: Crossroad, 2002.

Cahill, Lisa Sowle. *Sex, Gender, and Ethics*. Cambridge: Cambridge University Press, 1996.

Carson, Anne. "Putting Her in Her Place: Women, Dirt, and Desire." In *Before Sexuality: The Construction of the Erotic Experience in the Ancient Greek World*, edited by David M. Halpern, John J. Winkler, and Froma I. Zeitlin, 135–169. Princeton, NJ: Princeton University Press, 1990.

Cartagenas, Aloysius Lopez. "Provoking the 'Resident Evil': Feminist and Gender Provocations to Clericalism in the Philippine Context." In *Feminist Catholic Theological Ethics: Conversations in the World Church*, edited by Linda Hogan and A. E. Orobator, 85–96. Maryknoll, New York: Orbis Books, 2014.

Cawthorn, Katrina. *Becoming Female: The Male Body in Greek Tragedy*. London: Bloomsbury, 2008.

Clark, Elizabeth. *Women in the Early Church*. Collegeville, MN: Liturgical Press, 1983.

Crossan, John Dominic. *Jesus: A Revolutionary Biography*. New York: HarperCollins Publishers, 1992.

Douglas, Mary. *Natural Symbols: Explorations in Cosmology*. Barrie & Rockliff: The Cresset Press, 1970.

———. *Purity and Danger: An Analysis of Concepts of Pollution and Taboo*. New York and Washington, D.C.: Frederick A. Praeger Publishers, 1966.

Exum, Cheryl. *Fragmented Women: (Sub) Versions of Biblical Narratives*. Valley Forge, PA: Trinity Press International, 1993.

Fowler, Don. "Vergil on Killing Virgins." In *Homo Viator: Classical Essays*, edited by M. Whitby and P. Harder, 185–198. Bristol: Bristol Classical Press, 1987.

Goodman, Martin. *The Ruling Class of Judaea: The Origins of the Jewish Revolt Against Rome A. D. 66–70*. Cambridge: Cambridge University Press, 1987.

Grabowski, John S. "Mutual Submission and Trinitarian Self-Giving." *Angelicum* 74, no. 4 (1997): 489–512.

Hanson, Ann Ellis. "Conception, Gestation, and the Origin of Female Nature in the 'Corpus Hippocraticum." *Helios* 19, nos. 1–2 (1992): 31–71.

John, Paul II. "On the Dignity and Vocation of Women." *Origins* 18, no. 17 (October 6, 1988): article 7.

King, Helen. *Hippocrates' Woman: Reading the Female Body in Ancient Greece.* New York: Routledge, 1998.

Lacey, W. K. *The Family in Classical Greece.* Ithaca, NY: Cornell University Press, 1968.

Leigh, Matthew. "Wounding and the Popular Rhetoric at Rome." *Bulletin of Institute of Classical Studies* 40, no. 1 (1995): 195–215.

Loraux, Nicole. *The Experiences of Tiresias: The Feminine and the Greek Man.* Translated by Paula Wissing. Princeton, NJ: Princeton University Press, 1995.

Murphy, Yolanda, and Robert F. Murphy. *Woman of the Forest.* New York: Columbia University Press, 1974.

Neusner, Jacob. *Purity in Rabbinic Judaism: A Systematic Account, the Sources, Media, Effects, and Removal of Uncleanness.* Atlanta: Scholars Press, 1994.

Ortner, Sherry B. "Is Female to Male as Nature is to Culture?" In *Woman, Culture, and Society*, edited by Michael Zimbalist Rosaldo and Louise Lamphere, 67–88. Stanford: Stanford University Press, 1974.

Padel, Ruth. "Women: Model for Possession by Greek Daemons." In *Images of Women Antiquity*, edited by Averil Cameron and A. Amélie, 3–19. London: Croom Helm, 1983.

Plaskow, Judith. "Embodiment and Ambivalence: A Jewish Feminist Perspective." In *Embodiment, Medicine, and Morality*, edited by Lisa Sowle Cahill and Margaret Farley, 23–36. Dordrecht and New York: Kluwer Publishers, 1995.

Power, Kim. *Veiled Desire: Augustine on Women.* New York: Continuum, 1996.

Ruether, Rosemary Radford. *Sexism and God Talk: Toward a Feminist Theology.* Boston: Beacon Press, 1993.

Saldarini, Anthony J. *Matthew's Jewish-Christian Community.* Chicago and London: The University of Chicago Press, 1994.

Smith, Daniel L. *Religion of the Landless: The Social Context of the Babylonian Exile.* New York: Meyer Stone Books, 1989.

Spelman, Elizabeth V. "Woman as Body: Ancient and Contemporary Views." *Feminist Studies* 8, no. 1 (Spring 1982): 109–131.

Stanford, W. B. *Greek Tragedy and the Emotions: An Introductory Study.* London: Routledge and Kegan Paul, 1983.

The Tragedies of Sophocles. Translated by Richard C. Jebb. Cambridge: At the University Press, 1928.

Trible, Phyllis. *God and the Rhetoric of Sexuality.* Philadelphia: Fortress Press, 1978.

———. *Texts of Terror: Literary-Feminist Readings of Biblical Narratives.* Philadelphia: Fortress, 1984.

Vernant, J.-P. *Myth and Society in Ancient Greece.* Translated by Janet Lloyd. New York: Zone Books, 1990.

Zeitlin, Froma I. *Playing the Other: Gender and Society in Classical Literature.* Chicago: University of Chicago Press, 1996.

Chapter 6

Does Christian Catechesis Have a Gender Problem?

Toward a Catechesis of Wholeness

Valerie D. Lewis-Mosley

Voice, agency, and action and consent are the themes of concern when I ponder the role of Black Catholic lay women in the Church of the twenty-first century. At the centenary of the Women's Suffrage Movement, I reflect on how the voice, agency, and action of women led to a paradigm shift within society. Because of their active engagement and fearless challenges to structures of injustice and inequity, the Nineteenth Amendment was adopted and ratified on August 18, 1920. Consent was given and (all) American women were guaranteed the right to vote. This victory took many years of protest, agitation, and struggle. Actions that led to women being shunned, scandalized, and even vilified for seeking out that which was considered an inalienable right for men but denied to women solely on their gender. Yet, in the end, truth and justice prevailed. One hundred years later, women celebrate this jubilee that availed them of the very rights that they fought to obtain in society.

The turn of the nineteenth century ushered in the times of change for women. Activist and educator Anna Julia Hayward Cooper used her voice, agency, and action to affirm the rights and needs of Black women and their access to the very causes being addressed by the Women's Suffrage Movement. "Her wrongs are thus indissolubly linked with all undefended woe, all helpless suffering and the plentitude of her "rights" will mean the final triumphs of all right over might, the supremacy of the moral forces of reason, and justice, and love in government of the nation. God hasten the day."[1] The 1920s is often referred to as the Roaring Twenties. A time of change and casting off the restrictive social codes that held people to a traditional standard. The changes arose from popular culture—the grassroots movement so to speak. It was not generated by the hierarchy of society. It was in a sense, out of the people and it was an expression of the signs of the times. It was a wave that spread globally and simultaneously a sort of synergy so to speak. Synergistic change is often described as the principle of integrality by nursing theorist Martha Rodgers.[2] This change impacted not only personal lives, but also systems—for example, the arts (music and literary arts such as Jazz and the Harlem Renaissance). Even transportation (automobile production and aviation advances) evolved into the social sphere allowing for freedom of movement and access. Women's clothing attire, as well, evolved, providing women a release from the restrictive sphere of corsets and petticoats. The iconic image of the flapper—dancing free and unrestrained (e.g., Josephine Baker performing the Charleston)—was more than representative of a change in outerwear. It was symbolic of the freedom that women were embarking upon—no longer seen as chattel tied to the choices made by their husbands or fathers—but moving toward having their own agency and ability to act and speak with their own voice. The advent of the talking moving pictures (no more silent screen), radio, and the telephone all gave voice to the times of change. It is in this context of time that the voice of the people was being heard during this Progressive era of social activism and political change. The Women's Suffrage Movement came of age during this era. The voices of women were no longer bridled through their marriage contract to their husbands. They could voice their own agency "when and where they entered" into action that was for and about them as women.[3] "Only the Black woman can say 'when and where I enter, in the quiet, undisputed dignity of my womanhood, without violence and without suing or special patronage, then and there whole Negro race enters with me.'"[4] Cooper was born into the state of enslavement on August 10, 1858, in Raleigh, North Carolina. She married George A. G. Cooper, a teacher of theology in 1877. He was one of the first Black priests to be ordained into the Episcopal Church in North Carolina in 1879.[5] After the death of her husband, two years after their marriage, she went on to pursue her college education. Cooper dedicated her life to education. She served as a high school teacher, a principal, and the president of Frelinghuysen University in Washington, D.C. Cooper was the fourth African American woman to earn a doctoral degree. She was in her sixties when she earned a doctorate from the University of Paris-Sorbonne in 1925. She died in 1964 at the age of 105.

During the time of the Women's Suffrage Movement and the ratification of the Nineteenth Amendment, Cooper was in her sixties. She had been roaring with an unbridled tongue on the issues concerning women for quite some time—addressing women's rights, racial progress, and the education of African American women. Being a member of the Episcopal Church, she critiqued the Church for neglecting the education of African American women and argued that this was one reason why the Church had struggled to recruit large numbers of African Americans. She also cited the African Methodist Church as making great headway with its institutions of learning.[6] As a young girl of about nine years of age, Cooper challenged the faculty of St. Augustine Normal School. She voiced her displeasure because she was prevented from studying Greek, Latin, and Mathematics simply because she was a girl. Although this was a customary practice of the time to educate only males in these studies of the classics, Julia challenged the disordered practice. She was successful and gained admission and was a top student in the curriculum. The voice of Cooper was also a change agent at Oberlin University. She called attention to the discriminatory policies of the institution that prevented women from studying theology. It is this voice, action, and agency of Cooper that merges the context of Christian Theology and the Women's Suffrage Movement.

Although Cooper engages in this dialogue from a time span shortly after the Emancipation Proclamation and pursued the core concern of women—education, their access to ministry, and voting rights and equality for Black People throughout her life—the narrative of concern continues to plague us even as we celebrate the Centennial of the Women's Suffrage Movement. Even on the heels of the Centennial, women and African Americans are disenfranchised still in the voting booth and in the pulpit of far too many faith traditions. It is well established that various faith traditions continue to deny ordination to women purely based on gender. How is it that in the Church of the twenty-first century, gender is the sole determining factor on when and where women can enter the ministries of the Catholic Church? I preface this ongoing dialogue paraphrasing Cooper's historical quote: "Only the Sophia Wisdom of the Holy Spirit can authentically say when and where a woman can enter into the quiet undisputed dignity of the Creator's beck and call to a ministry of service."

The Catholic Church of the twenty-first century continues to bridle the voice, impede the agency, and deny consent for women to act in ministerial roles. Women are still denied the right to preach and teach within the liturgical celebration. *Kerygma* is the proclamation of the Gospel. It is the primary mission of the Church. Yet, women are limited in the capacity of serving in this ministry. As recently as January 11, 2021, the Church, under the direction of Pope Francis, has finally given permission for women to be officially installed in the ministries of Lector and Acolyte. Although women have been reading at the liturgical celebrations, they were not allowed to be officially installed into the ministry.[7] Concerning these two ministries, Pope Francis notes ". . .that since they are based on the Sacrament of Baptism, they may be entrusted to all suitable faithful, whether male or female . . . a doctrinal development has been arrived at in these last years that has brought to light how certain ministries instituted by the

Church have as their basis the common condition of being baptized and the royal priesthood received in the Sacrament of Baptism."[8] Women are still denied the right to serve as ordained clergy (Priesthood and Permanent Diaconate). It would seem that by right of Baptism, when one is received into the inclusive Kin-dom, and claimed by Christ as Prophet, Priest, and Royal Kinship, one should have full access to serve in all the ministries of the Church.[9]

The five distinct movements that occur in the Church's ministerial life are:

1. *Kerygma*: Proclamation and Preaching of the Gospel.
2. *Liturgia*: Liturgical public worship, and praise.
3. *Didache*: Teaching and Training passing on the faith doctrines, dogma, and practices.
4. *Diakonia*: Service to the community, spiritual and corporal needs.
5. *Koinonia*: Communion and community, sharing in love and unity the Eucharistic Celebration.

Catechesis is the ministry of teaching the Word to those who are willing to hear and accept it. It leads to the development of a mature faith. Catechesis is a major catalyst for evangelization.[10] Catechesis is the teaching with fidelity and respect, the Scripture, Doctrine, and Dogma of the Catholic faith. Yet, what happens when catechesis (that is intended to further the mission of evangelization through the proclamation of the Gospel) has some restrictions? When one teaches on the Sacraments (gifts instituted by Christ to give grace)—and then prefaces the Sacrament of Holy Orders as only for men— how is it that even young children old enough to understand, are able to raise the question: why are women excluded? I raise the following question, if we as members of the Body of Christ are also to mirror the radical equality (radical unity) of the Trinity, why do we set up distinctions about who is called to serve based solely on gender? How does this reflect the Wisdom (*Sophia*) of a God who created male and female in the image and likeness of God?

Christ came to delegitimize all structures of marginality in our world. John 12:1-8 provides a prototype of how women are called and confirmed to participate without restriction.[11] Just as women acted with conviction to challenge age-old restrictions against their right to vote, women who serve in ministry must point out and challenge age-old paradigms, disordered theologies, and praxis that inhibit the beck and call of the Lord from being actualized in their witness. The Anointing at Bethany is a substantive and prophetic matrix that affirms tradition, culture, and the human experience of a woman acting in her own agency in accordance with the beck and call of the Lord. It is through this lens that a catechesis of wholeness—mind, body, and spirit—is engaged.

The mission of the Church is to evangelize. It is the established call for every baptized Christian to spread the message of salvation, to share the Good News of the Gospel, and to lead others to a life centered on Christ. The waters of baptism initiate us into the mission of the Church and the Oil of Chrism seals, and anoints us for the mission. It is at the baptismal font that we are initiated into the mission, and given full authority to stand on the promise of full inheritance into the Body of Christ. We are reminded in Galatians 3:28 that in the Body of Christ, "there is neither Jew nor Greek, slave nor free, male nor female, for you are all one in Christ Jesus." Even with these Pauline injunctions, divisions are so clearly evidenced by the gender issues that continue to plague the Church. Black women, and women in general, are treated as unopened gifts and are often left to feel undaughtered, orphaned by the Church.[12] Similar experiences of being undaughtered and rejected are the historical exclusion of Black and Brown women from the Motherhouses of Catholic convents in the United States; due to racism and exclusion, these women were barred from religious life and ministry.[13] Women are invisible most often to the hierarchy. Even when they have received the relevant formation, most women are not allowed to participate in the Church's ministerial life. One particular example of their being treated as guests in their own homes is noted by Carmel McEnroy.[14] Her discussion about the women of Vatican II gives a historical backdrop to the circumstances of Catholic women not having a voice and not being included at the beginnings of the sessions of Vatican Council II. "This was not surprising, since no women were permitted to vote at Vatican II."[15] Writing about the women of Vatican II, McEnroy stated a sad truth that Catholic women, "were so conditioned that we did not expect to find ourselves there, and we did not miss ourselves when we were left out."[16] Catholic women were not allowed attendance at the very beginning stages of the Council, although the wives of clergy from the other Christian faiths were accorded a seat in the back, and, as the Council progressed, the locale of their seating was progressively moved forward. Yet, Catholic women were not provided such accommodation.[17]

As an African American woman, whose people were consistently delegated to the back of all accommodations, even that of the back of the Church, this common circumstance for the women of Vatican II speaks of the marginalization that occurs beyond race and is a gender and class issue as well. These twenty-three women invited by Pope Paul VI as auditors to Vatican Council II were not given voice nor vote; they were there as listeners. McEnroy describes these women in the time of the preconciliar Church, as being treated as minors, unequal, and unheard and ignored. Yet these women were indispensable collaborators in its mission.[18] The lens of my social location is that of a Black Catholic laywoman. A Christian woman called in every fiber of my being to give witness to the mission of Jesus Christ through the triple charism to Preach/Praise, to Teach, and to Bless according to the Order of Preachers as a Lay Associate of the Caldwell Dominicans. The teaching office and the blessing office through the ministry of catechesis to children and youth are the point of origin for this discourse. It begins with a question raised by children—yes children. It is this theological question; faith seeking reasoning and understanding presented by the children during sacramental formation that has tugged at my reasoning for over thirty years. It is also the reasoning behind my using the voice and experiences of Cooper in this discourse. She, at the tender age of nine, was able to reason that something was inherently wrong with the limitations placed on girls and women to study or participate in the theological sphere simply because of their gender.

The question raised in the title of this chapter is one that was inferred by the children of my catechetical ministry as they prepared for Baptism and reception of the Sacrament of Holy Communion. It was my own question as well fifty-nine years ago (ironically at the beginning of Vatican II). Albeit a question that was not voiced for fear that the nuns would deem me heretical in raising a question that challenged the instruction that "only men could be ordained." There was another question that I dared to ask. Why could I not be an altar server, when my male classmates were chosen? My male classmates in my early years of faith formation all relied on me to help them with understanding the Latin pronunciation and meaning of the words on the instructional placard given to them by the priest, as they studied to be altar boys. My question elicited a look of anger and an instruction for me to go to Confession. I did not obey because I did not think there was any sin involved with me asking a question. The answer I was given then was: "No you cannot serve because you are a girl, and girls cannot be priests or serve at the altar." This made no sense. Feeling powerless, I just learned to accept it. Many years later, reading about the life of Cooper left me feeling quite vindicated. Yet, for many decades, I skirted the question (pun intended) raised by the children and the youth, as to why women could not be ordained? My response was always, "This is the teaching of the Church." I did not deviate from the prescribed response. The desire to engage the children and the youth in faith formation came at a price: adhering to what the Church called orthodoxy— right teaching on matters of who could and could not receive the Sacrament of Holy Orders. It was, for many decades, a question I buried deep within the recesses of my own spirit. I did not give much credence to the nagging question that had gone unanswered. The priesthood was for men only, case closed. But why? There was no burning desire within me personally to engage in the discussion or the pursuit of the Call to the Priesthood. It was actually nothing more than a philosophical question. What had been a philosophical issue took on a more directed concern. The impediment of racism to the evangelization mission began to be the lens that led me to reevaluate the various teachings and history of my faith. The intersectionality of my Catholic identity (Black and Catholic) brought me to the crossroads of when and where I entered into ministry as a Black Catholic woman in the American Catholic Church. Gender, race, and faith were points of being of my existence that were irreducible. I was more than the sum of my parts.

The catechist in me, a teacher of the faith, was a ministry and call that I had embraced. It was in keeping with the orthodoxy of the faith. It was acceptable that I teach the faith. "Although the role of teacher was never institutionalized as a church office, teachers within the Christian community enjoyed an authority that sometimes put them in competition with their bishops."[19] For the Christian community, the work of teachers fell into two categories: catechizing the converts and instructing the faithful. The role of teacher itself was not gendered as noted by Karen Jo Torjesen.[20] Along my journey as a catechist, something strange happened to challenge my own accepted understanding of orthodoxy. In the Spring of 2000, I was asked to participate in a Holy Week Seder meal and liturgy and give an accounting for my faith in Christ (Fr. Judge Center—Shrine of St. Joseph Retreat Center for the Missionary Servants of Most Holy Trinity in Sterling, New Jersey). My understanding was that I would give a reflection at the evening liturgy. I presumed that this would be a reflection given after reception of the Eucharist prior to the closing of the liturgy. Shortly after the Proclamation of the Gospel, the celebrant beckoned for me to come forward. I ignored him at first because I thought I had misunderstood him. My husband nudged me and said, "Father Dennis is calling for you." I shook my head and said, "No, I cannot speak now. It is not acceptable. I have to wait until after Communion during the meditation." My husband, at the time, was a new convert to the faith and was still learning the nuance of all things Catholic. He responded, "I am not sure what you are troubled about, but you better move fast because you are holding up the service."

As I reflect on this twenty-plus years later, I realize just how indoctrinated I was with what I thought was orthodoxy—right teaching; and orthopraxy—right action. My reasoning then was that women could neither preach nor be ordained to Holy Orders in the Catholic Church. Suffice it to say that the movement of the Holy Spirit, which is perfected in orthopraxy—right action—began to stir within me and invite me to critically discern and evaluate what I had been taught and left unchallenged. My spirit wrestled with this. It would not let me be at peace until I began to allow the Holy Spirit to trouble the spiritual waters of my heart—a movement toward orthopathy. I began to acknowledge the feelings and emotions about this subject were neither strange nor disordered but valid and warranted. This stirring of the spiritual waters began to birth within me a new epistemology, and, yes, even a new pathos, so to speak. I began to think about my personal philosophical statement on Catechesis as it related to my ministry to Black and Brown children. It was imperative that the teaching be rooted in a theology that was pluralistic and reflective of Black Catholic Theology. A theology that contributed to the teaching and learning (*Didache*) a genuine enrichment of doctrine and faith through the lens of the culture of the people. It was my belief that this led to a mature faith out of which evolves true conversion. A conversion that was open to a ministry of service and outreach (*Diakonia*), and commitment to proclaiming the Word (*Kerygma*), in a way that led to a vibrant worship and committed prayer life (*Liturgia*), and the building up of the community of believers and celebration of the ecclesial fellowship (*Koinonia*).[21]

Catechesis, from an Afrocentric way of knowing, is rooted in a Black mindset. It is the Black perspective that is reflective of positive Black cultural experiences. Catechesis, through Black epistemology, needs to embrace teaching and learning principles that reflect the learning styles of African Americans. A catechesis with a Black epistemology allows for an African American learner to see herself in the image and likeness of God. This view links the individual to the salvation story of God. It acknowledges the participation of Black people in the salvation story.[22] The Black way of knowing—Black epistemology, and experiencing the Gospel reflects a historical Jesus of the people—Jesus Christ Liberator.[23] This is a tangible and embraceable reality for African Americans because it is linked to their cultural experiences. It is not an abstract construct of something alien or unrelated to their way of being.[24] Black Catholic Theology that comes out of this way of knowing gives rise to a faith of a people embodied in the Christ of the People.

This call to ministry as a catechist, from an Afrocentric worldview, addresses faith formation in a way that allows for Black Catholic spiritual development. Inculturated catechesis impacts the Black human development of right feeling and affect. It leads the believer to see herself as a part of the salvation story. This produces the true conversion and renewal with understanding and acceptance of God's fundamental truth; that all people are created in the image and likeness of God. An inculturated catechesis from an Afrocentric lens allows the believer to be empowered with the Word of God, a living example that Black Catholic Theology is Black articulation to the Catholic experience.[25]

This authentic catechesis gives a call to the faithful that esteems the African American learner and enables one to see oneself as God's creation fully equipped. This response of empowerment enables the believer to creatively cope and overcome life's hardships. This type of catechesis enables, sustains, and guides the learner to discover positive options for believing and acting.[26] This is the path to religious faith in action; a life like new wine poured into new wineskins. This is the substance that provides for the people to be the change agents of social structures and attitudes. They are then armed with the tools to challenge and address social structures and attitudes, for example, the structural and social sins of racism and sexism.

Racism represents a serious obstacle to the African Americans' encounter with Christ through the Catholic Church. Racism is an impediment to the evangelization mission.[27] It is a hindrance to the ministry of fellowship (*koinonia*). We are called to be one, just as God the Father, the Son, and the Holy Spirit are one. Racism severs this communion of the Body of Christ as one people. It seriously challenges the Church's mission of being truly Catholic and truly universal.

The Good News of the Gospel is supposed to be liberating. The Incarnation of Christ entering into the human condition is the Perfected Inculturation. Jesus takes on the experiences of humanity. He enters into the culture of the people and engages them in their social location. It is through the lens of their worldview that Jesus leads them and guides them and empowers them. It is in the vernacular, the language, and the ways of the people, that Jesus meets them and cares for them. This is the liberating experience of an inculturated catechesis. It is a reciprocal exchange of Black culture and the Catholic faith. This exchange allows for the religious experience to rise within the person and to be: (1) Poured out in service (*Diakonia*) to the community (*Koinonia*) and (2) Manifested in authentic worship and prayer (*Liturgia*). Catechesis from an Afrocentric perspective allows the people to engage God in their Blackness, in God's image and likeness. It expresses God in the Black Aesthetic. The inculturation of the Catholic witness with Black spirituality, through Black art, drama, music, and language into the catechetical process leads to a Black Aesthetic. The gift of Blackness enriches the doctrine, liturgy, and faith of the Church according to Pope John Paul II. This authentic expression of faith encompasses the full dignity of the African American worshiper. This is full witness of faith in the Church. It is fellowship (*Koinonia*) for it allows an illumination of relationship with God and neighbor. This Afrocentric paradigm of catechesis leads to social and critical analysis of our faith, church, and world. Catechesis, from this vantage point, empowers the believer for leadership.

LEADERSHIP REQUIRES ACTION

It is here that I realize that my discussion of catechesis from the lens of being Black and Catholic was a bit myopic—to say the least. Nowhere in the discussion was the aspect of my gender taken into account. The fierceness and holy boldness that I embraced to dismantle cultural biases were bridled on the topic of how I was marginalized as a woman. I was a Black Catholic woman. I addressed concerns that were not inclusive of the Holy through the lens of Blackness. Yet I did not address the obvious disparity of women in the leadership roles of the Church. I continued to skirt (pun intended) the obvious disparity of women in leadership until a sequence of events forced me to confront the situation. I wonder now if I was hedging my bets. (Rita Nakashima Brock uses this same language of hedging one's bet in her discussion on the paradoxical choices one may make to both reject and keep, while navigating through areas of ambiguity as one's refusal to discard something that might retain some power.)[28] The reality of the matter was if I did not engage it, then I did not have to do anything about it. Somewhat in the same manner that agnostics do not engage in the dialogue of is there a God—for fear that if they respond yes—then they may have to do something about the impact this might have on their life. Just as "agnosticism is content to leave the question unanswered, because it is judged difficult, irrelevant, or threatening."[29] I had avoided the question of why not the women for the very same reason. The matter was placed before me by an ordained member of the Permanent Diaconate.

The late Deacon Leon Johnson was among the first group of men ordained as Permanent Deacons. He was an activist who was involved in the Civil Rights Movements of the 1960s. He was involved with the Black Catholic community in the Archdiocese of Newark, when Rev. Dr. Martin Luther King, Jr. was granted permission to speak at the Black Catholic Church of Our Lady Queen of Angels. It was Johnson who sparked the inquiry for me with the following comment. "When they begin to ordain women, I am going to pass on the first entourage that comes running through the doors. Then I am going to submit your name for inquiry." I looked at him as if he had lost his mind. First, I had absolutely no interest in being a priest (I was married and of course that brings up a whole other discourse), and second, there was no way that this was even a viable conversation. When I expressed this to him, Deacon Johnson stated that he was not really talking about the priesthood, although he had no qualms against women priests. His focus was on the Permanent Diaconate. My response to him was, "you know the Catholic Church does not believe in ordaining women into either the Priesthood or the Diaconate." Johnson countered with a simple question; "Why not?" I had been dancing around this question most of my life. I was now being asked to dig deep and engage in a dialogue that went beyond the usual response of: "the Church teaches that only men can be ordained." Johnson raised three questions. First, "As someone who prepares children and youth for the Sacrament of Baptism, what would you say if girls were told they could not be baptized because they were misbegotten souls with defects of being?" Second, "What if you were told that you could not teach catechism because as a woman you lacked wisdom and authority?" Third, "What if you were prohibited from the ministry of Lector because only men were permitted to serve in this capacity?" Johnson phrased his questions with words that he knew would irk my sensibilities as a woman. He also infused the conversation with the very reasoning used by Thomas Aquinas that fostered this disordered Aristotelian premise of women as defective and misbegotten. It was this conversation that sent me on a quest to seek out the answer to "Why not the women?"

Discussing the topic of the role of women in the Church, Elizabeth Johnson notes the following:

> Since the soul informs the body, woman's defective physical state leads Aquinas to the conclusion that woman's soul is likewise deficient, her mind weak in reasoning and her will fragile in choosing the good . . . . Aquinas reasonably deduces a host of consequences . . . woman may not be ordained as priest since priesthood signifies the eminence of Christ and women do not signify what pertains to eminence; women should not preach since this is an exercise of wisdom and authority of which they are not capable; and so on.[30]

Elizabeth Johnson states that it is Aquinas' cultural prism of patriarchy and the androcentrism of the Christian tradition that allow for this problematic argument to be accepted as truth. She surmises that the "bias against the genuine humanity of women is not superficial but is intrinsic to inherited religious structures and paradigms of thought that are firmly in place."[31] It is further indicated in Elizabeth Johnson's work that this theology of Aquinas' embeds within the Catholic Church a structure that "marginalizes women and justify structures that exclude them from full and equal participation."[32]

Earlier on I argued for the necessity of addressing the social sin of racism due to its impact on Black and Brown people in the evangelization mission of the Church. It did not escape me from re-reading the premise that sexism was not included in the original assessment. It is this which Deacon Johnson called me out on. The fact that the marginalization of my being in the witness and ministry was not just because of my Blackness but equally because of my being a woman as well. Appropriating the insights from Elizabeth Johnson, "From the margins feminist liberation theology sees clearly that society and the church are pervaded by sexism with its twin faces of patriarchy and androcentrism. This social sin has debilitating effects on women both socially and psychologically, and interlocks with other forms of oppression to shape a violent and dehumanized world."[33] Elizabeth Johnson cites Bell Hooks when she writes, "To be in the margins, is to be part of the whole but outside the main body." Elizabeth Johnson notes that "It is not an unnecessary place, but a place of systematic devaluing. Being there signifies being less, being overlooked, not having as much importance."[34]

It was this internal battle that was taking place within me. I had absolutely no qualms in calling the Church out on systemic and institutionalized racism. What was it that had me so hesitant in being a voice of challenge as to what was becoming revealed as an inconvenient truth that these traditions of men that exclude women from full and active participation may not be so divinely established? The ability to sanction or silence a voice of discord has been the arm of authority exercised by the hierarchy of the Church for millennia. The Church has historically excommunicated, sanctioned, or silenced its members who spoke or taught with a different perspective. Yves Congar, Pierre Teilhard de Chardin, and even Galileo (theologians and philosophers) suffered for the use of their voice, action, and agency in bringing forth new bodies of knowledge. Even in more recent times, in 2012, the Missionary Maryknoll priest, Roy Bourgeois was excommunicated and laicized because of his support of the ordination of women. What happened to Bourgeois scared me because, at that same period, I was working on my doctoral studies and was working on the passage of The Anointing at Bethany by Mary in John 12:1-8 to argue for women's ordination.

The silencing of women who challenged authority was not without precedent. As noted by the Black Womanist Theologian, Diana L. Hayes, "Historically, women have been the unheard voices calling for recognition and the freedom to speak of their lives in words of their own choosing. Women of color have especially suffered from the oppression of others, both male and female, of their own and other races and ethnicities, speaking for and about them."[35] Biblical context continues to be used as an embedded understanding that women should be seen and not heard. I hated this quote when it was directed at children, and I disliked it even more as a mature and self-determined woman. The scales had begun to fall from my eyes. I began to seriously look at the role of women in the history of the Church and see that the restrictions on ordination and preaching and ministry were not so much the inspired word of G*d as it was the interpretation of men that was seeped into the Aristotelian/Aquinas myth on women. "Being humble, silent, and unassuming has been extolled throughout the centuries as a feminine virtue... Deprecation and vilification: Wo/men who do not adapt to the *kyriarchal* ethos of malestream society are vilified, maligned, and slandered as bad women."[36] I was no longer content with allowing my mouth to be bridled to adhere to a restriction that was becoming more of a stumbling block. I was ready to embrace my calling to proclaim and teach in the Church.

Furthermore, I was consistently being sought out to speak at ministry programs on spirituality and faith witnessed through the lens of women. These ministerial events were not isolated to Catholic communities. Over the course of time, I have been invited to speak at various Catholic liturgies (Sunday Mass) as the reflectionist although the talk would take place immediately after the proclamation of the Gospel. The nuance of this was always finessed with the pastor providing a very short commentary on the major theme of the Gospel and then turning over the pulpit to me for my spiritual talk. On some occasions, the invitation to speak would be situated at the end of the Mass for fear that the local ordinary might get news that there was a woman preaching at Sunday Mass. Yes, the nuances (of reflectionist versus preaching, location of the talk after Communion with the announcements versus pride of place in the pulpit after the Gospel is proclaimed) began to weigh on my conscience. I began to ask the question: what difference does it all make?

I have been asked by Lutheran and Episcopal houses of worship to participate in various ministry programs and liturgies. It was an encounter with a Lutheran pastor and an Episcopal pastor, who was a former Catholic priest, that finally challenged me to get off the fence with regard to the question. Also, it was the following statement from a Franciscan priest after hearing me preach on *Women in the Scripture* that also got me thinking of the need to engage the question: "This is why women are needed in the preaching ministry." He was responding to my reflection on the Gospel of Luke 24:11 and the male disciples' response to the proclamation by Mary of Magdala and the women at the tomb. "The Women were said to be crazy for proclaiming Jesus resurrected from the dead." Could it be, just as they were in error then, that male hierarchy is in error now about the role of women in the proclamation and preaching of the Gospel? Once I had voiced this question, my entire being responded with a resounding embodiment of the truth will set you free, woman, thou art loosed. Theologian and womanist preacher, Rev. Dr. Prathia Hall engages the marginalization of women in the biblical text and context and calls for a dismantling of patriarchy. She restates a quote by Renita Weems: "Because it [the message] came from women, they thought it was gossip. When, in fact, it was the Gospel."[37] Hall also notes that "many of us . . . are still missing the Gospel, because God chooses a messenger who is a woman."[38]

It was at the urging of both the Lutheran and Episcopal priests that I entered the seminary for theological studies. Although they both felt that the Catholic Church would never allow me to participate actively in ordained ministry simply because of my gender, I was adamant that I would not leave the Catholic Church. Both of these ordained men of God spent time engaging me in spiritual direction and theological reflection to challenge me to discern for myself the anointing and the call that the Holy Spirit had for my life. So emphatic was the Episcopal priest, that he set up an appointment for me to meet with his bishop (an appointment that I declined), and with the women priests at their convent in Mendham, New Jersey. The wisdom of the women I met was that they could clearly see that even though I had a calling for preaching and possibly ordination, I would not choose conversion to another faith tradition in order to fulfill the calling.

Many years of theological reflection and studies in Biblical theology, Black theology, and Catholic theology have empowered me to unbridle my tongue and to no longer be afraid of engaging in the dialogue and answering emphatically: Women too!

The continued delay of the Church's affirmative response to the ordination of women to the Permanent Diaconate sounds so much like the response of the confused men when the women shared the Good News: He is Risen! The continued resounding no on the question of women priests begs the question; what are they afraid of? Church tradition relies on the teaching that Jesus did not call women! The Church's hermeneutical interpretation of the sign and symbol of the foot washing of the disciples by Jesus in John 13:1-17 is that it represents the call to the priesthood—ordination! Elisabeth Schussler Fiorenza notes:

> We must assume that wo/men were present and active in history until proven otherwise. Hence, we have to read kyriocentric texts in an inclusive fashion unless it is explicitly stated that wo/men were not present . . . texts and injunctions that seek to censure or limit wo/men's behavior must be read as prescriptive rather than as descriptive of reality. If women are forbidden from a certain activity, we can safely assume that they might actually have engaged in it so much that it became threatening to the kyriarchal order. [39]

Cheryl Townsend-Gilkes challenges the only male priesthood doctrine by her creative use of the Spirituals of the African Diaspora. She writes: "One of the basic contradictions that emerges in this model is that an ordaining body that insists that only men are called to the ministry is forced to argue that God does not speak to women in the same way that God speaks to men. The problem is that the spirituals about Mary Magdalene and the sisters, Mary, and Martha, insist that not only does God speak to women but that God speaks to women to give messages to men."[40] Scripture has been the foundation upon which women have been excluded from participating in priestly ministries. Yet, it was not Scripture, but its interpretation that provided the arguments for gender bias. If catechesis, understood as the authentic teaching of the faith is to be rooted in Scripture, as one of the foundational pillars, then it must have a Biblical hermeneutic that is consistent with seeing women as God sees them.

Earlier in this chapter, I referenced John 12:1-7 as an example of how Jesus saw the role of women in the witness and ministry of service. Let us look with a new eye at how this particular text can provide a new epistemology and teaching on the role of women in ministry:

> Six days before Passover Jesus came to Bethany, where Lazarus was, whom Jesus had raised from the dead. They gave a dinner for him there, and Martha served, while Lazarus was one of those reclining at table with him. Mary took a pound of costly perfume oil made from genuine aromatic nard and anointed the feet of Jesus and dried them with her hair; the whole house was filled with the

fragrance of the oil. Then Judas the Iscariot, one of his disciples, and the one who would betray him, said "Why was this oil not sold for three hundred days' wages and given to the poor?" He said this not because he cared about the poor but because he was a thief and held the money bag and used to steal the contributions. So, Jesus said, "Leave her alone. Let her keep this for the day of my burial."

The Anointing at Bethany involves the very dear friends of Jesus, Lazarus, and his two sisters, Martha and Mary. Yet, the pivotal character is Mary (point of clarification, this is Mary of Bethany not to be confused with Mary of Magdala). It is necessary to understand the historical background as to the role and status of women in the society of this particular time. The knowledge of the cultural norms is imperative to understand and interpret the significance of the actions of this woman. Knowledge of the cultural expectations and taboos of the time gives clarity to the actions of Mary of Bethany. The purpose of the anointing must be considered. What was the Jewish tradition in relation to anointing? Was the action within the scope of a woman's role and was the technique of the anointing of particular interest? What is the symbolism of the ointment nard?

Mary of Bethany is identified as the woman who performs the anointing. What is the relevance of her being called by name? What is the significance of the use of Mary's hair (a woman's crowning glory) to wipe off the excess of the expensive ointment? She anointed his feet. Was there a specific purpose for the anointing? The Scripture notes that the scent of the fragrance filled the whole house! What is the relevance of this and is there a connection to any other scriptural text? The placement of the event within the Gospel of John is strategic. The event takes place after the miracle of the raising of Lazarus from the dead and before the triumphant entry of Jesus into Jerusalem. It is my belief that the sweet fragrance that fills the house, and the use of the woman's hair all speak to the glory of the Lord, that is to come through his death and the Resurrection. The literary positioning of the anointing between the raising of Lazarus from the dead and the beginning of the Passover leads us to the real glory not being of this world but of the heavenly kingdom that is to come.

Mary is the one who sits at Jesus's feet in Luke 10:38-42. Jesus acknowledges that her position to learn from him is the better part of serving in his ministry. Mary is the one who falls at his feet when Jesus comes to visit the family after the death of Lazarus. Mary is the one at Lazarus' tomb who the people follow to comfort her. Her actions lead them to faith (*pistis*) when they follow her as she follows Jesus. The anointing of Jesus by Mary of Bethany points to his being the "Anointed One" (truly the Messiah the Anointed One referenced in John 1:41). Mary was prophetic in her actions and acknowledgment that Jesus was the King of Glory. Her actions are those of true discipleship and witness. Yet, they also portray so much more.

The act of anointing has a historical and cultural context. Exodus 29:7 gives the instruction for the consecration of a priest: "Take the anointing oil and anoint him with it pouring it on his head." Daniel Fleming argues that "The particular association of royal anointing with designation by God . . . may itself be rooted in the old practice of consecrating priests for divine service, set apart as sacred to God."[41] Isaiah 61:1 makes note of the anointing of the prophet, as well as Psalm 105:15.[42] The practice of cultures in the ancient Near East consisted of anointings of women upon betrothal.[43] Anointings were regularly performed by wives for their husbands in ancient Greek customs. Song of Songs 1:2 and 4:14 allude to the anointing of the bridegroom by the bride.[44] Women were also sent to anoint a dead body for burial.[45] The celebration of a meal was often accompanied by an anointing of those participating as a diplomatic sign of sharing hospitality and friendship.[46] It calls to mind Psalm 23:5: "you prepare a table before me in the presence of my enemies, and you anoint my head with oil."

The norms related to a woman's unbound hair in first-century Jewish culture were similar to the wider society; unmarried Roman and Greek girls wore their hair free.[47] Marriage required a change in hairstyle for a woman. Thus, the hair was bound in public.[48] It is noted that when a woman wears her hair unbound in the ancient Mediterranean world, it can portray an expression or sign of mourning, a symbolic expression of distress or grief. It can also be representative of religious devotion, and one presenting herself in a natural state for religious initiation.[49] Although ancient Greek society shunned the public appearance of women at banquets in the presence of men, the early Roman society was undergoing cultural changes. These changes in women's meal customs were allowing for the public appearance of respectable women at meals with men. These changes did incur some criticism. Jewish cultural norms were not unaffected by the changes in the social customs of Greco-Roman society.[50]

The symbolism and the customs around the legitimacy of women are relevant. They provide some context to the women during the time of Jesus. What is interesting is the fact that unbound hair could represent religious devotion and preparation for a religious initiation. The example of Mary who sat and studied as a disciple at the feet of Jesus could be symbolic of this above-noted religious devotion and initiation. Studying closely the actions of Mary as she later anoints the feet of Jesus, one is compelled to ask, could her actions have been more than just the symbolic preparation for his impending death and burial? She provided a prototype of discipleship of service that is later mirrored when Jesus washes the feet of his disciples and dries them with a towel. The actions that are noted of Jesus in the Gospel of John 13:1-17 are interpreted by the Church as the foundation for the institution of the priesthood.

The foot washing took place in the chapter following The Anointing at Bethany. Just as Mary sat at his feet and learned from the teachings of her friend Jesus, is it inconceivable to think that Jesus also modeled that which he saw as the selfless outpouring of love and service for another? Is it conceivable that Mary, knowing that Jesus's hour of death was approaching, was preparing herself to step into full ministry of service to carry on the faith? The outpouring of self and precious gifts to honor Jesus is noted. The term *pistikos* is a Greek description of the real nard and literally translates as faithful.[51] The word nard is unique to the Gospel of John. The only other time that it is used in the Scriptures is in the Song of Songs 1:12 and 4:14, which is a poem that describes spousal love. John the Baptist referenced Jesus as the bridegroom in John 3:29. Mary's actions are comparable to the bride's action in Songs 1:12 and 4:14: "pouring forth ointments of nard onto her bridegroom."

The irony of this Scripture's proclamation is that it is only proclaimed once in the liturgical year of the Church. The Monday of Holy Week is the designated day that the passage on The Anointing at Bethany in the Johannine Gospel is read during Mass. Supposedly, it is the symbolism of the anointing in preparation for his death (Good Friday) that positions it to be read the morning after Palm Sunday. Such a missed opportunity for this passage to not be proclaimed during a Sunday liturgy or, better yet, at a Holy Week Chrism Mass. The Chrism Mass, which occurs during Holy Week, is when the Sacred Oils of the Church are blessed by the bishop with the local church gathered around him and distributed to the local churches for the edification and furtherance of the faith. What a powerful sign and witness this would be for The Anointing at Bethany to be the passage that is proclaimed as the Church prepares for the Sacraments of Initiation at the Easter Vigil.

The perspective on the reading through the eyes of a woman allows for a hermeneutic that sees beyond gender limitation. To see as Mary of Bethany saw, as Mary of Magdala saw, as the Syrophoenician woman and the Samaritan woman saw, allow for all in the Church to embrace the sight of faith. It is worth noting also that there was wisdom in Jesus's command: "Leave her alone . . . . Why do you trouble the woman? For she has done a beautiful thing to me . . . . Truly I say to you wherever this Gospel is proclaimed in the whole world, what she has done will also be told in memory of her" (Matthew 26:6-13; Mark 14:3-9; Luke 7:36-50 and John 12:1-8).

CONCLUSION

I began this discourse from a place of bondage. A bridled tongue tied up in not proclaiming the fullness of what was so clear to the spiritual eyes of children; that the Lord instituted all of his gifts (sacraments) to give grace.

There is no restriction on God's grace. I take particular note that it was the youth to whom I was teaching the faith, that challenged the gender restrictive norms. They are responsible for planting the seed for my Intellectual Conversion. According to Bernard Lonergan, it is defined as "the shift from a very erroneous myth concerning reality, objectivity, and human knowledge," as it relates to intellectual, moral, and religious conversion.[52] I close this discourse with the instruction of Jesus of Nazareth to the woman who anointed his feet in Luke 7:50 "Your faith has saved you, go in peace!"

NOTES

1. Anna Julia Cooper, *A Voice from the South by a Black Woman of the South* (Xenia, OH: The Aldine Printing House, 1892), 125.

2. Elizabeth Ann Manhart Barret, ed., *Visions of Rogers' Scienced-Based Nursing* (New York: National League for Nursing, 1990), 8, 35, 47.

3. Charles Lemert and Esme Bhan, eds., *The Voice of Anna Julia Cooper: Including A Voice from The South and Other Important Essays, Papers and Letters* (Lanham, MD: Rowman & Litttlefield Publishers, Inc., 1998), 63.

4. Ibid.

5. Vincent W. Lloyd, *Black Natural Law* (New York: Oxford University Press, 2016), 34.

6. See Andrew Leiter, "Summary Anna J. Cooper (Anna Julia), 1858-1964 A Voice from the South- Documenting the American South" (Xenia, OH: The Aldine Printing House, 1892), https://docsouth.unc.edu/church/cooper/summary.html.

7. Vatican News, "Pope Francis: Ministries of Lector and Acolyte to Be Open to Women," *Vatican News. Daily World News*, January 11, 2021, https://www.vatican-news.va/en/pope/news/2021-01/pope-francis-opens-ministries-lector-acolyte-women.html.

8. Francis, *Apostolic Letter Issued "Motu Proprio" By the Supreme Pontiff Francis: "Antiquum Ministerium." Instituting the Ministry of Catechists* (Rome, May 10, 2021), https://www.vatican.va/content/francesco/en/motu_proprio/documents/papa-francesco-motu-proprio-20210510_antiquum-ministerium.html.

9. The use of inclusive language of Kin-dom vs. Kingdom supports a change in orthopraxy from a patriarchal language context of gender designated. See Reta Halteman Finger, "From Kingdom to Kin-dom and Beyond," *Christian Feminism Today* (2013), https://eewc.com/kingdom-kindom-beyond/.

10. Giles Conwill, "Black Catechesis," in *Taking Down Our Harps: Black Catholics in the United States*, ed. Diana L. Hayes and Cyprian Davis (Maryknoll, NY: Orbis Books, 1998), 200.

11. All biblical citations in this chapter are taken from *The New American Bible* (Wichita, KS: Fireside Bible Publishers, 1987).

12. Miroslav Volf, *Exclusion and Embrace: A Theological Exploration of Identity, Otherness and Reconciliation* (Nashville: Abingdon Press, 1996), 158 (un-daughtered is a paraphrase of the language unsonned used by Volf about marginalization.)

13. See the detailed critique of the racial exclusion of Black women from women religious orders in the United States of America by Shannen Dee Williams in *Subversive Habits: Black Catholic Nuns in the Long African American Freedom Struggle* (Durham, NC: Duke University Press, 2022).

14. Carmel McEnroy, *Guests in Their Own House: The Women of Vatican II* (New York: Crossroads, 1996), 3.

15. Ibid.

16. Ibid., 3, 5.

17. Ibid.

18. Ibid., 3, 4.

19. Karen Jo Torjesen, "Reconstruction of Women's Early Christian History," in *Searching the Scriptures: A Feminist Introduction, vol. 1,* ed. Elisabeth Schussler Fiorenza (New York: The Crossroad Publishing Company, 1993), 300.

20. Ibid.

21. Eva Marie Lumas, "The Nature and Goals of Africentric Catholic Catechesis," in *God Bless Them...Who Have Their Own: African American Catechetical Camp Meeting: A Gathering to Chart a New Course* (Washington, DC: Department of Education United States Catholic Conference, Inc., 1995), 30.

22. Giles Conwill, "A Unique People," in *Tell It Like It Is: A Black Catholic Perspective on Christian Education* (Oakland, CA: The National Black Sisters' Conference, 1983), 25–34.

23. Conwill, "Black Catechesis," in *Taking Down Our Harps,* 212.

24. Toinette Eugene, "Black Theology" in *Tell It Like It Is, A Black Catholic Perspective on Christian Education* (Oakland, CA: The National Black Sisters' Conference, 1983), 99.

25. Jamie T. Phelps, "A Doctrinal Perspective: Implications for an Africentric Catechesis," in *God Bless Them...Who Have Their Own: African American Catechetical Camp Meeting: A Gathering to Chart a New Course,* 20.

26. Eva Lumas, "Leaning on the Word," in *Tell It Like It Is: A Black Catholic Perspective on Christian Education,* 18–24.

27. Warren J. Savage, *Project Reach Out: Evangelization Leading the Way to Eradicate Racism* (Westfield, MA: National Black Catholic Evangelization Forum, 1998), 1.

28. Rita Nakashima Brock, "Dusting the Bible on the Floor: A Hermeneutics of Wisdom," in *Searching the Scriptures: A Feminist Introduction, vol. 1,* ed. Elisabeth Schussler Fiorenza (New York: The Crossroad Publishing Company, 1993), 64.

29. Kathleen Fischer and Thomas Hart, *Christian Foundations: An Introduction to Faith in Our Time, revised edition,* (Mahwah, NJ: Paulist Press, 1986), 28.

30. Elizabeth Johnson, *She Who Is: The Mystery of God in Feminist Theological Discourse* (New York: The Crossroad Publishing Company, 1992), 24–25.

31. Ibid.

32. Ibid.

33. Ibid., 24.

34. Ibid.

35. Diana L. Hayes, "And When We Speak: To Be Black, Catholic, and Womanist," in *Taking Down Our Harps: Black Catholics in the United States*, ed. Diana L. Hayes and Cyprian Davis (Maryknoll, NY: Orbis Books, 1998), 102.

36. Elisabeth Schussler Fiorenza, *Wisdom Ways: Introducing Feminist Biblical Interpretation* (Maryknoll, NY: Orbis Books, 2001), 110.

37. Donna E. Allen, *Towards a Womanist Homiletic: Katie Canon, Alice Walker and Emancipatory Proclamation* (New York: Peter Lang Publishing, Inc., 2013), 60.

38. Ibid.

39. Fiorenza, *Wisdom Ways*, 185.

40. Cheryl Townsend-Gilkes, "'Go and Tell Mary and Martha' The Spirituals, Biblical Options for Women, and Cultural Tensions in African American Religious Experience," in *Womanist Theological Ethics*, eds. Katie Geneva Cannon, Emilie M. Townes, and Angela D. Sims (Louisville, KY: Westminster John Knox Press, 2011), 232.

41. Daniel Fleming, "The Biblical Tradition of Anointing Priests," *Journal of Biblical Literature*, vol. 117, no. 3 (1998): 401–414.

42. Ibid., 407.

43. Ibid., 405, 407.

44. Kathleen Corley, "The Anointing of Jesus in the Synoptic Tradition," *Journal for the Study of the Historical Jesus*, vol. 1, no. 1 (2003): 61–72.

45. Ibid.

46. Fleming, "The Biblical Tradition," 407.

47. Charles H. Cosgrove, "A Woman's Unbound Hair in the Greco Roman World," *Journal of Biblical Literature*, vol. 124, no. 4 (2005): 675–692.

48. Ibid., 682.

49. Ibid.

50. Corley, "The Anointing," 64.

51. Raymond Brown, *The Gospel According to John: 1-12: translated, with introduction, notes, and commentary, Anchor Bible Reference*, vol. 29 (Garden City, NY: Doubleday, 1966), 448.

52. Bernard Lonergan, *Method in Theology* (New York: Herder and Herder, 1972), 238.

FURTHER READINGS

Canon, Katie Geneva. *Katie's Canon: Womanism and the Soul of the Black Community*. New York: Continuum, 1995.

Cutter, Elissa. "Toward a Feminist Historical Theology: Part I, Hamilton." *womenintheology.org*, July 3, 2021.

———. "Toward a Feminist Historical Theology: Part II, Feminist Biblical Interpretation." *womenintheology.org*, October 27, 2021.

Hayes, Diana L. *No Crystal Stair: Womanist Spirituality*. Maryknoll, NY: Orbis Books, 2016.

Thistlethwaite, Susan Brooks. *Women's Bodies as Battlefields: Christian Theology and the Global War on Women.* London: Palgrave MacMillan, 2015.

Trible, Phyllis. *Text of Terror: Literary-Feminist Readings of Biblical Narratives.* Philadelphia: Fortress Press, 1984.

Williams, Delores. *Sisters in the Wilderness: The Challenge of Womanist God-Talk.* Maryknoll, NY: Orbis Books, 2000.

REFERENCES

Allen, Donna E. *Towards a Womanist Homiletic: Katie Canon, Alice Walker and Emancipatory Proclamation.* New York: Peter Lang Publishing, Inc., 2013.

Barret, Elizabeth Ann Manhart, ed. *Visions of Rogers' Scienced-Based Nursing.* New York, NY: National League for Nursing, 1990.

Brock, Rita Nakashima. "Dusting the Bible on the Floor: A Hermeneutics of Wisdom." In *Searching the Scriptures: A Feminist Introduction, Volume 1*, edited by Elisabeth Schussler Fiorenza, 64–75. New York: The Crossroad Publishing Company, 1993.

Brown, Raymond. *The Gospel According to John: 1–12. Translated, With Introduction, Notes, and Commentary: Anchor Bible Reference, Volume 29.* Garden City, NY: Doubleday, 1966.

Conwill, Giles. "A Unique People." In *Tell It Like It Is: A Black Catholic Perspective on Christian Education.* Oakland, CA: The National Black Sisters' Conference, 1983.

———. "Black Catechesis." In *Taking Down Our Harps: Black Catholics in the United States*, edited by Diana L. Hayes and Cyprian Davis, 199–231. Maryknoll, NY: Orbis Books, 1998.

Cooper, Anna Julia. *A Voice From the South by a Black Woman of the South.* Xenia, OH: The Aldine Printing House, 1892.

Corley, Kathleen. "The Anointing of Jesus in the Synoptic Tradition." *Journal for the Study of the Historical Jesus* 1, no. 1 (2003): 61–72.

Cosgrove, Charles H. "A Woman's Unbound Hair in the Greco Roman World." *Journal of Biblical Literature* 124, no. 4 (2005): 675–692.

Eugene, Toinette. "Black Theology." In *Tell It Like It Is, A Black Catholic Perspective on Christian Education.* Oakland, CA: The National Black Sisters' Conference, 1983.

Finger, Reta Halteman. "From Kingdom to Kin-dom and Beyond." *Christian Feminism Today.* 2013. https://eewc.com/kingdom-kindom-beyond/.

Fiorenza, Elisabeth Schussler. *Wisdom Ways: Introducing Feminist Biblical Interpretation.* Maryknoll, NY: Orbis Books, 2001.

Fischer, Kathleen, and Thomas Hart. *Christian Foundations: An Introduction to Faith in Our Time. Revised Edition.* Mahwah, NJ: Paulist Press, 1986.

Fleming, Daniel. "The Biblical Tradition of Anointing Priests." *Journal of Biblical Literature* 117, no. 3 (1998): 401–414.

Francis. *Apostolic Letter Issued "Motu Proprio" By the Supreme Pontiff Francis: "Antiquum Ministerium." Instituting the Ministry of Catechists.* Rome, May 10,

2021. https://www.vatican.va/content/francesco/en/motu_proprio/documents/papa-francesco-motu-proprio-20210510_antiquum-ministerium.html.

Hayes, Diana L. "And When We Speak: To Be Black, Catholic, and Womanist." In *Taking Down Our Harps: Black Catholics in the United States*, edited by Diana L. Hayes and Cyprian Davis, 102–119. Maryknoll, NY: Orbis Books, 1998.

Johnson, Elizabeth. *She Who Is: The Mystery of God in Feminist Theological Discourse*. New York: The Crossroad Publishing Company, 1992.

Leiter, Andrew. *Summary Anna J. Cooper (Anna Julia), 1858–1964 A Voice From the South-Documenting the American South*. Xenia, OH: The Aldine Printing House, 1892. https://docsouth.unc.edu/church/cooper/summary.html.

Lemert, Charles, and Esme Bhan, eds. *The Voice of Anna Julia Cooper: Including a Voice From the South and Other Important Essays, Papers and Letters*. Lanham, MD: Rowman & Litttlefield Publishers, Inc., 1998.

Lloyd, Vincent W. *Black Natural Law*. New York: Oxford University Press, 2016.

Lumas, Eva Marie. "The Nature and Goals of Africentric Catholic Catechesis." In *God Bless Them...Who Have Their Own: African American Catechetical Camp Meetin': A Gathering to Chart a New Course*. Washington, D.C.: Department of Education United States Catholic Conference, Inc., 1995.

McEnroy, Carmel. *Guests in Their Own House: The Women of Vatican II*. New York: Crossroads, 1996.

Phelps, Jamie T. "A Doctrinal Perspective: Implications for an Africentric Catechesis." In *God Bless Them...Who Have Their Own: African American Catechetical Camp Meetin': A Gathering to Chart a New Course*, 15–27. Washington, D.C.: Department of Education United States Catholic Conference, 1995.

Savage, Warren J. *Project Reach Out: Evangelization Leading the Way to Eradicate Racism*. Westfield, MA: National Black Catholic Evangelization Forum, 1998.

The New American Bible. Wichita, KS: Fireside Bible Publishers, 1987.

Torjesen, Karen Jo. "Reconstruction of Women's Early Christian History." In *Searching the Scriptures: A Feminist Introduction, Volume 1*, edited by Elisabeth Schussler Fiorenza, 290–310. New York: The Crossroad Publishing Company, 1993.

Townsend-Gilkes, Cheryl. "'Go and Tell Mary and Martha' the Spirituals, Biblical Options for Women, and Cultural Tensions in African American Religious Experience." In *Womanist Theological Ethics*, edited by Katie Geneva Cannon, Emilie M. Townes, and Angela D. Sims, 217–236. Louisville, KY: Westminster John Knox Press, 2011.

Vatican News. "Pope Francis: Ministries of Lector and Acolyte to Be Open to Women." *Vatican News, Daily World News*, January 11, 2021. https://www.vaticannews.va/en/pope/news/2021-01/pope-francis-opens-ministries-lector-acolyte-women.html.

Volf, Miroslav. *Exclusion and Embrace: A Theological Exploration of Identity, Otherness and Reconciliation*. Nashville: Abingdon Press, 1996.

Williams, Shannen Dee. *Subversive Habits: Black Catholic Nuns in the Long African American Freedom Struggle*. Durham, NC: Duke University Press, 2022.

Chapter 7

Gender, Race, God

A Case for a Pragmatic Theological Anthropology

Anthonia Bolanle Ojo

Women have been unjustly held back from achieving full equality with men for much of human history in many societies around the world. The age-long experience of women being regarded as inferior to their male counterparts is more evident in modern times, when they are being discriminated against because of their gender, jobs, race, and so on. According to Strachan Owen:

> The oppression of women in the 21st century is perhaps more multi-faceted and developed than it has been historically. This shows that modern society has re-envisioned its conception of the human person. For ages, humanity was understood in light of God; humankind was made in the image of God, and thus the human race had certain duties before God. All these have changed. The modern society no longer bases its thinking of the human person on God, but on the qualities possessed by individuals.[1]

Although most of the theological anthropologies that have been developed in modern times purport to apply to all human beings, recent theologians representing the causes of feminism, such as marginalization of women, the need to assert oneself, and so on, the liberation of the poor and oppressed, and so on, have repeatedly complained that mainstream theologies exclude or at least fail to include these causes among their concerns. The oppressive patterns toward women and other subjugated people do not come from specific doctrine but from patriarchal-dominated system.[2]

Gender is a characteristic that does go to the core of what it means to be a human person. The revelation of God about the meaning of the human person as taught by the Catholic Church reveals that we are creatures, lovingly created in God's image and likeness (Gen 1: 26-27).[3] This passage does not imply that God is "androgynous." On the contrary, the writer makes an important two-sided distinction by means of the pronouns they choose to employ. The first of these pronouns is singular: "in the image of God He created him." The second is plural: "male and female He created them." Herein lies an extremely significant truth. Viewed in terms of the Godward relation, "man" or "mankind" is one: all of us, men and women alike, are created equally "in His image" (see Galatians 3:28). But amongst ourselves we are differentiated by sex as a race, we are divided into two groups, halves, or component parts—male and female. God, of course, is neither male nor female. He transcends all such categories. Indeed, the concept of an "androgynous" God is not only foreign but actually offensive to Christian theology. It is not God but we who are marked and set apart from one another in terms of sex. And according to Genesis 1:27, it is only as these two distinct halves of humanity come together that the image of God in man is most fully and completely revealed.[4] The very idea that we are God-like is specifically revealed through our maleness and femaleness, not through any other characteristic ascribed to each by the society.[5] Thus, this chapter argues that sexual differences are accidental when considered from the perspective of nature, but essential on the level of human personhood. There is a single human nature that is always embodied in two irreducible modes in existing human persons—either male or female. This affirms the genuine equality that coexists with utterly unique personal differentiation.

Also, although the Church has engaged in numerous attempts to remedy racism, theology still seems to witness a God that stands relatively unopposed to the status quo of racial injustice and marginalization. Considering the cultures that always prioritized theological anthropology that does not circulate in universal notions of value, hence, this chapter, argues for a theological anthropology that specifically opposes the dehumanizing axiological systems that denigrate those who are regarded as second-class citizens. The inclusive theological anthropology will help to liberate the Gospel from its patriarchal bondage and transform our lives into an inclusive form that might more effectively summon our sinful world. I argue that this kind of theology will free both men and women from the estrangements brought about by patriarchal traditions, and will also help in eradicating racial prejudice.

CONCEPTUAL CLARIFICATION

This section deals with the clarification of some concepts as they will be used in this paper.

These include Gender and Gender Racism.

Gender

Broadly speaking, the term "gender" refers to the socially constructed differences that assign the attitudes and opportunities of males and females and their social interaction and relationships between them. It also determines what is culturally or/and socially accepted, permitted, and valued for both women and men at any given time, and it differs from context to context, thus being context-specific. It is good to point out that some cultures recognize the third gender, such as Hinduism in India. In Hindu Philosophy, there is a boundary-less spiritual world embodied in images such as the Ardhanareshwara, where Shiva presents himself as half woman, where Vishnu transforms himself into a damsel who enchants everyone, or as Durga, the goddess who performs the traditional male role of a warrior and matches into battle on a lion bearing lethal weapons in her hands.[6] Gender is fluid here—god is goddess and goddess is god. Also, the concept of the third gender is common among the Hijras who are often born male but look and dress in traditionally female ways.[7]

Gender is social status, a legal designation, and a social and/or personal identity. Through the social processes of gendering, gender divisions and their accompanying norms and role expectations are built into the major social institutions of society, which include the economy, the family, the state, culture, religion, and the law. Woman and man, girl and boy are terms used when referring to categories of gender.[8] According to the World Health Organization (WHO), gender refers to "the characteristics of women, men, girls and boys that are socially constructed. This includes norms, behaviors and roles associated with being a woman, man, girl or boy, as well as relationships with each other. As a social construct, gender varies from society to society and can change over time."[9] Gender, therefore, refers to the socially given attributes, roles, activities, responsibilities, and needs connected to being men (masculine) and women (feminine) in a given society at a given time, and as a member of a specific community within that society. Women's and men's gender identities determine how they are perceived and how they are expected to think and act as human beings. Furthermore, gender is also one of the principal intersecting variables (along with race and caste or class) deployed in the distribution of privilege, prestige, power, and a range of social and economic resources.[10]

Gender Racism

Gendered racism is a form of oppression that occurs due to race and gender. It is perpetuated due to the prevalence of perceptions, stereotypes, and images of certain groups. "Racism" is defined as the belief that all members of each race possess characteristics or abilities specific to that race.[11] Racism functions as a way to distinguish races as inferior or superior to one another. Gendered racism pertains specifically to racial and ethnic understandings of masculinity and femininity, as well as along gendered forms of race and ethnic discrimination.[12]

THEOLOGICAL ANTHROPOLOGY ANALYZED

Christian anthropologies have been of vital importance throughout the history of the Church because at each point in history there are cultural assumptions and philosophical perspectives about the nature of humanity that call the Gospel into question, that question God's Lordship, humanity's servanthood, and their genuine fellowship in Jesus Christ. Although in Thomas Aquinas' *Summa Theologiae*, there can be found theological opinions that present women as inferior to men, one has to acknowledge the fact that he was writing based on the cultural, philosophical, and religious biases against women that were the dominant view of his time. Nonetheless, the question under consideration that Aquinas was attempting to address was whether the female, because of her inherent imperfection, should not have been part of the original creation. Aquinas' response to the question reveals his bias. He argues that "woman should have been produced in the Eden, since she is necessary for the generation of the species."[13] He then goes on to cite with approval Aristotle's infamous affirmation that "the female is a misbegotten male."[14] Aquinas himself declares that women are *"deficiens et occasionatus"*—defective and misbegotten.[15] In reply to the question of whether the female should be subject to the male, Aquinas asserts that females are inherently subordinate to males and that this "subjection existed even before sin." Female subordination, for Aquinas, is not a result of the fall, but part of the created order. Such female subordination, he argues, is actually "for their own benefit and good." Following Aristotelian logic, Aquinas adds that without female subordination, "good order would have been lacking in the human family if some were not governed by others wiser than themselves. By such a subjection, therefore, woman is naturally subject to man, because in man the discretion of reason predominates."[16]

Aquinas' views on female inferiority were doubtlessly influenced as well by Aristotle's reproductive biology, with its understanding of the relation between male and female as one of active (perfect) principle to passive (imperfect) principle. Aristotle saw the sperm as the formative agent in reproduction; the mother simply supplied raw material to be incorporated into the developing child. He also thought the sperm was directed to producing only male offspring and that when this did not result it was because something interfered with the active principle within the sperm.[17] In the view of Aquinas about women, Mary Daly points out that his conclusions are defective. "Thomas of course shares the feeling that women are not quite human. However, leaving all questions of graces aside, there is indecision in his thought on the level of nature itself."[18] Fundamentally, age, class, and gender are intersecting categories of experience that affect all aspects of human life. Thus, they simultaneously structure the experiences of all people in society. Anthropology lies at the center of contemporary controversies both inside and outside the Church. Differing judgments about what it means to be human inform different approaches to race and sexuality, religion and politics, animating discussions and debates in homes, schools, churches, and larger society.[19]

Anthropology concerns itself with understanding human experience. Theology is concerned with God—God and humanity. In an attempt to understand the whence and the wither of human's existence, one must first look to humanity's origin—humanity is created in the image of God. This is anchored on the fundamental teaching of Gen 1: 27 that every human being comes into existence when God said "Let us make humankind (*adam*) in our image, after our likeness: . . . . And God created humankind in his own image, in the image of God he created him; male and female he created them." What follows then is a theological anthropology; an understanding of human experience which acknowledges that all human experience is rooted in the light of God's revelation. This passage clarifies that the Hebrew term *adam* stands for the generic species of humanity which is composed of men and women. Gen 5:2–3 further clarifies this understanding that: "When God created humankind, he made him in the likeness of God. Male and female he created them, and he blessed them and named them humankind when they were created." Hence Maryanne Horowitz points out that:

> The "image of God in man and woman" opens us to transcend both the masculine and feminine metaphors for God which abound in the Bible and to transcend our historical selves and social institutions in recognition of the Holy One. It would appear that whatever one's interpretation of the "image" and "likeness" of God, one would have to recognize that the biblical text makes explicit that in our resemblance to the Divinity and in our dominion over the earth and animals, men and women share a common human dignity.[20]

The question, "What does it mean to say that humanity has been created in God's image," is, simultaneously, both theological and anthropological. It would be one-sided to say that it is primarily a theological question or to suggest that it is essentially an anthropological question. It is both theological and anthropological. This is the question of theological anthropology.[21]

Theological anthropology concerns human beings and their relationship with God. It addresses humans as created in the image of God with a special qualitative relation to God compared to other species. Theological anthropology also deals with the restoration of the human relationship, tarnished by sin, with God through the life, death, and resurrection of Jesus Christ. It looks at human experience with a view to catching glimpses of God's glory, the glory of his purpose for humanity. Theological anthropology is "our search for a wholesome and meaningful way of being human as well as in the elaboration of what human being is all about."[22] Theological anthropology presents a framework by which "what race is" as a concept can be distinguished from "what it means to be human" as an embodiment. This distinction is calibrated through a theologizing about God from the meaningfulness of "what it means to be human" beyond "what race is." More importantly, this differentiation is respectively between "what race is" in theory and "what race is" in praxis as what it means to be human, to the extent that what becomes specifically existential in the meaningfulness of race is translated by what becomes generally existential in the meaningfulness of human embodiment.[23]

Therefore, where God is excluded from anthropology, everything is viewed in a horizontal dimension. Anthropology grounded in despising other people, in what Hue Woodson calls the "wretched of the earth,"[24] should be a fluid anthropology, composed of several fragmentary anthropology from those excluded from theological thinking and writing by virtue of their subhuman status in practice. The argument of Charles Cameron that anthropologies are theological insofar as they take their cues from the doctrines of God and creation is relevant here. The basis for humanity's life is participatory fellowship with the Living God. Christopher L. Fisher makes an assertion that "fellowship and relationship with God are realized in the light of the incarnation. Human beings discover who they were meant to be in relationship to God through the incarnate Son. He validates the claim that the creation's relationship to the Creator finds its supreme and final realization in humanity."[25] Theological anthropology deals with the horizontal and the vertical dimensions, the reality of God in human experience. This divine reality is not located within a single, clearly defined, and limited part of human life. Rather, we see the whole of life being shaped by the fact that humanity is the creation——albeit fallen——of God, the creation which he has not abandoned, the creation which he purposes to redeem. It is with this wide-ranging view of the reality of God within human experience that we address ourselves to the subject of theological anthropology. This is a theology that is deeply interested in God but also interested in the life of humanity. Theological anthropology is interested in both, the Creator and the creation, the Redeemer and the redeemed.[26]

SOCIOCULTURAL EXPERIENCES OF WOMEN

There is no gainsaying that women generally have suffered untold hardship under gender socialization. The roles and uniqueness of women experiences in society are actually a societal creation as against biological history. Women, generally, are born into the social circumstances that socialize them in pure gender roles. Subjugation and arbitrariness masquerading as cultural practices, religious edicts, and gender perception continue to be the existential issues facing women. Discrimination triumphs over equality, the much-touted sustaining element of our social fabric. Frequent use of the language of discrimination for perpetuating gender inequity produces a trail of exclusions stretching to multiple spheres of life.[27]

Gender inequality and stereotyping are integral part of history and go all the way back to Adam and Eve in the Genesis story. Stereotypical generalizations are passed on from one generation to the other, and include ideas such as that women are born with inferior status; women are Eve incarnated; girls are seen as property; men and women are not equal; men are superior because God ordained them to be superior; sin originates from women's embedded wickedness and weakness; and women may not be leaders because of their fragility. Eve was even believed to be made from and for Adam, and as the lesser of the two created genders, she persuaded Adam to eat the forbidden fruit.[28] Gender inequality manifests as one of the most prevalent forms of social construction all over the world, and it is culturally and socially created differences between men and women when both sexes do not have the same share in the decision-making and wealth of a society.[29] Inequality is the result of cultural and historical developments, geographic setting, and religious customs predominant in society.

The problem of patriarchy is one major social and cultural challenge that women face, most especially in Africa. Patriarchy presented and shaped societies in the history of humanity, both in the past and the present. Kinsey Nyisome defines patriarchy as a social system in which men dominate. It is a social system in which men are regarded as the authority within the family and society, and in which power and possessions are passed on from father to son. It is a social system through which, as a group, men receive more power and privileges than women on the basis of gender, and in which traditionally male activities are valued more highly than traditionally female activities.[30] As an ideology, patriarchy upholds the view that the male has superior control over women and all others under their care. Generally, the concept of patriarchy is denoted as the "rule of men over women," and mostly it refers to economic, political, social, and religious ideologies that have enforced the domination of women.[31]

Patriarchy, as a discriminatory force, has a long history that sweeps across national and cultural boundaries. It is a system that constrains women by means of male dominance.[32] John Stott gives an illuminating description of the nature of patriarchy and specifically of its portrayal of women in various cultures and ages. Plato, according to Stott, stated that a bad man's fate would be reincarnation as a woman. Aristotle viewed women as imperfect, mutilated males. The Jewish writer Josephus described women as inferior to men in every way. In the history of the Church, theologians, at times, also spoke disparagingly about women.[33] Stott quotes Tertullian as an example: "You are the devil's gateway; you are the unsealer of that (forbidden) tree; you are the first deserter of the divine law; you are she who persuaded him whom the devil was not valiant enough to attack. You destroyed so easily God's image, man. On account of your desert—that is death—even the Son of God had to die."[34] Patriarchy can therefore be seen as 'a hierarchical system of social organization which causes women to internalize a sense of inferiority to men, and when this very conditioning of their inferiority to men is not accepted, men resort to coercion, intimidation and violence."[35]

Harmful and traditional cultural practices contribute to women's suffering and often result in violence in the patriarchal context. Within marriage, patriarchy makes male power felt even more because of its obvious minute-to-minute application. Marriage enables men to assume the identity of the head of the family with all its trappings.[36] It has been uttered as the rule of the father where fathers are ultimately respected in the society or can be observed as the dominance of males in simple terms.

Within faith communities, patriarchy is one of the main stumbling blocks that prevent women to be fully equal to men in their own right. Frederick Engels argues that religion fosters oppression of women in a smooth way that hinders their active consciousness. Religion as a set of beliefs and norms governs human lives through desired ways of conduct it administers. The participation of women in church activities is limited due to the belief that men are the true leaders. Some Christian churches hold to the fact that their leader who is Jesus Christ is a man and most of the iconic figures of the religion such as Moses and Abraham were also males; hence, it instills submission to women as they pave the way for male dominance.[37] The above verdict has led many women who have the potential not to join leadership but only to be oppressed by men as they are viewed as inferior when it comes to Church leadership. Accordingly, John Paul II, in *Mulieris Dignitatem*, points out that "A woman represents a particular value by the fact that she is a human person, and, at the same time, this particular person, by the fact of her femininity.

This concerns each and every woman, independently of the cultural content in which she lives, and independently of her spiritual, psychological and physical characteristics, as for example, age, education, health, work, and whether she is married or single."[38]

Many theorists of patriarchy normally base their argument on the teaching of St. Paul: "For man was not made from woman, but woman from man. Neither was man created for woman, but woman for man" (1 Cor. 11:8-9). Man was viewed to be created in the image of God; Adam was created first and then Eve from Adam's rib; and not only was she guilty of tempting Adam, she was weaker and lesser than him and she became the cause of the Fall. According to Paul, there is a natural order built into God's creative design for men and women that the church should reflect in its ministry (cf. 1 Tim 2:13-14). For the sake of the present discussion, it is important to observe that Paul does not stop there. After reiterating his judgment that "a wife ought to have a symbol of authority on her head" when she prophesies (1 Cor. 11:10); Paul adds: "Nevertheless, in the Lord woman is not independent of man nor man of woman; for as woman was made from man, so man is now born of woman. And all things are from God" (11:11-12). In addition to the authority-relation between men and women, there is a dependence-relation between men and women that must be taken into account as well, and both of these relations may be understood properly only when viewed in the context of their underlying relation of dependence on God. Woodson points out that "We find numerous texts in the Bible that deal with the differences between men and women and their different roles. However problematic these texts may be, they do not represent a checklist for stereotyping what each gender should do or not do. Instead, they teach us how to relate to each other in, and through, God."[39]

Mercy Amba Oduyoye offers a brief but insightful description of the effects of patriarchy on women in Africa. She states that the predominant view of women in Africa is that they are persons first and foremost in relation to whose mother or whose wife they are. She also refers to various cults and practices that African women are not allowed to participate in. Although women can participate in economic life, the work and products of women are viewed as inferior.[40] Since the modernization and technologization of women's work are viewed with suspicion, "African women still grind and pound their hours away."[41] In the same vein, Louise Du Toit highlights rape as one of the most dehumanizing consequences of patriarchy. She describes the rape of women by men as first and foremost an assertion of power through an act of supreme humiliation. The sexual pain and humiliation involved in the act of rape serve to affirm manhood and demonstrate masculine power.[42] This brief description of the nature and consequences of patriarchy suggests that anthropology of independence and power underlies patriarchy. This is reflected in Jürgen Moltmann's definition of patriarchy as, "the term for an institutionalized system of sexual hierarchy and a psychological mechanism for its justification, according to which the man is born and made to rule, while the woman is born and made to serve."[43]

Sexism is another way women are marginalized in society. Sexism is prejudice or discrimination based on a person's sex or gender, especially, discrimination against women and girls. Sexism has been linked to stereotype and gender roles, and includes the belief that one gender is intrinsically superior to another.[44] In her reflection on the anthropology of independence and power, Nyambura Njoroge points out that historically, gender roles—the socially constructed roles of women and men—have been ordered hierarchically, with men exercising power and control over women.[45]

Nevertheless, Kwadwo Okrah points out that generally, in precolonial African societies, interdependency and mutual sustenance marked gender relations. Even though the patriarchal system in Africa cannot be denied, yet, the African woman possesses the power that binds the society together. In precolonial African societies, the survival of the family and the future of marriage depended a great deal on the African woman. Thus, the African woman played a key role in the education and the teaching of children social, ethical, and moral values which were part of the cultural standards for evaluating proper societal behavior. While the obvious area of authority in the polity is in the custody of men, women control the base of men's public authority. Men are seen on the thrones and in official settings as rulers, yet perceived as unable to stand without the help of women.[46] In other words, the position of women was complementary to that of men.

Society generally ascribes to each sex different duties. In Africa, for example, men are expected to tackle their chosen "male jobs; like felling trees, repairing roofs and generally cracking the 'hard nuts'"; while women are to be concerned with cooking, taking care of the children, and keeping and cleaning the house. Also, the patriarchal ideologies in Africa value male children at the expense of females who are given access to societal essentials. Female schooling is regarded as a waste of money as the population always considers the fact that one day the child will be married out of the family where benefits are not guaranteed, hence females are restricted from attaining proper education. Edith N. Njiri explains that "education was meant for boys, girls were to stay at home, learning domestic skills from their mothers and grandmothers; which were assumed to be relevant to their domestic roles. Girls were made to believe that education comes second to marriage."[47] This has brought women such opprobrium that it engendered the largest illiteracy amongst their rank and file.

Many women experience specific forms of gender discrimination where they are vulnerable because of their race/class or ethnicity. Marginalized women may be subject to specific forms of racial discrimination simply because of their gendered location within their communities. In traditional conceptions of race and gender discrimination, certain specific problems or forms of discrimination faced by marginalized women are rendered invisible. For example, according to Kingsley Omoyibo and Benedict Ajayi, the trafficking of women and young girls is mainly targeted at African girls who seek asylum in developed countries. Many African girls have been brought to the UK en route to Italy where they are coerced by human traffickers to work in the sex industry. The combination of their gender, socioeconomic position, and race renders them vulnerable to economic and sexual exploitation. Thus, the racism they experience may affect them in ways that are different from that experienced by men in their communities.[48]

Black women are both Black and women at the same time. As such, Black women typically experience racial oppression on the one hand, and gender oppression on the other in ways that are distinct from those who are either Black or woman alone. As such, Black women's experience of inequity is compounded in ways that are foreign to that of Black men and white women out of the experience of being both subjugated by race and subordinated by gender in church, the academy, and society. Since Black women's bodies sit at the intersection of racialized subjugation on the one hand, and gendered subjugation on the other, their experiences and distinct contributions are not only marginalized and caricatured, but often rendered fictitious, as if Black women do not know for themselves that their stories are true.[49]

Stereotyping of women holds back women's full potential and must thus be labeled as one of the worst forms of violence against women. Not only does it get in the way of women participating fully and equally in all spheres of their society, it also demeans and lessens women's dignity. Stereotyping of women results in them being marginalized and discriminated against, which brings about unfair and inequitable conduct against them—whilst their human rights are being constrained.[50]

THE DYNAMICS OF RACISM

The contemporary society wrestles with continuing scandal of racial injustice. This is the era of growing racial pride. "Race is a physical indicator that shows differences among different groups of people. It is a group of people having physical characteristics that are specific and perceptible."[51] For instance, according to Shi Long, in the United States, white supremacy has made it possible to widely spread the white ideologies within a variety of groups. The ideology of white beauty confirms the physical characteristics of white women as the criteria for assessing the level of one's beauty. For black women, the standard of beauty has placed them at a disadvantage since their physical features do not match those that are idealized.[52] It is unfortunate that the color of skin becomes one of the main features of white beauty. It is for this reason that black women are not regarded as being parts of the wide majority and they become inferior citizens in their own country. The supremacy of the whites brings about oppressing discrimination and injustice, especially for the black-skinned people who are regarded as inferior in that country.

The overlap of race and gender brings about multiple oppressive impacts on women. For black women, racial injustice gives them experiences that are different from those of white women. The white supremacy places them in a lower position. Meanwhile, gender inequality gives black women different experiences from black men. The American patriarchal society treats women as subordinate to men. It is for this reason that African American women are vulnerable to injustices not only because of their race but also because they are women.[53] Black women live at the bottom of the society; they suffer from oppression of both sexuality and racial discrimination. Although blacks have fought for their equal rights all the time, they are still not treated as equal citizens by the society. Blacks couldn't enjoy equal opportunity for better education, nor could they get equal chances for better jobs. They also do not have the right to vote or be voted. The severe discrimination from whites results in the humblest living situation for black people.[54]

The supremacy of the white ideology puts the position of African descendants below that of the whites. The whites identify themselves with anything civilized, having high values, and being beautiful. On the other hand, they identify blacks with anything low, having poor values, and being ugly. The dominant ideology puts the blacks and the whites in different strata. They even see them as having opposite images.[55] The social construct of color gives a contribution to forming the ideology that white, or bright, represents anything that is sacred, clean, and decent while, on the other hand, black represents anything evil, dirty, and indecent.[56] It is by this construct that white is more preferable because it is regarded as having positive values while black is not because it has negative values. To resist the oppressive injustices, Collins stresses the importance of attempts that encourage personal drive of black women. She underlines self-consciousness as the primary factor to deal with the injustices. Self-consciousness is then strengthened by self-definition, self-valuation, self-reliance, and self-empowerment.[57]

It is unfortunate that many black people have been subjugated to the extent that they view God as a white man; they are also more likely to believe that white men/women are better than suited for positions of leadership and authority than women and Black people. This point is best articulated in the work of Steven Roberts.[58] Furthermore, pointing out that God is beyond race and gender, Bryan Massingale opines that this view challenges the innocence of the sacred icons in the vast majority of Catholic Churches' exclusive white images of God, Jesus, and Mary. This perpetuates a "dual brainwashing" convincing white people of their superiority and Black people of their inferiority.[59] Elizabeth Johnson observes that how we conceive of God shows how we understand the greatest good and the highest beauty. If God and the sacred images are presented mostly in white images, it is difficult to avoid concluding that those who most closely resemble those images reflect God's goodness, beauty, power, and authority in a way that people of "color" do not and cannot. [60]

Humanity in all of its expressions and dimensions—is sacred because all individuals bear the imprint of their Creator. Racism which is prejudice, discrimination, or antagonism directed against someone of a different race based on the belief that one's own race is superior to another is a direct assault on the sanctity and dignity of human life. Paul in Acts 17:26-27 reminds us that God "made from one man every nation of mankind to live on all the face of the earth, having determined allotted periods and the boundaries of their dwelling place, that they should seek God, and perhaps feel their way toward him and find him." This shows that as Christians, our identity in Christ unites us in ways that transcend race, class, culture, and even gender: "For as many of you as were baptized into Christ have put on Christ. There is neither Jew nor Greek, there is neither slave nor free, there is no male and female, for you are all one in Christ Jesus" (Galatians 3:27-28). The words of Nelson Mandela become relevant: "We must ensure that color, race and gender become only a God-given gift to each one of us and not an indelible mark or attribute that accords a special status to any."[61]

TOWARD A PRAGMATIC THEOLOGICAL ANTHROPOLOGY OF DEPENDENCE AND RELATIONALITY

No single biblical text has been more important in the understanding of theological anthropology than the first three chapters of Genesis, particularly Genesis 1:26-28. It reads:

> Let us make humankind in our image, according to our likeness; and let them have dominion over the fish of the sea, and over the birds of the air, and over the cattle, and over all the wild animals of the earth, and over every creeping thing that creeps upon the earth. So God created humankind in his image, in the image of God he created them, male and female he created them. God blessed them and said to them, "Be fruitful and multiply, and fill the earth and subdue it; and have dominion over the fish of the sea and over the birds of the air and over every living thing that moves upon the earth."

The importance of this passage, with its inclusion equally of men and women, is evident. The idea of human as the image of God is the basis of the theologically motivated reason for the dignity of the person. Phyllis Bird points out that "Women and men are representative of a collective humanity and are co-equally models for the human. A representing of this affirmation of human wholeness and mutuality is foundational for a renewed biblical and theological understanding of the fullness of human personhood for both women and men."[62] Accordingly, the most basic affirmation about humankind is that it is in relationship with God. The human being is thus only understood by reference to God. The passage, Genesis 1:26-28, does indeed present women and men equally. There is no hierarchy established here, and both are fully recognized as making up the image of God.

The "image of God" in relation to the fullness of humanity is revealed in Jesus. Jesus shows us what a human life actually reflecting the image of God looks like. Jesus images God, without distortion or blur, in a human life lived as intended at creation—a life fulfilling the vocation first given in Genesis 1. Marc Cortez shows why theological anthropology must begin with Christology. "Jesus constitutes true humanity. We cannot understand humanity without knowing Christ."[63] On this point, Cortez argues that instead of emphasizing maleness and femaleness as distinct realities that differ essentially as a consequence of underlying biological processes, the focus should be on the common human nature while simultaneously recognizing the "interdependence of human differences."[64] In this view, Christology alone lays the proper groundwork from which to consider the human creature, in its relation to God and its relation to others.

Jesus, in works and deeds, shows that humanity is one and equal. In view of this, Christopher P. Klofft points out that it was Jesus himself who openly and publicly went against the grain of the social norms of his time. For example, he openly reached out to women such as Mary Magdalen (cf. Luke 8:1-3) and the Samaritan woman at the well (cf. John 4: 1-25). He also reached out to those unnoticed women such as Peter's mother-in-law (cf. Matt 8:14-15, Mark 1: 29-31), the woman who touched his garment (cf. Matt 9:20-22), the widow of Nain (cf. Luke 7:11-17), and Jairus' daughter (cf. Matt 9:18-26; Mark 5:21-43). He also presented women such as Zarephath's widow (cf. Luke 4: 26), the Queen of the South (cf. Matt 12:42), and the poor woman's offering as models of faith (cf. Mark 12: 41-44). Furthermore, Jesus told parables about women such as the parable of the lost coin and the Leaven (cf. Luke 15: 8-10). The parables of the lost sheep (cf. Luke 15: 1-7) and the mustard seed (cf. Mark 4: 30-32) point to the growth of God's Kingdom in terms of women and their domestic work.[65] These acts of Jesus clearly show how Jesus defied the patriarchal mindset about women and his refusal to bend to Pharisaic pressures of his time. Jesus reacted against the patriarchal mentality based on sexual differences by calling women to follow him in his ministry.[66]

Against anthropology of independence and power, many theologians propose anthropology of relationality and dependence. Klofft argues that human beings are called to live in relationships. We are called to be partners of fellow human beings and of God. Through relationships, human beings are defined and developed. To live as humans, we need each other and we need God. To be human, therefore, is to live in relationships of dependence.[67] Various theologians base this dependence of human beings on the revelation of the triune God, making personhood primary to a notion of human being. From a Trinitarian perspective, persons are not autonomous individuals that are defined in terms of their separation from other individuals, but are understood in terms of their relations to other persons. Humankind is inherently social. Whatever the differences of emphasis, the origin and destiny of human beings are ultimately to be understood in the light of the triune God's creating, redeeming, and sanctifying activity. Gary Deddo states that the basic insights of a Trinitarian theological anthropology arise out of a consideration of the person and work of Christ. Jesus Christ reveals to us both who God is and who humankind is. "In Christ God is revealed to be the triune God, the God who exists from all eternity by virtue of the triune relations among Father, Son and Spirit."[68] Furthermore, "in Christ humanity is revealed also to exist by virtue of its relations, first with God and then with others and the rest of creation."[69] These relations, Deddo states, are not external or accidental to who we are. "Relationship is essential and internal to divine and human existence. God would not be God were God not triune. If humanity did not exist in relationship, originally and continually with God, there would be no humanity. Humanity has its existence in and through personal relations."[70] Being created in the image of God entails personally imaging in human relationships the divine love imaged between Father and Son in the Spirit. Human beings therefore are relational beings who are in need of God, each other, and also the nonhuman part of creation. Precisely through reconsidering what our humanity entails we are able to embark on the road of rehumanization.[71]

According to John Paul II, masculinity and femininity are relational terms. Neither can be understood apart from the other.[72] John Paul II argues that both sex and gender have transcendent and ontological meaning fashioned and intended by God in the original creation for all times. John Paul II's gender theory argues that a fundamental fact of human existence is that at every stage of its history, God "created them male and female." He contends that God always creates humanity in this way and that they are always such.[73] John Paul II starts his theology of the body with a consideration of the human person alone before considering sex as a human marker. He argues that the first human being, Adam, is not yet specifically sexed/gendered but embodies both male and female humanity.[74] Both male and female participate in the original solitude so that all that is said about the person before the duality of sex is affirmed in both the male and the female after the duality is established. This anthropology is based on God's plan in the creation of man and woman which, according to John Paul II, "is a plan that from the beginning has been indelibly imprinted in the very being of the human person—men and women—and, therefore, in the make-up, meaning and deepest workings of the individual."[75]

Sexism is an anthropological problem that does not allow for relationality. Today, society defines people based on their gender, race, and what, their occupation. It is good to point out that the sets of gender-specific roles ascribed to women by society are insufficient by themselves to shed light on the Christian teaching of the dignity of the human person. Sexism, according to Oduyoye, can therefore only be overcome if females and males become conscious of "the true nature of the human community as a mixture of those things, values, roles, temperaments, etc. that we dichotomize into feminine and masculine."[76] According to her, the exclusion of women from defining and determining what it means to be human makes all of us, female and male, losers. The concern is not only that the humanity of women is ignored because of this denial. Men are also dehumanized since they miss the opportunity to understand and experience full humanity.[77] This is why Moltmann invites men to develop a male or masculine liberation theology.[78] This theology has to free both men and women from the estrangements brought about by patriarchal traditions. This anthropology is in contradiction to the modernistic anthropology of power, autonomy, and independence. This theology has to free both men and women from the estrangements brought about by patriarchal traditions.[79]

In seeking to establish a framework for theological anthropology with respect to the question of gender, Swain Scott points out that the sets of gender-specific roles ascribed to women by the society should be looked at under the lenses of three other important social concepts, namely: (1) commonality and equality, (2) diversity and structure, and (3) mutual fellowship.[80]

1. Commonality and equality: Commonality is an anthropological concept that presents itself to us across the entire range of God's works in relation to human beings in nature, grace, and glory. Human beings have a common nature. God created both man and woman in his image and likeness (Gen 1:26-27; 2:18-25). The Hebrew term *adam* refers to both man and woman (5:2). Human beings are recipients of a common grace. Both men and women are recipients of a common baptism: "As many of you as were baptized into Christ have clothes yourselves with Christ. There is no longer Jew or Greek, there is no longer slave or free, there is no longer

male and female; for all of you are one in Christ Jesus." (Gal.3.27-28; cf. Eph 4:6). Both men and women are common heirs of "the grace of life" (1 Pet 3:7). Finally, human beings share a common destiny in glory. The common nature and status of men and women in nature, grace, and glory entail the notion of our equal standing before God.[81]

2. Diversity and Structure: In humanity's status as male and female, there are various forms of natural inequality that do not compromise or threaten human fundamental status as creatures made in God's image; baptized in the name of the Trinity; and destined for God's kingdom. All forms of social diversity and structure do not threaten the shared status as the special objects of God's creative, redeeming, and perfecting work. The differentiation in being created male and female are constructive and healthy for human existence. These natural forms of social order presuppose in their exercise our common nature as human beings and aim at our mutual fellowship.[82]

3. Mutual fellowship: Rooted in human common nature, ordered under God and to God, Christian social order is realized in mutual fellowship. Christian social order has an equalizing tendency. This tendency is rooted in the saving agency of Jesus Christ. In John 15:15, Jesus states: "No longer do I call you servants, for the servant does not know what his master is doing; but I have called you friends, for all that I have heard from my Father I have made known to you." All Christian social order has an equalizing tendency toward friendship; mutual agency; and mutual fellowship in the good things of God.[83]

CONCLUSION

From the foregoing, it is clear that women and men were created equally (Gen 1:27); they have equally fallen into sin (Rom 3:23); they are equally redeemable through Christ's life, death, and resurrection (John 3:16); both male and female are equal in participating in the new covenant (Gal 3:28) and they are equal heirs of God in Christ (1 Pet 3:7). Both men and women are equally responsible for life and ministry as empowered human beings through the Holy colonial Spirit (Acts 2:17).[84] Recognizing and becoming sensitive to gender in theology will help to deal with violence against women leading one to a theology that is liberative, one that does not remain theoretical but demands ethical choices that will empower the transformation of relationships that have been damaged by sexism and racism attitudes.[85] Undoing gender bias in theology requires both the Church and society to engage critically in the dynamics of patriarchy. Therefore, although a number of nongovernmental organizations (NGOs) and researchers have devoted considerable time and resources to understanding and addressing the effect of multiple forms of discrimination against women, much work remains to be done globally. A more holistic approach to discrimination that recognizes the simultaneous nature of women's experiences of various forms of discrimination is necessary if we are to ensure that human rights are a reality for all women. In the same vein, to prevent women's marginalization and victimization, the Church has a pivotal role and responsibility to redefine gender roles that affect justice and equality for women. The Church has to be an active participant in the restoration of women's dignity through addressing the complex and core principles of male control, dominance, identification, and centeredness that still prevail in the church and society. The Church has the task of dismantling and transforming the patriarchal roots in society into roots of empathy, caring, healing, and equality in order to protect women from all forms of discrimination.

NOTES

1. Strachan Owen, *Re-enchanting Humanity: A Theology of Mankind* (Nairobi: Mentor Publishing Company, 2019), 37.

2. Kingsley Omoyibo and Benedict Ajayi, "Understanding Gender and Global Africa: A Critical Perspective," *African Journal Online*, vol. 9 no. 1 (2011): 123.

3. All biblical citations are taken from *Revised Standard Version* (New York: Collins Bible, 2004).

4. Though this is the traditional view of the Catholic Church, social scientists and feminist scholars, like Simone de Beauvoir and Judith Butler among others, have called attention to the performative nature of gender construction. In her famous work, *The Second Sex,* de Beauvoir argues that "One is not born but becomes woman." See Simone de Beauvoir, *The Second Sex*, trans. Constance Borde and Sheila Malovany-Chevallier (New York: Alfred A. Knopf, 2010), 267. See also, Judith Butler, *Undoing Gender* (London and New York: Routledge, 2004).

5. Victor Anderson, *Beyond Ontological Blackness: An Essay on African American Religious and Cultural Criticism.* (New York: Bloomsbury, 2016), 123. It is important to state that Anderson's conclusion needs to be critiqued. Maleness and femaleness are themselves socially constructed identity markers. See footnote 4 above.

6. Devdutt Pattanaik, "On Gender Fluidity and its Place in Hindu Spirituality," October 19, 2018, https://www.vogue.in/magazine-story/devdutt-pattanaik-on-gender-fluidity-and-its-place-in-hindu-spirituality/.

7. Ibid.

8. Judith Lorber, *Gender Inequality: Feminist Theories and Politics* (New York: Oxford University Press, 2014), 15.

9. World Health Organisation, "Gender, Equity and Human Rights: Glossary of Terms and Tools," https://www.unicef.org/rosa/media/1761/file/Gender%20glossary%20of%20terms%20and%20concepts%20.pdf.

10. Omoyibo and Ajayi, "Understanding Gender," 123.

11. Allan G. Johnson, *The Gender Knot: Unravelling Our Patriarchal Legacy* (Philadelphia: Temple University, 1997), 79.

12. Anderson, *Beyond Ontological Blackness*, 125.

13. Thomas Aquinas, *The Summa Theologica of St. Thomas Aquinas* (London: Burns, Oates & Washburne Ltd, 1912), 1a, q. 92, a.1, Obj.1.

14. Ibid., 3.

15. Ibid., 1.

16. Ibid., 2.

17. See Michael Nolan, "What Aquinas Never Said About Women," *First Things* (November 1998), https://www.firstthings.com/article/1998/11/what-aquinas-never-said-about-women. See also, Marie I. George, "What Aquinas Really Said About Women," *First Things* (December 1999), https://www.firstthings.com/article/1999/12/what-aquinas-really-said-about-women.

18. Mary Daly, *The Church and the Second Sex* (Boston: Beacon Press, 1985), 92.

19. See Charles Cameron, "An Introduction to Theological Anthropology," *Evangel*, vol. 23, no.5 (2005): 56.

20. Maryanne C. Horowitz, "The Image of God in Man: Is Woman Included?" *The Harvard Theological Review*, vol. 72, no. 3–4 (1979): 175.

21. Cameron, "An Introduction to Theological Anthropology," 54.

22. Mercy Amba Oduyoye, quoted in Nico Koopman, "Theological Anthropology and Gender Relations," *Scriptura*, vol. 86 (2004): 191.

23. Hue Woodson, "The Existential Demands of Race: Dialogues in Theological Anthropology," *Journal of African American Studies*, vol. 11, no. 24 (2020): 225.

24. Ibid., 230.

25. Christopher L. Fisher, *Human Significance in Theology and the Natural Science: An Ecumenical Perspective with Reference to Pannenberg, Rahner, and Zizioulas* (Eugene, OR: Wipf & Stock Pub, 2010), 115.

26. Cameron, "An Introduction to Theological Anthropology," 54.

27. Bartholomew Chidili, *Pedagogy of Human Dignity through the Vision of Mercy Amba Oduyoye*. (Jos: Fab Educational Books, 2008), 52.

28. Ibid., 55.

29. Casmir A. Chukwuelobe, "The Church and Gender Equality in Africa: Questioning Culture and the Theological Paradigm on Women Oppression," *Open Journal of Philosophy*, vol. 4, no 6 (2014): 168.

30. Kinsey Nyisome, "Cultural Trends and Gender Relations in Africa," *Humanities and Societal Journal*, vol. 6, no. 2 (2005): 879.

31. Johnson, *The Gender Knot*, 79.

32. Loreen Maseno and Susan Kilonzo, "Engendering Development: Demystifying Patriarchy and its Effects on Women in Rural Kenya," *International Journal of Sociology and Anthropology*, vol. 3, no.2 (2011): 45.

33. John Stott, *The Spirit, the Church and the World: The Message of Acts* (Westmont, IL: InterVarsity Press, 1990), 255.

34. Ibid.

35. Maseno, and Kilonzo, "Engendering Development: Demystifying Patriarchy," 55.
36. Mercy Amba Oduyoye and Musimbi Kanyoro, *The Will to Arise: Women, Tradition and the Church in Africa* (Maryknoll, NY: Orbis Books, 2016), 68.
37. Fredrick Engels, *Religion and the Oppression of Women: A Marxist Interpretation* (New York. Routledge, 1984), 25.
38. John Paul II, *Dignity and Vocation of Women. Mulieris Dignitatem* (Nairobi: Paulines Publications, 2005), 65.
39. Woodson, "The Existential Demands of Race," 223.
40. Mercy Amba Oduyoye, "Feminism: A Pre-Condition for Christian Anthropology," *African Theological Journal*, vol. 3, no.2 (1982): 194.
41. Ibid., 196.
42. Louise Du Toit, "Rape Understood as Torture: What is the Responsibility of Men?" in *Rape: Rethinking male responsibility*, eds. Lindsay Clowes and Ernst M. Conradie (Stellenbosch; South Africa: EFSA Publications 2003), 38.
43. Jürgen Moltmann, *Experiences in Theology: Ways and Forms of Christian Theology* (London: SCM Press, 2000), 274.
44. Koopman, "Theological Anthropology and Gender Relations," 196.
45. Nyambura Njoroge, *Gender Justice, Ministry and Healing: A Christian Response to the HIV Pandemic* (London: Progressio, 2009), 7.
46. Kwadwo A. Okrah, "The Dynamics of Gender Roles and Cultural Determinants of African Women's Desire to Participate in Modern Politics," *Journal of Global Engagement and Transformation*, vol. 2. no. 1 (2018), https://scholarworks.iu.edu/journals/index.php/joget/article/view/24395.
47. Edith N. Njiri, "Women's Hospitality and Economic Development," *Transforming Power: Women in the Household of God*, ed. Mercy Mba Oduyoye (Accra: Sam-Woode Limited, 1997), 132.
48. Omoyibo and Ajayi, "Understanding Gender," 3729.
49. Koopman, Theological Anthropology and Gender Relations," 199.
50. Woodson, "The Existential Demands of Race," 156.
51. Ruth Sean, "Understanding Oppression and Liberation," *Studies*, vol. 77, no. 308 (Winter 1988): 440.
52. Shi Long, "Black Feminism in Their Eyes Were Watching God," *Advances in Literary Study*, vol. 8, no. 1 (2020): 6.
53. Ibid.
54. Ibid.
55. Mark Hill "Skin Color and the Perception of Attractiveness among African-Americans: Does Gender Make a Difference?" *Social Psychology Quarterly*, vol. 65, no. 1 (2002): 77.
56. Vetta Sanders Thompson, "African American Body Image: Identity and Physical Self-Acceptance," *Humbold Journal of Social Relations*, vol. 30, no. 2 (2006): 48.
57. Patricia Hill Collins, *Black Feminist Thought* (New York: Routledge, 2000), 119.
58. Steven Roberts et al., "God as a White Man: A Psychological Barrier to Conceptualizing Black People and Women as Leadership Worthy," *Journal of Personality and Social Psychology*, vol. 85, no. 9 (2020): 1290–1315.

59. Bryan Massingale, "God is beyond Race and Gender. Our Sacred Art Should Be Too," *US Catholic*, vol. 85, no. no 9 (2020): 41.
60. Ibid.
61. Nelson Mandela, "Address by President Nelson Mandela of South Africa to the Forty-Ninth Session of the General Assembly," *United Nations* (New York City, October 3, 1994), https://www.polity.org.za/article/sa-mandela-address-to-the-49th-session-of-the-general-assembly-03101994-1994-10-04.
62. Phyllis Bird, "Male and Female He Created Them: Gen. 1:27b in the Context of the Priestly Account of Creation," *Harvard Theological Review*, vol. 74, no. 2 (1981): 135.
63. Marc Cortez, *ReSourcing Theological Anthropology: A Constructive Account of Humanity in the Light of Christ* (Grand Rapids, MI: Zondervan Academic, 2018), 67.
64. Ibid., 210.
65. Christopher P. Klofft, "Image and Imago: A Rational Defense of a Theological Anthropology of Gender," *Studia Gilsoniana*, vol. 3 (2014): 525.
66. Patricia Hill Collins, *Black Sexual Politics: African Americans, Gender, and the New Racism* (New York: Routledge, 2010), 87.
67. Klofft, "Imago Dei: A Rational Defense of a Theological Anthropology of Gender," 525.
68. Gary Deddo, "Persons in Racial Reconciliation: The Contributions of a Trinitarian Theological Anthropology," in *The Gospel in Black and White: Theological Resources for Racial Reconciliation*, ed. Dennis l. Okholm (Westmont, IL: InterVasity Press, 2007), 56.
69. Ibid., 59.
70. Ibid.
71. Ibid., 69.
72. Anthony Chundelikkat, *The Theology of the Body in John Paul II* (Bangalore: St. Pauls, 2009), 43.
73. Ibid., 44.
74. Ibid.
75. Ibid., 46.
76. Oduyoye, "Feminism: A Pre-Condition for Christian Anthropology," 194.
77. Ibid.
78. Moltmann, Experiences in Theology, 269.
79. Ibid., 271.
80. Swain Scott "Thoughts on Theological Anthropology: Man as Male and Female," *The Journal of Reformed, Faith and Practice*, vol. 5, no.1 (2020): 60–63.
81. Ibid., 60.
82. Ibid., 62.
83. Ibid., 63.
84. Rebecca M. Groothuis "Equal in Being, Unequal in Role: Exploring the Logic of Woman's Subordination," in *Discovering Biblical Equality: Complementarity without Hierarchy*, eds. Roland Pierce and Rebecca M. Groothius (Westmont, IL: InterVarsity Press, 2014), 13.

85. Ibid.

FURTHER READINGS

Abraham, Andrea C. *God and Blackness: Race, Gender and Identity in a Middle Class Afrocentric Church*. New York: New York University Press, 2014.
Amartya, Sen. *Many Faces of Gender Inequality*. Bombay: Delhi Publishing House, 1994.
Congregation for Catholic Education. "'Male and Female He Created Them' Towards a Path of Dialogue on the Question of Gender Theory." *Vatican City*, 2019. https://www.vatican.va/roman_curia/congregations/ccatheduc/documents/rc_con_ccatheduc_doc_20190202_maschio-e-femmina_en.pdf.
Jantzen, Matt R. *God, Race and History: Liberating Providence*. Lanham, MD: Lexington Books, 2021.
Massingale, Bryan N. *Racial Justice and the Catholic Church*. Maryknoll, NY: Orbis, 2010.
Peterson, Ryan. *The Imago Dei as Human Identity: A Theological Interpretation*. Winona Lake, IN: Eisenbrauns, 2016.
Thistlethwaite, Susan Brooks. *Sex, Race and God: Christian Feminism in Black and White*. Eugene, Oregon: Wipf and Stock Publishers, 2009.

REFERENCES

Anderson, Victor. *Beyond Ontological Blackness: An Essay on African American Religious and Cultural Criticism*. New York: Bloomsbury, 2016.
Aquinas, Thomas. *The Summa Theologica of St. Thomas Aquinas*. London: Burns, Oates & Washburne Ltd, 1912.
Bird, Phyllis. "Male and Female He Created Them: Gen. 1:27b in the Context of the Priestly Account of Creation." *Harvard Theological Review* 74, no. 2 (1981): 129–159.
Butler, Judith. *Undoing Gender*. London and New York: Routledge, 2004.
Cameron, Charles. "An Introduction to Theological Anthropology." *Evangel* 23, no. 5 (2005): 54–68.
Chidili, Bartholomew. *Pedagogy of Human Dignity Through the Vision of Mercy Amba Oduyoye*. Jos: Fab Educational Books, 2008.
Chukwuelobe, Casmir A. "The Church and Gender Equality in Africa: Questioning Culture and the Theological Paradigm on Women Oppression." *Open Journal of Philosophy* 4, no. 6 (2014): 166–173.
Chundelikkat, Anthony. *The Theology of the Body in John Paul II*. Bangalore: St. Pauls, 2009.
Collins, Patricia Hill. *Black Feminist Thought*. New York: Routledge, 2000.
———. *Black Sexual Politics: African Americans, Gender, and the New Racism*. New York: Routledge, 2010.

Cortez, Marc. *ReSourcing Theological Anthropology: A Constructive Account of Humanity in the Light of Christ*. Grand Rapids, MI: Zondervan Academic, 2018.

Daly, Mary. *The Church and the Second Sex*. Boston: Beacon Press, 1985.

de Beauvoir, Simone. *The Second Sex*. Translated by Constance Borde and Sheila Malovany-Chevallier. New York: Alfred A. Knopf, 2010.

Deddo, Gary. "Persons in Racial Reconciliation: The Contributions of a Trinitarian Theological Anthropology." In *The Gospel in Black and White: Theological Resources for Racial Reconciliation*, edited by Dennis l. Okholm, 57–70. Westmont, IL: InterVasity Press, 2007.

Du Toit, Louise. "Rape Understood as Torture: What is the Responsibility of Men?" In *Rape: Rethinking Male Responsibility*, edited by Lindsay Clowes and Ernst M. Conradie, 36–66. Stellenbosch; South Africa: EFSA Publications 2003.

Engels, Fredrick. *Religion and the Oppression of Women: A Marxist Interpretation*. New York. Routledge, 1984.

Fisher, Christopher L. *Human Significance in Theology and the Natural Science: An Ecumenical Perspective With Reference to Pannenberg, Rahner, and Zizioulas*. Eugene, OR: Wipf & Stock Pub, 2010.

George, Marie I. "What Aquinas Really Said About Women." *First Things*, December 1999. https://www.firstthings.com/article/1999/12/what-aquinas-really-said-about-women.

Groothuis, Rebecca M. "Equal in Being, Unequal in Role: Exploring the Logic of Woman's Subordination." In *Discovering Biblical Equality: Complementarity Without Hierarchy*, edited by Roland Pierce and Rebecca M. Groothius, 10–27. Westmont, IL: InterVarsity Press, 2014.

Hill, Mark. "Skin Color and the Perception of Attractiveness Among African-Americans: Does Gender Make a Difference?" *Social Psychology Quarterly* 65, no. 1 (2002): 77–91.

Horowitz, Maryanne C. "The Image of God in Man: Is Woman Included?" *The Harvard Theological Review* 72, nos. 3–4 (1979): 175–206.

John, Paul II. *Dignity and Vocation of Women. Mulieris Dignitatem*. Nairobi: Paulines Publications, 2005.

Johnson, Allan G. *The Gender Knot: Unravelling Our Patriarchal Legacy*. Philadelphia: Temple University, 1997.

Klofft, Christopher P. "Image and Imago: A Rational Defense of a Theological Anthropology of Gender." *Studia Gilsoniana* 3 (2014): 523–535.

Koopman, Nico. "Theological Anthropology and Gender Relations." *Scriptura* 86 (2004): 190–200.

Long, Shi. "Black Feminism in Their Eyes Were Watching God." *Advances in Literary Study* 8, no. 1 (2020): 1–7.

Lorber, Judith. *Gender Inequality: Feminist Theories and Politics*. New York: Oxford University Press, 2014.

Mandela, Nelson. "Address by President Nelson Mandela of South Africa to the Forty-Ninth Session of the General Assembly." *United Nations*, New York City, October 3, 1994. https://www.polity.org.za/article/sa-mandela-address-to-the-49th-session-of-the-general-assembly-03101994-1994-10-04.

Maseno, Loreen, and Susan Kilonzo. "Engendering Development: Demystifying Patriarchy and Its Effects on Women in Rural Kenya." *International Journal of Sociology and Anthropology* 3, no. 2 (2011): 45–55.

Massingale, Bryan. "God is beyond Race and Gender. Our Sacred Art Should Be Too." *US Catholic* 85, no. 9 (2020): 40–41.

Moltmann, Jürgen. *Experiences in Theology: Ways and Forms of Christian Theology*. London: SCM Press, 2000.

Njiri, Edith N. "Women's Hospitality and Economic Development." In *Transforming Power: Women in the Household of God*, edited by Mercy Mba Oduyoye, 118–133. Accra: Sam-Woode Limited, 1997.

Njoroge, Nyambura. *Gender Justice, Ministry and Healing: A Christian Response to the HIV Pandemic*. London: Progressio, 2009.

Nolan, Michael. "What Aquinas Never Said About Women." *First Things*, November 1998. https://www.firstthings.com/article/1998/11/what-aquinas-never-said-about-women.

Nyisome, Kinsley. "Cultural Trends and Gender Relations in Africa." *Humanities and Societal Journal* 6, no. 2 (2005): 874–890.

Oduyoye, Mercy Amba. "Feminism: A Pre-Condition for Christian Anthropology." *African Theological Journal* 3, no. 2 (1982): 193–208.

Oduyoye, Mercy Amba, and Musimbi Kanyoro. *The Will to Arise: Women, Tradition and the Church in Africa*. Maryknoll, NY: Orbis Books, 2016.

Okrah, Kwadwo A. "The Dynamics of Gender Roles and Cultural Determinants of African Women's Desire to Participate in Modern Politics." *Journal of Global Engagement and Transformation* 2, no. 1 (2018): 1–15. https://scholarworks.iu.edu/journals/index.php/joget/article/view/24395.

Omoyibo, Kingsley, and Benedict Ajayi. "Understanding Gender and Global Africa: A Critical Perspective." *African Journal Online* 9, no. (2011): 3729–3752.

Owen, Strachan. *Re-Enchanting Humanity: A Theology of Mankind*. Nairobi: Mentor Publishing Company, 2019.

Pattanaik, Devdutt. "On Gender Fluidity and its Place in Hindu Spirituality." October 19, 2018. https://www.vogue.in/magazine-story/devdutt-pattanaik-on-gender-fluidity-and-its-place-in-hindu-spirituality/.

Revised Standard Version. New York: Collins Bible, 2004.

Roberts, Steven, Kara Weisman, Jonathan D. Lane, Amber Williams, Nicholas P. Camp, Michelle Wang, Mishaela Robison, Kiara Sanchez, and Camilla Griffiths. "God as a White Man: A Psychological Barrier to Conceptualizing Black People and Women as Leadership Worthy." *Journal of Personality and Social Psychology* 85, no. 9 (2020): 1290–1315.

Scott, Swain. "Thoughts on Theological Anthropology: Man as Male and Female." *The Journal of Reformed, Faith and Practice* 5, no. 1 (2020): 54–65.

Sean, Ruth. "Understanding Oppression and Liberation." *Studies* 77, no. 308 (Winter 1988): 434–444.

Stott, John. *The Spirit, the Church and the World: The Message of Acts*. Westmont, IL: InterVarsity Press, 1990.

Thompson, Vetta Sanders. "African American Body Image: Identity and Physical Self-Acceptance." *Humbold Journal of Social Relations* 30, no. 2 (2006): 44–67.

Woodson, Hue. "The Existential Demands of Race: Dialogues in Theological Anthropology." *Journal of African American Studies* 11, no. 24 (2020): 223–237.

World Health Organisation. "Gender, Equity and Human Rights: Glossary of Terms and Tools." https://www.unicef.org/rosa/media/1761/file/Gender%20glossary%20of%20terms%20and%20concepts%20.pdf.

Chapter 8

Recovering an Ecologically Embodied Humanity

Insights from Native American Women's Experiences

Lisa Ann Dellinger

Defining an ecologically embodied humanity and why understanding this concept of what it means to being human using Native American cosmologies as a framework motivates the substance of this chapter. Contemplation of Indigenous cosmologies reveals significant differences to the Euro-American worldviews that are heavily influenced by overarching tropes found in Western Christianity in its numerous articulations. In explicating what is meant by ecological embodiment, my work examines how nature and women are objectified and commodified within Western philosophy and Christian notions of reality as a hierarchy of being. The organization of this great chain of being situates Man existing above creation and only falling below God and the angels. This configuration of human primacy demands reconsideration given the environmental and patriarchal violence reported globally with a common frequency. The language of being *caretakers of the earth* or having *dominion over the earth* by Divine appointment creates a division of humanity from creation. The recovery of Indigenous cosmologies offers a window into possibilities for imagining ways to heal this rupture. This work utilizes a wealth of scholarship from Native American studies and spiritualities found in traditional and contemporary epistemologies. These ways of knowing root themselves in an essential reverence for all sentient and nonsentient beings which form an interdependent web of relationships. In reconstructing the foundational expressions of radical relationality with Native American perspectives, which honor the sacred contributions of nature and women, a space is created which is a starting point for making new ways of being that do not rely on hierarchy and imbalances of privilege and power. The commitment to

Western narratives of human supremacy led to a dogma of supremacy. This ideology functions to naturalize the institutions that uphold racism, classism, heteropatriarchy, and commodification of land and women. A new vision is needed to reshape a reality where all beings share lives that make tangible actions toward justice while foregrounding the sacredness of all beings. The focus of this chapter is to highlight the differences and the potential contributions that Indigenous cosmologies embody and may inspire for creating a new way of being human in collaboration with all life.

THE RUPTURING OF THE ECOLOGICAL FROM THE ANTHROPOLOGICAL

The division made between ecology and anthropology in the Western academy thereby created two distinct disciplines of inquiry. Broadly defined, ecology is the study of biological systems' interactions and lifecycles within specific environments. Anthropology, as a field, lends itself to the study of human social and cultural developments and contexts; each discipline branching off into categories and taxonomies to label and explain the objects of inquiry. This tendency toward compartmentalization of living and nonliving beings through systems of ranking importance often bleeds into uninterrogated popular culture and social practices. While this gaping chasm between disciplines establishes an artificial construct, this division often contributes to a false presumption of an indisputable hierarchy that places humanity as superior to and demands the controlling of environments for sustenance, adventure, and/or profit. The impulse to cast humanity as the subject and the ecological as the object lends status to a specific metanarrative, which is invested in the toxic conventions that covet power and in making institutionalized capitalism, racism, and heteropatriarchy so systemic they are viewed as unremarkably *normal*. Within the logic of white colonial rhetoric, there is a tendency to form oppositional binaries that use the language of conflict. Examples of these binaries are found in common tropes such as male versus female, light versus darkness, and good versus bad which permeate American culture to normalize antagonism as an appropriate response to difference. The ability to recognize existing or imagine new alternatives to a system of thoughts and behaviors, which rank and pit earth, creatures, and humanity against one another, is lost. Native American religious scholar Vine Deloria Jr. describes two core beliefs of Christian doctrine that influence the social milieu of the United States concerning the nature and function of creation. The first idea is that humanity and creation are constitutionally corrupt/sinful and consequently operate within an adversarial relationship.[1] This concept of a fallen creation that cannot redeem itself through its own agency establishes a reality based on alienation. "The second aspect of the Christian doctrine of creation that concerns us today is the idea that man receives domination over the rest of creation," Deloria tells us, going on to say, "It is this attitude that has been adopted wholeheartedly by Western peoples in their economic exploitation of the earth. The creation becomes a mere object when this view is carried to its logical conclusion—a directly opposite result from that of Indian religions."[2]

The overarching cloud of Western cultural Christianity encompasses society in such a way that forecloses seeing the viability of Indigenous cosmologies. A self-imposed blindness results in the inability to perceive a way of living that is both conscious of the interconnection of ecology to anthropology and honors the interrelational nature of the cosmos. The symbiosis of humanity within the totality of Indigenous cosmologies predates the colonized imposition of its *civilized reality* but remains largely invisible or discounted as fanciful. Winona La Duke sums up this dichotomy in her consideration of what is considered sacred within U.S. cultural practice:

> We have a problem of two separate spiritual paradigms, and one dominant culture-make that a dominate culture with an immense appetite for natural resources. The animals, the trees, and other plants, even the minerals under the ground and the water from the lakes and streams, all have been expropriated from Native American territories. Land taken from Native peoples either by force or the colonists' law was the basis for an industrial infrastructure and now a standard of living that consumes a third of the world's resources.[3]

This bifurcation of the environment from the sphere of humanity is a dichotomy that contributes to disorienting people from recognizing their dependence and place within the living world as cocreating companions. This ideological separation of creation from humanity mutates nature into material goods and humans into individual consumers. This paradigm is one of separation where creation becomes an inanimate *thing*, lacking status as a multivalent web of sacred living beings. This severance does not exist within non-Christian, Native American knowledges and is not seen as viable or desirable. The fullness of the universe is active, inventive, and responsive. The privilege of the human creature is not the primary consideration. As the Laguna Pueblo and Sioux writer, poet, activist, and professor, Paula Gunn Allen explains, "[f]urther, tribal people allow all animals, vegetables, and minerals (the entire biota, in short) the same or even greater privileges than humans. The Indian participates in destiny on all levels, including that of creation."[4] She later states that a radical egalitarianism is reflected in the structure of American Indigenous literature as a mirror of traditional American Indian societies,' "of tribal understandings, and its relation to the unitary nature of reality."[5] The flourishing of all beings, both sentient and nonsentient, is opposed by adherence to the cosmology of consumption and dominance. The growing concerns about environmental disasters and shifting climate changes speak to the destruction of the earth and its viability for all life, constructing an ecological anthropology that not only recognizes but also tangibly respects the interrelated and interdependence of All Our Relations. The phrase, "All Our Relations," refers to the cosmological reality of reciprocal being. This term recognizes the entwined and communal relationship of human beings with respect to one another and everyone else that sustains life.[6]

Indigenous Peoples, who, despite the pressures of settler colonial hegemony, maintained their cultural and spiritual ceremonies and cosmologies are living examples of resistance to exploitation and destruction of biodiversity, material resources, and other human beings. To be clear, I am not suggesting that the United States appropriate the Indigenous sacred ritual practices or arrogate methods of communal governance. What I am proposing is the legacy of White presumptions of heteropatriarchal and racialized superiority to Native American civilizations has not led to imagining realities that palpably benefit All Our Relations.[7] This existing disconnect between humanity and all things destroys the planet, squanders resources, and alienates humankind from one another. Recovering imagination is not a fanciful diversion from the consequences of this estrangement of humans from the universe. Remembering that the embedded Western notions of civilization are not a universal and unchangeable inevitability might be the beginning to accomplish mutual healing and flourishing for All Our Relatives.

There are limitations to what can be done within the scope of one chapter or even in one lifetime. For this reason, I want to clarify a challenge that arises as I attempt to share broad Indigenous understandings of the non-Indigenous term, *ecological anthropology*. Primarily, over 562 federally recognized Native American tribal nations live in the United States.[8] Each is a society with its own languages, cultural traditions, and spiritual practices that are continually negotiated within ever-changing sociological contexts. There is not one, universal Indigenous cosmology. The spiritual beliefs held by Native Peoples, however, do share certain values and ethics in common even with their extreme diversity of expression. Consider all the religions of the world and the variety of ways that each varies under the same title of affiliation. For example, Christianity is not the unified monolith that it appears to be to escape critical interrogation of its many variant denominations and doctrinal conflicts. Yet the framework of Christianity's heterogeneous Protestants and Catholic hold to certain overarching themes that allow for conversations to be held.

This chapter utilizes the work of Barbara Alice Mann (Haudenosaunee) and other Indigenous women to investigate the complexity and brilliance of the Indigenous epistemologies that share overarching themes that reflect a North American Indian cosmology. Mann explains the logic, ethics, philosophy, and metaphysics of Indigenous knowledge across Turtle Island (recognized now as North America) by explicating what she terms the Twinned Cosmos.[9] These foundations of Indigenous knowledge detail how Native American spiritualties and intellectual traditions, obscured by settler colonialism's gendered, raced, and monotheist interpretations, can clarify an ecological anthropology that brings humankind back into kinship with All Our Relations. Likewise, Paula Gunn Allen's work is referenced highlighting the importance of women to Indigenous life, using the term cosmogyny. She coined cosmogyny by combining the Greek words *kosmogonia*, or the creation of the world, and *gyné,* meaning woman.[10] Allen's oeuvre stresses the importance of women as integral to Indigenous identity and the creation of life within, "Gynocentric communities (that) tend to value, peace, tolerance, relationship, balance, harmony, and just distribution of goods."[11] Prior to colonial invasion, Indigenous civilizations practiced traditional rituals and customs that interpret binary opposites in terms of complementarity. Through the stories of Indigenous women, an understanding of the wideness of an ecological anthropology may connect us to All Our Relations.

THE INTERRELATED RESILIENCE OF INDIGENOUS COSMOLOGIES

The Indigenous way of Twinship, as its name suggests, does not rely on monotheism. In contrast to a monotheistic view, the cosmos, along with everything and everyone, is composed of the interactive Spirits of Place in the sky and on the earth.[12] Mann begins by illustrating the most basic concept of Twinship as follows:

> Let us all traipse back to kindergarten, then looking first at our hot and sticky little hands, palms down, please. No, that will not 'automatically' lead us to "ten," unless we are already atomizing Westerners. Otherwise, the two hands will lead us to the Twinned Cosmos, for like the rest of our body, our hands are mirrored yet cooperative, so that, right off, we see that Twinship is central to consciousness.[13]

Mann then demonstrates that the thumbs are equal in function even if they face opposite directions. Though different in position, each functions in a complementary manner. Thumbs are more independent and stronger than the other digits and are considered the elders. This title of elder does not make its bearer better than the other fingers. The thumbs cannot accomplish as much as a lone individual. The elders, as leaders, are the sensible choice because the thumbs can bear the heavier responsibilities in the collective action/task of the hands, which sustains the community. The pointer fingers also mirror each other and are considered the associate leaders as the next strongest digits. All the other twinned fingers are expected to lend support to one another because cooperation is vital to success. "Finally, the fingers and thumbs of the two hands interlace perfectly, so that the mutuality reinforcing interdependence of the combined whole of the Twinship must be the central organizing principle of reality."[14]

Our hands also indicate numerical patterns of relationship through their mirrored and grouped extremities: two thumbs, bundles of four fingers, and then, when clasped, a bundle of eight. This two-based system becomes the foundation for Indigenous relationships and praxis. Even numbers indicate balance; odd numbers are dysfunctional. "In the Twinship system, 'one' is incomplete, not a whole number, but a fraction, one-half of the twinned collective."[15] The number one is considered suspect, as it does not fulfill the evident twinned nature of the cosmos. Likewise, anything counted in threes is incomplete or out of balance and potentially dangerous. Occurrences appearing in sets of three demand the careful attention of the observer. Encountering events in a sequence of threes can also be a warning to correct a present or impending imbalance and restore the cosmos to relational equilibrium.[16] The Twinship system does not characterize one or three as evil or sinful; instead, these uneven observations expose a material reality, which must be attended to thoughtfully.

There is no judge/king deity that determines if a human soul is worthy of paradise because the Twinned Cosmos relies on a pervasively relational approach in which all things are connected. Indigenous relationships were not formulated as a pyramid hierarchy with human beings at the zenith of creation. American Indian civilizations regard the cosmos as a complex web of interdependent relationships. This network regards all things animate and inanimate—rock, plants, animals, humans, sky, earth, wind, and divine mystery—as relatives. Turtle Island's practices of Twinship dismantle the Platonic and Aristotelian categories that cause human beings to feel alienated and seek escape from a fallen creation/nature.[17] God, as the sole creator who formed the world out of nothing, is not the universal panacea that Christianity assumes.

Twinship's devotion to symmetries of communal relationship renders the Christian obsession with the oneness of God illogical. God or the divine being in Native theologies is not identical to the Christian God. Instead, the divine maintains its unknowable alterity, a Sacred Other/Mystery who acts in the best interests of the whole of creation. Native Peoples experience the Sacred Other/Mystery in specific manifestations, which are male, female, and genderless in form.[18] Indigenous Peoples recognize the existence of this sacred force that infuses all life and that reveals its energies through all manner of tangible and intangible experiences. Indigenous Spiritualties are more than the pantheistic nature worship or proto-environmentalism that is often purported by Eurocentric observers. Instead, Native Peoples developed complex, relational philosophies about the cosmos in which divine beings are multiple and linked to all other beings.

Sky and earth are recognized as the Sacred Other's life-giving spirits/energies of Breath and Blood. These related halves correspond to one another, expressing the balance of the Twinned Sacred Mystery; Breath/sky and Blood/earth Spirits are linked and function in roles of leadership, decision-making, nurturing, and providing for the community's wholeness.[19] Everything is comprised of these bonded pairs that are at once self-governing but always interdependent. This web of mutual vulnerability builds a social structure reliant on collaboration and cooperation as its prime ethical tenets.[20] The observance of maintaining balance makes the pairings of matched and doubly matched sets indispensable for the wellbeing of all life.

The practice of maintaining balance is exemplified in two common Indigenous creation stories. One is a tale of descent from the sky and the other is of emergence from the earth. These stories are both different by design and both are considered valid. The Origin stories of Turtle Island significantly deviate from the Euro-Christian conceptions of an autonomous Creator/God. Creation in many Indigenous cultures is a communal act that encompasses both a divine person or being and animals. Creation stories rooted in earth/blood teachings record humans emerging from caves and tunnels. Breath/Sky creation stories also tell of people falling from the sky. Both stories are held together as authentic. Traditions surrounding creation stories are specific to the locale and, as a result, vary in their depictions of how the world was brought to life. Some creation stories include the figure of the Coyote; some include the Heron, Loon, Eagle, Snapping Turtle, a host of animals, Falling Sky Woman, her daughter, and her twin grandsons; and others include Old Spider Woman, Serpent Woman, Corn Woman, and Earth Woman.[21] One creation story of the Chickasaws says that the land is formed by Crawfish bringing mud up to the surface of the water and Raven terraforming the earth and creating the skies because Ababinili, a divine spirit associated with the sun, asked for their help.[22] These tales reflect the sacred belief that creation itself is made to be a collaboration of a heterogeneous community, a world birthed by the spirits of Breath/sky and Blood/earth and not the sole accomplishment of an individual God.

Eurocentric, Western educators fail to perceive the essential significance of paired sets. In the rush to unify and reconcile the perceived discrepancies, they categorized these differences as errors.[23] This assumed that Native Peoples were unable to properly remember their own histories, science, and spiritualities. Upon hearing the American Indians' origin stories, Christian settlers promptly severed the twinned stories to compose a fable more in keeping with their own cultural preconceptions by pronouncing the Breath/sky "God" to be their One True God. The Chickasaw's Ishahollo/Ababinili, once an unknowable "composite force consisting of the Four Beloved Things Above, which were the Sun, Clouds, Clear Sky, and He that Lives in the Clear Sky," became the Christian God. The spirits of the earth, the HottukOokproose, residing in the dark regions of the West, were labeled as evil. Furthermore, the spirits of the higher regions, the HottukIshtohoollo, were good.[24] The entire concept of complementary binaries in a relationship of interdependence is elided. The European hermeneutic comprehended binaries only existing in oppositional relationships and driven by competitive conflict.

Collaboration, as a principle of righting relationships, is a vital component of every aspect of Indigenous life. The idea of original sin or "human depravity" is alien to Indigenous understandings of what it means to be human.[25] I want to be clear that Native American Indians do not believe that human beings are infallible, incapable of inappropriate behavior, or neglecting ethical responsibilities. But error is seen as a temporary condition that can be repaired by actions of purification, self-sacrifice, or acts of respect. Native Peoples have the capacity to reestablish a balanced and harmonious relationship. There is no pronouncement of the human being as inherently evil or superior because humans are only one part of the cosmos. Humans are not privileged over or above the rest of creation. The Eurocentric language surrounding the loci of sin, theological anthropology, and the fallen state of creation in Christianity does not have translatable equivalents in American Indian languages. Indigenous epistemologies take seriously the material reality of the Twinned Cosmos, as described above. The Sacred Mystery, or life force that animates all things, provides for human understanding of and participation in balancing ceremonies that uphold the ethics of reciprocity. Any failures to contribute to maintaining balance do have material consequences. Whether these outcomes are a natural product of behavior or whether it is community prompted, any ill effects experienced by an unobservant person do not result in his or her eternal, punishing damnation. The responsibility to act individually with an ethic of reciprocity establishes that all persons have communal importance and value. Identity is spatial for Indigenous Peoples. The land one inhabits instructs one to his or her place and role within the cosmogyny.

LAND AS LIFE AND BEING

Native American epistemologies position land/place as the establishing principle for organizing all domestic relationships. This emphasis on attunement with the tangible world provides the framework for historic, religious, and self-understanding that evades Christian teleological emphasis on salvation apart from the Earth in heaven.[26] As previously alluded to, traditional Indigenous beliefs about human beings and the land invert a dominant system of property ownership. For Indigenous Peoples, Mann informs us, "Spatiality is a spiritual, not a geopolitical issue."[27] The land gave birth to human beings and all our relatives, and the land itself is composed of the dust of our ancestors. Because of these tenets, the people do belong to the land. Mann continues:

> The physical place in which one resides molds all of consciousness, including that of non-human animals, plants, minerals and the water around them (on the Blood side), as well as that of winds, stars, constellations and the spaces around them (on the Breath side). The interactions and relationships formed among things residing in any space- say, in the desert southwest or on the moon-create a specific spiritual consciousness that is simply not transportable or transferrable to any other locale.[28]

The specificity of location circumscribes rhythms, responsibilities, and rites that create the social structures of each Indigenous culture, clan, tribe, or nation. Attentiveness to the processes of the natural world led human beings to recognition of and admiration for the coherence of the Twinned cosmos. The bonded pairs of Blood/earth and Breath/spirit establish ethical and aspirational goals for social relationships.

The Indigenous social structures also rely on place/space for the markers of belonging. Unlike the hierarchical formulations favored by visions of a Christendom where Christ is King and humans rank below angels and above all of creation, Indigenous identity is rooted in interdependence that is expressed through systems of kinship. Kinship is about more than lineage. Kinship involves the local: the person (individual), clan (family), and tribe (community), but it also considers the wider vision of the affiliations we have with All Our Relatives, which includes an underrepresented transcontinental element.[29] One must understand the importance of kinship as the practice that maintains the balance of creation. The following is a general primer on how Indigenous cultures honor kinship principles in local and continent-wide relationships.

First, familial bonds are recognized and honored. When a person is born, he or she acquires two sites of self-identification. This identity is a twinned relationship that mirrors the larger union of Breath/Sky laying over Blood/earth to create life. This cosmic procreation is a pattern repeated in nature. The mother provides the child with his or her Blood/earth connection understood as the clan. The father contributes the Breath/Sky affiliation to the Peoples usually translated as tribe. The human being is not only determined by genetic contributions. Each parent contributes to the child a name and a set of communal obligations that are based on the Peoples' ties to their specific location. For example, Jeannette Armstrong (Okanagan), director of the En'owkin Center, explains how the method of introducing oneself is a detailed process that reveals more than just one's name and place of habitation. Armstrong begins by describing the name and location of her birthplace. She then details the climate and physical features of this area, two mountain ranges, and a main river with four tributaries. Next, she describes her mother as a river Indian from Kettle Falls. The river Indians are caretakers of the fisheries. She goes on to explain that her father's family is from the mountain area, Okanagan Valley. The mountain Indians are hunters and do not live in the river basin. The mountain culture is distinctive from the river culture. She is named after her father's great-grandmother, describing herself as associated with her paternal family but her right and responsibility are through her mother's birth and family education. All this information is necessary, as Armstrong explains:

> So that is who I am and where I take my identity from. I know the mountains, and by birth, the river is my responsibility: They are part of me. I cannot be separated from my place or my land.
>
> When I introduce myself to my own people in my own language, I describe these things because it tells them what my responsibilities are and what my goal is. It tells them what my connection is, how I need to conduct myself, what I need to carry with me, what I project, what I teach and what I think about, what I must do and what I cannot do.[30]

Armstrong also explains what it means to call oneself by the name of her People, Okanagan. Like most other Indigenous cultures, the name of the People is a variation on a translation of "the people of the land."[31] Okanagan is the self-identification as "the ones who are dream and land together," meaning "Before anything else, we are the living, dreaming Earth pieces." This is your humanity and point of connection to each other and the world.[32]

Respecting and participating as individuals and communities in the ceremonies, which balance the complementary pairs of Blood (Earth) and Breath (Sky) is how the Twinned Cosmos is made whole. Being becomes an ongoing labor of love. Paula Gunn Allen explains, "The ceremony is the ritual enactment of a specialized perception of a cosmic relationship, while myth is a prose record of that relationship."[33] From the perspective of the community, each individual ceremony is not performed in isolation. Instead, the belief is that each rite connects to all other ceremonies in the dynamic processes of living as part of a whole creation. Wholeness creates all the good, the healthful, and the beautiful. This reverent striving for wholeness extends beyond the capacity for human knowing. "The purpose of ceremony is to integrate: to fuse the individual with his or her fellows, the community of people with that of other kingdoms, and this larger communal group with the worlds beyond this one."[34]

THE ROLE OF WOMEN IN THE WEB OF LIFE

The universe is a multitude of connected pairs recognized as different but of equal importance to maintaining holistic and universal wellbeing. Gendering of the bonded pairs of creation is evidenced by the stories across Turtle Island of "the Creatrix as She Who Thinks rather than She Who Bears, of woman as creation thinker and female thought as origin of material and non-material reality . . . But 'she is the supreme Spirit, both Mother and Father to all people and all creatures.'"[35] The Creatrix illustrates that Indigenous women are esteemed as a source of life in this symbiotic, bonded system and not solely for their reproductive potential.

Women, in the Indigenous view, are equally capable and expected to attend to governmental, financial, legal, and spiritual obligations. For example, the Haudenosaunee, "Iroquois," had the wise matron *Gantowisas*, a title that roughly translates to "indispensable woman."[36] Mann's work tells us:

> The Gantowisas enjoyed sweeping political powers ranged from administrative and legislative to the judicial. The Gantowisas ran the local clan councils. They held the lineage wampum, nomination belts and titles. They ran the funerals. They retained exclusive rights over naming, i.e., the creation of new citizens and instillation of public officials. They nominated all male sachems as well as all Clan Mothers to office and retained the power to impeach wrongdoers. They appointed warriors, declared war, negotiated peace, and mediated disputes.[37]

Mann goes on to later say:

> These League Clan Mothers met in the gendered counterpart of the Men's Grand Council. They operated at the local level of government, balancing and replicating the federal government operated by the men . . . the terms 'local' and 'federal' may be misleading to the reader. When used to describe modern American government, they denote lesser and greater powers, respectively. Among the Haudenosaunee, however, no such hierarchy was implied. The organizing principle behind the local-federal mechanism was Twinship in the form of gendered balance.[38]

Likewise, Indigenous Peoples in the Southeast, including the Cherokee, Choctaw, Muscogee, Seminole, and Chickasaws, lived in matriarchal societies. The women of this region participated in gendered councils too. The

Cherokee referred to the female clan heads with the title of Beloved Woman. In Choctaw and Chickasaw societies, Beloved People embodied exceptional qualities that made them not only respected and admired, but also sacred. Beloved women who had moved past the powerful time of childbearing could handle medicine, attend funeral ceremonies and rituals, collect the first fruits of a new harvest, or perform any duty that required a high degree of purity. This purity involved an absence of blood, so for men returning from war or a hunt where blood had flowed, a ritual of purification was required. This male observance mirrored the women's seclusion and washing after childbirth and menses.[39] In a matriarchal system, women farmed the crops and worked for the good of the people through food distribution and trading their harvests. Women of the Southeast also owned their property, even after marriage. The men who married came to live in the woman's clan home. The children's lineage was always traced through the mother's clan. A marriage could be dissolved without the woman losing her home or her children. There was no disgrace associated with divorce, the practice of sexual freedom, or childbearing out of wedlock.

In Native cultures, both genders are necessary for the other to be whole. Identifying as female links one to the realm of Blood and as such determines how one supports the well-being of the community. Story, nature, ceremony, spirituality, identity, economics, and relationship are not compartmentalized discreet functions. Like Mother Earth, women give life. This life-giving is not limited to reproductive capacity. Women tended to the earth by planting, caring for, and distributing of the crops. Corn in oral traditions was a gift of the Blood spirits. It is also an example of how balance is a participatory process that necessarily permeates all aspects of life.

The imposition of patriarchy over Indigenous systems disturbed Indigenous community wholeness by excluding women from the sociopolitical processes and prohibiting ceremonies that are as ancient as Turtle Island itself.[40] After European intrusion, colonists enforced changes like refusing to trade with women or only negotiating with the Native men. Women were further marginalized by the colonial insistence on the *morality* of male supremacy, private property, and Christianity. Viewing their Eurocentric customs and worldview as superior to the Indian practices of egalitarianism, radical relationality, and gifting economies that characterize epistemologies of the Twinned Cosmos, colonists committed to erasing knowledge about women's position of authority and their stories. It is important to acknowledge Native Peoples' recognition of the importance of the aspects of both male and female energies, present within each being/relative. As previously discussed, all things and beings are perceived as coming in complimentary twos, fours, and doubles. The twinned world, made up of bonded pairs of Earth/Blood/female spirits and Sky/Breath/male spirits, comprises all philosophical, pragmatic, and material aspects of life, death, and life after death. Each pair is part of a whole that is inseparable and mutually joined to maintain harmony. Indigenous theologies did not credit Father God without a balancing Mother counterpart. Monotheism's lack of symmetry indicates that the adoration of the "One" leads to destruction and implies cosmic dysfunctional nonsense.[41] This complimentary system also confounds the binary gender stereotypes and roles of Western masculinity and femininity. Many societies were matrilineal, and sexism was not practiced. Instead of placing rigid boundaries between or around male and female roles, Indigenous cosmologies recognize that each person is composed of both spirit energies. Unlike Christians who only have one spirit or "soul," in Indigenous cultures, everyone has two spirits. Everyone received these two spirits through his or her parents. The mother gives her child the Blood spirit, which resides in the bone marrow. The father provides that same child with the Breath spirit that dwells in the cranium.[42] These two spirits constituted the mirrored halves of the cosmos within oneself.

INDIGENOUS RE-MEMBERING THE ECOLOGY AND ANTHROPOLOGY DIVIDE

I began this chapter reflecting on the ways in which constructs of Western colonial thought and theology in the United States established an intellectual, spiritual, and physical disconnection between humanity and the world. I proposed that the taxonomies that elevate the human being as the apex of creation and render the world as consumable things fail to sustain life. Relationship between the human being, the earth, and other creatures is severed on such a fundamental level that toxic social systems continually seek to assert dominance through the destructive forces of capitalism, racism, and heteropatriarchy. Moving away from the conflict-driven rhetoric of individualism is vital to reversing the environmental and psychosocial wounds. Damage is inflicted by using only one lens that advances an antagonistic, oppositional vision of reality. I sought to encourage recovery from cosmological alienation through sharing traditions animating the Indigenous ethic of interdependent, complementary, and egalitarian relationality. In Native cosmologies, there is the recognition of everything as being sacred and valuable, sometimes more so than even the human creature. While I do not believe Indigenous spiritual or cultural practices should be appropriated by the dominant American culture, I do believe that the Traditions of the Twinned Cosmos and its Creatrix offer possibilities for healing the human and nature divide.

The Indigenous practice of keeping All Our Relations as an inviolable tenant becomes an opportunity for envisioning and enacting a re-membering of the vivisection that severed humanity from creation becomes viable. Points of intersection between the aspirations of Western culture and Christianity and this Creatrix-centered interrelationality seem incompatible, however, tenuous resonances are detectible. For Native American Peoples, who continue living within the traditions of their cultures under the surveillance of settler colonial science and governance, there is the tension of inhabiting an environment where institutions of Western civilization work to erase or reduce the authority of Indigenous cosmologies and spiritualities. While I presented these views of reality and meaning-making in stark contrast for the purpose of this chapter, the nature of existence is one in flux. Interaction and mutual contamination of thought and experiences impact both Native and non-Native Americans. The fact of proximity makes the flourishing of our communities one of mutual concern. We are vulnerable to our interconnection with other human beings and creation. Environmental changes as the result of global warming and pollution highlight the precarious nature of a creation that is far from a state of balance. This imbalance occurs through acts that feature a lack of respect and reciprocity toward All Our Relatives within the cosmos. The system of hierarchy lauded through the cultural conventions of settler colonialism's civilization is destructive to the preservation of life. Points of resonance between many peoples would include clean air, pure water, arable land, and a prospering biodiversity. The compartmentalizing of the ecological world into things or tools separated from humanity for human consumption prevents the changes necessary to obtain a balanced and holistic way of being in the world. The Indigenous intellectual and spiritual philosophies, which are a form of radical egalitarian interdependence, offer the means to care for political and economic needs of communities. Native women held positions of authority in domestic and governmental matters to uphold the sacredness of the cosmological necessity to recognize oneself as kin to all things in word and deed. This commitment to justice through relationality continues as Indigenous women continue to act through community organization and leadership in the struggles against impoverishment, oppression, eco-genocide, and the systems of heteropatriarchy. The Native American methodologies are a springboard for reimagining humanity's self-awareness as an integral piece of creation but only a piece. The schism hinders methods for formulating collaborative and responsible actions to empower and resist the alienation of humanity from All Our Relations.

NOTES

1. Vine Deloria, Jr., *God is Red: A Native View of Religion, 30th Anniversary Edition* (Golden: Fulcrum Publishing, 2003), 80.
2. Ibid., 81.

3. Winona LaDuke, Recovering *the Sacred: The Power of Naming and Claiming* (Cambridge: South End Press, 2005), 14.

4. Paula Gunn Allen, *The Sacred Hoop: Recovering the Feminine in American Indian Traditions* (Boston: Beacon Press, 1992), 57.

5. Ibid, 58–59.

6. Winona LaDuke, *All Our Relations: Native Struggles for Land and Life* (Cambridge: South End Press, 1999), 2.

7. I realize that not every US citizen is of Anglo European heritage. I do not use "White" as a descriptor of phenotype or race. Instead, I deploy the term to describe an individual or collective acceptance of a Western European ideology that privilege concepts of democracy, empire, Christianity, and teleological progress as universal and empirically true.

8. David E. Wilkins, *American Indian Politics and the American Political System, second edition* (New York: Rowman & Littlefield Publishers, Inc., 2007), 108.

9. Barbara Alice Mann, *Spirits of Blood, Spirits of Breath: The Twinned Cosmos of Indigenous America* (New York: Oxford University Press, 2016), 4.

10. Paula Gunn Allen, *Grandmothers of the Light: A Medicine Woman's Sourcebook* (Boston: Beacon Press, 1991), xiii.

11. Ibid., xiv.

12. Mann, *Spirits of Blood*, 39.

13. Ibid., 41–42.

14. Ibid., 42.

15. Ibid.

16. Ibid., 43.

17. Deloria, *God is Red,* 90–91.

18. George E. Tinker, *American Indian Liberation: A Theology of Sovereignty* (Maryknoll, NY: Orbis Books, 2008), 61–70.

19. Barbara Alice Mann, *Iroquoian Women: The Gantowisas* (New York: Peter Lang, 2004), 59–112.

20. Ibid., 89.

21. Referring to creation accounts from several works: George E. "Tink" Tinker, "Why I Do Not Believe in a Creator," in *Buffalo Shout, Salmon Cry: Conversations on Creation, Land Justice, and Life Together*, ed. Steve Heinrich (Waterloo: Herald Press, 2013). 167–183; Mann, *Iroquoian Women*, 1–10, 59–60. Allen, The *Sacred Hoop, 13.*

22. I have heard this story on multiple occasions throughout my life. In some tellings, Ababinili (a more Christianized understanding of God) does not appear. Ishtahollo', Worker of Sacred Wonders, is also used to refer to the divine force. This version is documented in a Chickasaw Nation sponsored video, Stephanie Scott, storyteller, "Creation Story: The Crawfish." www.chickasaw.tv/history/video/creation-story-the-crawfish/list/stories.

23. Mann, *Spirits of Blood,* 45.

24. Arrell M. Gibson, *The Chickasaws* (Norman: University of Oklahoma Press, 1971), 9–10.

25. Tinker, *American Indian Liberation*, 90.

26. Deloria, God *is Red*, 61, 65.
27. Mann, *Spirits of Blood*, 54.
28. Ibid., 55.
29. Allen, *The Sacred Hoop*, 59.
30. Jeannette Armstrong, "Community: 'Sharing One Skin,'" in *Paradigm Wars: Indigenous Peoples Resistance to Globalization*, eds Jerry Mander and Victoria Tauli-Corpuz (San Francisco: Sierra Club Books, 2006), 35.
31. Ibid., 35–36.
32. Ibid., 35.
33. Allen, *The Sacred Hoop*, 61.
34. Ibid., 62.
35. Ibid., 15.
36. Mann, *Iroquoian Women*,16.
37. Ibid, 116–117.
38. Ibid, 161.
39. Michelene E. Pesantubbee, *Choctaw Women in a Chaotic World: The Clash of Cultures in the Colonial Southeast* (Albuquerque: University of New Mexico Press, 2005), 23–24.
40. Kay Givens McGowan, "Weeping for the Lost Matriarchy," in *Daughters of Mother Earth: The Wisdom of Native American Women*, ed. Barbara Alice Mann (Westport, CT and London: Praeger, 2006), 53–68.
41. Mann, Spirits of Blood, 242–243.
42. Ibid., 96–97.

FURTHER READINGS

Allen, Paula Gunn. *Grandmothers of the Light: A Medicine Woman's Sourcebook*. Boston, MA: Beacon Press, 1993.

Goeman, Mishuana. *Mark My Words: Native Women Mapping Our Nations*. Minneapolis, MN: University of Minnesota Press, 2013.

Hixson, Walter L. *American Settler Colonialism a History*. Basingstoke: Palgrave Macmillan, 2013.

Rifkin, Mark. *When Did Indians Become Straight?: Kinship, the History of Sexuality, and Native Sovereignty*. New York: Oxford University Press, 2011.

Tinker, George E. *Missionary Conquest: The Gospel and Native American Cultural Genocide*. Minneapolis, MN: Fortress Press, 1993.

Wilson, Angela Cavender. *What Does Justice Look Like?: The Struggle for Liberation in Dakota Homeland*. St. Paul, MN: Living Justice Press, 2008.

REFERENCES

Allen, Paula Gunn. *Grandmothers of the Light: A Medicine Woman's Sourcebook*. Boston: Beacon Press, 1991.

———. *The Sacred Hoop: Recovering the Feminine in American Indian Traditions.* Boston: Beacon Press, 1992.

Armstrong, Jeannette. "Community: 'Sharing One Skin.'" In *Paradigm Wars: Indigenous Peoples Resistance to Globalization*, edited by Jerry Mander and Victoria Tauli-Corpuz, 35–39. San Francisco: Sierra Club Books, 2006.

Deloria, Vine, Jr. *God is Red: A Native View of Religion, 30th Anniversary Edition.* Golden: Fulcrum Publishing, 2003.

Gibson, Arrell M. *The Chickasaws.* Norman: University of Oklahoma Press, 1971.

LaDuke, Winona. *All Our Relations: Native Struggles for Land and Life.* Cambridge: South End Press, 1999.

———. *Recovering the Sacred: The Power of Naming and Claiming.* Cambridge: South End Press, 2005, p. 14.

Mann, Barbara Alice. *Iroquoian Women: The Gantowisas.* New York: Peter Lang, 2004.

———. *Spirits of Blood, Spirits of Breath: The Twinned Cosmos of Indigenous America.* New York: Oxford University Press, 2016.

McGowan, Kay Givens. "Weeping for the Lost Matriarchy." In *Daughters of Mother Earth: The Wisdom of Native American Women*, edited by Barbara Alice Mann, 53–68. Westport, CT and London: Praeger, 2006.

Pesantubbee, Michelene E. *Choctaw Women in a Chaotic World: The Clash of Cultures in the Colonial Southeast.* Albuquerque: University of New Mexico Press, 2005.

Scott, Stephanie. "Creation Story: The Crawfish." www.chickasaw.tv/history/video/creation-story-the-crawfish/list/stories.

Tinker, George E. *American Indian Liberation: A Theology of Sovereignty.* Maryknoll, NY: Orbis Books, 2008.

———. "Why I Do Not Believe in a Creator." In *Buffalo Shout, Salmon Cry: Conversations on Creation, Land Justice, and Life Together*, edited by Steve Heinrich, 167–183. Waterloo: Herald Press, 2013.

Wilkins, David E. *American Indian Politics and the American Political System. Second Edition.* New York: Rowman & Littlefield Publishers, Inc., 2007.

Part 3

TOWARD A HERMENEUTIC OF LIBERATION

Chapter 9

The Human Person as a Polyphonic Being

Giving Voice to the Experiences of Black Women

SimonMary Asese A. Aihiokhai

To speak of the human is to give voice to a polyphonic being, one that embodies the ability to fantasize. In the words of Judith Butler, "fantasy is what allows us to imagine ourselves and others otherwise; it establishes the possible in excess of the real; it points elsewhere, and when it is embodied, it brings the elsewhere home."[1] This ability of the human to fantasize allows for "new modes of reality to be instituted through the scene of embodiment, where the body is not understood as a static and accomplished fact, but as an aging process, a mode of becoming that, in becoming otherwise, exceeds the norm, reworks the norm, and makes us see how realities to which we thought we were confined are not written in stone."[2]

In this chapter, I will articulate a more inclusive theological vision of the human by appropriating the insights of Black women in the global south and north. In doing this, I will resist the temptation of writing a monologic script. In my engagement with the topic of being human from the two worlds, north and south, I will appropriate insights from religious and cultural traditions within and outside of Christianity. Methodologically, I will retell our human stories from the existential locus of Black women. Retelling our stories allows for the possibility to hear what has been silenced and to silence that which has the power to negatively manipulate the cognitive abilities of the listener.

EXPERIENCES OF BLACK WOMEN: SEEKING AN INCLUSIVE ANTHROPOLOGY

Traditional theological anthropology makes ontology its starting point. By speaking of inherent dignity, devoid of existential qualifiers, it reifies cultural preferences in ways that they are accepted as the will of God without any serious critique. When these cultural preferences are themselves dehumanizing, they are legitimized theologically and with such arguments like, if God wanted something different, God would have made it so. This type of reasoning was used to justify the Apartheid policies of South Africa. For example, Stephanus Jacobus du Toit, an Afrikaner nationalist and theologian of the Dutch Reformed Church in South Africa went to great lengths to justify the racial policies during the Apartheid era and to articulate a theological anthropology that gave dignity to White South Africans at the expense of non-whites. He held the belief that "the church had a divinely ordained duty to protect the cultural identity of Afrikaners."[3] For him, Apartheid was described as a great commandment by God. He believed that "it was within God's ordinances and that there should be no one who should try to make equal that which God had not made equal."[4] Let me state briefly here that rather than uphold a rigid ontological view of the dignity of the human person, it is better to embrace a weak ontology, one that affirms alterity as the locus for identity derivation. To speak of ontological dignity, one ought to weigh the statement alongside the conditions of the concrete human of history. How is human dignity to be understood in the era of ethnic cleansing, genocide, and mass murders of the innocent? These abnormalities demand that theologians reengage that which they have taken for granted. Human dignity is not only to be spoken of, it ought to be experienced existentially in all its surplus *epiphanies*. By experience, I do not mean encountering a rigid idol that reflects back what it receives. No! To experience humans in their dignity as images of God is to encounter infinite possibilities; possibilities that evoke an ethical responsibility for the ones being encountered. In other words, "to be in the image of God does not signify being the icon of God, but finding oneself in his trace . . . Going toward him is not following this trace that is not a sign. It is going toward Others who stand in the trace of illeity. It is by that illeity, situated beyond the calculations and reciprocities of the economy of the world, that being has sense. Sense that is not a finality."[5]

In Africa, any discourse on the dignity of women must necessarily begin with a critique of religion, colonialism, and culture. These continue to give life and legitimacy to patriarchy in contemporary African societies. Prior to the introduction of Islam and Christianity to the continent, sub-Saharan societies were known to be deeply matriarchal in social structures, economy, and religious worldview. I must state quickly that by matriarchy, I do not mean a female version of patriarchy. The latter is by its nature exclusive and manipulative as it has played out in human history. Matriarchy is inherently linked to a cosmic understanding of surplus and generosity that allows for all to find meaning and purpose. For example, "among the Tiv of Northeastern Nigeria, a woman is regarded as both a symbol of communal continuity and as a sacred representation of cosmic harmony. The Tiv believe that God has given them the knowledge of manipulating the *Akombo* (sacred object that links the community/family/individual with the divine) for personal protection as well as for the protection and survival of the community/tribe/nation."[6] Furthermore,

> women who have reached puberty are seen as the greatest Akombo among the Tiv people. This point is reflected in the tattoos drawn on the body of a pregnant woman. These tattoos are similar to the scarification on the great communal Akombo to protect the community when it is faced with grave danger that might lead to its extinction. The body of the woman becomes both the symbol of purification and continuity of the tribe. She bears on her body the past, present, and future of the tribe. In her body lies the meaning of existence of the Tiv people and becomes a testament for the entire tribe to be virtuous and holy.[7]

The struggle of African women to reclaim their stolen identities and roles in society is one that is fought on several fronts. It involves a re-reading of African histories in ways that they are retold as "her-stories." It involves a critical evaluation of cultural practices that have been legitimized by appeals to religious heritage. It involves a critical and public denouncement of the vestiges of colonialism that erased the traces of African women and their roles in their societies from the collective memories of Africans and their descendants. It involves an intentional pushback at Western feminist imperialism, one that universalizes the interests and concerns of middle-class White women without paying much attention to the particularities defining the very existence of African women. In fact, these struggles are best described by Ifi Amadiume who argues that "Third World women can ignore historical and cultural differences only at their own peril in view of the damage done already by colonialism and still being inflicted by neo-colonialism and Western feminist imperialism."[8] In addition to Amadiume's insight, Teresia Mbari Hinga paints a vivid picture of what confronts African women as they attempt to reclaim their place in society. In her words:

> African women's struggle is against the imperialism implicit in the efforts of others, particularly Westerners, to represent them, a struggle that they share with male theologians. For African women, however, their critique of Western paternalism includes the critique of Western women insofar as they, too, may presume to speak on their behalf. African women insist that the right to speak

for themselves is a necessary condition for their emancipation and must be respected by all.[9]

The need to deconstruct the effects of colonialism and neocolonialism on the psyche of Black women transcends the context of Africa. On that note, let me explore the context of African American women in the United States and by extension, the Americas. Looking closely at the context of African American women in the United States and the Americas in general, Rosemary Radford Ruether writes, "in the liberation struggles of the black community and of women, black women find themselves the double minority, or triple minority, if the fact that most black women are poor is taken into account. Poor black women are the group on which the triple jeopardy of oppression by race, class, and gender converge."[10] I should add here, religion. It is thus a quadruple "jeopardy" that confronts African American women. Renita J. Weems has called for a reading of the Bible by African American women in ways that allow for them to intentionally deconstruct the veils of race, gender, and class that tend to be used to justify their oppression and erasure from the history of their communities.[11] I label this a triple-consciousness; one that calls for a critical "re-re-reading" of the text to allow for the tri-silenced voices of African American women to be heard in the texts.

CRITIQUING THE CARTESIAN MODEL OF THE HUMAN

Looking critically at the western notions of self, one notices the radical influence of the Cartesian primacy of the individual. The ideology that presents the individual as a being capable of attaining self-realization without the assistance of the community is a false myth. This false myth presents hard work as the ability to go it alone; rather than working with others. Jean-Luc Marion states it clearly when he writes, "before the *cogito* exists, the *ego* would be well and truly already established in its unconditioned existence as *corpus et sensus* . . . . The *ego* gives itself as flesh, even if one wants to hide it."[12] As Emmanuel Levinas has argued, the other is the bearer of the gift of identity for the self. Levinas offers a relevant critique of ontology as it pertains to identity construction, one that is relevant to the argument being articulated in this chapter. In his words, "When I speak of first philosophy, I am referring to a philosophy of dialogue that cannot not be an ethics. Even the philosophy that questions the meaning of being does so on the basis of the encounter with the other."[13] Levinas argues that at the core of identity is vulnerability. In "vulnerability lies *a relation to the other* . . . . From the moment of sensibility, the subject is *for the other*: substitution, responsibility, expiation."[14] By moving away from identity as static to identity as constituted within the realm of encounter, Levinas gives voice to the prophetic by calling to question identities that do not birth-forth life for others.

Why this critique of Cartesian ontology that has defined Western approaches to identity construction? I will offer three responses; one from Levinas himself, another from Molefi Kete Asante, and a third from Homi K. Bhabha. For Levinas, the barbarism inherent in the Holocaust calls to question notions of identity that privilege the self. Looking closely at European history and its role in global politics, one notices a close link between the evils of history and the primacy of ontology in European intellectual traditions, hence he laments:

> But the conscience of Europe is a bad conscience, because of the contradiction that tears her apart at the very hour of her modernity, which is probably that that of ledgers set up in lucidity, that of full consciousness. That history of peace, a freedom and well-being promised on the basis of a light that a universal knowledge projected on the world and human society—even unto the religious messages that sought justification for themselves in the truths of knowledge—that history is not recognizable in its millennia of fratricidal struggles, political or bloody, of imperialism, scorn and exploitation of the human being, down to our century of world wars, the genocides of the Holocaust and terrorism; unemployment and continual desperate poverty of the Third World; ruthless doctrines and cruelty of fascism and national socialism, right down to the supreme paradox of defense of man and his rights being perverted into Stalinism . . . . The shattering of the universality of theoretical reason, which arose betimes in the 'Know thyself,' and sought the entire universe within self-consciousnes.[15]

Asante's focus is on the existential realities defining Black existence in the United States that eventually led to the "Back-to-Africa Movement of the early twentieth century."[16] As he notes, this "was African Americans' radical critique of the American Dream . . . . The language, scope, and arguments of the Back-to-Africa Movement were tantamount to crusades for freedom and sanity, underscoring the African's essential search for dignity and cultural renewal in a strange land."[17] Furthering the discourse on identity construction that challenges the Eurocentric (Cartesian) model, Asante argues that "Afrocentric interpretation introduces a new, critical perspective into the nature of human discourse, especially when that discourse emerges from the cutting edges of rejection and resistance."[18] Critiquing Eurocentric thought process further, Asante calls to question notions of objectivity in the hermeneutic discourse. This, he argues, has "often protected social and literary theory from the scrutiny that would reveal how theory has often served the interests of the ruling classes . . . . More damaging still has been the inability of European thinkers, particularly of the neopositivist or empiricist traditions, to see that human actions [and identities] cannot be understood apart from the emotions, attitudes, and cultural definitions of a given context."[19]

Furthering the critique of identity construction as inherited from the Cartesian worldview, Bhabha engages Franz Fanon as his interlocutor in a chapter of his work he titled, "Interrogating Identity." In it he concludes the following:

> The struggle against colonial oppression not only changes the direction of Western history, but challenges its historicist idea of time as progressive, ordered whole. The analysis of colonial depersonalization not only alienates the Enlightenment idea of 'Man', but challenges the transparency of social reality, as a pre-given image of human knowledge. If the order of Western historicism is disturbed in the colonial state of emergency, even more deeply disturbed is the social and psychic representation of the human subject. For the very nature of humanity becomes estranged in the colonial condition and from that 'naked declivity' it emerges, not as an assertion of will not as an evocation of freedom, but as an enigmatic questioning. With a question that echoes Freud's *'What does woman want?'*. . .[20]

Bhabha's engagement with the colonial reality as it has played out in the world calls to question notions of universal personhood or in the theological context, *imago Dei*. Stated differently, the unfolding realities of human histories have shown that many humans have not been accorded the dignity that befits one made in God's image. On that note, one has to ask, who comes to mind when the words, *imago Dei* are uttered? African women, Blacks in America, especially African American women, members of the LGBTQIA+ community worldwide, and migrant communities in contemporary societies find themselves constantly being denied that dignity. Asante has posited a question, one worth repeating here; "how can the oppressed use the same theories as the oppressors?"[21] It is on that note that I now attempt to articulate a more inclusive understanding of human dignity that affirms the lives of Black women.

TOWARD AN INCLUSIVE ANTHROPOLOGY: VOICES FROM THE MARGINS

At the heart of African anthropological vision is personalism. This, Asante describes as "an ideal ideological commitment to harmony and the fundamental Afrocentric response to phenomena."[22] Refuting the bias for the spirit over matter, or the preference for the real as found in the positivist tradition, Asante insists that "personalism, in the African and African American sense, is neither spiritualism nor materialism, but the activating energy contained in the person .... Each person contains these energies; some cultivate them more than others, but they inhere in all of us."[23] The beauty of personalism is that it evokes relationality in a saturated manner. Thus, Asante concludes that "there is no 'great tradition' of withdrawal in the African or African American tradition; ours is preeminently a tradition of remarkable encountering with others."[24] Bénézet Bujo attests to this notion of personalism by speaking of an African identity that is at its core relational and communal. Critiquing the Cartesian view of insular self-identity that has prevailed in the Western world for centuries and traceable back to the philosophical propositional claim "I think therefore I am," Bujo argues that "In the African conception, there is no separation between "being" and "doing"; consequently, one may say that the human person is what he does."[25] He goes further to stress the community in the shaping of African notions of identity. This approach demonstrates the fact that identity points to the concept of belonging. One does not exist alone. Rather, one always belongs to a community. The community defines itself by its link to its ancestors.[26]

The art of storytelling is closely linked to an African sense of belonging. It is the responsibility of African women to pass on the narratives that validate the African sense of belonging. They are the storytellers. Mercy Amber Oduyoye has called for the need for African women to reclaim their roles as storytellers and retell the stories that have been silenced by the patriarchal stories handed down to Africans by religious and secular agents from Europe and the Arab world. In her groundbreaking work, *Daughters of Anowa: African Women and Patriarchy*, Oduyoye seeks to deconstruct traits of oppression in African cultures and religions. She engages head in the narratives of subjugation that African women have been taught to embrace for centuries as the only valid stories defining their roles in society. She insists on telling the older story that speaks of the roles of African women as leaders of their communities. Prior to the advent of Islam, Christianity, and colonial rule, women's roles in the political, economic, religious, and cultural spheres were highly regarded. In postcolonial Africa, African women have become the social donkeys whose only purpose is to be the beast of burden for the beneficiaries of patriarchy. Oduyoye's work forces Africans to pause and ask themselves, what type of identity do the nostalgic memories of Africa's precolonial, colonial, and postcolonial pasts seek to create? Does it affirm the dignity of African women?[27] This question is pertinent when one takes seriously the caution raised by Musimbi R. A. Kanyoro as she sheds light on the dilemma faced by African women as they attempt to retell Africa's stories in ways that seek to change the oppressive structures inherent in the colonized narratives currently present in the continent. This dilemma is tri-faced: westernized, indigenous, and religious.[28]

Hinga joins Oduyoye in her call for African women to empower themselves and thus tell their cultural stories in ways that give voice to their experiences, wisdom, and virtues. Hinga does this by re-membering the prophetic witness of Kimpa Vita (Dona Beatrice), who, prior to her conversion to Christianity, was a *Nganga* (a medium between the physical and spiritual worlds). Though Kimpa Vita fell victim to the religious and political intrigues of the Capuchins present in the then Kingdom of Kongo, who accused her of heresy and had her burned at the stake for witchcraft and heresy, her prophetic vision and agency of connection between the indigenous religion of her people and Christianity, along with her vocation to be a conduit between the material world and the spiritual world, serve as a reminder of what it means to be a woman in Africa.[29] African womanhood is the source of life, knowledge, memory, tradition, and transformative change for African people. For Hinga, any discourse of African notions of identity must necessarily involve the experiences of African women and their roles in all the spheres of life. This means that the stories of Africa must also be told by African "her-storians." To deny African women the opportunity to tell Africa's stories is to tell an incomplete story, one that cannot give life and freedom both to the storytellers and the audience.

What are the stories being told by African women? The female voice that has been long silenced by the oppressive agenda of patriarchy in the continent is being heard not only in Africa but in the global community. African women within the continent and in diaspora carry on the legacy of defining what it means to be human. I am conscious of persons like Chimamanda Ngozi Adichie, who deliberately explores issues related to pluralistic identities and migrant identities. In one of her novels, *Purple Hibiscus*, Adichie, as it were, sees it as her rightful place to give the female perspective of Africa's stories. In this novel, Adichie explores the theme of African face of Christianity through the fictional character, Father Amadi. This young Nigerian priest embraces the vibrancy of life that characterizes what Asante describes as African personalism.[30] Adichie's work can comfortably be juxtaposed with Achebe's *Things Fall Apart*. In Achebe's work, the indigenous worldview of African people prior to colonial rule has been shattered by the colonizing agenda of the British colonial presence and the introduction of Christianity.[31] Where Achebe sees hopelessness, Adichie sees hope. Where Achebe sees discontinuity, Adichie sees a new form of continuity, a hybridity characterized by the creativity of the indigenous people of Africa who, faced with the new colonial order, must make sense of it in ways that the pragmatic openness to reality, inherent in African worldview, is allowed to take form.

From the context of Southern Africa, NoViolet Bulawayo reflects on what it means to be a Zimbabwean in her novel, *We Need New Names*.[32] Bulawayo's work is best described by Margaret Busby's words, "Bulawayo immerses us in the world of 10-year-old Darling and her friends Sbho and Bastard and Chipo and Godknows and Stina—a child's—eye view of a world where there is talk of elections and democracy but where chaos and degradation become everyday reality, where death and sickness and the threat of violence lurk."[33] Bulawayo showcases the excellent storytelling skills of African women by giving voice to the perspective of those patriarchal systems have judged to be irrelevant. Children see everything. They speak the unredacted truth that adults have learned to sanitize. For Bulawayo, if Zimbabwe is again to be the home of all Zimbabweans, the stories of the country ought to be told exactly as they are. Violence occurs in society when only partial stories are told of how reality unfolds before the faces of all.

From Eastern Africa, an African story is being told by an African woman. In her case, she is a theologian who refuses to be silenced by the life-denying stories told by some ordained members of her faith tradition. Her name is Haregewoin Cherinet, a theologian of the Ethiopian Orthodox Tewahedo Church. She has called for a critical reading of the Bible within her church. She argues that this can become the strategic approach to deconstructing cultural patriarchy that has held Ethiopian societies hostage.[34] As she once said in 2013, during a meeting we were both attending in Nairobi, Kenya; "In Ethiopia, women are called donkeys. But Ethiopians forget that the most prominent animal in the salvific narratives in the scriptures is the donkey itself. If women are donkeys, then women are the favorite of God's creatures." She has given dignity to the ones that society has denied their legitimate dignity, just as Jesus did to the Samaritans; one he called good (Lk. 10:25-37), and the other he shared his true identity with, while she gladly bore witness to what she heard and who she encountered at the well (Jn. 4: 4-26). Her witnessing has historically been attested to by the name that tradition has come to identify her with, Saint Photina or the luminous one.

From the context of the African Diaspora, Petina Gappah has chosen to reflect in her collection of short stories titled, *An Elegy for Easterly*, on the resilience of fellow Zimbabweans who have chosen to remain behind and find ways of identifying with a country in chaos. Gappah wants to show not only how current political, cultural, economic, and social conditions play out in independent Zimbabwe, but also an aspect of what it means to be an African within the geopolitical space called Zimbabwe.[35] Gappah stands at the intersection of two worlds, Germany, her current home, and Zimbabwe, the land where her umbilical cord is buried, and from that location reflects on what ought to be in her beloved Zimbabwe. In Africa, stories are not just told. They are the pathways of discovering and claiming one's identity(ies). When African women tell Africa's stories, they are passing on to their audience, the gifts of African identities.

When one looks closely through the lens through which African women see the world they live in and the ways they give voice to their visions, one notices the following characteristics; they are visions and stories of unity. They give voice to all who in the past have been made voiceless. They make known all that has been hidden. They decenter the centers of power. They shed light on new horizons and new possibilities. Conscious of the African notion of the human person as a social being, I want to make a very bold claim. It is my conviction that if the human person is constitutive of webs of relationships, all identities derived from those relationships, be they economic status, social status, cultural status, philosophical and/or religious status, must be open at their core to the grace of generosity.

As noted by Michael Battle, "the concept of Ubuntu of necessity poses a challenge to persons accustomed to thinking of themselves as individuals."[36] In simple terms, *Ubuntu* means personhood. For those familiar with the trinitarian discourses of the early church, personhood is constitutive of relationality. "It is by opening up completely to one another that the hypostases are able to share *hoousios* (one nature or substance) without restriction, without being divided."[37] Applying this understanding of personhood to the African understanding of *Ubuntu*, personhood is always relational. Stressing the intended end result of this concept, Battle argues that "Ubuntu is the interdependence of persons for the exercise, development, and fulfillment of their potential to be both individuals and community."[38] This authentication of both the individual and community is something to be cherished by the global community, especially those in the Western world who have been trained to think that the individual has to define itself in opposition to the community.

African women's theological anthropology calls to question the fixation on maleness as representative of the fullness of the *imago Dei*, especially as articulated by Thomas Aquinas, whose bias for the maleness of Christ has led to an anthropology crafted to align itself with a male-biased Christology. A witty response to this bias toward the maleness of Christ as symbolic of our true humanity comes in the form of a rhetorical question, are we saved by the genitalia of the incarnate Christ? I do not think any theologian would want to respond in the affirmative. If that is the case, why then are we hesitant to see women as fully representing the *imago Dei*? The *Circle of Concerned African Women Theologians* is a group of African women theologians who came together when summoned by Oduyoye in 1989. By choice, they called themselves a *Circle* because it depicts fully an African sense of the human that is grounded in personalism. A circle is inclusive. A circle allows for growth. A circle calls for equity and justice for all. It rejects false notions of hierarchy. In their quest for holistic anthropology, the members of the *Circle* have "identified four themes to guide and nuance their research. They are women in the context of religious and cultural pluralism;

the history and agency of African women in religion; biblical and cultural hermeneutics; and issues in the theological and ministerial formation of African women."[39]

Turning to the global north, African American women, while reflecting on their endless experiences of violence from the larger racialized communities, their own Black community that reifies the oppressive structures inherent in the larger society, and from the Black Church where they ought to find a sense of belonging, seek to articulate a response to what it means to be a Black woman. As Kelly Brown Douglas notes, "Black women enlisted such terms as 'slave of a slave,' or 'double jeopardy' to point to what it meant to be an oppressed member of an already oppressed group. With the emerging 'womanist consciousness' Black women began to openly discuss their experiences as Black women and to search for ways in which to gain their freedom without becoming alienated from the Black community as a whole—particularly Black men"[40] Womanist anthropology is at its core an anthropology of surplus. It seeks to welcome all voices who are excluded while also highlighting their uniqueness. Alice Walker writes, "womanism gives us a word of our own."[41] Less, one thinks that Walker is advocating for a separatist ideology, womanism is a theory of bridge-building that intentionally aims to seek moments of intersectionality between African American women's perspectives and other feminist perspectives in their effort to critique the oppressive structures of race, gender, and class.[42]

Attesting to the notion of surplus inherent in womanist anthropology, Douglas, among others, continues to give voice to the experiences of members of the LGBTQIA+ community in the Black Church. What womanist theology is doing to address the anthropological discourse in theology that previously favored maleness, can be said to be what queer theology aims to do for members who identify with the LGBTQIA+ community. Previously, maleness/masculinity and heterosexuality were considered to be the full expressions of God's vision for humans. All that is changing. In the words of Patrick S. Cheng, " . . . queer theory challenges and disrupts the traditional notions that sexuality and gender identity are simply questions of scientific fact or that such concepts can be reduced to fixed binary categories such as 'homosexual' vs. 'heterosexual' or 'female' vs. 'male.' As such, this third definition... refers to the erasing or deconstructing of boundaries with respect to these categories of sexuality and gender."[43] Because of Butler's insights, scholars are beginning to understand that "identity categories tend to be instruments of regulatory regimes, whether as the normalizing categories of oppressive structures, or as the rallying points for a liberatory contestation of that very oppression."[44] Gender, "in other words, rather than being expressions of an innate (gender) identity, acts and gestures which are learned and are repeated over time create the illusion of an innate and stable (gender) core."[45] Her view is in line with the African and African American worldview that speaks of identity as actively expressed through performative relationality.

HIGHLIGHTS OF AN INCLUSIVE THEOLOGICAL ANTHROPOLOGY

Perhaps, to speak of the human through the eyes of Black (African and African American) women, one has to borrow insights from Mikhail Bakhtin. For many, the bias for the dialectic is strong. They long for an erasure of difference and seek to settle for a synthesis of the predictable.[46] On the other hand, Bakhtin reminds us of the realities that constitute the human condition, be they linguistic expressions or life encounters:

> We come into consciousness speaking a language already permeated with many voices—a social, not a private language. From the beginning, we are 'polyglot,' already in process of mastering a variety of social dialects derived from parents, clan, class, religion, country . . . . Finally we achieve, if we are lucky, a kind of individuality, but it is never a private or autonomous individuality in the western sense; except when we maim ourselves arbitrarily to monologue, we always speak a chorus of languages. Anyone who has not been maimed by some imposed 'ideology in the narrow sense,' anyone who is not an 'ideologue,' respects the fact that each of us is a 'we,' not an 'I.' Polyphony, the miracle of our 'dialogical' lives together, is thus both a fact of life and, in its higher reaches, a value to be pursued endlessly.[47]

This polyphonic existence that defines the human condition speaks truly to an *imago Dei* that is trinitarian and personal. To be a person is to be a being radically open to communion with others. To be in communion is to be open to endless possibilities. Though Butler was not thinking theologically when she called out the inadequacy of reducing the human to a "gender ontology," she is correct to conclude that "the viability of *man* and *woman* as nouns, is called into question by the dissonant play of attributes that fail to conform to sequential or causal models of intelligibility."[48]

Again, a Black woman's anthropological vision allows for Butler's performative identities.[49] Or what Amadiume has pointed out in the context of the Igbos of Eastern Nigeria; where social roles of husband and wife become fluid and can be assumed by a woman. In her words, "the flexibility of Igbo gender construction meant that gender was separate from biological sex. Daughters could become sons and consequently male. Daughters and women in general could be husbands to wives and consequently male. Daughters and women in general could be husbands to wives and consequently males in relation to their wives, etc."[50] During the years I worked amongst some Igbo communities in Eastern Nigeria, I came across this practice that the Igbos of Ezinifite, Nnewi of Anambra State, Nigeria refer to in Igbo language as *nwanyi ahahara*. Colloquially, it means a woman with many tricks. But on a serious note, this is existential *mimesis* at its best. The ability to transcend social expectations and thus be able to mediate a new existential meaning surrounds what it means to be woman in Igbo society.

Appropriating Bakhtin's insight of polyphonic existence, it is proper to conclude that the Western feminists' insistence on notions of autonomy and choice and the rights of the woman as an individual, the communal visions inherent in womanism, and African expressions of *Ujamaa* (familyhood) are not in themselves contradictory.[51] They are not to be synthesized in a Hegelian manner. Rather, their existence with all their tensions serves to show the multiple meanings derived from the discourse on what it means to be human when women's insights and experiences are given voice. When *Ujamaa* is fully embraced, it naturally leads to *Ubuntu*. "Ubuntu is the interdependence of persons for the exercise, development, and fulfillment of their potential to be both individuals and community."[52] African women theologians call attention to the intentional forgetfulness of Africans of their rich cultural heritage that has been replaced by patriarchal cultural and social systems.

Based on the above, I want to offer the following insights that ought to define an inclusive anthropology: first, if human dignity is ontological, then one ought to ask the following questions, how has this ontology been understood in the day-to-day lived experiences of women of color? How has human ontology been affirmed when women and children die in the thousands from negligence due to social systems designed to deprive them of any access to basic resources needed for their survival? I conclude that rigid ontology ought to be rejected by theologians interested in articulating healthy theological anthropologies. Ontology ought to be defined by the ethical. As Levinas rightly states, "I am I in the sole measure that I am responsible, a non-interchangeable I. I can substitute myself for everyone, but no one can substitute himself for me. Such is my inalienable identity of subject. It is in this precise sense that Dostoyevsky said: '*We are all responsible for all for all men before all, and I more than all the others.*'"[53] Thus, the ontological dignity of Black women ought to be defined by the inherent responsibility for women by men, women, and queer persons. This ought to be judged by how women are treated as embodied beings of history and not as an idea or a thought. God did not make humans to be an idea, but to be persons with bodies living in historical epochs.

Second, if the hermeneutics of suspicion that is being applied by women is leading to healthier understanding of biblical texts, what then should one do with the theological notion of biblical inerrancy that has sometimes been used to defend such oppressive structures? I conclude that all biblical texts should be read within the broader historical and cultural contexts from which they originate. This means that when problematic texts that silence the voices of women are being read, they ought to be read as texts that evoke "dangerous memories." They must not be glossed over. As M. Shawn Copeland rightly points out, "once the humanity and realities of poor women, particularly poor women of color, are moved to the foreground, a new question orients Christian reflection on anthropology: What might it mean for poor women of color to grasp themselves as human subjects, to grapple with the meaning of liberation and freedom? This new anthropological question seeks to understand and articulate authentic meanings of human flourishing and liberation, progress and salvation."[54] This realization ought to lead women to bring their own questions and not the questions of the power holders to the texts. In other words, the existential concerns of women are a legitimate starting place for doing biblical exegesis. The Bible, as the Word of God, ought to speak to us where we are in our lives and not speak to issues that have no bearing on our social locations. Furthermore, the Bible is both the Word of God and the work of a people living in a particular era with their sociocultural and political agenda. To deny these is to make the Bible a compendium of "The Satanic Verses," if I may use the title of Salmon Rushdie's 1988 novel.

Third, do human experiences have any role to play in defining human dignity? I conclude that the mere fact that God became human and lived amongst us legitimizes the claim that to speak of our human dignity, we must also explore how our experiences define how we come to understand ourselves. The incarnate Christ realized his humanity not as a moment but as a process through time. Thus, existence has primacy over essence. Furthermore, any discourse on the reclaiming of the dignity of women, especially women of color, must not be limited to the text. As rightly pointed out by Tamura Lomax in her insights on womanists' fetishization of texts written by Black women, "black women and girls simultaneously live outside of texts. Though they are textualized and often texts themselves, they are living, breathing, and walking subjects with complex lives, much of which has yet to be recorded."[55] In the United States, Lomax's claim is valid when she concludes that some Black women's lived experiences are "recorded via film, television, music, social media, iPhones, cameras, laptops, and other tools for our viewing."[56] But among the poor women of Africa and other parts of the global south, these lives can only be spoken of when one enters into a face-to-face encounter with them. Thus, the demand for an inclusive anthropology ought to lead theologians to always begin their discourse on the dignity of humans with the most marginalized, the "trice-silenced" ones amongst us. During my time working as a missionary in Nigeria, I met many women whose dignity as humans has been reduced to levels not even worthy of those of slaves. These women are married off at very young ages to much older men. Their plights are justified by appeals to religion and culture by the beneficiaries of such a dehumanizing system. These women labor every day just to be able to feed their families. They do not know what it means to have time for relaxation. When one encounters them, one sees persons who have only known the long nights of tears and sorrow. They lack the courage to tell their stories because religion and culture have been used to teach them that they are nobody. They live and die always in the shadows. They are the nameless ones whose experiences must necessarily be the starting place for speaking of theologies that affirm the dignity of humans as creatures who embody the "trace of the image of God." Their experiences ought to be accounted for and their conditions remedied. If these are not done, then the venture of theology is fruitless.

Fourth, is the dignity of humans as the image of God a given or something that unfolds over time? Let me engage Levinas as I attempt to address this question. Levinas writes:

> The God who passed by is not the model of which the face would be the image. To be in the image of God does not signify being the icon of God, but finding oneself in his trace. The revealed God of our Judeo-Christian Spirituality preserves all the infinity of his absence which is the personal 'order.' He shows himself only in his trace, as in chapter 33 of Exodus. Going toward him is not following this trace that is not a sign. It is going toward Others who stand in the trace of illeity. It is by that illeity, situated beyond the calculations and reciprocities of the economy of the world, that being has sense. Sense that is not a finality.[57]

Here, Levinas has turned the question on its head. For centuries, theologians simply understood Gen. 1:26 as referring to an ontological constitution of the human person. Question four of the *Penny Catechism* states: "Is this likeness to God in your body or in your soul?" The response is: This likeness to God is chiefly in my soul."[58] Question seven and its corresponding answer focused on a bias for the soul as the part of the human person that should be cared for. To buttress this point, a biblical text is cited (Matt. 16:26). These and lengthy theological and ecclesial traditions and spiritualities have been used to justify an understanding of ontology as the correct way to understand the biblical motif of *imago Dei*. Through the insights of Levinas, a different way of conceiving this is possible. Levinas speaks of one "finding oneself in his [God's] trace," which implies that it is always through a process of encounter that one finds oneself.

Furthermore, the human person, that is constituted in and through the humanity of Christ, the God-human, is a creature that is tasked with the ethical demand noted in the proclamation of Christ in the Johannine gospel: "I came so that they might have life and have it more abundantly" (Jn. 10:10). In other words, if Jesus Christ is the full expression of what it means to be the image of God, and he understands himself through his mission of being the medium of life for all, then humans cannot but understand their identity as the image of God only through the ethical commitment toward "others." By others, I am including the entire creation. The life of God that Christ mediates is not exclusive to humans. Rather, it is a gift given to all of creation. It is cosmocentric in its totality. With this understanding, when any woman or girl or anyone or thing has not experienced the fullness of life due to the structures of death that we have put in place to benefit the few, no one can truly speak of themselves as being the image of God. Again, being the image of God is what we become when we actively embrace that which constitutes the very core of our existence—caring for others.

CONCLUSION

No theology can exhaust Black women's visions of what it means to be human. This point is well stated by Isabel Apawo Phiri when she gives a response to the question, "Why theologies and not just theology?" In her words, "the word 'theologies' is used in its plural form because African women theologians want to acknowledge the fact that even within Africa, there is diversity of women's experiences due to differences in race, culture, politics, economy, and religions."[59] Just as Bakhtin speaks of "coexistence and interaction as the greatest strength of Dostoevsky's artistic capacity," so also it can be said that both womanist and African women theological views of the human is all about inclusivity.[60] Again, Phiri states it clearly, "despite the differences in terminology, all women would like to see the end of sexism in their lives and the establishment of a more just society of men and women who seek the well-being of the other."[61]

Black women's theological vision of the human insists on speaking of the embodied human. The temptation to want to speak ideally of ontological realities that are at best realities of the imagination must always be resisted. In fact, Black women's theologies arise from a refusal to be relegated to the realm of the mythical where unfounded notions have been given the power to dominate the lives of women by social structures put in place by those at the center of power, whether in the religious, social, cultural, political, or economic contexts. To speak of the human is to speak of the existential. To speak of the dignity of Black women as persons made in the image of God is to give voice also to "the bodies that suffer" in Asia, the Americas, Africa, Europe, and everywhere where people have been erased from the tapestry of history. In Africa, Asia, the Americas, and Europe, many of these are women, especially women of color. The solutions to these histories and memories of subjugation must begin with an embrace of the "hermeneutical subjects or bodies for these are bodies that resist. In breaking the silence on sexuality, these hermeneutical bodies [of women] generate new ways of seeing that are grounded, specific, and critical."[62] The demand for inclusivity is not the monopoly of Black women theologians. Walker's definition of womanist states that a womanist is "a woman who loves other women, sexually and/or nonsexually."[63] African women theologies are loudly silent on the issues dealing with sexuality outside of the boundaries of heterosexuality. Butler's insight must not be forgotten if oppressive structures are to be overcome. In her words, "to counter oppression requires that one understand that lives are supported and maintained differentially, that there are radically different ways in which human physical vulnerability is distributed across the globe."[64] Douglas speaks of "a spirituality of resistance" as the vital force that continues to be passed on by Black women to their children.[65] I conclude this chapter by stating that this "spirituality of resistance" ought to be inclusive of all persons. It ought to give voice to all women who are oppressed, whether heterosexual, homosexual, White, Black, Latina, Asian, rich, poor, able-bodied, handicapped, educated formally or informally, old, young, and whatever characteristics may define their lives. This is what it means to speak of being made in God's image. Or better put, being made in the image of Christ who takes on the identity of being Black and womanish!

NOTES

1. Judith Butler, *Undoing Gender* (London and New York: Routledge, 2004), 29.
2. Ibid.
3. Gwashi Freddy Manavhela, "An Analysis of the Theological Justification of Apartheid in South Africa: A Reformed Theological Perspective" (PhD diss., Vrije Universiteit, 2009), 56.
4. Ibid.
5. Emmanuel Levinas, *Humanism of the Other*, trans. Nidra Poller (Urbana and Chicago: University of Illinois Press, 2003), 44.
6. Bruce Lincoln, "The Religious Significance of Women's Scarification among the Tiv," *Africa: Journal of the International African Institute*, vol. 45, no. 3 (1975): 316. See also, SimonMary A. Aihiokhai, "The Place of Women in the Catholic Church of Africa: Using Inculturation as a Model for Inclusion of Women in the Ministerial Life of the Church," in *Theological Reimagination: Conversions on Church, Religion, and Society*, ed. Agbonkhianmeghe E. Orobator (Nairobi, Kenya: Paulines Publishers Africa, 2014), 263.
7. Aihiokhai, "The Place of Women in the Catholic Church of Africa," 263. Lincoln, "The Religious Significance of Women's Sacrifice among the Tiv," 325.
8. Ifi Amadiume, *Male Daughters, Female Husbands: Gender and Sex in an African Society* (London: Zed Books, 1987), 8.

9. Teresia Mbari Hinga, *African, Christian, Feminist: The Enduring Search for What Matters* (Maryknoll, NY: Orbis Books, 2017), 5.

10. Rosemary Radford Ruether, "Black Women and Feminism: The U.S. and South African Contexts," in *A Black Theology of Liberation. Twentieth Anniversary Edition*, ed. James H. Cone (Maryknoll, NY: Orbis Books, 1990), 175.

11. See Renita J. Weems, "Reading *Her Way* through The Struggle: African American and The Bible," in *Stony The Road We Trod: African American Biblical Interpretation*, ed. Cain Hope Felder (Minneapolis, MN: Augsburg Press, 1991), 57–78.

12. Jean-Luc Marion, *In Excess. Studies of Saturated Phenomena*, trans. Robyn Horner and Vincent Berraud (New York: Fordham University Press, 2002), 86–87.

13. Emmanuel Levinas, *Alterity & Transcendence*, trans. Michael B. Smith (New York: Columbia University Press, 1999), 97.

14. Levinas, *Humanism of the Other*, 64.

15. Ibid., 132.

16. Molefi Kete Asante, *The Afrocentric Idea. Revised and Expanded Edition* (Philadelphia: Temple University Press, 1998), 160.

17. Ibid.

18. Ibid., 161.

19. Ibid., 179–180.

20. Homi K. Bhabha, *The Location of Culture* (London and New York: Routledge, 1994), 59–60.

21. Asante, *The Afrocentric Idea*, 181.

22. Ibid., 202.

23. Ibid., 202–203.

24. Ibid., 203.

25. Bénézet Bujo, *Foundations of An African Ethic. Beyond the Universal Claims of Western Morality*, trans. Brian McNeil (New York: The Crossroad Publishing Company, 2001), 124.

26. Bénézet Bujo, *The Ethical Dimension of Community. The African Model and The Dialogue between North and South* (Nairobi, Kenya: Paulines Publications Africa, 1997), 15–16.

27. See Mercy Amba Oduyoye, *Daughters of Anowa: African Women and Patriarchy* (Maryknoll, NY: Orbis Books, 1995).

28. Musimbi R. A. Kanyoro, "Engendered Communal Theology: African Women's Contribution to Theology in the Twenty-first Century," in *Hope Abundant. Third World and Indigenous Women's Theology*, ed. Kwok Pui-lan (Maryknoll, NY: Orbis Books, 2010), 21.

29. Hinga, *African, Christian, Feminist*, xiii–xxv.

30. See Chimamanda Ngozi Adichie, *Purple Hibiscus* (Chapel Hill, NC: Algonquin Books, 2003).

31. See Chinua Achebe, *Things Fall Apart* (London: William Heinemann Ltd., 1958).

32. See NoViolet Bulawayo, *We Need New Names* (New York: Litle, Brown and Company, 2013).

33. Margaret Busby, "We Need New Names by NoViolet Bulawayo," The *Independent*, June 7, 2013, https://www.independent.co.uk/arts-entertainment/books/reviews/we-need-new-names-by-noviolet-bulawayo-8647510.html.

34. See Haregewoin Cherinet, *Women and Donkeys in Ethiopia: Gender and Christian Perspective* (Addis Ababa, 2015).

35. See Petina Gappah, *An Elegy for Easterly* (New York: Farrar, Straus and Giroux, 2009).

36. Michael Battle, *Ubuntu: I in You and You in Me* (New York: Seabury Books, 2009), 1.

37. Ibid., 125.

38. Ibid., 3.

39. Hinga, *African, Christian, Feminist*, 15–16.

40. Kelly Brown Douglas, *The Black Christ* (Maryknoll, NY: Orbis Books, 1994), 92.

41. See Wilma Mankiller, et al., "Womanism," *The Reader's Companion to U.S. Women's History* (Oakland, NJ: Houghton Mifflin Company, 2013).

42. See Stacey M. Floyd-Thomas, ed., *Deeper Shades of Purple: Womanism in Religion and Society* (New York and London: New York University Press, 2006).

43. Patrick S. Cheng, *An Introduction to Queer Theology. Radical Love* (New York: Seabury Books, 2011), 6.

44. Judith Butler, *Gender Trouble: Feminism and the Subversion of Identity* (New York: Routledge, 1990), 13–14.

45. Nikki Sullivan, *A Critical Introduction to Queer Theory* (New York: New York University Press, 2003), 82.

46. See Caryl Emerson, "Editor's Preface," in Mikhail Bakhtin, *Problems of Dostoevsky's Poetics*, ed. and trans. Caryl Emerson (Minneapolis and London: University of Minnesota Press, 1984), xxxii.

47. Wayne C. Booth, "Introduction," in *Problems of Dostoevsky's Poetics*, xxi.

48. Butler, *Gender Trouble*, 33.

49. See Judith Butler, *Bodies That Matter: On the Discursive Limits of "Sex"* (London and New York: Routledge Classics, 2011), 184–185.

50. Amadiume, *Male Daughters, Female Husbands*, 15.

51. For a history of Western feminist thought on autonomy and individuality, see Elizabeth Beck-Gernsheim, "On the Way to a Post-Familial Family: From a Community of Need to Elective Affinities," *Theory, Culture and Society*, vol. 15, no. 3–4 (1998): 53–70.

52. Battle, *Ubuntu: I in You and You in Me*, 3.

53. Emmanuel Levinas, *Ethics and Infinity. Conversations with Philip Nemo*, trans. Richard A. Cohen (Pittsburgh: Duquesne University Press, 1985), 101.

54. M. Shawn Copeland, *Enfleshing Freedom: Body, Race, and Being* (Minneapolis, MN: Fortress Press, 2010), 88.

55. Tamura Lomax, *Jezebel Unhinged: Loosing the Black Female Body in Religion & Culture* (Durham and London: Duke University Press, 2018), 88.

56. Ibid., 88–89.

57. Levinas, *Humanism of the Other*, 44.

58. See *The Penny Catechism: A Catechism of the Christian Doctrine* (Charlotte, NC: TAN Books, 1982), 1.
59. Isabel Apawo Phiri, "HIV/AIDS: An African Theological Response in Mission," in *Hope Abundant. Third World and Indigenous Women's Theology*, 220.
60. Bakhtin, *Problems of Dostoevsky's Poetics*, 30.
61. Phiri, "HIV/AIDS," 220.
62. Sharon A. Bong, "The Suffering Christ and The Asian Body," in *Hope Abundant. Third World and Indigenous Women's Theology*, 189.
63. Alice Walker, *In Search of Our Mothers' Gardens: Womanist Prose* (New York: Harcourt Brace Jovanovich, Publishers, 1983), xi.
64. Butler, *Undoing Gender*, 24.
65. Douglas, *The Black Christ*, 105.

FURTHER READINGS

Anderson, Ray S. *On Being Human: Essays in Theological Anthropology*. Pasadena, CA: Fuller Seminary Press, 1982.
Arabome, Anne. "When a Sleeping Woman Wakes . . . A Conversation With Pope Francis in Evangelii Gaudium About the Feminization of Poverty." In *The Church We Want: African Catholics Look to Vatican III*, edited by Agbonkhianmeghe E. Orobator, 55–63. Maryknoll, NY: Orbis Books, 2016.
Cannon, Katie G. *Black Womanist Ethics*. Eugene, OR: Wipf and Stock Publishers, 2006.
Hodgson, Dorothy L. *The Church of Women: Gendered Encounters Between Maasai and Missionaries*. Bloomington and Indianapolis: Indiana University Press, 2005.
Potter, Elizabeth. "Gender and Epistemic Negotiation." In *Feminist Epistemologies*, edited by Linda Alcoff and Elizabeth Potter, 161–186. New York and London: Routledge, 1993.
Pui-lan, Kwok. *Postcolonial Imagination & Feminist Theology*. Louisville, KY: Westminster John Knox Press, 2005.
Saporta, José. "Changing the Subject by Addressing the Other: Mikhail Bakhtin and Psychoanalytic Therapy." In *The Ethical Turn: Otherness and Subjectivity in Contemporary Psychoanalysis*, edited by David M. Goodman and Eric R. Severson, 209–231. New York and London: Routledge, 2016.

REFERENCES

Achebe, Chinua. *Things Fall Apart*. London: William Heinemann Ltd., 1958.
Adichie, Chimamanda Ngozi. *Purple Hibiscus*. Chapel Hill, NC: Algonquin Books, 2003.
Aihiokhai, SimonMary A. "The Place of Women in the Catholic Church of Africa: Using Inculturation as a Model for Inclusion of Women in the Ministerial Life of the Church." In *Theological Reimagination: Conversions on Church, Religion,*

and Society, edited by Agbonkhianmeghe E. Orobator, 256–268. Nairobi, Kenya: Paulines Publishers Africa, 2014.

Amadiume, Ifi. *Male Daughters, Female Husbands: Gender and Sex in an African Society*. London: Zed Books, 1987.

Asante, Molefi Kete. *The Afrocentric Idea: Revised and Expanded Edition*. Philadelphia: Temple University Press, 1998.

Battle, Michael. *Ubuntu: I in You and You in Me*. New York: Seabury Books, 2009.

Beck-Gernsheim, Elizabeth. "On the Way to a Post-Familial Family: From a Community of Need to Elective Affinities." *Theory, Culture and Society* 15, nos. 3–4 (1998): 53–70.

Bhabha, Homi K. *The Location of Culture*. London and New York: Routledge, 1994.

Bong, Sharon A. "The Suffering Christ and the Asian Body. Phiri, Isabel Apawo. HIV/AIDS: An African Theological Response in Mission." In *Hope Abundant: Third World and Indigenous Women's Theology*, edited by Kwok Pui-lan, 186–193. Maryknoll, NY: Orbis Books, 2010.

Booth, Wayne C. "Introduction." In *Mikhail Bakhtin, Problems of Dostoevsky's Poetics*, edited and translated by Caryl Emerson, xiii–xxvii. Minneapolis and London: University of Minnesota Press, 1984.

Bujo, Bénézet. *Foundations of an African Ethic: Beyond the Universal Claims of Western Morality*. Translated by Brian McNeil. New York: The Crossroad Publishing Company, 2001.

———. *The Ethical Dimension of Community: The African Model and the Dialogue Between North and South*. Nairobi, Kenya: Paulines Publications Africa, 1997.

Bulawayo, NoViolet. *We Need New Names*. New York: Litle, Brown and Company, 2013.

Busby, Margaret. "We Need New Names by NoViolet Bulawayo." *The Independent*, June 7, 2013. https://www.independent.co.uk/arts-entertainment/books/reviews/we-need-new-names-by-noviolet-bulawayo-8647510.html.

Butler, Judith. *Bodies That Matter: On the Discursive Limits of "Sex."* London and New York: Routledge Classics, 2011.

———. *Gender Trouble: Feminism and the Subversion of Identity*. New York: Routledge, 1990.

———. *Undoing Gender*. London and New York: Routledge, 2004.

Cheng, Patrick S. *An Introduction to Queer Theology: Radical Love*. New York: Seabury Books, 2011.

Cherinet, Haregewoin. *Women and Donkeys in Ethiopia: Gender and Christian Perspective*. Addis Ababa, 2015.

Copeland, M. Shawn. *Enfleshing Freedom: Body, Race, and Being*. Minneapolis, MN: Fortress Press, 2010.

Douglas, Kelly Brown. *The Black Christ*. Maryknoll, NY: Orbis Books, 1994.

Emerson, Caryl. "Editor's Preface." In *Mikhail Bakhtin, Problems of Dostoevsky's Poetics*, edited and translated by Caryl Emerson, xxix–xliii. Minneapolis and London: University of Minnesota Press, 1984.

Floyd-Thomas, Stacey M., ed. *Deeper Shades of Purple: Womanism in Religion and Society*. New York and London: New York University Press, 2006.

Gappah, Petina. *An Elegy for Easterly*. New York: Farrar, Straus and Giroux, 2009.

Hinga, Teresia Mbari. *African, Christian, Feminist: The Enduring Search for What Matters*. Maryknoll, NY: Orbis Books, 2017.

Kanyoro, Musimbi R. A. "Engendered Communal Theology: African Women's Contribution to Theology in the Twenty-First Century." In *Hope Abundant: Third World and Indigenous Women's Theology*, edited by Kwok Pui-lan, 19–35. Maryknoll, NY: Orbis Books, 2010.

Levinas, Emmanuel. *Alterity & Transcendence*. Translated by Michael B. Smith. New York: Columbia University Press, 1999.

———. *Ethics and Infinity: Conversations With Philip Nemo*. Translated by Richard A. Cohen. Pittsburgh: Duquesne University Press, 1985.

———. *Humanism of the Other*. Translated by Nidra Poller. Urbana and Chicago: University of Illinois Press, 2003.

Lincoln, Bruce. "The Religious Significance of Women's Scarification Among the Tiv." *Africa: Journal of the International African Institute* 45, no. 3 (1975): 316–326.

Lomax, Tamura. *Jezebel Unhinged: Loosing the Black Female Body in Religion & Culture*. Durham and London: Duke University Press, 2018.

Manavhela, Gwashi Freddy. *An Analysis of the Theological Justification of Apartheid in South Africa: A Reformed Theological Perspective*. PhD Dissertation, Vrije Universiteit, 2009.

Mankiller, Wilma. *The Reader's Companion to U.S. Women's History*. Oakland, NJ: Houghton Mifflin Company, 2013.

Marion, Jean-Luc. *In Excess: Studies of Saturated Phenomena*. Translated by Robyn Horner and Vincent Berraud. New York: Fordham University Press, 2002.

Oduyoye, Mercy Amba. *Daughters of Anowa: African Women and Patriarchy*. Maryknoll, NY: Orbis Books, 1995.

Phiri, Isabel Apawo. "HIV/AIDS: An African Theological Response in Mission." In *Hope Abundant: Third World and Indigenous Women's Theology*, edited by Kwok Pui-lan, 219–228. Maryknoll, NY: Orbis Books, 2010.

Ruether, Rosemary Radford. "Black Women and Feminism: The U.S. and South African Contexts." In *A Black Theology of Liberation: Twentieth Anniversary Edition*, edited by James H. Cone, 174–184. Maryknoll, NY: Orbis Books, 1990.

Sullivan, Nikki. *A Critical Introduction to Queer Theory*. New York: New York University Press, 2003.

The Penny Catechism: A Catechism of the Christian Doctrine. Charlotte, NC: TAN Books, 1982.

Walker, Alice. *In Search of Our Mothers' Gardens: Womanist Prose*. New York: Harcourt Brace Jovanovich Publishers, 1983.

Weems, Renita J. "Reading *Her Way* Through the Struggle: African American and the Bible." In *Stony the Road We Trod: African American Biblical Interpretation*, edited by Cain Hope Felder, 57–78. Minneapolis, MN: Augsburg Press, 1991.

Chapter 10

Religion, African American Women, and the Suffrage Movement

The Journey to Holistic Freedom

Kathleen Dorsey Bellow

The centennial anniversary festivities, media specials, and retrospectives that marked the 2020 celebration of women's suffrage in the United States give the impression that the 100-plus-year struggle to win the vote was actually won with the 1920 ratification of the Nineteenth Amendment. Today, record-breaking numbers of U.S. female officeholders representing diverse backgrounds, perspectives, and experiences have grabbed the baton passed on from previous generations. They boldly jumped the conventional hurdles to run for and win local, state, and national elections and in so doing, managed, some against incredible odds, to cross a finish line in the struggle for equal voting rights.[1]

However, while cheers go out for these individual victories, many hard-fought and meaningful community wins, there are many more miles to run before women suffrage is secured in the United States. The suffragist run up to 1920 demanded monumental struggles, strategy, and collaboration by women to finally validate the Nineteenth Constitutional Amendment and win the opportunity for enfranchisement for all women. Despite historic efforts, the opportunity has yet to be fully realized. A general scan of 2021 news reports on U.S. electoral politics by the author reveals continuing challenges to women's rights and responsibility to vote. For example, there exist multiple inconsistencies between local, state, and national electoral policies, laws, and regulations, including those governing voter qualifications and registration, poll locations, and ballot access. Additionally, the tremendous costs—economic and personal—of running for office, disproportionately deny the voting rights of people of color and the poor, many of whom are women and their children.

For historical clarity, it makes sense to review the celebrated suffrage movements of the nineteenth and early twentieth centuries in order to chart a potential twenty-first-century course forward. However, careful reading of the record confirms that although the push for voting rights for women grew out of anti-slavery activism, support for Black enfranchisement throughout the movement, was unreliable at best. Few White suffragists maintained more than a passing solidarity with African American women in their fight for social equality that began during enslavement and endures until today. There is an anti-black bias in the "official" record. In all but the most recent and local histories of the suffrage movement, Black women are virtually invisible despite their active engagements at the national, regional, and community levels. Despite great hardships and challenges, their remarkable examples of moral and civic leadership are largely ignored.

The contemporary season of celebrating the passage of the Nineteenth Amendment for Women's Suffrage presents a salient opportunity to assess the nation's continuing advancement toward universal suffrage by highlighting the valiant efforts of pioneering African American political activists. They carried the baton from the beginning, through some perilous laps of the race to make the United States a more perfect union, more of a democracy that works for all the people. When Black women could not vote, they lobbied, campaigned, volunteered, lectured, raised funds, wrote, reported, created art, and testified on behalf of the cause. Their contributions made a way for those yet to come, the generations that will see the race through to its authentic conclusion.

This work asserts that African American women, empowered by God with gifts of Black culture and faith are responsible in large measure for the progress of the suffrage movement in the United States from its anti-slavery beginnings through its current ongoing phase. This work unfolds with (1) a portrayal through the lens of Black culture and religion of the Black heritage with which African American women have been blessed, a shared legacy that inspires their continued engagement and leadership in a society that aggressively challenges the rights of Blacks to full citizenship; (2) the philosophical idea of the United States as a democratic government and the response of Black suffragists' involvement in the passage of the Nineteenth Amendment, demanding the lofty promises of liberty and justice for all; and (3) with the hidden legacy of African American participation in the suffrage movement in clearer historic view, the conclusion will outline a strategic path forward toward the U.S. ideal and the mission of African American suffragists—electoral freedom for all.

THE HERITAGE OF BLACK WOMEN IN SERVICE TO VOTING RIGHTS

if we only look for African American woman suffragists in organizations put together by white American women, we're going to be disappointed in the sense that their numbers will be small—or, in the example of Seneca Falls, non-existent. At the same time, if we follow African-American women to where they are and listen to what they have to say and watch what they do, turns out they are as interested in political power and the problem of sexism as any community of American women—but they're doing that work on their own terms.[2]

In this assertion offered in an August 2020 *Time Magazine* interview, Martha S. Jones emphasizes the importance of cultural context in examining history. Every people that comprises society has a particular culture, whether or not it is taken into official account. Culture which refers to the comprehensive way that a people or community organizes itself to manage, master, and make sense of life is complex. Human cultures are constituted of core elements such as beliefs, worldviews, values, ways of relating, affective patterns, codes of behavior, experiences, symbols, and spirituality. The material aspects of culture, generally referred to as "the arts"—for example, music, cuisine, dance, dress, literature, architecture, fashion, and rituals—are not culture itself; these reflect the aforementioned constitutive elements of culture.[3] African American cultures are generally "an admixture of the prevailing worldview, normative assumptions, and conceptual frame of reference of West African cultures which have developed in reaction to, and in cooperation with, the prevailing worldview, normative assumptions, and conceptual frame of reference of America's dominant culture."[4] In other words, Black Americans are Africans living in America—African Americans.

Attuned to African American cultures, Jones and other contemporary historians, theologians, and artists have explored the hidden record of history to learn how African women organized themselves to make sense of life in the United States. Their revised narratives of the U.S. suffrage movement lift up the remarkable contributions of many unheralded Black women activists as they bring into more accurate focus the particular situation of the African American community in the national struggle for women's rights.[5]

THE RELIGIOUS HERITAGE OF BLACK SUFFRAGISTS AND THE COMMUNITY

Africa is an ancient land, a vast continent covered by very different geographies and climates. In terms of land mass and population, it is second only to Asia. The African population is remarkably diverse in culture, language, and faith traditions. Colonialism has made its mark throughout the continent. Despite the depth and breadth of diversity that is Africa, indigenous scholars attribute common and enduring cultural features, including spiritualities, beliefs, customs, and values to African life on the continent and in the diaspora. In the *Spirituality of African Peoples: The Search for a Common Moral Discourse*, theologian Peter Paris highlights shared "features implicit in the traditional worldviews of African peoples as foundational for an African and African American moral philosophy."[6] Primary among them is the reality that "religion permeates every dimension of African life. In spite of their many and varied religious systems the ubiquity of religious consciousness among African peoples constitutes their single most important common characteristic."[7] Paris further argues that, "contrary to the opinions of most of their predecessors, contemporary scholars of African religion generally agree that all peoples throughout the continent believe in a self-existent supreme deity who...constitutes the primary cohesive power in every African cosmology: the power that unites the realms of nature, history and spirit."[8] One's ethnic or tribal community is the "paramount social reality apart from which humanity cannot exist. Similarly, all agree that the community is a sacred phenomenon created by the supreme God, protected by the divinities, and governed by the ancestral spirits. Thus, full participation in the community is a fundamental requirement of all humans."[9] Paris states: "the destiny of each person affects the well-being of the whole community, for better or worse. Thus, nothing is taken more seriously by African communities than the moral nurture and guidance of children, who belong to the whole community. The community is teacher, parent, guardian, advocate, legislator of all."[10] Paris makes explicit foundational traditions of African religion that continue as cultural expressions in African and African American communities, adapted to the particular times, situations, and understandings of Black peoples throughout the world. African American suffragists may have lived generations away from a physical connection with the Motherland, yet they embodied the religious-cultural beliefs of their ancestors and employed them to manage, master, and make sense of life—demanding, troubling, bewildering, and mean as it was—in the United States.

THE BLACK SPIRIT OF GOD EMBODIED IN BLACK WOMEN

Enslaved Black women were especially important in the retention and passing down of Black culture. Both womanist and Black feminist scholars use the phrase *bearers of culture* to depict the role they played in their communities. They taught much needed skills and also preserved African traditions of song, and story, thereby helping to develop, nurture and perpetuate the emerging Black community during slavery and after. They also knew how to bide their time and "hunker down" until a better time for action arose rather than risk lives in a futile gesture of rebellion. For Black women, liberation was not the only goal, nor was it the most important goal. These women recognized their need to survive as the most important factor and then their need to have a reasonable quality of life while still enslaved so that they and their families could indeed survive until freedom was theirs.[11]

African American suffragists, from the iconic Sojourner Truth—abolitionist and preacher of the nineteenth century—to the contemporary Stacy Abrams—politician and author from the state of Georgia—have brought the timeless resources of African heritage to bear on the U.S. political system to build Black community and engage others of good faith in the fight for the rights of the disenfranchised. The Judeo-Christian traditions of the nation gradually exemplified in the Black Church, have been inculturated by African religious traditions, and African American life experiences. For example, as Black women became familiar with the Word, relating Scripture to real life,

> ... they invoked the Bible as the moral basis upon which they argued the absurdity of their subordination. Moreover, they underscored their humanity and their subjectivity vis-à-vis their statuses as God's children, and did so to inscribe themselves into the body politic as subjects, to affirm their access to God's promises (which included civil rights), to situate their political concerns as valid and worthy of address, and to explore the daily survival tactics they employed to negotiate a world that was simultaneously racist and sexist.[12]

Black faith and Black culture empowered the self-determination of African American women and their people.

In each generation, African American suffragists strategized to win the vote relying on the providence of God, recalling the examples and tactics of those in the struggle before them and demanding the people's active participation in the life of the community to bring about change. Black women undertook the liberating role of "bearers of culture" to form themselves and the entire community in the quest for the full and free citizenship of all African Americans. Theirs was collective work and responsibility toward establishing, for a stubbornly White supremacist nation, the humanity and agency of God's beloved Black people made in the divine image and likeness.

THE DEMOCRATIC IDEAL AND THE SUFFRAGIST STRUGGLE

"Life, Liberty and the pursuit of Happiness" did not apply to fully one-fifth of the country. Yet despite being violently denied freedom and justice promised to all, black Americans believed fervently in the American creed. Through centuries of black resistance and protests, we have helped the country live up to its founding ideals. And not only for ourselves—black rights paved the way for every other rights struggle, including women's and gay rights, immigrant and disability rights. Without the idealistic, strenuous and patriotic efforts of black Americans, our democracy today would most likely look very different—it might not be a democracy at all.[13]

In the ideal world, democracy is a style of government in which the people rule by choosing in free, regular, and fair elections, representatives to govern on their behalf. Those elected officials are expected to be accountable to the people, to work toward the promises made during their run for office, and to act and make decisions and policies that ensure the participation of the citizenry in the development of their respective communities. The authors of "Voting Counts: Participation in the Measurement of Democracy" maintain that "ancient and modern philosophers have struggled to describe the democratic 'ideal', a governance system in which every citizen participates in the political process that shapes society's fate and through it, his or her own."[14] Their international analysis demonstrates the extent to which all adults, regardless of gender, have equal access to the ballot box is an inarguably decisive indicator of democratization. Broad participation by the people results in a political system that effectively attends to democracy's highest goals—social justice and equality that apply across boundaries of class, gender, and ethnicity. The research suggests that when high percentages of the community independently and regularly exercise their right to vote, the electorate fashions for itself a government that provides for basic human needs, serves the common good, and contributes to the self-actualization of the individual citizen, specifically her/his freedom, independence, and agency. In the process, gender equality is achieved.[15]

Although the founders of the United States were not privy to the insight of the previously cited research, they expressed similarly high ideals in documents that established the new nation. The 1776 Declaration of Independence upholds the undeniable equality of persons who have rights endowed by the Creator, including life, liberty, and the pursuit of happiness. The Constitution of the United States, ratified in 1789, prescribes how the government is to be structured and operated. Its preamble pronounces: "We the People of the United States, in Order to form a more perfect Union, establish Justice, ensure domestic Tranquility, provide for the common defense, promote the general Welfare, and secure the Blessings of Liberty to ourselves and our Posterity, do ordain and establish this Constitution for the United States of America." In their rhetoric, the Founding Fathers intellectually appreciated the noble nature of democratic rule and championed representative government as they laid the groundwork for the hybrid political system that is generally recognized today as a democratic republic.

Their practice of leadership, rooted in the culture of their times, however, produced a socially discriminating and oppressive effect by centering governing power in their own hands and those recognized as their posterity. For as long as they could, White men preserved the benefits of the democratically guaranteed franchise for their kind: literate, land-owning, financially endowed European American males. By the 1830s, for reasons philosophical and expedient, most states had extended the vote to all White men regardless of socioeconomic standing. Voting was categorized as a gender-specific right, disenfranchising the few women and free Blacks who had access to the ballot in some American colonies.

If voting rights, liberty, and participation in government were considered the prerogative of White male citizens, there was resistance to (1) the wretched legacy of slavery; (2) societal ills that were the side-effect of the nation's industrial growth; and (3) the sheer willpower of U.S. patriots. These forces activated segments of the disenfranchised population who took the country's fundamental issues of democracy, liberation, and participation to heart. Free Blacks living in northern cities as well as enslaved persons in the South built in their respective communities, mutual aid societies that buried the dead, cared for the needy, and tended the sick. Beginning in 1830, activists met regularly in "colored" conventions held in northeastern cities to deliberate the pressing political issues of the day. The abolition of slavery was uppermost on the agendas of these gatherings that were attended by "colored" and white conventioneers of both genders. Reform organizations—temperance leagues, religious crusades, and morality groups—also proliferated during the 1820s and 1830s; many of these depended on the leadership of Black women, although the particular issues and organizational skills that they brought to the table were not highly appreciated.[16]

In 1848, male and female abolitionists convened in Seneca Falls, New York where they asserted in wording from the U.S. Declaration of Independence, the equal rights of women, including the right to the ballot. During the following decade, a national women's rights movement was born and gradually included prominent Black suffragists who among them had resolute histories of promoting universal suffrage. Although faced with steady opposition from men and women, suffragists tenaciously sought enfranchisement believing that access to the ballot would finally grant women full U.S. citizenship, equal rights, and the political power to reform society. Among the many social issues of nationwide concern was the lack of economic and educational opportunities for women, political corruption, intemperance, consumer abuses, and rampant crime. The emancipation of millions of enslaved Africans in the United States was not a universal aim of suffrage campaigns.[17]

The Civil War between the North and the South (1861–1865) interrupted the momentum of the suffrage movement and in the years after the war, the ongoing calculation of the country's northern dominant class—White, male, and rich—to preserve political power for themselves, and those most like them, played out. In the aftermath of the Civil War, when the Confederacy was dissolved and the southern states readmitted to the Union, Congress passed the Thirteenth, Fourteenth, and Fifteenth Amendments to the Constitution to respectively abolish slavery (1865), grant citizenship to all U.S. men born or naturalized, including the enslaved (1868), and prevent states from withholding the right to vote to citizens on the basis of race (1870).

During post-war Reconstruction (1863–1877), these new laws temporarily shifted Southern politics to include the formerly enslaved. With the new opportunity, Black leadership, male and female, flourished. Public education systems were formed and Black colleges were founded across the country. Some few African American men were able to vote, run for office, govern, legislate, and shape policy at federal, state, and local levels. African American women influenced political systems from every vantage point possible to uplift and make a way for the four million newly freed Black people. Reconstruction was an invigorating taste of freedom for the Black community; the almost immediate rollback of Reconstruction progress was yet another dehumanizing devastation. White supremacy and anti-blackness in the South fueled the rampant violence of the political, civil, and social backlash, emboldened by the withdrawal of northern U.S. troops assigned after the war to protect the formerly enslaved population. The systematic lynching of African American males and wanton sexual violence against African American females, most perpetrated in southern states, were intended to humiliate and subordinate the Black community. "Between 1882 and 1968, 4,743 lynchings were recorded, including that of fifty African American women victims, between 1889 and 1918."[18] State and local governments arrogantly violated Black federally guaranteed rights. The right to vote was effectively nullified by the enforcement of state and local poll taxes, literacy tests, and Jim Crow laws. Violence and other means of intimidation moderated, but did not subdue the militancy, advocacy, and political action aspirations of Black Americans after Reconstruction.

On the women's suffrage scene, the campaign to pass the Fifteenth Amendment in 1870 effectively neutralized the already tenuous mixed-gender, cross-cultural coalitions of the early women's rights movement in the United States. The issue of universal enfranchisement for men was the deal breaker for suffragists who could not abide the idea of Black men gaining the vote before White women. Black women in general would not sacrifice the promised representation of their community through the enfranchisement of their men by demanding that women go first. Here, at the critical intersection of gender and race, the suffrage movement fractured.

The break would prove to be fatal. "African American women were in a difficult position. Sometimes they worked in their own clubs and suffrage organizations, sometimes with White suffragists. Black women did not accept their exclusion from White suffrage organizations or the racist tactics employed by White suffragists. In the twentieth century, more and more Black women joined the ranks of suffragists as the movement progressed."[19] However, once the Nineteenth Amendment had been ratified in 1920 and the ballot secured for their own, White suffragists dropped out of the race for universal enfranchisement in favor of other political issues of the day. Abandoned, Black allies in the movement were quickly disenfranchised in the face of state and local Jim Crow laws and public terror authorized by White supremacist southern governments. In Black communities, White supremacy severely limited the potential of the Nineteenth Amendment until the Civil Rights Movement of the mid-twentieth century prevailed. From the margins, African American women continued to push through social challenges presented by the system to progress their people and demand that the nation live up to its promise. As it turned out, universal suffrage and freedom in the context of life in the United States represent profoundly different realities for White and Black women.

THE BLACK SUFFRAGIST JOURNEY: INSPIRATION AND STRATEGY FOR A RELUCTANT NATION

> An authentic faith—which is never comfortable or completely personal—always involves a deep desire to change the world, to transmit values, to leave this earth somehow better than we found it. We love this magnificent planet on which God has put us, and we love the human family which dwells here, with all its tragedies and struggles, its hope and aspirations, its strengths and weaknesses.[20]

Pope Francis' quote from his 2013 *The Joy of the Gospel: Evangelii Gaudium* is a universal wisdom that speaks in this setting to the investment of faith and culture that Black suffragists made in the early campaign for women's rights and affirms the ongoing commitment of present-day Black voting rights advocates to secure universal enfranchisement in the United States. In their respective eras, fidelity to God and country and the uplift of their people have motivated Black women activists to keep on struggling, strategizing, and collaborating in the firm belief that God justifies their efforts to hold the nation to the constitutional promise made to its people. In their spirit of perseverance—suffragist self-determination—a strategy for moving forward begins to take shape.

The strategy involves truth-telling. The revisionist narratives of the suffrage movement uncover the historical contributions of many unheralded Black women's rights activists and bring into more accurate perspective the particular inspirations and situations of the various participant groups involved in the struggle. In their rigorously researched telling of this national story, a community of notables is lifted up, including Fannie Lou Hamer, the founders of the 100 Black Women Clubs, Diane Nash, and Maggie Lena Walker whose remarkable examples of moral and civic leadership have meaning for all contemporary Americans and deserve a rightful place in the legacy of the U.S. suffrage and larger civil rights movements.

Besides lifting up hidden heroines, recent research into the true history of the women suffrage movement sets the record straight, revealing that anti-black racism, expressed in attitudes and behaviors of dismissal, betrayal, and denigration was present from its beginnings. The failure of White suffragist solidarity nearly obliterated the hope of Black suffragists to liberate themselves and their community through the power of the vote. It lives. The truth of the matter is that, in the process, White suffragists failed to achieve their own aspirations of equal rights for U.S. women; the fracture of the suffrage movement in the early twentieth century has delimited the progress of the feminist movement even until today.

In its examination of the 2020 Biden election, the *Pew Report* reiterates a stark disunity between Black and White women voters. During the two last national elections, significant numbers of White women backed Donald J. Trump for president of the United States while 9 out of 10 African American female voters in 2016 and 2020 voted against the candidate who flaunted misogyny, White supremacy, and xenophobia in his private life and public policy for all to see. In 2016, White women voters threw significant weight against a powerful, White female candidate for the office of U.S. President: Hillary Clinton. In 2020 (the hundredth anniversary of the U.S. suffrage movement), White women voted by an even larger percentage for Trump, rejecting a formidable woman of color, Kamala Harris, who ran for Vice-President alongside Joe Biden who nevertheless was elected President of the United States.[21]

It appears that enough of the generational daughters of White suffragists typically vote to maintain the status quo agenda of the Republican Party. There they enjoy the privileges of whiteness despite the fact that many White women grievously suffer discrimination based on sexism and economic injustice.[22] When it comes to electoral politics, the sisterhood between Black and White voters remains tenuous, at best. Although alliances exist, a general lack of will yields to gerrymandering and legislative efforts to purge voter rolls, restrict voting registration, and suppress the vote in targeted neighborhoods.

The way forward to universal suffrage remains full of the same human obstacles that short-circuited the nineteenth- and twentieth-century efforts to enfranchise women in the United States.

The strategy to bring about universal voting rights, to realize the national value of "one person, one vote"—equal representation in the electoral process—demands an understanding of human cultures and a regard for cultural diversity in the life of the United States.

Black culture and Black faith feature prominently in the tenacious commitment of Black suffragists to liberate their people and, in so doing, contribute to the advancement of the oppressor class. The persistence of African peoples, so despised and feared, in their allegiance to the American experiment calls the nation to collective, critical thought on culture, self-identity, community-identity, and national identity. Considered the underdog in most societal situations, including the fight for enfranchisement, African American women continue to tackle the prevalent socioeconomic factors—race, gender, and class—that are stubbornly embedded deep in U.S. cultures, systems, and social capital.

Black women are neither paragons nor superwomen but they have managed to self-actualize within institutional structures designed to accommodate the needs, temperaments, and leadership styles of the most independent, privileged, and well-resourced members of society. They survive and thrive on what some describe as "Black Girl Magic" but, at its core, is the supernatural combination of Black culture, Black community, and Black faith.

In truth, there is no magic strategy to make our nation live up to its promise before God. African American suffragists have brought along their own community and dragged the country at large toward the original democratic ideal of universal suffrage. Throughout the course of the country's development, Black women have battled in the midst of terrible injustice to see just how power works in the United States. Like other marginalized peoples, they have fought against the meanest of odds to participate fully in U.S. civic life—to register to vote, gain access to the ballot, run for office, and elect candidates who look like them to govern with equity. From the past right up to the very present, African American women fearlessly champion their own liberation and, in so doing, bring along the rest of the community.

NOTES

1. Rutgers Eagleton Institute of Politics. "Women in Elective Office 2020," *Center for American Women and Politics*, https://cawp.rutgers.edu/women-elective-office-2020.

2. Olivia B. Waxman, "'It's a Struggle They Will Wage Alone.' How Black Women Won the Right to Vote." https://time.com/5876456/black-women-right-to-vote/.

3. Eva M. Lumas, "The Nature and Goals of Africentric Catholic Catechesis," in *God Bless Them Who Have Their Own: African American Catechetical Camp Meetin': A Gathering to Chart a New Course*, ed. Therese Wilson Favors (Washington, DC: Dept. of Education, United States Catholic Conference, 1995), 31.

4. Ibid.

5. Refer, for example, to Martha S. Jones' *Vanguard: How Black Women Broke Barriers, Won the Vote, and Insisted On Equality for All* (New York: Basic Books, 2020); Rosalyn Terborg-Penn, *African American Women in the Struggle for the Vote: 1850-1920* (Bloomington: University of Indiana Press, 1998); Ann D. Gordon, et al., eds., *African American Women and the Vote, 1837-1965* (Amherst: University of Massachusetts Press, 1997) for the narratives of Black suffragists.

6. Peter J. Paris, *The Spirituality of African Peoples: The Search for a Common Moral Discourse* (Minneapolis, MN: Fortress Press, 1995), 19.

7. Ibid., 27.

8. Ibid., 28.

9. Ibid., 51.

10. Ibid. 112.

11. Diana L. Hayes, *Forged in the Fiery Furnace: African American Spirituality* (Maryknoll: Orbis Books, 2012), 137–138.

12. Robert J. Patterson. "A Triple-Twined Re-Appropriation: Womanist Theology and Gendered-Racial Protest in the Writings of Jarena Lee," in *Religion and Literature*, vol. 45, no. 2 (2013): 58.

13. Nikole Hannah-Jones, "America Wasn't a Democracy, Until Black Americans Made It One," *The New York Times*, 4, https://www.nytimes.com/interactive/2019/08/14/magazine/black-history-american-democracy.html.

14. Bruce E. Moon, et al., "Voting Counts: Participation in the Measurement of Democracy," *Studies in Comparative International Development*, vol. 41, no. 2 (Summer 2006): 4.

15. Ibid., 6. The report makes no mention of racial justice in terms of participation and democracy.

16. See, Jones, *Vanguard: How Black Women Broke Barriers, Won the Vote, and Insisted on Equality for All*; Paula Giddings, *When and Where I Enter: The Impact of Black Women on Race and Sex in America* (New York: Amistad, 1984). These works detail the burgeoning political activism of Black women in the 19th century.

17. See Sally Roesch Wagner, *The Women's Suffrage Movement* (New York: Penguin Books, 2019).

18. Darlene Clark Hine, "African American Women and their Communities in the Twentieth Century: The Foundation and Future of Black Women's Studies," *Black Women, Gender + Families*, vol. 1, no. 1 (Spring 2007): 6–7.

19. Edith Mayo, ed. "African American Women Leaders in the Suffrage Movement," *Turning Point Suffragist Memorial Association*, 1, https://suffragistmemorial.org/african-american-women-leaders-in-the-suffrage-movement.

20. Pope Francis, *The Joy of the Gospel: Apostolic Exhortation* (Washington, DC: United States Conference of Catholic Bishops, 2014), 183.

21. Ruth Igielnik, Scott Keeter, and Hannah Hartig, "Behind Biden's 2020 Victory," *Pew Research Center*, 6, https://www.pewresearch.org/politics/2021/06/30/behind-bidens-2020-victory.

22. Coleen Butler-Sweet, "White Women's Bad Bargain," *U.S. News and World Report*, https://www.usnews.com/opinion/civil-wars/articles/2017-12-14/roy-moore-donald-trump-and-white-women-voting-for-misogyny.

FURTHER READINGS

Chambers, Veronica, and the Staff of the New York Times. *Finish the Fight: The Brave and Revolutionary Women Who Fought for the Right to Vote*. New York: Versify, 2020.

Dionne, Evette. *Lifting As We Climb: Black Women's Battle for the Ballot Box*. New York: Viking Books for Young Readers, 2020.

Hayes, Diana. *Standing in the Shoes My Mother Made: A Womanist Theology*. Minneapolis, MN: Fortress Press, 2010.

Hubbard, LaRese. "Anna Julia Cooper and Africana Womanism: Some Early Conceptual Contributions." *Black Women, Gender + Families* 4, no. 2 (Fall 2010): 31–53.

Stavney, Anne. "'Mothers of Tomorrow': The New Negro Renaissance and the Politics of Maternal Representation." *African American Review* 32, no. 4 (1998): 533–561.

REFERENCES

Butler-Sweet, Coleen. "White Women's Bad Bargain." www.usnews.com/opinion/civilwars/articles/2017-12-14/roy-moore-donald-trump-and-white-women-voting-for-misogyny.

Francis. *The Joy of the Gospel: Apostolic Exhortation*. Washington: United States Conference of Catholic Bishops, 2014.

Giddings, Paula. *When and Where I Enter: The Impact of Black Women on Race and Sex in America*. New York: Amistad, 1984.

Gordon, Ann, Bettye Collier-Thomas, John H. Bracey, Arlene Voski Avakian, and Joyce Avrech Berkman, eds. *African American Women and the Vote, 1837–1965*. Amherst: University of Massachusetts Press, 1997.

Hannah-Jones, Nikole. "America Wasn't a Democracy, Until Black Americans Made It One." www.nytimes.com/interactive /2019/08/14/magazine/black-history-american-democracy.html.

Hayes, Diana L. *Forged in the Fiery Furnace: African American Spirituality*. Maryknoll: Orbis Books, 2012.

Hine, Darlene Clark. "African American Women and Their Communities in the Twentieth Century: The Foundation and Future of Black Women's Studies." *Black Women, Gender + Families* 1, no. 1 (Spring 2007): 1–23.

Igielnik, Ruth, Scott Keeter, and Hannah Hartig. "Behind Biden's 2020 Victory." www.pewresearch.org/politics/2021/06/30/behind-bidens-2020-victory.

Jones, Martha S. *Vanguard: How Black Women Broke Barriers, Won the Vote, and Insisted on Equality for All.* New York: Basic Books, 2020.

Lumas, Eva M. "The Nature and Goals of Africentric Catholic Catechesis." In *God Bless Them Who Have Their Own: African American Catechetical Camp Meetin': A Gathering to Chart a New Course*, edited by Therese Wilson Favors, 28–38. Washington, DC: Department of Education, United States Catholic Conference, 1995.

Mayo, Edith, ed. "African American Women Leaders in the Suffrage Movement." https://suffragistmemorial.org/african-american-women-leaders-in-the-suffrage-movement.

Moon, Bruce E., Jennifer Harvey Birdsall, Sylvia Ciesluk, Lauren M. Garlett, Joshua J. Hermias, Elizabeth Mendenhall, Patrick D. Schmid, and Wai Hong Wong. "Voting Counts: Participation in the Measurement of Democracy." *Studies in Comparative International Development* 41, no. 2 (Summer 2006): 3–32.

Paris, Peter J. *The Spirituality of African Peoples: The Search for a Common Moral Discourse.* Minneapolis, MN: Fortress Press, 1995.

Patterson, Robert J. "A Triple-Twined Re-Appropriation: Womanist Theology and Gendered-Racial Protest in the Writings of Jarena Lee." *Religion and Literature* 45, no. 2 (2013): 55–82.

Rutgers Eagleton Institute of Politics. "Women in Elective Office 2020." https://cawp.rutgers.edu/women-elective-office-2020.

Terborg-Penn, Rosalyn. *African American Women in the Struggle for the Vote: 1850–1920.* Bloomington: University of Indiana Press, 1998.

Wagner, Sally Roesch. *The Women's Suffrage Movement.* New York: Penguin Books, 2019.

Waxman, Olivia B. "'It's a Struggle They Will Wage Alone.' How Black Women Won the Right to Vote." https://time.com/5876456/black-women-right-to-vote/.

Chapter 11

Deep Down in My Soul

Black Women and the Spirituality of Freedom: Reading the Signs of the Times

C. Vanessa White

> I believe there are as great possibilities in women as there are in men .... We are marching onward grandly .... We love to think of the great women of our race—the mothers who have struggled through poverty to educate their children .... There are many wives who are now helping to educate their husbands at school, by taking in sewing and washin .... I believe in equalizing the matter. Instead of going to school a whole year, he ought to stay at home one half, and send his wife the other six months .... I repeat, we want a grand and noble womanhood, scattered all over the land. There is a great vanguard of scholars and teachers of our sex who are at the head of institutions of learning all over the country. We need teachers, lecturers of force and character to help to teach this great nation of women.[1]

These powerful words by Hallie Quinn Brown in 1889 at the African American Episcopal[2] (AME) Conference eloquently address the power and the determination of Black[3] women who strived to be free in a society that worked to diminish their value in the United States. Note that her words were in a Black church and not at the earlier 1848 women's meeting in Seneca Falls, New York. For Black women, the struggle for equal rights, to be granted the right to vote, did not take place at women's conventions, which were primarily for white women only but in Black Churches. This also gives testament to the intersections of justice movements and religious movements that have been prevalent in the struggle for civil rights for Black people. This resistance to separating the sacred from the secular is a characteristic of the journey of Black women to achieve and sustain their value in an oppressive society. Traditionally as women of faith, Black women have strived to be free while all that is around them reinforces the notion that they are called to be submissive to male voices and actions. In spite of this oppression, Black women have been leaders of human rights movements and associations such as the National Association of Colored Women (NACW), the Negro Council of Women, Black Women's Defense League, The Black Women's Health Imperative, and the National Black Women's Justice Institute. This chapter will look at the characteristics of Black women's spirituality of freedom that have sustained Black women and provided hope to the community from the time of enslavement through the suffragette and civil rights movements to today. Let us not forget that it is primarily Black women who have shaped the current Black Lives Matter movements as well as other social justice movements and have sustained many of the ministries in churches today. What has been characteristic of their spiritual strivings and strength? What biblical texts have provided a source of hope? How has Mary, the mother of God, a woman of color, and a strong mother provided a model to Black women as they strive to say their own yes in the midst of oppression and struggle? What stories of Black women suffragettes such as Hallie Quinn Brown, Nannie Helen Burroughs, Sojourner Truth, and Helen Quinn Brown can be models for women of color as they strive for freedom in today's society?

BLACK SPIRITUALITY AS RESILIENCE AND RESISTANCE

From the time of enslavement to the present day, Black women have been engaged in a close relationship with the Spirit of God that dwells within and among the community. This spirituality has deep African roots. The ways of searching for God and experiencing God's presence in the lives of Black people are not done within a vacuum but in a cultural context. Black spirituality is a response to and a reflection on Black life and culture.[4] It is rooted in the African heritage and is colored by the Middle Passage from Africa to America, slavery, the Caribbean and Latin experience, segregation, integration, and the ongoing struggle for liberation. It permeates and is ingrained in the fabric of Black life and is at once God awareness, self-awareness, and other awareness[5]. Furthermore, "African American spirituality is grounded in devotion to the Holy Spirit and her ability to create possibility in the face of denial . . . . It is a spiritual story of hope in the face of despair, of quiet determination in the face of myriad obstacles, of a quiet yet fierce dignity over against the denial of humanity."[6] Ultimately African American spirituality is a liberating spirituality of resistance and resilience.

In understanding African American spirituality, it is useful to consider four persons who write about the marginalization and devaluation of African

Americans and the effect of such marginalization on the psyche and spirit of a people—W.E.B. Dubois, Jamie T. Phelps, Paul Gilroy, and Emilie Townes.

W.E.B. DuBois, founder of the National Association for the Advancement of Colored People (NAACP) and one of the leading African American intellectuals in the twentieth century, states:

> The Negro is a sort of seventh son, born with a veil and gifted with second sight in this American world—a world that yields him no true self-consciousness, but only lets him see himself through the revelation of the other world. It is a peculiar sensation, this double—consciousness, this sense of always looking at one's self through the eyes of others, measuring one's self through the eyes of others, measuring one's soul by the tape of a world that looks on in amused contempt and pity. One ever feels the twoness—an American, a negro, two souls, two thoughts, two unreconciled striving, two warring ideals in one dark body, whose strength alone keeps it from being torn asunder.[7]

Jamie T. Phelps, a womanist systematic theologian, builds upon DuBois' insights in considering African American Catholics:

> African American Catholics experience a double invisibility, marginalization and devaluation. In the Black world, we are marginalized because our religious identity as Catholics, and in the Catholic world, we are marginalized because of our racial identity as African Americans . . . . Black Catholics simply wish to make it possible to be Black, Catholic, and American without being cursed and spit upon, devalued and marginalized by other Blacks, Catholics or Americans.[8]

Paul Gilroy expresses how the struggle for personhood in the nineteenth and twentieth centuries has shaped the psyche of African Americans. In writing about the tension to survive as persons of value he states: "They had to fight—often through their spirituality—to hold on to the unity of ethics and politics sundered from each other by modernity's insistence that the true, the good and beautiful had distinct origins and belong to different domains of knowledge."[9]

Finally, Emilie Townes writes of Black spirituality and specifically of Black women's spirituality as a spirituality of social witness that seeks to cross the yawning chasm of hatred and prejudices and oppressions into a deeper and richer love of God as we experience Jesus in our lives, it is a love that extends to self and to others.[10] All four authors share in their own unique way, the tension of the merging of African culture and Western culture in these times of modernity and postmodernity. They offer a lens for journeying into the spirituality of Black peoples and more specifically Black women.

Cyprian Davis notes that the context of Black spirituality is the African experience lived out in America.[11] This experience, of marginalization and devaluation, has shaped African American religious experience over the past centuries and continues to have an impact today.

The above-noted writers have articulated some aspects of Black spirituality, particularly its context of marginalization within the United States reality. But how is Black spirituality further defined and expressed? The next section will focus on the five key characteristics of Black spirituality.[12]

EVERY TIME I FEEL THE SPIRIT: CHARACTERISTICS OF BLACK SPIRITUALITY

GOD IS: God-Centered Spirituality

God is central in the life of many people of African descent. This God is one who is both immanent and transcendent. God dwells within as well as sits on the throne. As Diana Hayes states the immanent God loves us and nurtures us like a parent bending low over a child, yet as transcendent God is free to judge those who oppress us and to call us forth into freedom.[13] The relationship that Black people have with Jesus is also an example of the personal and immanent God. It is not uncommon for Black people to wake up in the morning and their first thought is to say, "thank you, Jesus." For African Americans as immanent humanity Jesus is brother, sister, and friend who journeys with the one who is suffering the pain of oppression while as transcendent Son of God will come forth in glory leading followers to the promised land.[14]

The ancestors, grandmothers, grandfathers, aunts, and uncles, have testified to the power of God in their lives. Such phrases as "God don't ever change" and "there will always be God" infuse the language and speak of Black people's concept of God. African Americans furthermore have always relied on the belief in a God of sanctity, mercy, and transformation.[15] This trifold belief in God has historically led to an ongoing practice of mercy and even forgiveness toward white racists and a belief in the justice of God who will ultimately prevail.

Let My People Go: Spirituality of the Holy Word

Black spirituality is a spirituality of the Word.[16] Any serious discussion of African American spirituality must consider the importance of Christian scripture in the identity, formation, and empowerment of black life.[17] The African Americans' sense of self is based upon their understanding and integration of the sacred scripture. Even during the times of enslavement, the Bible was not foreign to the experience of African Americans. The stories were told and retold in sermons, spirituals, and shouts.[18] African Americans historically have had a personal relationship with scripture. The Bible gave African Americans a language to articulate their thoughts, ideas, and feelings about their life and their lives in God, who was for them very present in their daily journey.[19] The Bible is not foreign to the lives of Black people. It has had both a liberating and humanizing function in African American life as well as remaining a reliable source of information for black survival.[20] The ecumenical nature of African American family life (where one could have members who are Catholic, Baptist, Lutheran, AME Zion, Apostolic, and Pentecostal, to name a few) speaks to the commonality and importance of scripture in bridging the religious gap. Though families could come from many faith traditions, if there was a personal relationship and love of the Sacred Scriptures, this gap could be lessened and the relationship with scripture affirmed.

Spirit Fall Fresh on Me: Spirituality of Joy, Contemplation, and Wholeness

Joy is a hallmark of black spirituality.[21] As fruit of the spirit, this sense of joy among peoples of African descent has sustained them even during the most difficult of times. African American people are able to experience joy even in the midst of suffering. The experience of funerals in the Black community is one of sorrow, as well as a celebration that the person has finally "made it over." This does not negate the suffering of individuals but is focused on the belief in the hope of Jesus Christ. This joy is expressed in movement, dance, song, art, and sensation as well as in thanksgiving and exultation.

Black spirituality is holistic. Feelings are not separate from intellect, and the heart is not separate from the soul. Black people use their entire bodies to express their love of God. As noted by the Black bishops, "Divisions between intellect and emotion, spirit and body, action and contemplation, individual and community, sacred and secular, are foreign to us."[22]

African American people are also a contemplative people. Contemplation has to do with an awareness of the presence of God apprehended not by thought but by love.[23] For African American people, God's presence is experienced at all times and in a variety of different ways. It is not uncommon to hear African Americans speak of "resting in the Lord" or to observe the elders rocking or humming in deep prayer. These indescribable moments of deep spiritual abiding bear all of the marks of contemplative practice.[24] Lifted up by God's presence, African Americans respond by surrendering and basking completely in marvelous mystery, whether in church on bended knee or at home in labor or at rest.[25] Today we live in a time of great noise and busyness. The emergence of cell phones, zoom meetings, and the deluge of emails have created an environment that disrupts the ability to listen and dwell in the spirit of God. This lack of contemplative abiding time has created a restless longing in Black people.[26]

At the same time, it is not uncommon to hear people in the African American community speak of being led by the spirit which propels them in their actions and in their decisions. Also, frequently African Americans during worship and prayer are moved to tears, shouts, and raised hands that attest to the deep joy and sense of peace that is felt by the Spirit of God. The impulse in black spirituality to abandon oneself to the divine will and the indwelling spirit lends itself to a particularly intimate experience of God.[27] Black spirituality has taught Black people what it means to "let go" and "lean on the Lord."

Walk Together: Communal Spirituality of Welcome and Hospitality

In West African tradition, the "I" is defined by the "We." At the base of African cosmology is the understanding that the individual exists, or identity defined in relation to the community, which is expressed in the saying, "I am because we are and because we are, I am."[28] Individual identity is found in the context of community. The communal aspect of Black spirituality is quite evident in Black churches, worship, and Eucharistic celebrations in the African American community. One cannot enter an authentically Black church and not feel welcomed. No one stands alone in prayer. Hospitality and community are gifts of Black folk. All are welcome in the House of God and in Black community associations and organizations. This communal aspect of spirituality shapes the community and in turn is shaped by the community.[29]

This person- and community-centered component shapes the African American's sense of the sacredness of human life.[30] Since all human life is sacred and the individual and community are interdependent, it is the responsibility of the persons to become good representatives of their respective communities. A common caution in African American communities is to not bring shame onto the community (or the admonishment in the recent past to be "a credit to the race").

Oh Freedom, Oh Freedom: Spirituality of Liberation and Justice

African American spirituality leads to freedom. The journey in the spiritual life and closer union to God not only leads to personal freedom and authenticity but invokes a community to strive for freedom from oppression in all its forms. Authentic black spirituality leads to prophetic action on behalf of justice, a justice that requires liberation from sin and its effects.[31] The community- and person-focused nature of African American spirituality profoundly affects how Black people treat one another. It affects the quality of one's life and the way one relates to others. It infuses one with a sense of social concern and spirituality that moves the person and community to action. This sense of right relationship inspires African Americans to do right, act right, and be right.

In all human activities, African peoples have been concerned primarily with the following forms of justice: (1) the individual's obligations to the community as mediated through the many dealings individuals have with one another and (2) the community's obligations to its members and itself.[32]

In committing to liberation and justice, those imbued with spirit must stand for the truth. They must walk the path of Jesus, who was a man of justice who announced the gospel to the poor, the oppressed, and the marginalized in society and was called to set the captives free. They must promote justice not only in the pulpit, but in the schools, in the homes, and throughout the world.

The justice tradition in the African American community is rooted in the belief that God intervenes with the self in community[33] and thus is a spirituality that is embodied to promote justice and speak the truth to power.

The absolute criterion of the authenticity of African American spirituality is its impact on the quality of the believer's life.[34] The question becomes, do the actions of the community lead to right relationships? Does the person act right and call others to be right? Do the person and community struggle for the liberation of oppressed races and nations?"[35] Ultimately the spirituality of Black people provides individuals and the community with the tools to liberate themselves from the tyrannies that sequester the soul and destroy the mind. It finds its expression through the oral and aural tradition.

GO TELL IT: THE ORAL-AURAL TRADITION IN BLACK SPIRITUALITY

African Americans come from an oral-aural tradition. All the sounds of a people comprise their oral tradition.[36] In calling to mind the stories of faith and the history of a people, the Black person's main mode of communication has always been the oral tradition. Liturgist Clarence Rivers states in some ways the term oral-aural may be misleading because in oral-aural cultures all the senses are involved without the dominance of the eye over the others.[37] Rivers further explains the particularity of the oral-aural tradition with the following example:

> A people whose roots are in a "literate/literary tradition will tend to listen to the music." Their other senses are restrained by the tendency of the eye toward uninvolved observation and detachment. Whereas a people whose roots are in an oral tradition have no such restraints and they will inevitably tend to merge

with music, to become involved with it, to dance. And if not to actually dance, then a least to give oneself over entirely to the sentiment of the song.[38]

This does not negate the written word but brings attention to a preferred mode of expression. Oral people tend to be poetic in their use of language which can be seen among African American people, particularly in the oratorical style of preaching.

Clarence Rivers in speaking of this tradition states that Black spirituality finds its harbor in Black religious expression. Preaching, storytelling, music and song, prayer, drama, and art are all venues by which the black community expresses its deep connection to the divine.

MARY DON'T YOU WEEP: MARY, MOTHER OF JESUS, AND MARY MAGDALENE IN BLACK SPIRITUALITY

For Black women, Mary, the mother of Jesus and Mary Magdalene, the proclaimer of the Resurrection, have been strong models and guides for a spirituality of resistance, resilience, and freedom. Mary's strong yes, opened the gates and the door to a new way of being, a new way of living life in relationship to God and to others. Mary was the first disciple of Jesus. She is the mother of the one who was unjustly condemned and hung from a tree. In her role as mother of a son who was continually persecuted and reviled, she provided a place of comfort and steadfastness to not only Jesus but to his other companions on the journey. Her presence testified to the role of women in the salvation story as well as gave guidance to the Black women in the nineteenth and twentieth centuries who were themselves vilified and whose family members had also been hung from a tree or murdered in the streets. Mary experienced her son's death in the most famous state-initiated execution of all time.[39] Mary also gives witness to the struggle for freedom in her Magnificat. In this song of freedom, she proclaims the power of God, and this freedom song serves as an anthem for Black women declaring personal blessedness and worth along with intimate knowledge of God's preference for the oppressed.[40] Mother Mary, the Theotokos (God Bearer), ushers in a time of justice and an ordered social advocacy as she proclaims that God is on the side of the oppressed, the disenfranchised, the hungry, the poor, and the brokenhearted.[41] Generations of Black women have affirmed and acknowledged the agency of Mary who gave her consent in becoming the mother of Jesus. In a quote attributed to the great Sojourner Truth, she makes clear the role of Mary in the struggle for women's rights. *"And then that little man in black there, he says women can't have as much rights as men 'cause Christ wasn't a woman. Where did Christ come from? From God and a woman?*[42]

Mary Magdalen's story as a strong woman of faith has also been a model for Black women. Nineteenth-century African American evangelist, Jarena Lee, in her writings about preaching the Gospel, (a role that was denied women in the AME church at that time) poses the questions, *"If a man may preach, because the Saviour died for him, why not the woman? Seeing he died for her also. Did not Mary first preach the risen Saviour and is not the doctrine of the resurrection the very climax of Christianity—hangs not all our hope on this as argued by St. Paul? Then did not Mary, a woman preach the Gospel? For she preached the resurrection of the crucified Son of God."*[43] Her repositioning of the narrative of Mary from a woman inaccurately depicted as a prostitute and centering her in the Gospel narrative as the one who liberates through her testimony of Jesus's resurrection sheds light on the role and power of Black women to transform false narratives imposed on women of that day. Sojourner Truth and Jarena Lee in their words and actions exude the components of a Black Spirituality of Resistance, Resilience, and Freedom which will become more evident in the lives of the African American women whose stories will be highlighted in the next section.

I'M GONNA MOVE WHEN THE SPIRIT SAY MOVE: THE SPIRITUAL JOURNEYS OF BLACK WOMEN SUFFRAGETTES

Womanist theologian Emilie Townes states that womanist wisdom and spirituality springs out of the stories and experience of the survival of African American women as they have been daughters, wives, partners, aunts, grandmothers, mothers, other mothers, comrades, worshipers, protesters, wisdom bearers, murders, and saints in African American culture and society.[44] While many of their stories have been silenced, the Black women who participated and survived as leaders of the suffragette movement give testimony to the power of Black women's deep spiritual strivings and journey in resistance against the oppressive nature of racism that was evident during the late nineteenth and twentieth centuries. Black women were not welcomed into the suffrage movement even though many white women suffragists were abolitionists and anti-slavery advocates. White women feared that having Black women at their events would cause them to lose the support of Southern white politicians. In fact, many Black women were denied participation in the movement while also having to fight against stereotypes perpetuated by white women suffragists who reinforced negative images of Black women as uneducated and/or promiscuous[45]. In spite of the challenges to their participation in the suffrage movement, Black women viewed the vote as a means of protecting themselves against sexual exploitations as well as a way to boost education for African Americans by exerting influence on school boards and state legislatures.[46] In spite of many challenges, black women rooted in a strong biblical tradition and a spirituality that was spirit-filled and holistic, and which affirmed the dignity of their being and the goodness of their communities, continued to fight for justice and liberation despite tremendous odds. Supporting one another in the struggle, they began to organize themselves and by the late 1800s had formed the NACW. Their stories highlight their journey as proudly devout women of faith and action whose spirituality moved them to justice and political advocacy.

MARY ANN SHAD CARY (1823–1893)

"The crowning glory of American citizenship is that it may be shared equally by people of every nationality, complexion, and sex . . . "[47] Mary Ann Shad Cary was born free in the slave–holding state of Delaware but her family moved to Pennsylvania and later to Ontario Canada to avoid the Southern bans against educating children of color.[48] She later returned to the United States and began teaching black children in segregated Black schools. Propelled by her strong commitment to justice and education, she wrote an impassioned plea to Frederick Douglass about the "wretched conditions" of free Black Americans in the North.[49] Understanding the power of words, she soon was the publisher of a newsletter, *The Provincial Freeman,* that advocated for the rights of women to speak in public, control property, hold elective office, and obtain an education. and enter professions usually reserved for men. Throughout her life, her heart and mind remained fixed on the past, present, and future of America's former slaves, especially women.[50]

FRANCIS ELLEN WATKINS HARPER (1825–1911)

"Now is the time for our women to begin to try to lift up their heads and plant the roots of progress under the hearthstone."[51] Francis Ellen Watkins Harper was a suffragist who used poetry and the power of her voice to highlight the inequities of Black women in the mid to late nineteenth century. Building on the work of Sojourner Truth and other women who had been knocking on the doors of power for decades, Watkins-Harper constantly challenged her white counterparts and was continually parodied by Southern and anti-abolitionist journalists who dubbed her the "mulatto girl" while experiencing constant physical dangers to her person.[52] Acknowledging the work already done by Black women, Harper further pleaded for equal rights and equal access to education for African American women of the nation. Her support of the Fifteenth Amendment convinced her to ally herself with white women suffragettes, becoming one of the founding members of the American Woman Suffrage Association (AWSA). She would later become a delegate (Maryland) at their 1873 convention in which she gave a speech stating, "as much as the white women need the ballot, colored women need it more."[53] While the AWSA was at that time focused on one issue, women's suffrage, Harper's powerful words addressed the intersections of racism, feminism, and classism long before the civil rights movements of the 1960s and 1970s. Throughout her life, she would continue to address in words and actions the inequities faced by Black women which became for her a survival issue.

HALLIE QUINN BROWN (1845–1949)

"I repeat, we want a grand and noble womanhood, scattered all over the land. We need teacher, lecturers of force and character to help to teach this great nation of women."[54] Those remarks, before an African Methodist Episcopal Church helped to propel Hallie Quinn Brown to national leadership in her advocacy for Black women's right to vote in 1896. Brown, a powerful orator, and advocate for human rights worked throughout her life to break barriers and promote the human dignity of all persons. Born free in 1849 in Pittsburgh she fought tirelessly to promote the education of all children and the advancement of Black women's causes. She did not let the barriers of her gender inhibit her from advocating for equality. When she was admonished for wishing to hold the Office of Secretary of Education in the AME Church, she used it as a vehicle to enter women's politics along with her fellow "sisters" who strived to hold offices as ordained ministers. The sacred and the secular were tightly woven into her journey as a leader in the suffrage movement. She states, "Not until women had the ballot to be used for her protection and self-defense can she hope to secure the rights and privileges to which she is entitled." During 1911–1912, she headed the NACW's Suffrage department and later its presidency in 1920.[55] Quinn fought tirelessly against stereotypes placed on Black women specifically the "mammy" role. When a bill was introduced in Washington DC in 1922, to erect a "mammy statue" as a gift to the people of the United States, she joined luminaries such as WEB DuBois to oppose the bill. She like many others saw the bill as a way to distract the nation from real twentieth-century needs: adequate homes, schools, and health care. Luckily, the bill died in Congress.[56]

MARY CHURCH TERRELL (1863–1954)

"Lifting as we climb . . . we knock at the bar of justice, asking an equal chance."[57] In 1896, two Black women civil rights groups merged to form the NACW under the leadership of prominent Black women's civil rights activist and suffragist Mary Church Terrell. By the 1900s, Black suffrage clubs had been launched all over the country. She worked tirelessly with Ida B. Wells against anti-lynching which was terrorizing the Black communities in the early twentieth century. Terrell's life work was primarily focused on the notion of racial uplift, meaning if one person in the race is uplifted then it benefits all the community. This notion of racial uplift is also reminiscent of 1Cor. 12: 26: "If one part suffers, all parts suffer with it; if one part is honored, all the parts share its joy."[58] As one of the founders and later president of the NACW, Terrell's words—"Lifting as we Climb" became the motto of the NACW.[59]

NANNIE HELEN BURROUGHS (1879–1961)

"When the ballot is put into the hands of the American woman the world is going to get a correct estimate of the Negro woman. It will find her a tower of strength of which poets have never sung, orators have never spoken, and scholars have never written." [60] Nannie Helen Burrough devoted her life to the empowerment of Black women as an educator, church leader, and suffrage worker. She overtly articulated a religious perspective throughout her life. As a member of the National Baptist Women's Convention, she helped find and shape the National Baptist Women's Convention as well as led and shaped racial uplift and social activities with other Black club women. Her speech to the National Baptist Convention in 1900 in Richmond Virginia entitled "How the Sisters Are Hindered from Helping" significantly advanced the women's cause within the convention.[61] Her God-centered spirituality is evident in her later founding of the *WORKER*, a quarterly publication devoted to women's missionary societies. In this publication, she wrote: *"We realized that financial conditions are not altogether favorable to launch a magazine, but our church women need it. God will, therefore, make is possible for us to meet this definite need."*[62] Her person- and community-centered spirituality is further evident in Burroughs's identification of her activism as racial uplift work. She developed a National Trade and Professional School for Women and Girls whose focus in brochures is described as "an institution that would provide uplift of thousands of women and young girls throughout the country."[63] She further believed that churches should be involved in social activism in the communities. "Every church should attempt a definite program that projects itself into the community and no church should be allowed to stay in a community that does not positively influence community life."[64]

DAISY ELIZABETH ADAMS LAMPKIN (1884–1965)

"You cannot be neutral. You must either join with us who believe in the bright future or be destroyed by those who would return us to the dark past."[65] Daisy Elizabeth Adams Lampkin's life exemplifies the intersections of the sacred and the secular in the spiritual journeys of Black women. Originally born in Reading, Pennsylvania, she spent her adult life in Pittsburgh and married William Lampkin in 1917. She began promoting social justice as early as 1912 when she organized a suffrage tea. She later went on to organize the Black women in the area into consumer protest and social action clubs focused on providing clothing for the needy as well as persuading physicians to give free medical attention in church buildings in the late 1920s. As the Pittsburgh *Post-Gazette* states, Americans owe a debt to Mrs. Daisy Lampkin longtime civil rights leader. Not only did she struggle for Negro rights before the justice of the cause was popularly accepted but she was instrumental in advancing the cause of the NAACP and the desegregation of public schools. Her dynamic fundraising and relentless zeal were outstanding and uplifting.[66]

LET'S US WALK TOGETHER AND NOT BE WEARY: GLEANINGS FROM THE PAST—HOPE FOR THE FUTURE

The lives of these women affirm the power of Black spirituality to meet at the intersections of human experience, spiritual resilience, and prophetic action. It is at this intersection that Black women have been able to face those oppressive forces that have worked to dehumanize the Black woman's body and destroy the mind. Like many leaders in the civil rights movements that followed, these women were "birthed" from Black churches where they were formed in a religious tradition that promoted the dignity of Black people, and reinforced the primacy of God's presence and agency in their lives. Following a womanist ethic, they were not single-issue women but worked for change in voting rights legislation, education, prison reform, gender inequality in religious institutions, and the labor rights of working people. Viewing these stories through the lens of Black spirituality, we see women who believed in the power of the Spirit to make a change, and despite the oppression and racism of the nineteenth and early twentieth centuries, advocated for equity in home, church, and society. Imbued with a spirituality, rooted in their Black communal religious tradition, they chose not to work in isolation nor focus on individual achievements. Rather they promoted the value of working together in the forming of institutions such as the NACW and the NAACP that promoted the humanity and inherent rights of all Black people. Today as we journey anew in fighting racism in our nation and the promotion of voting rights, adequate health care, improved educational resources, and equitable employment opportunities for all people in our nation, may we look back at these women and learn from their stories which are rooted in a spirituality of resistance, resilience, and freedom.

NOTES

1. Martha S. Jones, "How Black Suffragists Fought for the Right to Vote and a Modicum of Respect," National Endowment for the Humanities, https://www.neh.gov/article/how-black-suffragists-fought-right-vote-and-modicum-respect.

2. African Methodist Episcopal Church was founded in 1816 in Philadelphia, PA, by Richard Allen. It is one of the oldest historically Black churches in the United States of America.

3. Throughout this chapter, several words will be used to designate those persons of African descent (Black, African American, Negro, Colored) whose history began in Africa, journeyed through the Middle Passage, and arrived on the continent of North America enduring centuries of Enslavement, Reconstruction, Jim Crow, Terrorism of Lynching, Civil Rights, Black Power and Black Lives Matter movement.

4. Thea Bowman, "Spirituality: The Soul of the People," *Tell It Like It Is: A Black Catholic Perspective on Christian Education* (Oakland, CA: National Black Sisters Conference, 1983), 84–85. Reprinted in *Sister Thea: Shooting Star*, ed. Celestine Cepress, (LaCrosse, WI: Franciscan Sisters of Perpetual Adoration, 1999), 39.

5. Bowman, *Shooting Star*, 40.

6. Diana Hayes, *Forged in the Fiery Furnace: African American Spirituality* (Maryknoll, NY: Orbis Books, 2012), 3.

7. W.E.B. DuBois, *The Souls of Black Folk* (Toronto, Canada: New American Library, 1903, 1963), 49.

8. Jamie T. Phelps, "African American Catholics: The Struggles, Contributions and Gifts of a Marginalized Community," in *Black and Catholic: The Challenge and Gift of Black Folk*, ed. Jamie T. Phelps (Milwaukee, WI: Marquette University Press, 1997), 21, 18.

9. Paul Gilroy, *The Black Atlantic* (Cambridge, MA: Harvard University Press, 1993), 39.

10. Emilie Townes. *In a Blaze of Glory: Womanist Spirituality as Social Witness* (Nashville, TN: Abingdon Press, 1995), 11.

11. Cyprian Davis, "Some Reflections on African American Catholic Spirituality," *U.S. Catholic Historian*, vol. 19, no. 2 (Spring 2001): 8.

12. Black Bishops of the United States, *What We Have Seen and Heard* (Cincinnati, OH: St. Anthony Messenger Press, 1984), 9. The Black Bishops in 1984 initially shared with the broader church, four components of African American spirituality: contemplative, holistic, joyful and communitarian.

13. Diana Hayes, *And Still We Rise: An Introduction to Black Liberation Theology* (New York: Paulist Press, 1996), 171–172.

14. Hayes, *And Still We Rise*, 172.

15. Carlyle Fielding Stewart III, *Soul Survivors: An African American Spirituality* (Louisville, KY: Westminster John Knox Press, 1997), 26.

16. Cyprian Davis, "The Black Contribution to a North American Spirituality," in *New Catholic World*, vol. 225 (July/August, 1982): 183.

17. Stewart, *Soul Survivors*, 10.

18. Black Bishops, *What We Have Seen and Heard*, 4.

19. Michael I. N. Dash, "The Bible in African American Spirituality," *Good News Bible with Deuterocanonicals/Apocrypha: Jubilee Edition* (New York: American Bible Society), 311.

20. Stewart, *Soul Survivors*, 11.

21. Black Bishops, *What We Have Seen and Heard*, 9.

22. Ibid., 8.

23. William H. Shannon, "Contemplation, Contemplative Prayer," in *The New Dictionary of Catholic Spirituality*, ed. Michael Downey (Collegeville, MN: The Liturgical Press, 1993), 209.

24. Barbara A. Holmes, *Joy Unbearable: Contemplative Practices of the Black Church* (Minneapolis, MN: Fortress Press, 2004), 7.

25. Wilton Gregory. *Plenty Good Room: The Spirit and Truth of African American Catholic Worship* (Washington, DC: National Conference of Catholic Bishops, August 28, 1990), 49.

26. Holmes, *Joy Unspeakable*, 2.

27. Jamie Phelps, "Black Spirituality," in *Spiritual Traditions for the Contemporary Church*, eds. Robin Maas and Gabriel O'Donnell (Nashville: Abingdon Press, 1990), 334.

28. Flora Wilson Bridges, *Resurrection Song: African American Spirituality*, The Bishop Henry McNeal Turner/Sojourner Truth Series in Black Religion (Maryknoll: NY: Orbis Books, 2001), 108.

29. Phelps, "Black Spirituality," 342.

30. Peter Paris, *The Spirituality of African Peoples: The Search for a Common Discourse* (Minneapolis, MN: Fortress Press, 1995), 135.

31. Phelps, "Black Spirituality," 344.

32. Paris, *Spirituality of African Peoples*, 152.

33. Flora Wilson Bridges, *Resurrection Song*, 83.

34. Phelps, "Black Spirituality," 344.

35. Jamie Phelps, "Black Spirituality," in *Spiritual Traditions of the Contemporary Church*, eds. Robin Maas and Gabriel O'Donnell, OP (Nashville: Abingdon Press, 1990), Location 7118.Kindle edition.

36. Bowman, "Soul of a People," 85.

37. Clarence J. Rivers, *Soulful Worship* (Washington, DC: National Office for Black Catholics, 1974), 21.

38. Rivers, *Soulful Worship*, 21.

39. Courtney Hall Lee, *Black Madonna: A Womanist Look at Mary of Nazareth* (Eugene, OR: Cascade, 2017), 79.

40. Lee, *Black Madonna*, 118.

41. Valerie Lewis Mosley, "Who Is Mary in the Life of a Social Justice Advocate?" *Black Catholic Messenger* (June 8, 2021), https://www.blackcatholicmessenger.com/who-is-mary/.

42. Sojourner Truth. "Ain't I A Woman" text attributed to Sojourner Truth. Women's Rights National Historical Park, https://www.nps.gov/articles/sojourner-truth.htm.

43. Jarena Lee. "The Life and Religious Experience of Jarena Lee, A Coloured Lady, Giving an Account of Her Call to Preach the Gospel, Revised and Corrected from the Original Manuscript, Written By Herself" (1836). In *Sisters of the Spirit*, ed. William L. Andrews (Bloomington: Indiana University Press, 1986), 36.

44. Townes, *In A Blaze of Glory*, 10.

45. For further information on the struggle for Black women and voting rights see. Martha S. Jones, *Vanguard: How Black Women Broke Barriers, Won the Vote, and Insisted on Equality for All* (New York: Basic Books, 2020), Rosalyn Terbog-Penn, *African American Women in the Struggle for the Vote*, 1850-1920 (Bloomington: Indiana University Press, 1998).

46. Sydney Trent, "The Black Sorority that Faced Racism in the Suffrage Movement and Refused to Walk Away," Washington Post, August 8, 2020, https://www.washingtonpost.com/graphics/2020/local/history/suffrage-racism-black-deltas-parade-washington/?utm_campaign=wp_main&utm_medium=social&utm_source=facebook.

47. National Museum of African American History, "Five You Should Know: Black Women Suffragists," https://nmaahc.tumblr.com/post/70901835372/five-you-should-know-african-american-suffragettes.

48. Jones. *Vanguard*, 73. For further information on Mary Ann Shad Cary see. Mary Ann Shadd, A Plea for Emigration; or Notes of Canada West (Peterborough, Canada: Broadview Press, 2016). Jane Rhodes, *Mary Ann Shadd Cary: The Black Press and Protest in the Nineteenth Century* (Bloomington: Indiana University Press, 1999); Willi Coleman, "Architects of a Vision: Black Women and Their Antebellum Quest for Political and Social Equality," in *African American Women and the Vote, 1837-1965*, eds. Ann D. Gordon, et al. (Amherst: University of Massachusetts Press, 1997), 24–40.

49. Megan Specia. "Overlooked No More: How Mary Ann Shadd Cary Shook Up the Abolitionist Movement, *New York Times,* June 6, 2018, https://www.nytimes.com/2018/06/06/obituaries/mary-ann-shadd-cary-abolitionist-overlooked.html.

50. Jones. *Vanguard*, 73–75.

51. National Museum of African American History. "Five You Should Know: Black Women Suffragists," see also The Archives of Maryland: Biographical Series. "Francis Ellen Watkins Harper." *MSA SC 3520-12499.* msa.maryland.gov/megafile

/msa/speccol/sc3500/sc3520/012400/012499/html/12499bio.html; Kerri Lee Alexander. "Frances Ellen Watkins Harper, National Women's History Museum, https://www.womenshistory.org/education-resources/biographies/frances-ellen-watkins-harper.

52. Jones, *Vanguard*, 91–92.

53. Terborg-Penn, *African American Women in the Struggle for the Vote*, 47–48.

54. Martha S. Jones, "How Black Women Fought for the Right to Vote and a Modicum of Respect," *HUMANITIES*, vol. 40, no 3 (Summer 2019), https://www.neh.gov/article/how-black-suffragists-fought-right-vote-and-modicum-respect. Moses E. Sauter, "Women, Her Influence," *Proceedings of the Quarto-Centennial Conference of the African Methodist Episcopal Church of South Carolina*, May 15, 16, 17, 1889, ed. Bishop Benjamin W. Arnett (Xenia, OH: Aldine Printing House, 1890), 82–83.

55. Jones, *Vanguard*, 193–195.

56. Ibid., 196.

57. National Museum of African American History. "Five You Should Know: Black Women Suffragists."

58. All scriptural texts are taken from *The Holy Bible, New Revised Standard Edition* (Iowa Falls, IA: World Bible Publishers, 1989).

59. Debra A. Michals, "Mary Church Terrell" National Black History Women's Museum, https://www.womenshistory.org/education-resources/biographies/mary-church-terrell.

60. National Museum of African American History. "Five You Should Know: Black Women Suffragists."

61. Rosetta E. Ross, *Witnessing and Testifying: Black Women Religion and Civil Rights* (Minneapolis, MN: Fortress Press, 2003), 23.

62. Ibid., 26.

63. Ibid., 24.

64. Ibid., 27.

65. National Museum of African American History. "Five You Should Know: Black Women Suffragists."

66. Pittsburgh Gazette Archives. March 10, 1965, and August 7, 1991, https://news.google.com/newspapers?nid=1129&dat=19910807&id=Pdc0AAAAIBAJ&sjid=aW4DAAAAIBAJ&pg=3094,1368651.

FURTHER READINGS

Berry, Daina Ramey, and Kali Nicole Gross. *A Black Women's History of the United States*. Boston: Beacon Press, 2020.

Dudden, Faye E. *Fighting Chance: The Struggle of Woman Suffrage and Black Suffrage in Reconstruction America*. Oxford: Oxford University Press, 2014.

McCluskey, Audrey. *A Forgotten Sisterhood: Pioneering Black Women Educators and Activists in the Jim Crow South*. Washington, DC: Rowan and Littlefield, 2017.

Rhodes, Jane. *Mary Ann Shad: The Black Press and Protest in the Nineteenth Century.* Bloomington: University Press, 1999.
Townes, Emilie. *In a Blaze of Glory: Womanist Spirituality as Social Witness.* Nashville: Abingdon Press, 1995.
Ware, Susan. *Why They Marched: Untold Stories of the Women Who Fought for the Right to Vote.* Boston, MA: Cambridge: Belknap Press, 2019.

REFERENCES

Alexander, Kerri Lee. "Frances Ellen Watkins Harper." *National Women's History Museum.* 2020. www.womenshistory.org/education-resources/biographies/frances-ellen-watkins-harper.
Black Bishops of the United States. *What We Have Seen and Heard.* Cincinnati, OH: St. Anthony Messenger Press, 1984.
Bowman, Thea. "Spirituality: The Soul of the People." In *Tell It Like It Is: A Black Catholic Perspective on Christian Education*, 84–85. Oakland, CA: National Black Sisters Conference, 1983. Reprinted in *Sister Thea: Shooting Star*, edited by Celestine Cepress, 39–40. LaCrosse, WI: Franciscan Sisters of Perpetual Adoration, 1999.
Bridges. Flora Wilson. "Resurrection Song: African American Spirituality." In *The Bishop Henry McNeal Turner/Sojourner Truth Series in Black Religion.* Maryknoll: NY: Orbis Books, 2001.
Coleman, Willi. "Architects of a Vision: Black Women and Their Antebellum Quest for Political and Social Equality." In *African American Women and the Vote, 1837–1965*, edited by Ann D. Gordon, 27–40. Amherst: University of Massachusetts Press, 1997.
Dash, Michael I. N. "The Bible in African American Spirituality." In *Good News Bible With Deuterocanonicals/Apocrypha: Jubilee Edition.* New York: American Bible Society.
Davis, Cyprian. "Some Reflections on African American Catholic Spirituality." *U.S. Catholic Historian* 19, no. 2 (Spring 2001): 7–14.
———. "The Black Contribution to a North American Spirituality." *New Catholic World* 225 (July/August 1982): 181–184.
DuBois, W. E. B. *The Souls of Black Folk.* Toronto, Canada: New American Library, 1903, 1963.
Gilroy, Paul. *The Black Atlantic.* Cambridge, MA: Harvard University Press, 1993.
Gregory. Wilton. *Plenty Good Room: The Spirit and Truth of African American Catholic Worship.* Washington, D.C.: National Conference of Catholic Bishops, August 28, 1990.
Hayes, Diana. *And Still We Rise: An Introduction to Black Liberation Theology.* New York: Paulist Press, 1996.
———. *Forged in the Fiery Furnace: African American Spirituality.* Maryknoll, NY: Orbis Books, 2012.

Holmes, Barbara A. *Joy Unbearable: Contemplative Practices of the Black Church*. Minneapolis, MN: Fortress Press, 2004.

Jones, Martha. "How Black Suffragists Fought for the Right to Vote and a Modicum of Respect." *Humanities* 40, no. 3 (Summer 2019). https://www.neh.gov/article/how-black-suffragists-fought-right-vote-and-modicum-respect.

———. *Vanguard: How Black Women Broke Barriers, Won the Vote, and Insisted on Equality for All*. New York: Basic Books, 2020.

Lee, Courtney Hall. *Black Madonna: A Womanist Look at Mary of Nazareth*. Eugene, OR: Cascade, 2017.

Lee, Jarena. "The Life and Religious Experience of Jarena Lee, A Coloured Lady. Giving an Account of Her Call to Preach the Gospel. Revised and Corrected from the Original Manuscript. Written By Herself (1836)." In *Sisters of the Spirit*, edited by William L. Andrews, 25–48. Bloomington: Indiana University Press, 1986.

Michals, Debra. "Mary Church Terrell." *National Women's History Museum*. 2017. https://www.womenshistory.org/education-resources/biographies/mary-church-terrell.

Mosley, Valerie Lewis. "Who is Mary in the Life of a Social Justice Advocate?" *Black Catholic Messenger*, June 8, 2021. https://www.blackcatholicmessenger.com/who-is-mary/.

National Museum of African American History. "Five You Should Know: Black Women Suffragists." June 18, 2019. https://nmaahc.si.edu/explore/stories/five-you-should-know-african-american-suffragists.

Paris, Peter. *The Spirituality of African Peoples: The Search for a Common Discourse*. Minneapolis, MN: Fortress Press, 1995.

Phelps, Jamie T. "African American Catholics: The Struggles, Contributions and Gifts of a Marginalized Community." In *Black and Catholic: The Challenge and Gift of Black Folk*, edited by Jamie T. Phelps, 17–42. Milwaukee, WI: Marquette University Press, 1997.

———. "Black Spirituality." In *Spiritual Traditions for the Contemporary Church*, edited by Robin Maas and Gabriel O'Donnell, 334–344. Nashville: Abingdon Press, 1990a.

———. "Black Spirituality." In *Spiritual Traditions for the Contemporary Church*, edited by Robin Maas and Gabriel O'Donnell. Nashville: Abingdon Press, 1990b. Kindle Edition.

Pittsburgh Gazette Archives. March 10, 1965, and August 7, 1991. https://news.google.com/newspapers?nid=1129&dat=19910807&id=Pdc0AAAAIBAJ&sjid=aW4DAAAAIBAJ&pg=3094,1368651.

Rhodes, Jane. *Mary Ann Shadd Cary: The Black Press and Protest in the Nineteenth Century*. Bloomington: Indiana University Press, 1999.

Rivers, Clarence. *Soulful Worship*. Washington, DC: National Office for Black Catholics, 1974.

Ross, Rosetta E. *Witnessing and Testifying: Black Women Religion and Civil Rights*. Minneapolis, MN: Fortress Press, 2003.

Sauter, Moses E. "Women, Her Influence." *Proceedings of the Quarto-Centennial Conference of the African Methodist Episcopal Church of South Carolina*, May

15, 16, 17, 1889, edited by Bishop Benjamin W. Arnett, 82–83. Xenia, OH: Aldine Printing House, 1890.

Shannon, William H. "Contemplation, Contemplative Prayer." In *The New Dictionary of Catholic Spirituality*, edited by Michael Downey, 209–214. Collegeville, MN: The Liturgical Press, 1993.

Specia, Megan. "Overlooked No More: How Mary Ann Shadd Cary Shook Up the Abolitionist Movement." *New York Times*, June 6, 2018. https://www.nytimes.com/2018/06/06/obituaries/mary-ann-shadd-cary-abolitionist-overlooked.html.

Stewart III, Carlyle Fielding. *Soul Survivors: An African American Spirituality*. Louisville, KY: Westminster John Knox Press, 1997.

Terbog-Penn, Rosalyn. *African American Women in the Struggle for the Vote, 1850–1920*. Bloomington: Indiana University Press, 1998.

The Holy Bible: New Revised Standard Edition. Iowa Falls, Iowa: World Bible Publishers, 1989.

Townes, Emilie. *In a Blaze of Glory: Womanist Spirituality as Social Witness*. Nashville, TN: Abingdon Press, 1995.

Trent, Sydney. "The Black Sorority that Faced Racism in the Suffrage Movement and Refused to Walk Away." *Washington Post*, August 8, 2020. https://www.washingtonpost.com/graphics/2020/local/history/suffrage-racism-black-deltas-parade-washington/?utm_campaign=wp_main&utm_medium=social&utm_source=facebook.

Truth, Sojourner. "Ain't I A Woman" Text Attributed to Sojourner Truth." *Women's Rights National Historical Park*. Originally Delivered in 1851 at Women's Rights Convention, Old Stone Church. https://www.nps.gov/articles/sojourner-truth.htm.

Chapter 12

A Theology of Women's Rights
Bridge-Building between Individual Rights and Communal Rights—Insights from Africa
Okechukwu Camillus Njoku

In the wake of World War II, the United Nations (UN), in 1948, promulgated the Universal Declaration of Human Rights. Clearly, the impetus for the recognition of such rights was already inchoate in the French Revolution of August 26, 1789 and in the American Bill of Rights of December 15, 1791. Many countries from around the world and Africa endorsed the UN Declaration. Furthermore, in 1981, African countries appropriated and expanded the Declaration to include what came to be known as the African Charter for Human and Peoples' Rights. This Charter ensured that not only the rights of the individual but also those of the people (community) were guaranteed and protected.

Notwithstanding all of these achievements on the human rights front, the total liberation of women and full recognition of women's dignity and rights remains an unfinished task in contemporary society. In this chapter, I will first revisit the prevailing Western Enlightenment notion of personhood rooted in modern philosophy. I contend that this notion, which is fundamentally individualistic, is what has undergirded the dominant construal of the notion of rights. Next, I will silhouette the contours of a trinitarian theology that valorizes relationality without marginalizing individuality. I argue that this theology provides the basis for theological anthropology that is capable of holding in creative tension the claims of both individuality and community. Additionally, I will mine useful insights from certain African religious anthropological worldviews which provide resources for further rethinking human, nay, women's rights. The next section is a critical evaluation of the state of women's rights in the United States. Finally, I submit that the convergence of insights drawn from both trinitarian theology and African religious anthropological worldviews provide hermeneutic tools for articulating a theology of women's rights in a way that is liberatory and life-giving.

WESTERN ENLIGHTENMENT NOTION OF PERSON

The eighteenth-century Western Enlightenment brought about a revolutionary turn to the self and privileged the individual as a rational and autonomous subject, who is imbued with rights. The individual was conceived as an autonomous thinking being who must be free and unfettered to speak, act, accumulate wealth, and legislate for oneself. René Descartes' axiom, "*cogito ergo sum*," which means, "I think, therefore, I am" lies at the explicit source of this autonomous, individualistic subject of modernity. But because the Cartesian *cogito* is inherently incapable of self-transcendence, I concur with Polycarp Ikuenobe, as he succinctly avers, that it is an "abstraction grounded in a solipsistic self-consciousness."[1]

Before the Enlightenment, there was its forebear, Hellenism. Hellenism had construed reality in terms of asymmetrical and hierarchical dualism that privileged spirit or soul over matter or body.[2] In Hellenistic worldview, the male was the quintessence of rationality and transcendence while the female epitomized materiality and irrationality. Invariably, this Hellenistic dualistic heritage paved the way for androcentric, patriarchal, misogynistic, and racist legacy that privileged male over female, and white over black. Descartes himself embraced and calcified this Greek heritage as he also privileged mind or consciousness (*res cogitans*) over body (*res extensa*). Indeed, the Cartesian valorization of mind over body allowed for the creation of modern structures of domination and subordination of women and nature by men. Elizabeth Johnson rightly notes that the construction of hierarchical dualism has profound implications for women and women's rights and dignity.[3] If women are ever to be totally emancipated and their rights and dignity fully recognized and protected, then rethinking the dualistic heritage of the Enlightenment is germane to refocusing the equality of all humans regardless of gender, sexuality, race, socioeconomic status, and so forth.

Furthermore, another dimension of construing personhood comes from certain Enlightenment thinkers such as Thomas Hobbes, John Locke, and Jean-Jacque Rousseau. For them, the person is conceived as enjoying an ontological anteriority to community with which she has only a contractarian relationship. In this ontology, relationship is not constitutive of personhood. Being thrives by suppressing alterity at best or at worst, strives to dominate and assimilate the Other for self-interest. This is the idea of the crass individualism that has become prevalent in American culture. Human rights are often seen through such individualistic prism. But such individualism always tends to threaten both the survival of the individual and society. In what follows, I will unpack a trinitarian paradigm that provides rich hermeneutical tools for embedding a theology of women's rights that is more liberatory.

TRINITARIAN FOUNDATIONS OF THE THEOLOGY OF WOMEN'S RIGHTS

Central to the Christian tradition is the doctrine of the Trinity, used to describe the God of Jesus Christ. The trinitarian metaphor finds its classic expression in the Gospel of John as, "God is love" (1 Jn 4:8, 16).[4] Here, I intend to articulate a theology of human rights, nay, a theology of women's rights by situating it within the matrix of trinitarian foundations of theological anthropology.

It is the affirmation of the Christian tradition that the one God of Christian confession is triune—Father, Son, and Spirit. Although various interpretations of this doctrine abounded in both the early and medieval church, it has remained central to Christian theology and practice.[5] But with the emergence of the Western Enlightenment, the doctrine of the Trinity became marginalized as it was viewed merely as little more than an abstract speculative theology. By the twentieth century, however, a renaissance of trinitarian theology spawned an array of studies aimed at new ways of understanding and recovering of the doctrine.[6]

One of the most important outcomes of the contemporary renaissance of trinitarian theology, to my mind, is the valorization of the category of relationality. Many scholars interested in contemporary trinitarian theology see it as offering an alternative to the dominant substance ontology that has influenced reflection on the doctrine for much of church history. Substance theology presented God, *inter alia*, as an isolated, solipsistic, and immutable solitary individual. Perhaps the goal of this theology was an attempt to preserve the immutability of divine essence. But clearly, in the process, what became the result was the obfuscation of divine relationality.

The Trinity, understood as agapic relationality, encapsulates self-transcendence, community of life, and love together in a way that respects distinctions devoid of homogenization, totalization, assimilation, or hegemonic appropriation of the "Other." The original point of the trinitarian doctrine, as Robert Jenson lucidly notes, is that "God's relations to us are internal to him and it is in carrying out this insight that the 'relation' concept was introduced to define the distinctions of identities."[7] Hence, I am in sympathy with Catherine Mowry LaCugna when she notes that *person* rather than *substance* is the proper category to characterize trinitarian relations.[8] God's triune relationality thus provides the basis for a nonlimiting understanding of *imago Dei*.[9]

THE IMAGE OF GOD

Christian theological reflection has traditionally constructed theological anthropology around the notion of the *imago Dei*. The core of this notion relates to the idea that human beings are created in the image of God. The Enlightenment constructed a notion of the self as atomistic, individualistic, and self-legislating. Perhaps one of the most important achievements of postmodernity in terms of identity formation is the decentering and reconceptualization of the self as a social reality. The self is a nexus of relationships. This postmodern achievement is precisely reflective of the divine image understood as a *koinonia*, a shared common life of fellowship of the three trinitarian persons.[10]

The biblical creation narratives provide the grounds for understanding the *imago Dei* as social, as a communal reality. More specifically, in Genesis 1:26-28, the biblical author presents God as creating a plurality of sexes within humankind in a manner that reflects the plurality found within the divine inner life. The divine self-reference, "Let us make humankind in our image," though not a reference to an explicitly and fully developed doctrine of the Trinity, is nonetheless, one of the earliest allusions to complexity within the God of biblical revelation. The divine self-reference suggests that the narrator here intends the reader to be able to link human plurality and relationality to the divine relationality as its foundation and which it represents. Thus, the creation of humankind in the divine image is nothing less than a vocation and an invitation to humans to express and reflect the relational, communal, and perichoretic dynamism of the God in whose image they are made.

However, it's worth noting that plurality and unity are coterminous in the Trinity. Consequently, the human community that truly reflects or represents the *imago Dei* and divine relationality is one that shows, as Daniel Helminiak writes, that, "the human phenomenon is always and simultaneously and inextricably both social and individual...there is no human being apart from the social group in which he or she participates and there is no group apart from the individual members who constitute that group."[11] To be clear, the trinitarian model helps us to acknowledge how a genuine human community can emerge only where differences are not obfuscated or reduced to sameness, and where independent self-expression is promoted within the matrix of relationality. As such, each human individual and each community is the subject of rights. Now, let me add to the robustness of a relational notion of personhood with some rich insights from a certain West African religious and anthropological worldview.

AN IGBO COSMO-RELIGIOUS WORLDVIEW AND THE NOTION OF PERSONHOOD

In many West African societies, social organization and engineering are shaped by a complex of relationships. By the same token, in these societies, the individual human person is also defined in terms of a complexity of relationships. Since West Africa is neither monolithic nor monocultural but varied, needless to say then that multiple and varied anthropologies do exist in the different regions and societies that make up the Continent. However, it has been observed that in the West African subregion, ranging from Ghana to Cameroon to Nigeria to Benin Republic to Mali, and so forth, many similarities do exist in terms of both interethnic and intra-ethnic group contextual conception of the human person.[12]

The most common significant characteristic of the conception of the human person among the various societies in the West African subregion is the category of relatedness. In this section, my focus is on Igbo cosmo-religious and anthropological worldview. The Igbo make up one of the three largest ethnic groups in Nigeria of West Africa. Among the Igbo, for example, the human person is linked to both the visible and invisible worlds. A person is defined in terms of relations to parents, siblings, relatives, departed ancestors, and to God as well as other spirit beings and Mother Earth. In many West African sacred narratives or myths, the person is viewed as being endowed by God from eternity with a destiny spirit. This destiny or guardian spirit opens the person up for relationship not only with the divine but also with others in the community. The destiny spirit is known by various names among the different ethnic groups in the subregion. It is called *chi* and *ori* (among the Igbo and Yoruba of Nigeria), *kra* or *okra* (Ewe and Asante of Ghana), and so forth. For the Igbo, "Through *chi*, God is ontologically linked to each person."[13]

The notion of personhood in Igbo *weltanschauung* is distinct from both the classical Greek substantialist and the Enlightenment notions. In this subregion, "personhood is not viewed primarily as being-in-itself or being-for-itself, but rather as being-with-others."[14] Relationality serves as the chief norm of being. In this worldview, to be is to be related; one is human, nay, a person, "because of others, with others, and for others."[15] Indeed, a Sotho aphorism encapsulates this view thus: *"motho ke motho kabatho ka bang"* which means "I am because we are, and since we are, therefore, I am."[16] In the Igbo worldview, the significance of the category of relationality is, according to Chinua Achebe, aptly capsulized in the Igbo maxim, *"Ihe kwuru, ihe akwudobe ya,"* meaning "Wherever Something stands, Something else will stand beside it. Nothing is absolute."[17] This dictum captures the multiplicity, complexity, and interrelatedness that characterize all of reality.

Personhood is, therefore, neither shaped nor attained in isolation. Rather, persons are products of society. At the same time, it is needful to point out that, albeit, most West African worldviews reserve an important place for community, they also value the agency of the individual whose creativity through interaction with others continues to reproduce culture and society. On this account, the Igbo, as Achebe writes, "postulate the concept of every man as both a unique creation and the work of a unique creator [*chi*]. Which is as far as individualism and uniqueness can possibly go."[18] Thus, the notion that each individual has a unique *chi* (guardian or destiny spirit), implying that no two individuals possess the exact same *chi*, speaks precisely to the unique individuality of each person. Being endowed with *chi* not only shapes the dignity of each person, but also, as the Nigerian theologian, Elochukwu E. Uzukwu writes, "this spiritual element [*chi*] is the basis of the creativity of the individual person in community."[19] In essence, "*chi* is [arguably the equivalent of] the *imago Dei* in each human being. Each person is, therefore, considered to be of value and no individual is swallowed up in the 'we.' Every person is irreplaceable and irreducible."[20] In this way, the Igbo balance the claims of both individuality and community. The implication here is that the multiplicity of personal *chi* which accounts for the multiplicity of unique individuals is what equips each with unique gifts for contributing to the building up of society in all its aspects—political, social, cultural, spiritual, economic, and so forth.[21] Clearly, the rich insights gleaned from both the trinitarian theology and Igbo religious anthropological worldview as I have articulated, provide a framework for building a bridge between a more communal-oriented and a more individual leaning conceptions of human/women's rights.

INTERROGATING HUMAN/WOMEN'S RIGHTS IN THE UNITED STATES

The theology of human rights in general and of women's rights, in particular, is rooted within the theological locus of the *imago Dei*.[22] Although initially slow in endorsing the basic human rights that came to be promoted in the wake of the nineteenth-century global revolutions and decolonization processes, the Catholic Church has increasingly accepted and sanctioned them. For example, Pope John XXIII, in his 1963 encyclical, *Pacem in Terris*, clearly enumerated and enunciated those human rights.[23] However, mindful of the plurality and complexity of the ways of organizing social life in various societies and cultures, the Catholic Church refrains from devising or endorsing any one particular model for social engineering. However, the church does not fail to hold up "the moral imperative of human rights as minimal social conditions which all nations must respect. . . . Yet the church calls upon all people to protect and promote human rights irrespective of the way that a community is structured. Human rights are the moral parameters within which a social order must be organized."[24] Perhaps what is important about the Christian framing of rights language is its grounding within a communal orientation in such a way that does not marginalize or destroy personal liberty and independence. As Michael Himes and Kenneth Himes write, "A right is a necessary empowerment for people to participate in community."[25]

While human rights encompass women's rights, in the context of the United States, a particular worldview or tradition with a distinctive set of values has shaped their construal. The dominance of liberal individualism and racist ideology, no doubt, shaped the understanding of personhood and citizenship. In this worldview, the individual is posited as enjoying a logical primacy and anteriority over community and all forms of social relations. Robert Bellah describes the basis of this tradition as ontological individualism. It is "the belief that the truth of our condition is not in our society or in our relation to others, but in our isolated and inviolable selves."[26] Undoubtedly, individualism, whether utilitarian or expressive,[27] according to Bellah and his associates, continues to hold a powerful sway in contemporary American society and consciousness, shaping how individuals see both life and themselves in America.

However, although American society prizes itself as upholding individual freedom, equality, and dignity, it is not every human person that seems to be included in these ideals. These ideals seem to have been forged ab initio within the context of whiteness and white supremacist ideology. It is important to keep in mind that the American Constitution which declared that all humans are equal and endowed by their creator with unalienable rights, was "a document initiated and signed into history by white male slave owners."[28] For example, Thomas Jefferson, claimed that blacks were inferior to whites because, among other things, they lacked independent rational and somatic endowments necessary for self-legislation. Consequently, they had no right to freedom.[29] To this end, it is legitimately arguable and as borne out by history, that the ideology of white supremacy has contoured the parameters for the interpretation of the ideals enshrined in the Constitution. Within this hermeneutic circle, one would only expect that such a notion as freedom can only be interpreted according to the parameters set by its inventors. In this way, it is not surprising that although freedom has been trumpeted as a great American ideal, and America itself has been idolized as the land of the free, but then some are not truly free because of the prevailing racial stratification anchored on oppositional hierarchization in American society. In other words, these ideals are not really applicable to all but to some groups only.

With regard to the issue of women's liberty and rights, and particularly, women's suffrage, the question is which women are we talking about? There is no question that the women's movements and the different waves of feminism sought liberty for White middle-upper-class women. White middle-upper-class women aimed to secure the right to vote, the right to exercise their own reproductive liberty, as well as to liberate themselves from the shackles of their husbands' domination and from their confinement to domesticity.[30] Although Black women were originally involved in the suffrage movement, but no sooner had White women secured the right to vote than they ignored the plight of Black women. This further demonstrated that white freedom was the ideal freedom; the freedom initially enjoyed only by white patriarchal heterosexual males but now incrementally extended to white women.

When the Declaration of Independence lays claim to the equality of all men and liberty for all, what does this really mean? As Cheryl Matias and Peter Newlove put it, "when the very concepts of freedom, independence, and equality are persistently construed to be for one group, at the cost of erasing both the suffering and the humanity of all others, there is no freedom writ large. There is only freedom for those 'who believe they are white' . . . who become white . . . and who receive the societal benefits of being white."[31] As people of color eventually secured the right to vote, that right has frequently been under the threat of disenfranchisement. The 2020 election and the big lies perpetuated by former President Trump about election fraud backed by vigorous attempts to discredit, invalidate, and disenfranchise predominantly Black voters speak to the fragility of the suffrage of Black women minorities. Indeed, it can be stated without fear of equivocation that "the United States has an illusion of freedom that masks deeply rooted racism, white supremacy, and whiteness."[32]

The solution, however, is not to abandon individualism completely as this would upend the foundations of American culture and life. Rather, it might lie in reconciling the claims of individuality and community, or simply holding both claims in creative tension. The trinitarian model and Igbo religious anthropological insights as teased out previously offer a hermeneutical framework for interfacing these apparent divergent claims.

WOMEN'S RIGHTS: CONVERGENCE OF TRINITARIAN AND AFRICAN ANTHROPOLOGICAL INSIGHTS AS A LIBERATORY HERMENEUTIC

From both the trinitarian and Igbo cosmo-religious anthropological viewpoints, it is clear that "to be" is "to be related"; to be connected to others, or "to-be-with-others." Thus, personal identity is shaped and attained within the matrix of relationality and community which always and logically precedes the individual. But each individual is also uniquely gifted and whose creativity contributes to the reproduction and building up of society. These insights are relevant to the question of women's rights. Against the backdrop of patriarchy, heteronormative masculinity, hegemonic whiteness, and White supremacist ideology, there is no question that women of all iterations have been discriminated against in all kinds of ways. Granted, feminist movements have challenged, deconstructed, and disrupted some of these discriminatory ideologies, but the gains that have been made do not seem to benefit all women. Obviously, it is the privileged White middle-upper-class women who have benefitted the most from the gains of feminist movements. Clearly, the majority of working-class women and women of color, particularly, Black women—who deal with triple discrimination on the basis of race, gender, and class—cannot be said to have benefitted equally from the gains of feminist movements including women's suffrage. As a matter of fact, womanist and intersectional theological approaches, as espoused by Black female theologians and scholars, are very critical of White feminist activism for ignoring Black women's experience and standpoint and for its overly White-centered and universalizing discourse.[33]

The theology of the Trinity, rooted, as it were, in life-giving and liberatory biblical narratives as well as the insights culled from Igbo religious anthropological worldviews, invite both church and society at large to address the need for the total emancipation and upholding of the dignity and rights of all women regardless of race, sexual identity/orientation, and class. That the Catholic Church has historically contributed to women's experience of discrimination and injury is unquestionable. I contend, nonetheless, that the church, as the witness to the Kingdom, remains the place for the recognition and defense of the rights of individuals, especially women, because it is quintessentially, though not exclusively, the locus of the operation of the Spirit of God.[34] Unfortunately, the church has not always been faithful to this prophetic task. Currently, however, the Church has come to recognize the equal dignity of women and men, while acknowledging that, as a consequence, women have special gifts to contribute to both church and society at large.[35] The insights drawn from a trinitarian and Igbo religious anthropological paradigms call for a more robust defense of the dignity and rights of all women by completing the unfinished task of working out their total liberation in church, family, workplace, and in social, cultural, economic, and political life in contemporary society.

CONCLUSION

In this chapter, I have mapped the contours of a theology of women's rights in a way that takes into consideration the seemingly paradoxical claims of individuality and community by holding them in creative tension. In order to accomplish this task, I first rethought the dualistic and individualistic legacy of the Enlightenment thinking with attention to its construction of the notion of personhood. Utilizing productive insights from a reconceptualized trinitarian theology and Igbo religious anthropological worldview, I argued that both individual claims and community claims with regard to women's rights are not mutually exclusive but coterminous.

Furthermore, I submitted that both the church and contemporary society have made giant strides in acknowledging women's rights and dignity. At the same time, I further pointed out that these enormous achievements in securing women's rights notwithstanding, the rights were not equally recognized for everyone, particularly, women's suffrage for Black women. Such rights seemed to have been secured mainly for White middle-upper-class women. In the United States, there is a lot of chatter about individual rights and freedom for all, but such seems only to be an illusion. Women have consistently been discriminated against due to oppressive strictures of patriarchy and white male chauvinism; racial minorities' rights are not too infrequently under ceaseless threats as was orchestrated by the Trump administration during the last 2020 presidential election. All in all, a trinitarian cum Igbo religious and anthropological perspectives offer us another paradigm for reimagining personhood; providing us with a hermeneutic tool for understanding women's rights in a not too strictly atomized sense but in a relational fashion that is liberatory and life-giving for each and all.

NOTES

1. Polycarp Ikuenobe, *Philosophical Perspectives on Communalism and Morality in African Traditions* (New York: Rowan and Littlefield Publishers, 2006), 55.

2. Elizabeth A. Johnson, *Women, Earth, and Creator Spirit* (New York/Mahwah: Paulist Press, 1993), 11.

3. See Johnson, *Women, Earth, and Creator Spirit*.

4. *The New Testament Bible in Contemporary Language* (Colorado Springs: NavPress Publishing, 2003).

5. For details on the various views, see Edmund Fortman, *The Triune God: A Historical Study of the Doctrine of the Trinity* (Philadelphia: Westminster Press, 1972).

6. See Catherine Mowry LaCugna, "Philosophers and Theologians on the Trinity," *Modern Theology*, vol. 2, no. 3 (April 1986): 169–181.

7. Robert W. Jenson, *The Triune Identity: God According to the Gospel* (Philadelphia: Fortress Press, 1982), 120.

8. Catherine Mowry LaCugna, *God for Us: The Trinity and Christian Life* (San Francisco: HapperCollins, 1991), 14.

9. Pamela Cooper-White, *Shared Wisdom: Use of the Self in Pastoral Care and Counseling* (Minneapolis: Fortress Press, 2004).

10. See Alistair I. McFadyen, *The Call to Personhood: A Christian Theory of the Individual in Social Relationships* (Cambridge: Cambridge University Press, 1990).

11. Daniel A. Helminiak, "Human Solidarity and Collective Union in Christ," *Anglican Theological Review*, vol. 70, no. 1 (January 1988): 37.

12. See Elochukwu E. Uzukwu, *A Listening Church: Autonomy and Communion in African Churches* (Maryknoll, NY: Orbis Books, 1996).

13. Okechukwu C. Njoku, "Translating the divine in the Encounter of the Gospel and Cultures: A Pneumatological Perspective," in *Translating Religion, College*

Theology Annual Volume 58, eds. Mary Doak and Anita Houck (Maryknoll, NY: Orbis Books, 2012), 80.

14. Okechukwu C. Njoku, "Igbo Communal Ethos: A More holistic Template for Rethinking the Principle of Patient Autonomy in Health Care Ethics and Biomedicine," in *Against All Odds: The Igbo Experience in Postcolonial Nigeria*, eds. Apollos O. Nwauwa and Chima J. Korieh (Glassboro, NJ: Goldline & Jacobs Publishers, 2011), 352.

15. Uzukwu, *A Listening Church*, 37.

16. See George O. Ehusani, *An Afro-Christian Vision "OZOVEHE": Toward a More Humanized World* (New York: University Press of America, 1991), 91–93.

17. Chinua Achebe, "Chi in Igbo Cosmology," in *African Philosophy: An Anthology*, ed. Emmanuel C. Eze (Oxford: Blackwell Publishing Company, 1998), 67.

18. Achebe, "Chi in Igbo Cosmology," 70.

19. Uzukwu, *A Listening Church*, 107.

20. Njoku, "Translating the divine in the Encounter of the Gospel and Cultures," 80.

21. Ibid., 82.

22. United States Conference of Catholic Bishops, *Economic Justice for All: Catholic Social Teaching and the U.S. Economy* (Washington, DC: United States Catholic Conference, 2006). 32.

23. See Pope John XXIII, Encyclical Letter, *Pacem in Terris* (Rome: Liberia Editrice Vaticana, 1963).

24. Michael J. Himes and Kenneth R. Himes, *Fullness of Faith: The Public Significance of Theology* (New York/Mahwah, NJ: Paulist Press, 1994), 64.

25. Ibid., 70.

26. Robert N. Bellah, "Community Properly Understood: A Defense of Democratic Communitarianism," in *The Essential Communitarian Reader*, ed. Amitai Etzioni (Lanham, MD: Rowman & Littlefield, 1998), 17.

27. Robert N. Bellah et al., *Habits of the Heart: Individualism and Commitment in American Life* (New York: Harper & Row, 1986), 33.

28. Cheryl E. Matias and Peter M. Newlove, "The Illusion of Freedom: Tyranny, Whiteness, and the State of the US Society," *Equity & Excellence in Education*, vol. 50, no. 3 (2017): 318.

29. See Emmanuel C. Eze, *Race and the Enlightenment: A Reader* (Oxford: Blackwell, 1998).

30. See Dorothy Roberts, *Killing the Black Body: Race, Reproduction, and the Meaning of Liberty* (New York: Vintage Books, 1997).

31. Matias and Newlove, "The Illusion of Freedom," 323.

32. Ibid., 321.

33. See Ruth Frankenberg, *The Social Construction of Whiteness: White Women, Race Matters* (Minneapolis: University of Minnesota Press, 1993), 8.

34. See Uzukwu, *A Listening Church*.

35. See Sara Butler, "Women and the Church," in *The Gift of the Church: A Textbook on Ecclesiology*, ed. Peter C. Phan (Collegeville, MN: The Liturgical Press, 2000), 424.

FURTHER READINGS

DuBois, Ellen C. Suffrage: *Women's Long Battle for the Vote*. New York: Simon and Schuster, 2020.
———. *Woman Suffrage and Women's Rights*. New York: New York University Press, 1998.
Franzen, Trisha. *Anna Howard Shaw: The Work of Woman Suffrage*. Urbana, Chicago and Springfield: University of Illinois Press, 2014.
Mayeri, Serena. "After Suffrage: The Unfinished Business of Feminist Legal Advocacy." *The Yale Law Journal Forum* 129 (2020): 512–534.
Terborg-Penn, Rosalyn. *African American Women in the Struggle for the Vote, 1850–1920*. Bloomington, IN: Indiana University Press, 1998.
Wagner, Sally R., ed. *The Women's Suffrage Movement*. New York: Penguin Classics, 2019.
Weatherford, Doris. *Victory for the Vote: The Fight for Women's Suffrage and the Century That Followed*. Coral Gables, FL: Mango Publishing, 2020.

REFERENCES

Achebe, Chinua. "Chi in Igbo Cosmology." In *African Philosophy: An Anthology*, edited by Emmanuel C. Eze, 67–72. Oxford: Blackwell Publishing Company, 1998.
Bellah, Robert N. "Community Properly Understood: A Defense of Democratic Communitarianism." In *The Essential Communitarian Reader*, edited by Amitai Etzioni, 15–20. Lanham, MD: Rowman & Littlefield, 1998.
Bellah, R. N., Madsen, R., Sullivan, W. M., Swidler, A., and Tipton, S. M. *Habits of the Heart: Individualism and Commitment in American Life*. New York: Harper & Row, 1986.
Butler, Sara. "Women and the Church." In *The Gift of the Church: A Textbook on Ecclesiology*, edited by Peter C. Phan, 415–433. Collegeville, MN: The Liturgical Press, 2000.
Cooper-White, Pamela. *Shared Wisdom: Use of the Self in Pastoral Care and Counseling*. Minneapolis: Fortress Press, 2004.
Ehusani, George O. *An Afro-Christian Vision "OZOVEHE": Toward a More Humanized World*. New York: University Press of America, 1991.
Eze, Emmanuel C. *Race and the Enlightenment: A Reader*. Oxford: Blackwell, 1998.
Fortman, Edmund. *The Triune God: A Historical Study of the Doctrine of the Trinity*. Philadelphia: Westminster Press, 1972.
Frankenberg, Ruth. *The Social Construction of Whiteness: White Women, Race Matters*. Minneapolis: University of Minnesota Press, 1993.
Helminiak, Daniel A. "Human Solidarity and Collective Union in Christ." *The Anglican Theological Review* 70, no. 1 (1988): 34–59.

Himes, Michael J., and Himes, Kenneth R. *Fullness of Faith: The Public Significance of Theology*. New York/Mahwah, NJ: Paulist Press, 1994.

Ikuenobe, Polycarp. *Philosophical Perspectives on Communalism and Morality in African Traditions*. New York: Rowan and Littlefield Publishers, 2006.

Jenson, Robert W. *The Triune Identity: God According to the Gospel*. Philadelphia: Fortress Press, 1982.

Johnson, Elizabeth A. *Women, Earth, and Creator Spirit*. New York/Mahwah: Paulist Press, 1993.

LaCugna, Catherine M. *God for Us: The Trinity and Christian Life*. San Francisco: HapperCollins, 1991.

———. "Philosophers and Theologians on the Trinity." *Modern Theology* 2, no. 3 (1986): 169–181.

Matias, Cheryl E., and Newlove, Peter M. "The Illusion of Freedom: Tyranny, Whiteness, and the State of the US Society." *Equity & Excellence in Education* 50, no. 3 (2017): 316–330.

McFadyen, Alistair I. *The Call to Personhood: A Christian Theory of the Individual in Social Relationships*. Cambridge: Cambridge University Press, 1990.

Njoku, Okechukwu C. "Igbo Communal Ethos: A More holistic Template for Rethinking the Principle of Patient Autonomy in Health Care Ethics and Biomedicine." In *Against All Odds: The Igbo Experience in Postcolonial Nigeria*, edited by Apollos O. Nwauwa and Chima J. Korieh, 347–364. Glassboro, NJ: Goldline & Jacobs Publishers, 2011.

———. "Translating the divine in the Encounter of the Gospel and Cultures: A Pneumatological Perspective." In *Translating Religion, College Theology Annual Volume 58*, edited by Mary Doak and Anita Houck, 71–84. Maryknoll, NY: Orbis Books, 2012.

Pope, John XXIII. "Encyclical Letter." In *Pacem in Terris*. Rome: Liberia Editrice Vaticana, 1963.

Roberts, Dorothy. *Killing the Black Body: Race, Reproduction, and the Meaning of Liberty*. New York: Vintage Books, 1997.

The New Testament Bible in Contemporary Language. Colorado Springs: NavPress Publishing, 2003.

United States Conference of Catholic Bishops. *Economic Justice for All: Catholic Social Teaching and the U.S. Economy*. Washington, D.C.: United States Catholic Conference, 2006.

Uzukwu, Elochukwu E. *A Listening Church: Autonomy and Communion in African Churches*. Maryknoll, NY: Orbis Books, 1996.

Part 4

TOWARD PEDAGOGIES OF WHOLENESS

Chapter 13

Toward the Flourishing of Women of Color through the Lens of Intersectionality and Neuropsychology

Sarina Saturn

This chapter attempts to address the intersectionality of gender, class, spirituality, and mental health in the well-being and flourishing of women of color in the United States. The concept of multiple marginality will be explored in women whose gender identity intersects with one or more marginalized identities, such as belonging to an ethnic minority, a nonheterosexual sexual orientation, physical disability, and low socioeconomic status. Those who experience multiple marginality, professionally and personally, need powerful guidance and advocacy and this chapter will cover the most effective and ineffective ways to accomplish this vital mentorship.

This chapter will also provide foundational knowledge on the neuroscience underlying social and emotional processing. This includes the underpinnings of implicit and explicit bias, prejudice, stereotypes, and sexism, racism, and colorism with a focus on neural architecture, evolutionary psychology, and neurochemistry. After unpacking the biology of trauma, depression, oppression, and anxiety, this section will cover ways of cultivating resilience with a variety of coping strategies, including through the cultivation of compassion for ourselves and others. The following questions will be relevant to this chapter: What strategies can be employed by women of color and their mentors that will promote the flourishing of their lives? In what ways can spirituality ensure holistic flourishing? How can the damage of destructive emotions, beliefs, and behaviors be repaired with the healing powers of understanding, forgiveness, and acceptance? How can the science of compassion and self-compassion inform us on the best ways to connect with one another to fuel a society of empathy and inclusion?

The fields of neuroscience and psychology were largely founded on the principles of "othering" and definitions of what qualifies as normal and abnormal. The colonization of the disciplines led to the production of knowledge through privileged, heteronormative, Eurocentric, and patriarchal lenses. Unfortunately, many of the first studies were geared to provide evidence that women and people of color are inferior as it comes to intellect, emotional stability, and subordination. It is important to have a critical view of the origins of our conceptions of social and emotional well-being in order to better understand the suffering, healing, and joy in ourselves and others. In the author's professional and personal journey as a woman of color (WOC) in the academy, she has moved from studying and living in emotional darkness, including trauma, fear, depression, and chronic stress, into the light of compassion, love, forgiveness, healing, and connection.

THE NEUROSCIENCE UNDERLYING SOCIAL AND EMOTIONAL PROCESSING

The Darkness

For millennia, scholars and laypeople alike have been pondering and investigating the nature and purpose of emotions. The ancient philosophical and theological notions centered on the idea that emotions are disruptive and interfered with cool-headed, rationale thinking. Neuroscience, which has an age-old conflict with religion, has provided evidence that emotions have evolved to aid in survival and well-being of the self and relationships with others. This is to say that emotions are functional and have a deep purpose in evolutionary biology.[1]

It is important to be scared during fearful events to instinctually allow self-preservation instincts to kick in, whether it be feeling, feigning, or freezing. It is also crucial to be angry to allow for the fight for autonomy and rights. There are many theories about the utility of sadness and many emphasize the need for this sickness response to restore energy. Many creatures have also evolved to have emotional memories of what has caused threats and harm in the past so that these recollections can assist in avoiding dangerous stimuli and contexts the next time they are encountered.

Nevertheless, emotions are designed to be most functional when they are fleeting. After perceiving environmental and existential threats, the brain activates survival mechanisms in the central and peripheral nervous system to deal with the situation at hand.[2] After this emergency response, the organism is designed to return to a resting and restorative state. The human condition, however, is especially prone to grudges and rumination due to the massive growth of our prefrontal cortex.[3] This structure, which sets us apart from other animals, is a double-edged sword. The prefrontal cortex gifts humanity with abstract thinking, creative problem solving, planning for the future, and emotion regulation. However, the prefrontal cortex also allows for emotions to endure and go haywire, as in cases of severe anxiety, violence, depression, and post-traumatic stress disorder.[4]

The manifestations of these chronic conditions cause isolating affective blinders and intense individual suffering. This suffering can manifest itself in psychological and somatic forms and can affect emotional, cognitive, and physical health in a variety of ways. When in the throes of anguish, this often leads to self-isolation, in both the mental and physical sense, and this further leads to a detachment from common humanity. Scientific evidence could argue that this suffering causes selfishness and a lack of perspective-taking. In turn, this can lead to many societal ills and selfish structures, including systemic oppression rooted in racism, sexism, queermisia, xenomisa, capitalism, grudge-holding, and more. Indeed, there are many examples of how systemic oppression and "othering" plays out in government, health care, business, religion, and education systems. This is a terrible outcome in the very systems purportedly designed to help and care for people.[5] These traumas endured by persons who suffer from social structures of injustice lead to institutional betrayal.

It becomes particularly nefarious when implicit biases from well-intended people lead to the marginalization of individual groups. This is a toxic combination with the stigma of mental illness, especially if the sickness of anguish is caused by afflictions of multiple systems of oppression in a patriarchal, heteronormative, and White supremacist world.[6]

The Light

Chronic dark emotional states can lead to harm to oneself and others due to the release of toxic and pro-inflammatory chemicals, especially stress hormones sparked by amygdala activation due to environmental threats. The prosocial nervous system, which incorporates the pillars of spirituality, compassion, love, and generosity, can lead to powerful movements related to healing, reparations, forgiveness, and justice. One of the most powerful elements of prosocial emotions is that it moves one from an inward, personal state of suffering into an outward light of common humanity. When individuals are in the weeds of despair concerning the details of their own specific narrative of suffering, it is very easy for them to lose sight of how billions of people across time and around the world have felt the searing pain of depression, isolation, anxiety, and ostracization. It can bring much solace and healing when one can enter the light of the interconnectedness of the human condition.

Concern for others—the motivation that guides prosociality—arises from neurophysiological processes that promote attachment and caregiving.

Prosocial behaviors are actions that benefit others, such as altruism, cooperation, and trust. This is due to the activation of prosocial networks that activate feel-good neurochemicals, such as dopamine, oxytocin, and serotonin, and calming and rewarding physiological circuitry, in both the giver and receiver of the prosocial bond. The biology underlying social connections has proven, in a variety of contexts, the intrinsic rewards that come from meaningful and nurturing social connections.

HEALING REMEDIES INSPIRED BY MORAL ELEVATION

Mentoring is a prosocial behavior in which a person with experience in a field guides another person with less experience. Although there are little or no direct studies of the neuroscience of mentorship, there is ample evidence from the neuropsychology of prosocial behavior, in addition to the psychology underlying effective and ineffective mentoring strategies, to thoughtfully explore the bases of transformative practices and studies of the science of mentoring.[7]

This focus is on mentoring in academia as the author is a WOC and serves as a scholar, teacher, and mentor at a university. However, many parallels can be drawn from what is shared here to other sectors of society. Despite an enormous amount of mentoring initiatives in higher education, the most effective prosocial endeavors will involve the engagement of the prosocial nervous system.

One distinct emotional state that has been shown to inspire mentorship is moral elevation. Moral elevation is elicited by watching acts of great virtue and benevolence. Elevation has been shown to promote altruistic acts through fostering compassion, hope, optimism about humanity, a desire to be a better person, and motivation to pay the altruism forward.[8]

On a biological level, moral elevation elicits neural and autonomic events by modulating the activity of the medial prefrontal cortex, a key brain structure involved in self-referential thought, as well as both the sympathetic (*flight, fright, freeze,* or *feign*) and parasympathetic (*feed* and *breed*; *rest* and *digest*) systems. It is uncommon for both branches of the autonomic nervous system to be significantly recruited simultaneously, though this uncommon pattern does arrive in unique situations that involve both stress arousal and social sensitivity, such as parenting and courtship. It is likely that mentoring also induces this dual activation due to a similar combination of challenge and encouragement.[9]

There is also indirect evidence that moral elevation induces oxytocin release, a hormone and neurotransmitter essential for nurturance and bonding.

Oxytocin probably modulates mentorship that involves warm and nurturing caregiving. Another key prosocial neuromodulator of mentorship is dopamine, which is responsible for the rush and reward of altruistic activities, such as teamwork, success, and charitable acts.[10]

Moral elevation can be induced very simply by reading stories or viewing videos of other people exhibiting moral excellence. This emotional state has been shown to boost positive attitudes toward mentoring and encourage the gathering of information about serving as a mentor in addition to promoting the act of mentoring itself. This implies that witnessing inspiring stories of the mentor-mentee relationship might be a very powerful way to motivate others to find avenues to mentor. Furthermore, moral elevation has been shown to reduce prejudice and isolation, thereby lowering two major stressors that marginalized identities face when persisting in a field where they are significantly outnumbered by a majority group. Therefore, not only can moral elevation inspire mentoring, but it can also reduce the negative emotions faced in predominantly white institutions.[11]

Witnessing so few successful individuals with a constellation of marginalized identities successful in ascending the ranks in academia leads to isolation, overidentification, and self-judgment. On the other spectrum of these elements are common humanity, mindfulness, self-kindness, and the pillars of self-compassion. The cultivation of compassion and self-compassion in the mentorship relationship would allow both the mentors and mentees to develop a sense of mastery and competence to override the negative emotions faced when navigating an uphill professional journey.[12]

HOW SPIRITUALITY LEADS TO FLOURISHING

When spirituality focuses on the cultivation of common humanity and the calling to help those who are suffering, this leads to an opening and recruitment of the prosocial nervous system. It is intrinsically rewarding to be altruistic, charitable, compassionate, and inclusive. It also allows for the reduction of self-other differentiation which fuels the fires of hate and judgment. Furthermore, the science of spirituality and contemplation has shown that loving-kindness practices can improve mental wellbeing by boosting positive emotions, immunity, and compassion and reducing bias, negativity, and depression. Indeed, people who make an effort to practice spiritual love and acceptance are much less likely to fall into the trap of othering and the drive to hurt others and themselves.

The oxytocin system evolved to promote spiritual bonds between sentient beings. When employed, it creates a chemical bond with others that are loved and cared for, and this extends from romantic, familial, and friendly bonds to love for fellow human beings, even complete strangers. When maximized endogenously, it connects others in beautiful ways and also reduces neurobiological and cardiovascular responses to social stress to calm the nervous system to allow for "tend and befriend" circuitry to do its magic.

Another key element of the social engagement system is a parasympathetic branch of the vagus nerve which is intimately tied to the oxytocin system. It is essential for recruitment of the periphery to show signs of nurturance, including eye contact, open body language, empathetic smiles, and putting the brakes on the heart rate to allow for calming during social interactions. Moreover, the myelinated vagus nerve plays a huge role in the benefits achieved through meditation, prayer and asana postures, chanting and singing in unison, and contemplative practices.[13] This can be a key differentiator in the interpretation and practice of religious doctrine, as well. If it is interpreted to impose judgment, condemnation, and dominance over others, this can lead to the emotional and physical maltreatment of those already suffering and marginalized. If it urges the faithful to be kind, charitable, and open-hearted to all, especially the less fortunate, this is a beautiful moral guide that can lead to wonderful flourishing and healing.

INTERSECTIONAL MARGINALITY: THE MENTORSHIP OF WOMEN FROM UNDERREPRESENTED MINORITIES

Multiple marginality exists in women and nonbinary people navigating multiple systems of oppression, especially those who identify as WOC. Thus, gender identity intersects with one or more marginalized and underrepresented minority identities, such as belonging to an ethnic or racial minority, a nonheterosexual sexual orientation (Lesbian, Gay, Bisexual, Transgender, Queer or Questioning, Intersex, Plus; LGBTQI+), physical disability, and low socioeconomic status. Those who experience multiple marginality need powerful guidance and advocacy. There are so many obstacles that people from sexual, physical, class, ethnic, and racial minorities face, and each of these identities deserves special attention.

While this chapter focuses on WOC, there is an undeniable need to recognize and care for all minorities who feel isolated and trapped in a toxic environment of an institution that continually endorses the superiority of majority statuses. Moreover, it is important to always bring intersectionality to the forefront since multiple marginality can lead to catastrophic outcomes. For example, transgender women of color from low socioeconomic backgrounds are exponentially more likely to die from homicide or suicide.[14]

SUPPORTING WOC IN THE ACADEMY

For WOC at all career stages in the academy, from undergraduate to full professor, the most effective strategies include transforming institutional culture and climate; building and sustaining critical mass of both students and faculty living in multiple marginality; ensuring, rewarding, and maximizing involvement; and building interinstitutional partnerships.

SUPPORTING WOC FACULTY

Top-down approaches that lead to campus transformation require a university's administration to recognize that there is a widespread need across the academy in supporting WOC and to commit to addressing the problem systematically and effectively. Although there are some great grant initiatives devoted to this from both the student and faculty end, these proposals are not funded unless there is very tangible and heartfelt financial backing and buy-in from university leaders. Furthermore, some granting agencies have a narrow scope of what they want the funding initiatives to achieve. Most grants can only work within certain systems in particular ways to address very specific problems. Thus, more radical and transformative ideas may be deemed too risky to finance. As a result, the awards are often given to safer bets and unfortunately, these are less likely to challenge the status quo.

Even with the best of intentions, most universities have institutionalized sexism and racism woven into the fabric of the culture due to the historical landscape of many centers of learning. As a result, most disciplines in higher education reflect colonization and the exploitation and domination of marginalized peoples. To further explain, particularly in the American academy, colleges and universities were built by and for wealthy White of high social class. Pedagogy and scholarship reflected thinking only substantiated by religions and other forms of thinking that sought to strengthen their place at the top of sociopolitical hierarchies. Therefore, this largely Eurocentric model of most of the humanities and social and natural sciences has played an integral role in how knowledge has been produced and disseminated. Although for many thousands of years, humans of all identities have been exploring, pondering, and investigating the nature and nurture of the world, this is not reflected in most textbooks and syllabi.

Thus, seams must be ripped to resew a more inclusive and welcoming fabric of education. In academia, this can be accomplished by powerful faculty and administrator professional development strategies with a lens of social justice. Boutique workshops and party programming lack efficacy and can cause more harm than good. Therefore, institutions must invest in deeper weeks-long development with accountability structures to demonstrate the cultivation of empathy and action items related to teaching, scholarship, and service. These trainings can continue for months or years and center on White fragility, ways to dismantle dominant narratives, microaggressions, inclusive pedagogy, racial and intergenerational trauma-informed knowledge, and repair practices. Rather than passive learning, they involve deep introspection, meaningful activities, group work across disciplines, and recognition of ways of being complicit in upholding White supremacy and patriarchy in the academy.

Accountability should involve action items with concrete outcomes and deadlines for endeavors. These can include a variety of ways to interrupt the systems of oppression. This includes decolonizing courses, creating bias-reporting systems, compassionate ways of calling in those who cause harm unintentionally, healing for those who are harmed, and punitive measures for repeat offenders with a track record of subjecting others to harm.

This also pertains to the strategies employed for hiring and retention. Professional development of search advocates and members of search committees can help with the tendency to resort to implicit biases and a lack of understanding of the obstacles faced by those who have faced multiple marginality, especially if they are nontraditional or first-generation students. Due to this continual replication, most departments and centers are predominantly White. Although hiring White women and queer and transgender academics is a step in the right direction, they can still contribute to systems of oppression, even with the best of intentions, as they are also subject to White fragility and are often unwilling to work on their own biases, prejudices, and self-awareness.

Indeed, White privilege is often used to leverage power to keep White supremacy intact, both consciously and unconsciously. A White person who belongs to a particular gender and/or sexual minority will undoubtedly encounter misogyny and queermisia in a patriarchal and cisheteronormative society and thus feel the pain and exclusion of belonging to a nondominant identity. This anguish can often make individuals develop a false sense of empathy for WOC.

It is a very dangerous situation when White people feel confident that they understand what it truly means to be a WOC due to their own marginalization. WOC carry deep unknowable scars from intergenerational trauma through slavery, stolen land, colonization, sexual violence, and genocide. This is combined with a lifetime of harm from systemic racism and sexism in societal constructions, including health care, education, economics, and housing. When White individuals who are members of other oppressed groups assume they have a basic understanding of the plight of WOC, this leads to fewer acts of compassion and antiracism which results in more isolation, gaslighting, and harm.

Although the percentage of WOC serving in faculty positions continues to grow each year, these are overwhelmingly nontenure-track, part-time positions. Thus, WOC are much more likely to be caught in academia's permanent underclass as an adjunct, instructor, or visitor. This lack of job security has devastating consequences for individuals who are members of marginalized groups. For those fortunate to have tenure-track positions, many are still excluded. It is worth noting that fewer than one in ten women faculty are full professors. Thus, inequities are rampant throughout academia. This affects WOC students who want to enter academia but cannot find themselves reflected in the tenure-track positions. This provides strong messaging for gatekeeping academia.

These stories and statistics should inspire more proactive hiring strategies that provide more job security, mentorship, and status. This includes avoiding cost-saving measures of paying numerous college teachers pennies on the dollar to do the same work required of tenured colleagues. It also involves open-rank hires so that new tenure-track lines are not all entry-level positions. In addition, cluster hires can lead to a built-in community of colleagues. Further, search committees should undergo thorough training on the application review and interview process to understand and override the tendency to use a biased rubric for sizing up worthiness. Also, a search advocate on each hiring committee devoted to diversity, equity, and inclusion can help articulate the unique experiences and perspectives that diverse candidates can bring to the classroom and laboratory. It is important to note that retention is a crucial element that is often overlooked for WOC students, staff, and faculty alike. Thus, this work requires constant progress with community building, affinity groups, and extra support. It cannot stop at the hiring decision or the statement of incoming WOC on the university websites.

Another crucial step is to implement structures, policies, and procedures with inclusive decision-making and power-sharing. This can be accomplished by revising archaic traditions by rewriting the rules and regulations adhered to in the past. Communal agreements can take place at the level of departments, colleges, schools, and the entire university to ensure fairness and transparency when it comes to hiring, promotion, and retention. Sadly, there are very few WOC in high ranks in the academy. They are severely underrepresented in both mid-level and upper administration, especially at faith-based institutions with religious foundations of misogyny, colonization, conversion therapy, and White saviorism. As a result, WOC at most institutions have little power or influence over governance and decision-making.

WOC students need more role models in faculty members that understand and live intersectional marginality. A critical mass of WOC faculty would help divide the unseen labor of advising students from diverse backgrounds that only resonate with one or two professors. This takes away from class preparation, research, email correspondence, and more, though it is a labor of love for most and considered an honor when students seek nurturance and understanding from certain advisors. One important aim is to reward WOC who take on the invisible labor with tenure and promotion and recognition.

In discussing the invisible labor of WOC faculty, Manya Whitaker states:

> On the days when I am tired of being "the only," or when I've experienced one too many microaggressions myself, a student visit always lifts my spirits. I am reminded that I am not here—on this campus or in this profession—for myself. I am here for the students. I am here to show them that people of color, queer people, disabled people, working class people—people like my students—can not only survive, but thrive at an institution that was not designed to meet their needs.[15]

SUPPORTING WOC STUDENTS

In the classroom, all instructors can thoughtfully integrate sources, assignments, and activities that are culturally relevant and meaningful to the students with a lens of social justice and decolonization. One example is to implement a community-based project catered to the discipline at hand, whether it be testing water quality in the laboratory, bringing the humanities from the ivory tower into the community, engineering accessibility devices for those with impairments, or using mathematics to study data related to mental health. Not only does this make the material more relevant and meaningful to students, but it cultivates a sense of mastery and contributes to the betterment of society.

In the laboratory, faculty scientists can be proactive in recruiting WOC into their research program in an assertive and encouraging manner by recognizing their potential through their coursework or initiatives outside the classroom. A study involving a team of students builds a strong social network and family away from home. Importantly, carving out and creating individual projects from a larger study inquiry often leads to pride-inducing mastery which then leads to conference presentations, capstone projects, and co-authorship on journal articles. This helps cultivate a strong scientific identity in students to encourage them to persist in the sciences as a professional path.

Finally, advising student clubs of identity groups and outreach endeavors to raise culture consciousness and sensitivity is another layer to complement initiatives in pedagogy, scholarship, and activism. This includes having meetings and events that bring in role models to campus, establishing service opportunities with local nonprofit organizations that serve marginalized populations, and establishing mentorship and club programs devoted to diversity, equity, and inclusion.

There is an undeniable magic when a senior WOC mentors a student WOC, but it is important to realize that these outlined strategies can be practiced by all faculty and will benefit all students. The author has had the great benefit of being mentored by feminist and antiracist white men. Infusing social justice and diversity, equity, and inclusion into curricula transformation, scholarship, and service cultivates understanding and advocacy in everyone.

Partnerships across institutions can help faculty and students cultivate well-developed senses of social competency and can help them recognize when race, ethnicity, and class identity affect student academic performance. External mentors can be more objective and unbiased and not affected by organizational dynamics. Moreover, these outside experts offer additional networking opportunities beyond the confines of the mentee's institution.

Potent catalysts to enact institutional shifts for WOC include peer mentoring and the support of advancement to decision-making roles inside or outside of administration. Moreover, faculty development on understanding multiple marginality can lead to curricula transformation and more meaningful and impactful courses and outreach. When students and faculty see their identities and histories reflected in their curriculum, diverse new perspectives are introduced into the field, which fosters new ideas and the growth of knowledge. One effective way is to promote accessibility to those inclusive designs for learning. This framework enhances usability and thus accessibility of curricular materials by taking advantage of technological advances to facilitate the development of hardware and software applications to assist students with disabilities. As a result, inclusive pedagogical strategies enhance learning for all students with the multimodal and flexible nature of this approach. Another key strategy is to incorporate the arts to increase achievement and knowledge through an interdisciplinary and decolonized approach.

Furthermore, faculty can promote inclusive and diverse perspectives in their syllabi, course materials, office spaces, and more. It is also important to emphasize that recognizing diversity is different from appropriating it, and that when this line is crossed, accept the harm done with humility. It is unfair to process shame and guilt with someone by imposing labor on diversity, equity, and inclusion education. Finally, institutions can provide a welcoming and nurturing environment inspired by a prosocial neuroscience lens with community-building bridge programs, inclusive spaces for marginalized groups to gather, and a visible and substantive commitment to address the leaky pipeline of WOC in the academy. In higher education, this includes entry-level college classes persisting throughout undergraduate and graduate studies to climbing the ranks as a faculty member. The so-called "leaky pipeline" which describes dropouts has been the topic of many papers, initiatives, and studies over the past decades, but there is no consensus on the best strategies to prevent WOC from leaving the broken system that is higher education.[16]

Unfortunately, most of the burden of invisible labor falls on WOC. A massive proportion of tenured women consider leaving academia and little scholarship focuses on the disproportionate burdens of invisible labor on women and faculty of color. Invisible labor consists of student-initiated and WOC-faculty-initiated mentorship, in which WOC faculty provide hands-on attention, guidance, and counseling to serve as role models, mentors, and even surrogate parents. This caregiving and emotional work are done by WOC devoted to diversification and inclusion. This time-consuming work often is overlooked and undervalued because it is considered unnecessary and voluntary, yet, it is absolutely necessary for the survival, well-being, and retention of students from marginalized and underserved backgrounds. Combined with rampant inequities in research and teaching, it is no surprise that women would consider alternative careers when overburdened with this service while remaining unacknowledged, underappreciated, and exhausted for it. There need to be more equity-minded faculty workloads. New policies can be created to make invisible labor visible and to reallocate service and teaching loads to recognize the cultural and emotional tax that WOC pay. Although it is immensely rewarding to mentor students from underserved backgrounds, it can lead to burnout because this spirit work is done on top of all the other faculty duties.

Furthermore, WOC disproportionally contributes to the activism, social justice, and equity work that is sorely needed during this time of reckoning in higher education. It is so inspiring when you see institutions empower, compensate, and recognize WOC for the time and energy spent on advising, emotional care, and equity initiatives. However, often times this transformational work by WOC rarely gains credit, praise, or acknowledgment, especially from upper administration. As so eloquently phrased by Nikole Hannah-Jones in her statement on the decision to decline a tenure offer at the University of North Carolina-Chapel Hill: "For too long, powerful people have expected the people they have mistreated and marginalized to sacrifice themselves to make things whole. The burden of working for racial justice is laid on the very people bearing the brunt of the injustice, and not the powerful people who maintain it."[17]

CONCLUSION

Flourishing of WOC involves building prosocial connections that allow for thriving in systems and structures that were built by and for those who have a different color and race. Developing a fundamental understanding of the colonized and dominant perspectives that exist in society, such as in higher education, can lead to personal growth and professional development on the individual and systemic levels. With prosociality comes the cultivation of humanity, benevolence, humility, and grace. These powerful spiritual tenets have the power to transform and thereby diminish selfishness, arrogance, greed, and judgment. This involves continual practice of contemplation and compassion to allow for the openings required to bring light and love into the darkness and contempt.

It is important for all to understand the neuropsychological and intersectional roots of oppression and compassion. As a result, mentorship for the marginalized, including WOC, can be provided with trauma- and healing-informed practices that lead to creating a culture of belongingness, acceptance, and liberation. It is not acceptable for WOC to do the majority of the work devoted to equity, retention, and community building. Now is the time for allies and accomplices to rise up and understand the impact of marginality in the academy and how WOC bear the brunt of the trauma and labor involved in their survival and the well-being of their mentees. An ally will mostly engage in activism by standing with an individual or group in a marginalized community. An accomplice will focus more on dismantling the structures that oppress that individual or group—and such work will be directed by the stakeholders in the marginalized group.

NOTES

1. See Sarina M. Rodrigues, Joseph E. LeDoux, and Robert M. Sapolsky, "The Influence of Stress Hormones on Fear Circuitry." *Annual Review of Neuroscience,* vol. 32 (2009): 289–313.
2. Ibid.
3. Ibid.
4. Robert M. Sapolsky, *Why Zebras Don't Get Ulcers: The Acclaimed Guide to Stress, Stress-Related Diseases, and Coping* (New York: Henry Holt and Company, 2004), 201.
5. See Ijeoma Oluo, *Mediocre: The Dangerous Legacy of White Male Power* (New York: Hachette Book Group Inc., 2020).
6. Ibid.
7. See Sarina Rodrigues Saturn, "Two Factors that Fuel Compassion: The Oxytocin System and the Social Experience of Moral Elevation," *Oxford Handbook of Compassion Science* (2017): 121–132.
8. Ibid.
9. See Sarina R. Saturn, "Mentorship of Female Faculty and Students from Underrepresented Minorities in STEM." *The Chronicle of Mentoring and Coaching* (2020): 657–661.

10. Saturn, "Two Factors that Fuel Compassion: The Oxytocin System and the Social Experience of Moral Elevation," 126.

11. Saturn, "Mentorship of Female Faculty and Students from Underrepresented Minorities in STEM," 658.

12. Ibid.

13. See Stephen W. Porges, "Vagal Pathways: Portals to Compassion." *The Oxford Handbook of Compassion Science* (2017): 189–204. See also C. Sue Carter, "The Oxytocin–Vasopressin Pathway in the Context of Love and Fear." *Frontiers in Endocrinology*, vol. 8 (2017): 356.

14. Human Rights Campaign, "Dismantling a Culture of Violence: Understanding Violence Against Transgender and Non-Binary People and Ending the Crisis." (2021): 3.

15. Manya Whitaker, "The unseen labor of mentoring." *Chronicle Vitae*, (June 12, 2017), https://www.chronicle.com/article/the-unseen-labor-of-mentoring.

16. Sarina Saturn, Carolina Cortes, Devonna Begay, "Peer, Reverse, and Reciprocal. Mentorship for Effective Diversity and Inclusion Advocacy and Care." *The Chronicle of Mentoring and Coaching* (2021): 109–113.

17. Defense, NAACP Legal, and Educational Fund, "Nikole Hannah-Jones Issues Statement on Decision to Decline Tenure Offer at University of North Carolina-Chapel Hill and to Accept Knight Chair Appointment at Howard University," (July 6, 2021), https://www.naacpldf.org/press-release/nikole-hannah-jones-issues-statement-on-decision-to-decline-tenure-offer-at-university-of-north-carolina-chapel-hill-and-to-accept-knight-chair-appointment-at-howard-university/.

FURTHER READINGS

Duncan, Patti, Reshmi Dutt-Ballerstadt, and Marie Lo. "Women of Color Faculty Reimagining Institutional Spaces During the COVID-19 Pandemic." *ADVANCE Journal: Individual and Institutional Transformation for Social Justice* 2, no. 3 (2021): 1–12.

Hamad, Ruby. *White Tears Brown Scars: How White Feminism Betrays Women of Colour.* New York, NY: Catapult Books, 2020.

Kandel, Eric R. *The Disordered Mind: What Unusual Brains Tell Us About Ourselves.* New York, NY: Farrar, Straus and Giroux, 2018.

Keltner, Dacher, Jason Marsh, and Jeremy Adam Smith, eds. *The Compassionate Instinct: The Science of Human Goodness.* New York, NY: Norton & Company, 2010.

Kristof, Nicholas D., and Sheryl WuDunn. *A Path Appears: Transforming Lives, Creating Opportunity.* New York, NY: Knopf Doubleday Publishing Group, 2015.

LeDoux, Joseph. *The Deep History of Ourselves: The Four-Billion-Year Story of How We Got Conscious Brains.* London: Penguin Books, 2020.

Reid, Rebecca A. "Retaining Women Faculty: The Problem of Invisible Labor." *PS: Political Science & Politics* 54, no. 3 (2021): 504–506.

REFERENCES

Carter, C. Sue. "The Oxytocin–Vasopressin Pathway in the Context of Love and Fear." *Frontiers in Endocrinology* 8, article 356 (2017): 1–12.

Defense, NAACP Legal, and Educational Fund. "Nikole Hannah-Jones Issues Statement on Decision to Decline Tenure Offer at University of North Carolina-Chapel Hill and to Accept Knight Chair Appointment at Howard University." *Legal Defense Fund*, July 6, 2021. https://www.naacpldf.org/press-release/nikole-hannah-jones-issues-statement-on-decision-to-decline-tenure-offer-at-university-of-north-carolina-chapel-hill-and-to-accept-knight-chair-appointment-at-howard-university/.

Human Rights Campaign. *Dismantling a Culture of Violence: Understanding Violence Against Transgender and Non-Binary People and Ending the Crisis*, updated October 2021. https://reports.hrc.org/dismantling-a-culture-of-violence.

Oluo, Ijeoma. *Mediocre: The Dangerous Legacy of White Male Power*. New York: Hachette Book Group Inc., 2020.

Porges Stephen. "Vagal pathways: Portals to Compassion." In *Oxford Handbook of Compassion Science*. Pp. 189–202. Edited by Emma M. Seppälä, Emiliana Simon-Thomas, Stephanie L. Brown, Monica C. Worline, C. Daryl Cameron, James R. Doty. New York: Oxford University press, 2017.

Porges S. W. "Vagal pathways: Portals to Compassion." In *Oxford Handbook of Compassion Science*, edited by E. M. Seppala, E. Simon-Thomas, S. L. Brown, M. C. Worline, C. D. Cameron, & J. R. Dot, 189–202. New York, NY: Oxford University Press, 2017.

Rodrigues, Sarina M., Joseph E. LeDoux, and Robert M. Sapolsky. "The Influence of Stress Hormones on Fear Circuitry." *Annual Review of Neuroscience* 32 (2009): 289–313.

Sapolsky, Robert M. *Why Zebras Don't Get Ulcers: The Acclaimed Guide to Stress, Stress-Related Diseases, and Coping*. New York: Henry Holt and Company, 2004.

Saturn, Sarina. "Two Factors that Fuel Compassion: The Oxytocin System and the Social Experience of Moral Elevation." In *Oxford Handbook of Compassion Science*. Pp. 121–132. Edited by Emma M. Seppälä, Emiliana Simon-Thomas, Stephanie L. Brown, Monica C. Worline, C. Daryl Cameron, James R. Doty. New York: Oxford University press, 2017

Saturn, Sarina R. "Mentorship of Female Faculty and Students from Underrepresented Minorities in STEM." *The Chronicle of Mentoring and Coaching* (2020): 657–661.

———. "Two Factors that Fuel Compassion: The Oxytocin System and the Social Experience of Moral Elevation." *Oxford Handbook of Compassion Science* (2017): 121–132.

Whitaker, Manya. "The Unseen Labor of Mentoring." *Chronicle Vitae*, June 12, 2017. https://www.chronicle.com/article/the-unseen-labor-of-mentoring.

Chapter 14

Defining the Contours of Pedagogies for Holistic Anthropologies

Dawn Michele Whitehead

Today's learners are living, working, and studying in globalized contexts. In this case, individuals in Nairobi, Paris, Buenos Aires, Tokyo, and Indianapolis are impacted by the same global issues, such as the current global health pandemic and global cries for racial justice. To be prepared to thrive in local, state, regional, national, or international settings, learners must be able to engage with diverse people in meaningful ways that recognize their full dignity and humanity. This chapter will examine key dimensions of a globalized classroom in order to propose strategic approaches that are relevant to today's learning context. The focus is to suggest a pedagogy that will be informed, framed, and guided by the human capabilities approach; cultural humility as well as community cultural wealth; and the power of high-impact practices. Such a pedagogy could create a rich resourceful learning environment to be able to address critical questions about oneself and society.

LEARNING IN A GLOBAL CONTEXT

A globalized classroom transcends disciplines and majors because it is based on essential skills and concepts that students need to thrive in work, life, and citizenship for today and for tomorrow. Many institutions have identified definitions of global learning that could be applied to a globalized classroom, an interdisciplinary team of faculty and other educational professionals; the American Association of Colleges and Universities' (AAC&U) Valid Assessment of Learning in Undergraduate Education (VALUE) project defined global learning as "a critical analysis of and an engagement with complex, interdependent global systems and legacies (such as natural, physical, social, cultural, economic, and political) and their implications for people's lives and the earth's sustainability."[1] This definition has been adopted, adapted, and used to start conversations to define global learning at institutions of all types. The team also developed six dimensions of global learning, which I put forward as essential for a globalized classroom.

1. Global Self-Awareness: Systemic understanding of interconnectedness of the self, local, and global communities and the natural and physical worlds.
2. Perspective-Taking: Learning and engaging from perspectives and experiences that are different from one's own and developing the capacity to understand the relationships between multiple perspectives.
3. Cultural Diversity: Recognizing origins of one's own cultural heritage, curiosity to respectfully learn about cultural diversity of others, and understanding power structures that determine hierarchies.
4. Personal and Social Responsibility: Recognizing responsibilities to one's local, national, and global communities and developing a perspective on ethical power relations across the globe.
5. Global Systems: Understanding worldwide systems, including natural world and human systems and how these systems influence how life is lived.
6. Knowledge Application: Applying and integrating systemic understanding of interrelationships between contemporary and past challenges facing cultures, societies, and the natural world.[2]

These dimensions offer a solid framework for broader global learning initiatives and for a globalized classroom. There has been a significant increase in global activity in college and university classrooms, from student mobility to greater integration of global perspectives across disciplines.[3] The literature on global learning has also grown and the six dimensions of global learning are well aligned with research and practice. The concepts of global citizenship, perspective-taking, and community-based learning[4] are a part of many definitions and frameworks for global learning, and they raise issues of social responsibility,[5] critical thinking about views of yourself and others,[6] perspective-taking[7], and consideration for intercultural competence.[8] These are all important components for student understanding of different conceptions of human dignity in diverse societies. This framing positions students to be open in their understanding and consideration of perspectives that are quite different from their own and to engage in thoughtful conversation to understand more from members of the societies or others. From a practical lens, institutions, such as Florida International University,[9] the University of South Florida,[10] and the University of California-Davis, have established global learning definitions and frameworks for globalized classrooms that affirm the six dimensions of global learning from AAC&U, and you can glean how university students might approach the concept of human dignity with this type of global framing regardless of their course of study.[11]

In a globalized classroom, students should have multiple opportunities to practice and apply key dimensions of global learning through assignments, in-class experiences, out-of-class experiences, evaluation, and/or assessment. Students should be presented with multiple opportunities to see the myriad of ways they are connected to their many communities and to the natural and physical world while also having opportunities to draw on different perspectives from regions and countries outside of their own as they attempt to solve problems and to apply their budding professional practices. It is also important that in a globalized classroom students have the opportunity to self-reflect on their own cultural heritage and how it can limit their understanding of the world as they seek to expand their knowledge. This self-reflection is done in concert with their learning about diverse perspectives from cultural groups within a particular community, such as gender, race, and/or people of faith and within countries. A critical reflection on examining hierarchies, inequities, and power dynamics from the lens of race, ethnicity, faith tradition, gender, class, and country of origin should also be undertaken in the context of a globalized classroom, and finally, the application of these global dimensions on current and past challenges is also key. Educators can apply all or some of the global dimensions to their course and integrate them with the learning outcomes to provide students with global experiences.

STRATEGIC PEDAGOGIES

In shaping the educational experiences of students, curriculum, the broader plan for what students will learn—purpose, content, organization, and evaluation—should align with strategic pedagogies to ensure students meet the overall learning goals of their institution, program, and course.[12] To ensure contemporary curriculum and pedagogies affirm the dignity of women and prepare students for learning in globalized contexts, the application of a human capabilities framework in the contexts of higher education is useful. This framing coupled with the concepts of cultural humility and community cultural wealth will prepare students to see the humanity of others through a lens of humility and to see their lived experiences reflected and valued in their courses. This type of holistic framing empowers students, which is also important in preparation for success inside and outside higher education.

Melanie Walker's human capabilities framework ensures considerations of dignity and humanity.[13] She argues that higher education can be an area for change with ethical inclusion, goals for development, and attention to the effects of higher education on the lives of humans.[14] In her argument, she builds on Amartya Sen and Martha Nussbaum's that dignity and equal worth to others are the basis for human capabilities[15] and Nussbaum's emphasis on freedom, choice, and attention to injustice and inequality[16] which are critical for the types of strategic pedagogies this chapter is advancing.

Following the death and destruction of World War II, there was a push to recognize and categorize human dignity through the United Nations Declaration on Human Rights. It declares that people are "free and equal in dignity and rights," and that "everyone has the right to education."[17] Others have also argued that human dignity cannot be lost or gained, and there is equal and inherent worth for every human.[18] This is the lens through which pedagogies must ensure students see themselves and other individuals they may encounter regardless of religious affiliation, race, color, economic status, or country of origin. The human capabilities framework is guided by these values of human dignity. Nussbaum argues that "a life that does not contain opportunities for the development and exercise of the major human capacities is not a life worthy of human dignity."[19] She also argues that conditions in which capabilities can develop and unfold are also essential for making the case to address the conditions under which individuals can demonstrate their capabilities.[20]

Walker's framework seeks to empower and reframe higher education into a capabilities model. Reexamining the functional capabilities of the university and the knowledge that is valued, from academic standards to the inclusion of those who have been marginalized.[21] Walker also argues that institutions of higher education could contribute to making more just societies with human dignity when higher education is centered on a public good.[22] Guided by a human capabilities approach, the curriculum could be transformative. While the curriculum frames "valid knowledge," with this transformative curricular shift, the range of learning opportunities could change and reflect wider views and perspectives with the human capabilities frame. Principles shaped by human development and capabilities and the civic and social roles of universities could be integrated into the curriculum and the pedagogies. With the human capabilities framework, curricula and pedagogies are redesigned for capabilities to be developed, and individual choice is involved in how they are exercised, and what students can do.[23]

Pedagogies could reflect team building, a skill valued in global learning, the development of friendships, that support learning to think critically and empower students to challenge what is learned, and recognition and respect, a core foundation of human dignity, through acknowledging others and respecting their viewpoints. Students should also have opportunities for active and experiential learning, which allows them to pursue their own interests and inquiries. This also helps students learn to find pleasure in learning. Finally, the development of active citizenship where students demonstrate their understanding of society and their contributions could also be reflected in these pedagogies.[24]

The human capabilities framework also seeks to empower students in their learning. Nussbaum makes a strong case for education as empowerment, especially for girls and women. She also asserts the importance of critical self-examination, the idea of a world citizen, and the development of the narrative imagination.[25] When students see themselves as world citizens, they learn about connections to people in distant communities and develop a "genuine curiosity" about the lives of these individuals, and it impacts their understanding and appreciation of issues of global inequities, justice, and other structural factors that they may not have realized without this framing.[26] Beyond the global implications, with a capabilities approach to education, there are also other dimensions of empowerment through participation, equality in opportunity, sustainability of opportunities to freely exercise capabilities, and community membership.[27]

Spaces for learning often reflect broader society where inequities and inequalities may be the norm instead of the exception. The human capabilities framework could offer a framework to combat these realities. Walker encourages a review of how identities such as gender, race, or culture may be devalued or diminished in learning environments, and it should push students to look at their own experiences and those of others with whom they engage.[28] Are the opportunities truly equal? Are individuals able to freely exercise their capabilities? If not, what is the hindrance? What are the barriers? Are the barriers from the student or the structure of the institution of higher education and/or society? These questions should be explored. There could be an overemphasis on one dimension and an underemphasis on another. For example, in Elaine Unterhalter's article on gendered education in South Africa, she found that while the Department of Education had been very attentive to equity issues overall, there was less attention given to issues of gender equity.[29] However, with intentionality, this framework could shape positive experiences for students, especially girls and women, with an emphasis on equitable gender policies and practices that impact their lives inside and outside the classroom. "Learning and learning achievements should contribute to well-being and quality of life. In higher education, it should be the case for all students, and this framework provides leaders of higher education with a foundation."[30]

CULTURAL HUMILITY AND COMMUNITY CULTURAL WEALTH

Cultural humility is an individual, lifelong process of reflection and inquiry to learn about yourself and others to build relationships. It requires an examination of an individual's values, beliefs, and cultural identities while also understanding and acknowledging biases and assumptions. It positions individuals to learn more deeply about cultural differences because the process often helps individuals understand how much they do not know about others.[31] It is a useful practice for students as they engage in cross-cultural interactions, and it contributes to their preparation for life and work.

Cultural humility grew out of clinical practice in health care as a response to cultural competence in patient care. Since it is a lifelong process, it affirms the need to revisit practice beyond a single class, experience, certificate, or degree program. In this ongoing process, a practitioner leads with humility throughout all stages. Cultural humility requires self-reflection, self-critique, and reflective practice; understanding and negotiating one's positionality and recognition of power imbalances; and a willingness for change toward more mutually beneficial partnerships.[32] This involves listening and observing with humility, examining your own positionality, and addressing systemic inequities to ensure dignity.[33] With this framing, educators provide students with opportunities to negotiate meaning as they encounter people in different cultural contexts.[34] This includes working with women in diverse contexts to ensure their dignity is preserved in all interactions and as experiences are formulated, implemented, and navigated by students and educators.

In the U.S. context, education has historically been seen as the "great equalizer," despite a valid counternarrative of gross educational inequities along racial, gender, and class lines. Students need to be prepared to understand the dignity of humanity and to engage ethically and equitably with individuals from walks of life, including those who come from different backgrounds. Cultural humility is an effective framework for their work on- and off-campus. It positions students to first understand and acknowledge themselves and their own beliefs, cultures, and biases before engaging with others on matters of culture and power. It also positions students to listen and observe before interacting and perpetuating preexisting stereotypes and/or assumptions about individuals or groups that may result in harmful and/or confrontational interactions. Finally, it situates students in a place of humility in their interactions, and this prepares them to respect the dignity of humanity in its many forms.

While women and people of color have been historically marginalized and/or diminished in higher education, Tara J. Yosso's concept of community cultural wealth focuses on the assets that students of color bring to their campus communities and classrooms and could transform education broadly, but elements could be applied to women.[35]

Yosso introduces six forms of capital that represent the community cultural wealth that students bring. Aspirational capital—maintaining hopes and dreams despite real and perceived barriers; linguistic capital—social and intellectual skills attained through communication experiences in language and/or style; familial capital—the knowledge carried among family including memory and cultural intuition; social capital—community resources, and networks of people for support in social and institutional navigation; navigational capital—maneuvering through social institutions; and resistant capital—development of knowledge and skills gained through oppositional behavior to challenge inequalities.[36]

Each of these forms of capital has the potential to build on the others, and with an orientation toward seeing students through these strength-based capital dimensions, those who have traditionally been viewed from a deficit perspective by institutions of higher education, are viewed as students bringing something to the table. These forms of capital should be communicated with students to affirm the value they bring with them to their institutions and their classes. Some students may not see the great value they bring or recognize the skills they already have before taking an initial course at the institution. By drawing on community cultural wealth, students may also see the value their peers and others they encounter bring to the educational space. This provides a new way of seeing assets, and it helps move students beyond traditional notions of value. Aspirational capital acknowledges the power of students to "dream of possibilities beyond their present circumstances" and achieve goals, linguistic capital values, the bilingual and/or bicultural experiences students bring while also acknowledging the value of different ways of communication, such as the oral tradition which has skills that have often been overlooked.[37] Familial capital affirms the value of family knowledge and reconceptualizes the notion of family in an inclusive way that again empowers students.[38] Social capital demonstrates the historical spirit of "Harambee" when families and communities come together to provide support while navigational capital also builds on the power to navigate spaces and places that were not created with students of color in mind.[39] Finally, resistant capital empowers students to take control of narratives that seek to diminish or denigrate them and allow them to rewrite the narrative into one of empowerment.

Through the lens of community cultural wealth, the lived experiences of women are valued and seen as assets. Women in many different contexts have demonstrated navigational capital in spaces dominated by boys and men and aspirational capital as they saw educational attainment beyond what they could see at the college or university, or within their communities. Through this lens, students will also be able to understand and see human dignity in different ways. If they only had experience seeing human dignity as a reflection of themselves or their own cultural group, this reorientation through an asset-based model will help students expand their ability to assess diverse forms of human dignity.

The framing of cultural humility and community cultural wealth situate pedagogies in a place of student-centered learning where students' lived experiences and their assets are valued in their educational experiences—classroom activities, assignments, and experiences. Students engage with each other and broader communities with an emphasis on humility and with confidence in their own strengths, and they are better prepared to explore critical questions in society and about themselves. They are also able to understand the dignity of humanity and to engage ethically and equitably with individuals from walks of life who are different from their own; this framing gives them the language, the tools, and the preparation to thrive.

HIGH-IMPACT PRACTICES

High-impact practices (HIPs) are educational practices that have been shown to benefit all students, but especially students of color, first-generation college students, and students from lower-income backgrounds in higher education.[40] There are eleven identified practices—First-Year Seminars and Experiences, Common Intellectual Experiences, Learning Communities, Writing-Intensive Courses, Collaborative Assignments and Projects, Undergraduate Research, Diversity/Global Learning, ePortfolios, Service Learning, Community-Based Learning, Internships, and Capstone Courses and Projects.[41] Institutions have redesigned their curriculum to ensure students have access to multiple HIPs, but intentionality is also very important. Tia McNair and Ashley Finley urge institutions to articulate the value of HIPs to students and to demonstrate the connections to preparation for life and work in assignments, activities, and experiences.[42]

Simply adding one of these practices to your program and/or course does not guarantee student success. George Kuh and Ken O'Donnell identified eight quality dimensions to make a high-impact. Interactions with faculty and peers about substantive matters reinforce dignity and student empowerment.[43] These interactions should include staff and members of the community who serve as coeducators who also inform students' development of cultural humility and community-specific social, economic, and cultural knowledge. In these one-on-one or small group conversations, students should also have opportunities to discuss their place in these situations and the role of women to gain additional perspective to inform their own. They should also have a chance to discuss questions or concerns about cultural diversity, personal and social responsibility, global systems, and any other dimension of global learning to affirm their understanding.

It is also critical that students have periodic, structured opportunities to reflect and integrate their learning.[44] These opportunities should be both written and verbal reflection, and there should be structured reflection activities that draw on course readings, lectures, and experiential learning opportunities. Self-reflection is an important component of cultural humility, and key questions to guide students along their development should also be included. Guided reflection should include an emphasis on dignity and humanity to ensure that students continue to keep these dimensions in mind. Students should also draw on multiple perspectives in their reflection—looking beyond their own experiences to those of others along with the writings, teachings, and experiences of others from diverse backgrounds and women. As students spend more time gaining knowledge from sources that represent different people and perspectives locally, the local media, and individuals who are different from themselves, it strengthens their ability to be global learners.

Students should have experiences with diversity where they interact and work with people and circumstances that they are unfamiliar with.[45] Again, with the framing of cultural humility, students will be ready to enter these situations attuned to listening and observing, seeking to avoid generalizations that lead to stereotyping, and will be ready to navigate their own positionality as they engage with people who are different from themselves. From a gender perspective, this includes understanding the diverse roles women may play in different contexts and being willing to understand and make connections to their own personal development and their course content. Students should also be guided toward the dimensions of cultural diversity. They should also be prepared to consider their own communities and cultures as well as the ones they have entered. Students should also be prepared to examine power structures that contribute to hierarchies.

Timely, constructive, and frequent feedback is also critical for students.[46] They should have continuous feedback from educators at various points throughout their experiences, and they should also receive constructive feedback to improve their work. This also affirms the human capabilities framework where students have an opportunity and the conditions to develop their capabilities.[47] Without an opportunity to learn where they stand and receive feedback, students' capabilities can be limited, and they deserve an opportunity to freely exercise their capabilities and feedback nurtures the process.

Ensuring students have the opportunity to apply their learning to real-world applications is another quality dimension.[48] Through these real world-applications, students can make direct connections from the courses and/or programs to experiences in work-based and/or community-based settings. With the framing of community-cultural wealth, students enter these situations with a sense of empowerment, as they know they bring powerful assets from their cultural experiences, and they couple this with their academic experience. It also affirms the global dimension of Knowledge Application.

Students should also have a significant investment of time and effort over an extended period to make a practice high impact.[49] For even a short experience, students should be engaged with dimensions of humanity, culture, and dignity of life well before an actual experience. Their assignments should also draw on connections with people from different walks of life, cultural experiences, faith traditions, and socioeconomic statuses, so their experiences do not evolve into stereotypes based on limited engagement. With a continued investment of time and effort, students will sustain their involvement with a topic and/or activity even when the activity may have ended through intellectual engagement with the topic. Educators can be more confident about their implementation of high-impact practices when they embed the quality dimensions. Students will also have a better understanding of course goals and why these practices will prepare them for their futures.

CONCLUSION

Today's learners are living, working, and studying in a globalized context, and higher education should prepare them to thrive. Through clear articulation of a global context, students will understand their own environment along with those of others, and they will understand the interdependent nature of our world. Their education will be empowering when the human capabilities framework is embedded across their educational experiences. Through pedagogies that encourage team building, critical thinking, and recognition and respect, students will be able to see their role in their local and global communities and exercise their capabilities to reach their full potential. This will also contribute to full participation by girls and women. Coupled with knowledge and skill development in cultural humility and community cultural wealth, students will also learn how to be more attentive to the full humanity of all individuals. By blending these frameworks with intentional, well-developed high-impact practices, students will be prepared to explore, analyze, and thrive in life, work, and citizenship.

NOTES

1. Association of American Colleges & Universities, "Global Learning VALUE Rubric," VALUE, 2015, https://www.aacu.org/value/rubrics/global-learning.
2. Ibid.
3. Philip G. Altbach and Jane Knight, "The Internationalization of Higher Education: Motivations and Realities," *Journal of Studies in International Education*, vol. 11, no. 3–4 (2007): 290.

4. Leslie A Bozeman et al., "Evolving Practices in the Development and Assessment of Global Learning," in *Trends in Assessment: Ideas, Opportunities and Issues for Higher Education*, eds. Stephen P Hundley and Susan Kahn (Sterling, VA: Stylus Publishing LLC, 2019), 47.

5. Fernando M Reimers, "Bringing Global Education to the Core of the Undergraduate Curriculum," *Diversity and Democracy*, vol. 17, no. 2 (2014), https://www.aacu.org/diversitydemocracy/2014/spring/reimers.

6. David C Braskamp, Larry A Braskamp, and Chris R Glass, "Belonging: The Gateway to Global Learning for All Students," *Liberal Education*, vol. 101, no. 2 (2015): 22–29.

7. Hilary Landorf and Stephanie Doscher, *Making Global Learning Universal* (Sterling, VA: Stylus Publishing, 2018), 31.

8. Bozeman, et al., "Evolving Practices in the Development and Assessment of Global Learning," 47.

9. Hilary Landorf and Stephanie Paul Doscher, "Defining Global Learning at Florida International University," *Diversity and Democracy*, vol. 18, no. 3 (n.d.): 24–26.

10. University of South Florida, "Being a Global Citizen," *USF*, 2021, https://www.usf.edu/gcp/being-a-global-citizen/index.aspx.

11. Bonnie Shea, "Global Education for All." *Global Affairs*, December 6, 2020, https://globalaffairs.ucdavis.edu/ge4a.

12. W. E. Toombs and W. G. Tierney, "Curriculum Definitions and Reference Points," *Journal of Curriculum and Supervision*, vol. 8, no. 3 (2021): 2, http://www.ascd.org/publications/jcs/spring1993/Curriculum-Definitions-and-Reference-Points.aspx.

13. M. Walker, "Universities and a Human Development Ethics: A Capabilities Approach to Curriculum," *European Journal of Education*, vol. 47, no. 3 (2012): 448.

14. Ibid.

15. M. Walker, "A Human Capabilities Framework for Evaluating Student Learning," *Teaching in Higher Education*, vol. 13, no. 4 (2008): 477.

16. Martha Nussbaum, *Creating Capabilities: The Human Development Approach* (Cambridge, MA Harvard University Press, 2011), 56.

17. United Nations, "Universal Declaration of Human Rights," https://www.un.org/en/about-us/universal-declaration-of-human-rights.

18. R. Andorno, "Human Dignity and Human Rights," in *Handbook of Global Bioethics*, eds. Henk A. M. J. ten Have and Bert Gordijn (Berlin: Springer, 2014): 45.

19. Martha Nussbaum, "Human Dignity and Political Entitlements," in *Human Dignity and Bioethics: Essays Commissioned by the President's Council on Bioethics* (Washington, DC: President's Council on Bioethics, 2008), 359.

20. Ibid.

21. Walker, "A Human Capabilities Framework for Evaluating Student Learning," 485.

22. M. Walker, "Universities and a Human Development Ethics: A Capabilities Approach to Curriculum," *European Journal of Education*, vol. 47, no. 3 (2012): 449.

23. Ibid., 457.
24. Ibid., 459.
25. Martha Nussbaum, "Education and Democratic Citizenship: Capabilities and Quality Education," *Journal of Human Development*, vol. 7, no. 3 (2006): 385–395.
26. Walker, "Universities and a Human Development Ethics,"458; Nussbaum, "Education and Democratic Citizenship: Capabilities and Quality Education," 389.
27. Des Gasper, "Is Sen's Capability Approach an Adequate Basis for Considering Human Development?," *Review of Political Economy*, vol. 14, no. 4 (2002): 435–461.
28. Walker, "A Human Capabilities Framework for Evaluating Student Learning," *Teaching in Higher Education*, vol. 13, no. 4 (2008): 485.
29. Elaine Unterhalter, "The Capabilities Approach and Gendered Education," *Theory and Research in Education*, vol. 1, no. 1 (2003): 7–22.
30. Walker, "A Human Capabilities Framework for Evaluating Student Learning," *Teaching in Higher Education*, vol. 13, no. 4 (2008): 479.
31. K. A. Yeager, S. Bauer-Wu, "Cultural Humility: Essential Foundation for Clinical Researchers," *Applied Nursing Research*, vol. 26, no. 4 (2013): 251–253.
32. Melanie Tervalon and Jann Murray-García, "Cultural Humility Versus Cultural Competence: A Critical Distinction in Defining Physician Training Outcomes in Multicultural Education," *Journal of Health Care for the Poor and Underserved*, vol. 9, no. 2 (1998): 117–125.
33. Eric Hartman et al., *Community-Based Global Learning: The Theory and Practice of Ethical Engagement at Home and Abroad* (Sterling, VA: Stylus Publishing, 2018): 95–96.
34. Eric Hartman et al., "Coloniality-Decoloniality and Critical Global Citizenship: Identity, Belonging, and Education Abroad," *Frontiers: The Interdisciplinary Journal of Study Abroad*, vol. 32, no. 1 (2020): 33–59.
35. Tara J. Yosso, "Whose Culture Has Capital? A Critical Race Theory Discussion of Community Cultural Wealth," *Race Ethnicity and Education*, vol. 8, no. 1 (2005): 69–91.
36. Ibid., 78.
37. Ibid., 77–78.
38. Ibid., 79.
39. Harambee was a historical Kenyan form of "pulling together" to support local initiatives or families in need.
40. See, George Kuh and Ken O'Donnell, *Ensuring Quality & Taking High-Impact Practices to Scale* (Washington, DC: Association of American Colleges and Universities, 2013). See also, Ashley Finley and Tia McNair, *Assessing Underserved Students' Engagement in High-Impact Practices* (Washington, DC: Association of American Colleges and Universities, 2013).
41. Charles Edward Watson et al., "Editorial: EPortfolios – The Eleventh High Impact Practice," *International Journal of EPortfolio*, vol. 6, no. 2 (2016): 65–69.
42. McNair and Finley, "Assessing Underserved Students' Engagement in High-Impact Practices." 31.

43. Kuh and O'Donnell, "Ensuring Quality & Taking High-Impact Practices to Scale." 10.
44. Ibid.
45. Ibid.
46. Ibid.
47. Nussbaum, *Creating Capabilities: The Human Development Approach*, 18.
48. Kuh and O'Donnell, "Ensuring Quality & Taking High-Impact Practices to Scale," 10.
49. Ibid.

FURTHER READINGS

de Andreotti, Vanessa Oliveira. "Soft Versus Critical Global Citizenship Education." *Development Education in Policy and Practice* (2014): 21–31. https://doi.org/10.1057/9781137324665_2.

———. "The Educational Challenges of Imagining the World Differently." *Canadian Journal of Development Studies/Revue canadienne d'études du développement* 37, no. 1 (2016): 101–112.

Felten, Peter, and Leo M. Lambert. *Relationship-Rich Education: How Human Connections Drive Success in College*. Baltimore, MD: Johns Hopkins University Press, 2020.

Oxley, Laura, and Paul Morris. "Global Citizenship: A Typology for Distinguishing Its Multiple Conceptions." *British Journal of Educational Studies* 61, no. 3 (2013): 301–325. https://doi.org/10.1080/00071005.2013.798393.

Stein, Sharon. "Critical Internationalization Studies at an Impasse: Making Space for Complexity, Uncertainty, and Complicity in a Time of Global Challenges." *Studies in Higher Education* (2019): 1–14. https://doi.org/10.1080/03075079.2019.1704722.

REFERENCES

Altback, Philip, and Jane Knight. "The Internationalization of Higher Education: Motivations and Realities." *Journal of Studies in International Education* 11, nos. 3–4 (2007): 290–305.

Andorno, Roberto. "Human Dignity and Human Rights." In *Handbook of Global Bioethics*, edited by Henk A. M. J. ten Have and Bert Gordijn, 45–57. Berlin: Springer, 2014.

Association of American Colleges & Universities. "Global Learning VALUE Rubric." *Value*, 2014. https://www.aacu.org/value/rubrics/global-learning.

Bozeman, Leslie, Dawn M. Whitehead, Darla K. Deardorf, and Gil Latz. "Evolving Practices in the Development and Assessment of Global Learning." In *Trends in Assessment: Ideas, Opportunities and Issues for Higher Education*, edited by

Stephen P. Hundley and Susan Kahn, 45–59. Sterling: Stylus Publishing LLC, 2019.

Braskamp, David, C., Larry A. Braskamp, and Chris R. Glass. "Belonging: The Gateway to Global Learning for All Students." *Liberal Education* 101, no. 3 (2015): 22–29.

Farrelly, Denise, Daniel Kaplin, and Delia Hernandez. "A Transformational Approach to Developing Cultural Humility in the Classroom." *Teaching of Psychology* 49, no. 2 (2021): 185–190.

Finley, Ashley, and Tia McNair. *Assessing Underserved Students' Engagement in High-Impact Practices*. Washington, DC: Association of American Colleges and Universities, 2013.

Gasper, Des. "Is Sen's Capability Approach an Adequate Basis for Considering Human Development?" *Review of Political Economy* 14, no. 4 (2002): 435–461.

Hartman, Eric, Nora Pillard Reynolds, Caitlin Ferrarini, Niki Messmore, Sabea Evans, Bibi Al-Ebrahim, and John Matthias Brown. "Coloniality-Decoloniality and Critical Global Citizenship: Identity, Belonging, and Education Abroad." *Frontiers: The Interdisciplinary Journal of Study Abroad* 32, no. 1 (2020): 33–59.

Hartman, Eric, Richard Kiely, Christopher Boettcher, and Jessica Friedrichs. *Community-Based Global Learning: The Theory and Practice of Ethical Engagement at Home and Abroad*. Sterling, VA: Stylus Publishing, 2018.

Hilary, Landorf, and Stephanie Doscher. *Making Global Learning Universal*. Sterling: Stylus Publishing, 2018.

Hilary, Landorf, and Stephanie Paul Doscher. "Defining Global Learning at Florida International University." *Diversity and Democracy* 18, no. 3 (2015): 24–26.

Kuh, George. *High-Impact Educational Practices: What They Are, Who Has Access to Them, and Why They Matter*. Washington, DC: Association of American Colleges and Universities, 2013.

Kuh, George, and Ken O'Donnell. *Ensuring Quality & Taking High-Impact Practices to Scale*. Washington, DC: Association of American Colleges and Universities, 2013.

Nussbaum, Martha. *Creating Capabilities: The Human Development Approach*. Cambridge: Harvard University Press, 2011.

———. "Education and Democratic Citizenship: Capabilities and Quality Education." *Journal of Human Development* 7, no. 3 (2006): 385–395.

———. "Human Dignity and Political Entitlements Essay." In *Human Dignity and Bioethics: Essays Commissioned by the President's Council on Bioethics*, 351–380. Washington, DC: President's Council on Bioethics, 2008.

Reimers, Fernando M. "Bringing Global Education to the Core of the Undergraduate Curriculum." *Diversity and Democracy* 17, no. 2 (2014). https://www.aacu.org/diversitydemocracy/2014/spring/reimers.

Shea, Bonnie. "Global Education for All." *Global Affairs*, December 6, 2020. https://globalaffairs.ucdavis.edu/ge4a.

Tervalon, Melanie, and Jann Murray-García. "Cultural Humility Versus Cultural Competence: A Critical Distinction in Defining Physician Training Outcomes in Multicultural Education." *Journal of Health Care for the Poor and Underserved* 9, no. 2 (1998): 117–125.

Toombs, William E., and William G. Tierney. "Curriculum Definitions and Reference Points." *Journal of Curriculum and Supervision* 8, no. 3 (1993): 175–195.
United Nations. "Universal Declaration of Human Rights." *United Nations.* 2021. https://www.un.org/en/about-us/universal-declaration-of-human-rights.
University of South Florida. "Being a Global Citizen." *USF*, January 4, 2021. https://www.usf.edu/gcp/being-a-global-citizen/index.aspx.
Unterhalter, Elaine. "The Capabilities Approach and Gendered Education." *Theory and Research in Education* 1, no. 1 (2003): 7–22.
Walker, Melanie. "A Human Capabilities Framework for Evaluating Student Learning." *Teaching in Higher Education* 13, no. 4 (2008): 477–487.
———. "Critical Capability Pedagogies and University Education." *Educational Philosophy and Theory* 42, no. 8 (2010): 898–917.
———. "Universities and a Human Development Ethics: A Capabilities Approach to Curriculum." *European Journal of Education* 47, no. 3 (2012): 448–461.
Watson, C. Edward, George Kuh, Terrel Rhodes, Tracy Penny Light, and Helen Chen. "Editorial: EPortfolios – The Eleventh High Impact Practice." *International Journal of ePortfolio* 6, no. 2 (2016): 65–69.
Yeager, Katherine A., and Susan Bauer-Wu. "Cultural Humility: Essential Foundation for Clinical Researchers." *Applied Nursing Research* 26, no. 4 (2013): 251–253.
Yosso, Tara J. "Whose Culture Has Capital? A Critical Race Theory Discussion of Community Cultural Wealth." *Race Ethnicity and Education* 8, no. 1 (2005): 69–91.

Chapter 15

Discursive Interventions toward Gender Justice

The Academic Study of the Bible in the Neoliberal Age

Susanne Scholz

When the Human Rights Campaign (HRC), one of the largest LGBTQ advocacy and political lobbying organization in the United States, calls upon "corporate America" to oppose anti-equality bills at the state level and "to rise up and stand by the principles and values" they espouse in their administrative manuals and on their website, perhaps Teresa J. Hornsby is correct.[1] She states in 2011 that the development from a women-centric focus to a more broadly conceptualized gender and queer agenda is not indicative of a subversive positioning of biblical studies. Rather, both women-centric and queer approaches need to be recognized as accommodating the forces in the economic-capitalist globalized world in which we live, since "sexuality and gender are constructed in collusion with capitalist power."[2] The decision of the HRC to pay for a one-page advertisement that addresses CEOs and other corporate business leaders, asking them to denounce discriminatory state legislation against LGBTQ and "transgender athletes," illustrates such an accommodation to the economic status quo. HRC argues from within the political-economic system.

In addition, the call of the HRC also proves the validity of three assumptions outlined by Hornsby. They are, first, that "power produces sexual normatives;" second, that "the dominant form that this power takes in Western Euro cultures is neoliberal capitalism;" and third, that "Christianity (indeed, organized religion) is an arm of power that aids in this production."[3] The acceptance and inclusion of nonheteronormative and queer sexualities thus may not be deconstructive moves of resistance to patriarchy, homophobia, or heteronormativity, but accommodations, even if unintentionally, to capitalism's need for a different kind of sexual/economic subject. Neoliberal capitalism needs bodies willing to submit and even enjoy "masochistic" positions in the societal-economic interplay of power.[4] "Gender equality" is on the list of concerns. The vision statement of the German Green Party illuminates this interplay of power. Steven Erlanger explains: "Alone among the main parties, the Greens have a vision for a Germany that is digital, climate neutral, deeply committed to the European Union, to democratic values and *gender equality*."[5] Gender equality stands next to democratic values as if Western democracies had always upheld the former. Of course, nothing could be further from the historical or geopolitical truth.

Unsurprisingly, then, today's neoliberal Western politicians bemoan the absence of gender equality. For instance, observers note that the withdrawal of American military troops from Afghanistan threatens "nation-building, democratization, establishing an effective internal security force, defending the *rights of women* and minorities."[6] Women's rights—next to the rights of "minorities"—are claimed as part of Western values, practices, and goals, as if women's rights were an integral part of neoliberal interests. Yet the mention of gender equality veils hegemonic capitalist ambitions, and so the insight that Hornsby articulates in 2011 is in full bloom by 2021. Is Hornsby thus correct that exegetical explorations into women, gender, and queer issues represent accommodations to neoliberal-capitalist demands? Have feminist, womanist, queer, and gender Bible scholars served the wrong "lords," not realizing that their work is part of the sociopolitical, cultural, and economic developments of the past fifty years? After all, cultural critics define neoliberalism as an all-embracive structural reality for all dimensions of society, from economics to ontology.[7]

This essay discusses this provocative possibility in three steps. The first section reflects on the development of feminist, womanist, queer, and gender biblical research to illuminate the difficulties of recognizing such scholarship as an accommodation to neoliberal capitalism. The second section considers the possibility of viewing current biblical scholarship on the Bible as an adaptation to the neoliberal status quo. The third section suggests ways for articulating feminist, womanist, queer, and gender biblical studies as a challenge to the neoliberal logic, especially since the latter has begun moving into what Greek economist and former Greek finance minister, Yanis Varoufakis, classifies as the advent of the "techno-feudalist" era.[8] Overall, the essay asks how to read the Bible in an era in which neoliberal principles morph increasingly into authoritarian practices, as economic-social precarity is shifting intellectual discourse, including in biblical studies, to the political right.

REFLECTIONS ON THE DEVELOPMENT OF FEMINIST, WOMANIST, QUEER, AND GENDER BIBLICAL STUDIES

When feminist Bible scholars gathered with their feminist colleagues of theological and religious studies in Atlanta, Georgia, during the annual meeting of the American Academy of Religion in November 1971, the neoliberal-capitalist agenda was not on their minds.[9] They had probably never even heard of it. They had grown up during the Bretton Woods era, and President Nixon had just decided to decouple the U.S. dollar from the gold standard, the starting point of the neoliberal-capitalist system.[10] The modest goal of the gathered scholars in Atlanta was to establish "a woman's caucus in the field and to demand that program time be allotted to papers and panels on women and religion."[11] Yet importantly, the scholars gathered at a meeting within the United States, a location signifying an end to European-German hegemony in biblical studies. In other words, almost thirty years after the Second World War, scholarly innovation and exegetical vibrancy in biblical studies had moved across the Atlantic Ocean. Despite still existing academic, institutional, or personal connections to the European and German traditions, the emergence of socially located biblical scholarship, such as feminist exegesis, in North America indicated that Eurocentric biblical research did not shape the present and future of the field anymore. The scholarly leadership role had shifted to the English-speaking academic world, in accordance with other socioeconomic and political developments.

During the past fifty years, feminist, womanist, queer, and gender biblical exegesis has spread to many other Bible-reading contexts across the globe, including to Europe.[12] Throughout these decades, such scholarship has not always been welcomed into the exegetical mainstream although some first-generation White feminist Bible scholars remember being nudged into teaching "Women in the Bible" courses by their White male department chairs.[13] At that time, mainline Christian denominations and Jewish liberal movements in the United States had implemented the ordination of women, and so these organizations began appreciating feminist, womanist, sometimes queer, and gender-oriented exegesis, always depending on how academically or religiously liberal or progressive the respective institutions positioned themselves. International student and faculty exchanges to U.S.-American theology schools and departments—if they had a sizeable presence of feminist, womanist, queer, or gender researching faculty—ensured that the new exegetical developments reached audiences far beyond North America.[14] Yet even today, feminist, womanist, queer, and gender biblical research is not mainstream, and many Bible textbooks still do not devote even a single chapter to such scholarship.[15]

Perhaps one of the most significant accomplishments of feminist, womanist, queer, and gender biblical scholarship consists in its speedy diversification. The original focus of rediscovering women's roles in the biblical canon and cognate works of literature expanded soon into comprehensive and intersectional exegetical, hermeneutical, and methodological concerns.[16] The extensive feminist, womanist, queer, and gender scholarship is impressive, especially in light of the considerable obstacles encountered by early feminist Bible scholars. They had been educated within the White, male, heteronormative, and Eurocentric scholarly framework, and have been of mostly White, U.S.-American, Protestant, Catholic, Jewish, or secular backgrounds. All of them had earned academic credentials in a field that had nothing to say about feminism, heteronormativity, or androcentrism intersecting with other structures of domination, such as racism, colonialism, or classism. The first generation of feminists and mostly White Bible scholars literally invented the field.

Some endured academic "horror" stories. One such tale comes from Athalya Brenner-Idan, which illustrates the outrageous disrespect the pioneering generation of feminist exegetes faced. In 2013, Brenner-Idan (*1943) explains why she had left her native land of Israel for a successful career in the Netherlands. By then, she had become an internationally renowned scholar who also served as the SBL President in 2015. Brenner-Idan elaborates on the turning point in her early academic career:

> After I got my Ph.D. at the University of Haifa, I wrote *The Israelite Woman* which was published in 1985. There was a strong grass-roots feminist movement in Haifa at that time, started mostly by American immigrants . . . . From experience I knew there had not been much written on women in the Hebrew Bible and I wanted to write an introductory text. I was not at that time theoretically a feminist, only in my real life and in what I was doing and how I was living. There was a quiet knowledge that women in the Bible felt different than men, and it had to be pointed out. I wanted to fill in this gap. In my innocence (this is how non-feminist I was) I thought everyone, even my institution, would welcome it. I didn't believe for a minute that I wasn't scientific, academic, and important. I was up for tenure, and until then I was a bright-eyed star. It was a very tame book, but as soon as it came out my committee decided it was *not* scientific or academic enough. I could not get tenure, which effectively meant I was thrown out of the system. I became an adjunct, and had a series of jobs for the next eleven years, which was a real formative experience for me. After the first shock—which lasted about two years, anger set in and I just knew I was going to do feminist studies. I was angry enough to get out of my depression. I'd done a Hebrew book (a commentary on Ruth) and was beginning to think about the *Feminist Companion*, because I thought there was a real need . . . . I thought unless other people knew what others were doing, this feminist approach would continue to be considered not scientific or important. So, for the next twelve

years from 1989-2001, most of my resources went into that project, the *Feminist Companion* series.... In 1992, I was in Utrecht for a six-month visiting professorship. This is where I met Fokkelien [van Dijk-Hemmes] and she had a lot of influence on me . . . . A total of 19 volumes came out in less than four years . . . . People bought the books.[17]

Brenner-Idan recovered from the academic harm she had encountered. Other feminist scholars experienced similar academic insults, yet they were not always so lucky. Often their careers ended prematurely, and some careers never took off due to sexism, homophobia, or other misogynist and exclusionary practices.

When one hears about the scholarly obstacles of early feminist Bible scholars, one is hard-pressed to see their scholarship as an accommodation to the neoliberal-capitalist framework. Well-established scholars tried to end the careers of young feminist scholars, such as Brenner-Idan. Yet she, and others like her, persisted by producing research that dismantles patriarchy, homophobia, or heteronormativity in biblical interpretation. Did the mere fact that their scholarly work attended to gender mean that it imagined a different kind of sexual/economic subject submissive to the neoliberal order? The answer to this question will only come from a differentiated understanding of the field of biblical studies.

What one needs to understand is that the field of biblical studies moves slowly and often indulges in quaint antiquarianism and proud references to its impressive past. The scholarly practice, established centuries ago, that requires students to master several languages, either "dead" or contemporary, as a prerequisite for advanced study has contributed to the tendency of cultural-intellectual isolationism and academic-scholarly sentiments of intellectual superiority. To introduce new ideas beyond conventionally defined exegetical standards, approaches, or methodologies is thus difficult. That many biblical scholars are closely connected to religious organizations whose positions are often grounded in exclusionary doctrines and religious teachings contributes to the field's cautious relationship to academic, sociocultural, or political-religious changes. Additionally, many Bible scholars are affiliated with the Christian right since the 1990s.[18] In short, several factors explain why biblical scholarship is slow to adopt contemporary concerns and standards and why the inclusion of feminist, womanist, queer, and gender biblical scholarship has yet to be fully accepted in the field.[19]

The resistance to systemic change and the clinging to a bygone academic worldview in biblical studies is perhaps surprising. Yet even more astounding is that feminist, womanist, queer, and gender research has produced so many publications. Engagement with other socially located hermeneutical approaches, such as postcolonial, anti-racist, or cultural studies, has contributed to productive collaboration and understanding.[20] Hornsby's observation that feminist, womanist, queer, and gender-related scholarship represents an accommodation to the neoliberal economic framework thus requires a differentiated view for understanding the challenges that such scholarship has encountered in the neoliberal-capitalist era.

CRITIQUE OF CURRENT GENDERED BIBLE APPROACHES

After the first generation managed to gain academic rank and status, an increasing number of mostly White women have entered the field since the 1990s. Sometimes the younger scholars nurture explicit interests in feminist, womanist, queer, or gender matters. Often, however, they do not have such concerns in mind, just like the early 1970s scholars when they entered the field as doctoral students. The statement of Katherine Doob Sakenfeld (*1940) is instructive in this regard because it articulates what often brings students to the advanced study of the Bible. Sakenfeld remembers:

> In my first year in college, a Hebrew Bible course was required. My professor told the story of Micaiah ben Imlach (1 Kings 22), where Ahab and Jehoshaphat are together and the 400 prophets tell him to go ahead. The whole drama of the scene hooked me on the Hebrew Bible. There are no women in the story, but it was one of the defining moments that made me think, "Wow! I could spend a lot of time studying this part of the Bible." It was not so much the material as the way this professor brought it to life.[21]

Sakenfeld's academic "conversion" story illustrates what is probably true for many Bible scholars. They fall in love with the academic study of the Bible for reasons relatively independent of consciously held political, sociocultural, or economic convictions. As they discover biblical studies, the disconnect to neoliberal-capitalist principles of viewing and being in the world remains intact. They learn to please the "fathers" of the field, "perpetuating the willing collusion of women with patriarchal ideology," and they come to serve hegemonic interests and structures of the neoliberal-patriarchal regime.[22] They also learn to rationalize and advance the powerful status quo in the field, whether by content analysis done, methodologies assumed, or positions taken. Readings disruptive of the hegemonic discourse are rare and perhaps only available when exegetes "ask the question 'why' or '*cui bono*.'"[23]

When Hornsby's challenge is correlated to the demand for disruptive biblical scholarship, some feminist, womanist, queer, or gender interpretations can be recognized as exhibiting acquiescent tendencies to neoliberal "capitalist power."²⁴ As the interpretations focus on individual biblical, especially female, characters,²⁵ they treasure personal experience. They also emphasize autonomy and authority of biblical characters while they produce literalist, historicized, or literary readings absent of substantive critical theoretical interrogation. They promise "market" inclusivity in which everybody can participate, as they locate themselves in specific readerly settings. Yet often such interpretations disconnect biblical meanings from specific readerly purposes, and so biblical meanings appear to pertain to anybody everywhere. As Esther Fuchs puts it so succinctly:

> In neoliberal terms, feminist research in biblical studies creates new products for the company. It expands the consumer base and the volume of production . . . . It does not question or interrogate the procedures that are supposed to produce knowledge about biblical women or women in ancient Israel . . . . This neoliberal presentation framed difference in feminism as diversity, plurality, and heterogeneity, and as a desirable commodity for potential consumers who sought in the academe what they found in the late capitalist marketplace: a rich selection of enticing products competing for readers and students.²⁶

The tendency of some feminist, womanist, queer, and gender biblical scholarship to accommodate to the neoliberal mindset is perhaps best illustrated with two concrete examples. The first example relates to several essays that explore "Gendered Historiography: Theoretical Considerations and Case Studies," appearing in the *Journal of Hebrew Scriptures* and edited by Shawna Dolansky and Sarah Shectman.²⁷ The introduction and four essays rely on what Fuchs classifies as the "historicizing strategy" of neoliberal feminist studies.²⁸ Focused on the historical analysis of biblical gender, the essays employ the hegemonic methodology of the field. The editors also reject feminist biblical scholarship as biased, political, "presentist," and "theological-literary."²⁹ Predictably, Dolansky and Shectman do not acknowledge the hegemonic status of historical criticism but employ what Elisabeth Schüssler Fiorenza characterizes as the colonizing, imperial, and hegemonic method of biblical studies. Schüssler Fiorenza explains that historical criticism's claim of scientific rationality, assertion of kyriarchal objectivity, and alignment with the Western empire has enabled "elite Western educated clergymen" to articulate "the interests of imperial cultural and political benefits."³⁰ Methodologically, then, the editors and contributors place themselves into this conceptual framework that relegates emancipative discourses and movements to the intellectual space of "cultural relativism."³¹ The interpreters set out to describe the authorial meaning of the Bible, and in the process, they reinforce the power system of the phallogocentric economy that makes women's perspectives invisible and silences feminist approaches as culturally relative. Validating unjust and oppressive theories and practices about women and sexuality, they do not analyze critically the power system articulated in the text and in the interpretation of history.

This methodological strategy also relies upon another neoliberal strategy that Hornsby classifies as the "neoliberal capitalist ideology and theologies of suffering, submission, and redemption."[32] The essay by Alison L. Joseph on "'Is Dinah Raped?' Isn't the Right Question: Genesis 34 and Feminist Historiography" demonstrates how far removed some interpreters are from taking key feminist insights into consideration, such as reading biblical texts from the perspectives of victim-survivors. Accordingly, Joseph asserts: "[A]s feminists, our modern sexual values are so in conflict with those of the story, imposing those values on ancient Israel and their story is not methodologically responsible."[33] Since Joseph identifies a huge gap between contemporary feminist and ancient Israelite values, she affirms the view that Dinah is not raped because biblical Hebrew does not have a specific word for rape and consent is a contemporary standard.[34] Since Joseph aims to reconstruct authorial biblical meaning—apparently never having heard of the "intentional fallacy" or of Roland Barthes' assertion that "the author is dead,"[35] she asserts that "historically, we cannot call this rape, neither linguistically nor conceptually,"[36] because "our modern definition of rape does not exist in ancient Israel."[37] Joseph thus rejects the question as "wrong" whether Dinah is raped. Relegating her readerly responsibilities into the hermeneutical dustbin, she believes to interpret biblical sexual violence within an imagined Israelite past that she reconstructs as separate from contemporary notions about sexual violence. Predictably, then, her reading reinforces the power system of the phallogocentric logic that marginalizes and even silences Dinah's perspective. Observing that Dinah does not speak, Joseph demands that contemporary feminist interpreters not speak for Dinah or "invent" her voice.[38] Still, Joseph worries whether her reading "sanctions" contemporary rape culture,[39] and she asks whether "[i]n denying Dinah's 'rape,' do we silence her and other victims." I would say, yes, Joseph silences Dinah, similar to the disregard for sexual violence as a "side effect" of total lockdown orders during the coronavirus crisis. In these and similar interpretations, then, biblical characters and texts turn into examples of female suffering and submission in service of hegemonic-masculinized powers not only within biblical texts but also within the neoliberal order.

A second example of accommodating tendencies in feminist, womanist, genderqueer, and gender exegesis is Caryn Tamber-Rosenau's book, entitled *Women in Drag: Gender and Performance in the Hebrew Bible and Early Jewish Literature*, published in 2018. This study presents the story of Judges 4-5, and related works of literature, as a heightened military tale in which the female immigrant character commits the murder of the enemy general.[40] The female character, Jael, "bring[s] down a man "by putting on a heightened feminized role like other ancient Near Eastern, biblical, or Hellenistic female characters. Like the other ancient female characters, they "execut[e] an over-the-top performance of expected femininity" and thereby "parody these very expectations."[41] Tamber-Rosenau claims to read from a queer perspective, and so, in her view, the female characters are "[j]ust as dragsters and burlesque performers [who] reveal the artifice of all gender through their exaggerated depictions of 'woman' or 'man.'"[42] They "unsettle what we think the Bible and early Jewish texts say about gender and sexuality."[43]

Yet Tamber-Rosenau's claim of reading female characters from a queer perspective does not convince. She defines as queer "anything that blurs or transcends categories, not just in matters of sex and gender," although her reading does not foster blurring or ambiguity.[44] Instead, her reading argues for clear-cut depictions of the various "lethal" women. For instance, Anat who is a Jael-like Ugaritic character appears in full feminine regalia when she kills her male opponent. To Tamber-Rosenau, she looks like "a fellow [male] warrior."[45] Moreover, Tamber-Rosenau maintains that Jael "does not serve the patriarchy but destabilizes it" because she "exposes the oppressiveness of patriarchal strictures of gender by parodying them through drag."[46] Yet how does Jael destabilize patriarchy when her gender performance includes the murder of the powerful enemy military leader and so ensures the success of the Israelites over the Canaanites? Does the immigrant woman not rather reinforce Israelite supremacy by putting up a "gender performance?" It seems likely that a male, heteronormative Israelite audience would have welcomed the narrated support from a Kenite woman whom they imagine as a "naturalized" sex object living in their midst.[47] Thus, should she not be compared to Rahab who is also a foreign woman moving into the "heterosexual, mono-loving mentality of only one nation, one God and one faith," as Marcella Maria Althaus-Reid maintains?[48] If seen accordingly, Tamber-Rosenau's interpretation does not challenge "discursive psycho-social-political regimes" of White-culturalist-androcentric-classist methodologies and practices, abstaining from a "different orientation to interpretation itself."[49] Rather, it reinforces those regimes.

In sum, various publications illustrate that contemporary feminist, womanist, queer, or gender readings do not always challenge hegemonic views of biblical characters. Such interpretations do not investigate, uncover, unmask, or unveil what is at stake in androcentric-ethnocentric fantasies. Yet many questions arise: what are the politics of such stories? How do past and present interpreters rationalize the stories of the selected female, queer, or otherwise gendered biblical characters? How do readers reinterpret them and for what purposes? Why do such studies matter, and what is at stake in studying them? Even further, where do we find such characters today? In prison? In academia? Why here and not there? How are readers continuously manipulated into fantasizing about female, queer, or otherwise gendered characters? And why, how, and for what purposes would "a woman happily married to a man"[50] be interested in reading such characters? As long as methodological frameworks and analytical categories reinforce what Hornsby classifies as obedient, submissive, and masochistic subject-object positions in the economic/social order, the focus on female, queer, or otherwise gendered characters tends to reinforce the neoliberal logic, even when biblical interpreters project biblical texts into the ancient past. The same is true for Bible scholars. If they classify their work as feminist, womanist, queer, or gendered while their interpretations surrender to the hegemonic imaginary of gendered characters as hypersexualized killer machines, what is feminist, womanist, queer, or gendered about such readings?[51] The publications in the *Journal of Hebrew Scriptures* and Tamber-Rosenau's study demonstrate that feminism "loses purchase on a reality fully subsumed by capital."[52] Everything can turn into a feminist, womanist, queer, or gender study when it rehearses the status quo in which female characters are imagined as enjoying their positions as sex objects while killing powerful military men. In light of this bleak present, how can feminist, womanist, queer, or gender biblical approaches be developed in resistance to or even in disruption of the neoliberal order? Is it possible, or does such work remain stuck within a submissive object position? In short, the question is how to move into a vibrant exegetical future while envisioning resistance to and disruption of the neoliberal logic.

HOW TO BECOME PART OF THE "ALTERNATIVE PRESENT"?

This question is not easy to answer.[53] As Varoufakis, the Greek economist and former finance minister of Greece, explains, we have already left the neoliberal capitalist order since 2008 and have begun to live in technofeudalism.[54] He asserts that "[t]he democracy we have is simply a piece of propaganda. We have an oligarchy with elections and the elections are bought by the oligarchy."[55] Said differently, the situation in which feminist, womanist, queer, and gender Bible scholars find themselves is probably even worse than Hornsby assumes in 2011 when she considers the impact of neoliberal forces upon biblical studies. Mitchum Huehls, an English professor at the UCLA English department, diagnoses that nowadays neoliberalism is surrounding everything and everybody in a totalitarian way. Based upon his analysis of contemporary U.S.-American novels, he subscribes to "the impossibility of generating any critical representation of the world that doesn't in some way reinforce neoliberalism."[56] Any critique reinforces neoliberal power so that any political critique of neoliberalism is necessarily "circular and impotent."⁵⁷ The only remaining option is to engage neoliberalism "on its own ontological terms."⁵⁸ He calls it "swimming with the zombies"⁵⁹ or becoming neoliberal without becoming neoliberal, although it "frequently look[s] like capitulation, but I think they [the novels he examines in his book] hold out some promise."⁶⁰ What must be done is to approach neoliberalism ontologically, and only when we become neoliberal subjects and objects can we form an ontologically grounded opposition.⁶¹ Said differently, Huehls suggests that critique as a strategy of resistance is futile.

As devastating as this assessment seems, it is also "overly hasty," as Ursula McTaggert puts it.⁶² Critics of structures of domination, whether related to class, race, or gender, have indeed "produced sophisticated and non-reductive strategies for navigating" binaries of these and other social categories.⁶³ Does Huehl's critique not veil a liberal positionality in the disguise of "exomodernism" by ignoring already existing modes of hybridity and ambiguity that are part of any critical evaluation?⁶⁴ Meanwhile, other literary critics insist, similar to Huehl, on a renewed value of surface readings,⁶⁵ as they reject the merits of the hermeneutics of suspicion as a twentieth-century literary-critical convention. Postcritics urge readers to let go of critique during this postcritique era by reestablishing an aesthetic pleasure of reading but not by "champion[ing] aesthetics over politics."⁶⁶ As the current all-pervasiveness of neoliberalism has produced various critical reading strategies and standpoints, some critics seem to succumb to neoliberal ideology while others insist on building an "alternative present." Yet all of them agree that individual and collective action is required in the totalizing era of neoliberalism. The neo-feudalistic regime of power requires theoretical focus and deliberation.

Yet the situation gets worse when one ponders the idea of living in a postnormative world. The era of a prescribed set of beliefs, values, behaviors, or practices is long over, as postmodernists already established in their rejection of the notion of grand narratives, that is, comprehensive, universal, and objective theories about history and knowledge. Master narratives do not convince anymore, as postnormative neoliberalism has gained power and influence in the world. Any explanation is countered with a counter-explanation, because "we challenge normative thought and behavior by offering competing representations of the world that critique the normative status quo."⁶⁷ The situation is even more complicated, as Huehls explains so well: "What seem like opposing arguments actually fit together to form a circle in which neoliberal values always triumph."⁶⁸ The subject becomes the object and the object becomes the subject because "the neoliberal circle actually precludes the production of meaningfully distinct positions."⁶⁹ Any position reinforces "in some way" neoliberal representations, values, or convictions. It becomes impossible to speak truth to power because neoliberal power has already incorporated the many versions of potential truths. Huehls describes the situation by explaining:

> On the one hand, neoliberal rhetoric cynically ventriloquizes leftist idealism, readily portraying the systematized neoliberal cog exploited by his university as either a selfless team player or a farsighted student committed to self-improvement through education. On the other hand, neoliberal rhetoric is quick to idealize leftist cynicism, readily portraying the entrepreneurial subject's big payday as either a win for a worker freed from his exploitative labor relationship with the university or as a moment of economic and social uplift. Neoliberalism speaks the language of the greater communal good as a cover for its systematic exploitation of individual-objects, and it speaks the anti-exploitative language of social justice as a cover for its championing of entrepreneurial individual-subjects. In the name of economic rationality, market logic, and maximized self-interest, neoliberalism makes all of the left's arguments for it.[70]

The HRC calling on corporate America illustrates this dynamic at the beginning of this essay. In other words, the relentless and unavoidable cooptation into neoliberal rhetoric, schemes, and processes is the problem. As the Borgs articulate it in *Star Trek: The Next Generation*: "Resistance is futile."[71]

Postcritics, however, also offer a way out of the problem of cooptation. As the "post-normative neoliberal ontology"[72] assumes a neat distinction between subject and object, postcritics suggest accepting the "muddled mix"[73] in which everything and everybody is a hybrid of both subject and object. The solution is to "no longer think of ourselves as discursively normativized constructs of the system."[74] We are simultaneously feminist and nonfeminist, womanist and nonwomanist, queer and nonqueer, or gendered and nongendered. What is at stake are not our identities, beliefs, or commitments, but the mapping of our relationships, our likes, clicks, and connections made. Since there is not "any evil apparatus for us to represent, reveal, and resist," post-critics like Huehls argue that the neoliberal "serial" culture requires us to "move from the critical to the ontological."[75] We have to engage neoliberalism "on its own ontological terms," and so we should consider "altering the given configuration of specific social, economic, and cultural formations; rearranging the established distribution of bodies, and reshaping geographies of inclusion and exclusion."[76]

What, then, does this "ontological turn" mean for interpreters working in feminist, womanist, queer, and gender biblical studies?[77] Three succinct suggestions are in order. First, interpreters need to recognize that the neoliberal age is ideologically secular and heterogeneous. Thus, a postnormative approach respecting "alterities" also pertains to the Bible.[78] When norms are constantly contested, and beliefs, including the belief in religious fundamentalism or in science and rationality, proliferate as "one sign of a secular age," the Bible must be recognized as only one of many texts to be studied or not.[79] Most importantly, the results of such study will never produce any singular norm to be followed by everybody, whether or not they are religious adherents of this text. This insight is not particularly new although religious or even historical-critical claims often assert singular authority over biblical meanings.

Second, the notion that we live in a changed context of the techno-feudalist era has methodological implications for the academic study of the Bible. As Felski puts it: "Rather than looking behind the text—for its hidden causes, determining conditions, and noxious motives—we might place ourselves in front of the text, reflecting on what it unfurls, calls forth, makes possible. This is not idealism, aestheticism, or magical thinking but a recognition—long overdue—of the text's status as coactor" so that "reading [becomes] a coproduction between actors rather than an unraveling of manifest meaning, a form of making rather than unmaking."[80] Although I am not entirely sure about Felski's claim of textual "agency," the idea of reading in front of the text as the locus of meaning is important though not new. This idea moves biblical interpretation from the conventional text-fetishized approach to a readerly orientation that exists already on the margins but not in the center of the field.[81]

The postcritical insistence on reading in front of the text emphasizes the study of historical, social, political, economic, and religious connections between biblical texts and readers, as both readers and texts are located in "a larger network of legible social notes."[82] The task becomes to map the transmitted information or data, to take account of what appears on the page, and to assess what to do with all of it. This task is not entirely new either, as McTaggart asserts rightly. She observes that "liberal discourses" have indeed been too weak to combat neoliberalism, but radical challenges to neoliberalist capitalism exist that postcritical proponents seem to underestimate.[83] The observation is also true for feminist exegesis: radical challenges to biblical androcentrism exist, but the focus on naturalized biblical women's strength, power, autonomy, or social status continues to dominate, perhaps because they project so successfully and assimilate so smoothly into neoliberal desires and dreams.

Yet a postcritical methodology also requires more when it suggests analyzing networks of meaning between texts and readers as a method of tracing networks of meanings. As Huehls states: "[P]olitics would involve repositioning oneself in the social configuration and forging new alliances within a set of rationalized parameters, absent neoliberalism's insistence on efficient profit."[84] The work entails following ideas and groups, as well as examining their enmeshment and investigating "the formation of the social *itself*."[85] Ultimately, then, neither text nor readers are central but the connections between them. The work turns into a "bricolage" or a "patchwork"[86] for the purposes of both pleasure and activism ("praxis"). Previously, I called for a feminist sociology of biblical interpretation that takes seriously the notion of a fragmentary, transitory, and pluralistic sense of contemporary identities.[87] In my view, postcritical demands align with my idea for such a methodological shift in feminist biblical studies. What has to be abandoned in the era of techno-feudalism is biblical research that affirms biblical women as having a natural, commonsense, real, collective, or individual presence. Similarly, presuppositions of gender as a stable unchanging essence or reality or the uncritical assimilation into neoliberal market forces must be abandoned.

Third and finally, in light of postcritical discussions in literary studies, biblical scholars ought to recognize the Bible as an inherited text that remains largely unread although it is still loudly proclaimed. How we read this text as feminist, womanist, queer, or gender-critical readers says much about how we view this text and ourselves as readers in the techno-feudalist era. The analysis of this context remains one of the most important and challenging tasks that demand critical acumen. Thus, feminist, womanist, queer, and gender approaches need to become part of methodological conversations and explore "how we are doing what we are doing and why and how we might want to do things differently given present conditions" which, after all, is "the basic impulse of critique."[88] Surely, more is required than one more publication on this or that biblical woman.

READING THE HEBREW BIBLE IN THE AGE OF TECHNO-FEUDALISM: TOWARD A CONCLUSION

The current transition toward techno-feudalism makes clear that we need to question and interrogate the procedures that supposedly create historical or literary knowledge about the meanings of biblical texts. To add this or that biblical woman or man into the mix will not suffice because such an approach only reinforces the endless neoliberal hunger for a diverse product selection within the neoliberal marketplace. The historical-critical adaptation to gender issues also only reinforces the hegemonic status quo that prevents critical examinations of what needs to be done in the field and for the billions of Bible readers in the world. The quick and easy assimilation into neoliberalism makes it difficult to identify ways of reading biblical texts, characters, or themes in resistance to or in disruption of what Huehls characterizes as the neoliberal circle. How can we escape the Borgs? This question haunts me since I watched the science fiction show that wrestles with this problem after Captain Piccard's rescue from the Borgs.[89] Can we read the Bible in ways that offer strategies out of the techno-feudalist moment? In the past few decades, feminist biblical interpreters aimed to dismantle patriarchal, androcentric, and heteronormative regimes of power, but are these readings still valid today? Perhaps the raising of this question is a first step toward figuring out how to escape the neoliberal circle as it morphs into techno-feudalism. An inheritance from our various ancestors, the Bible is surely an unsuspecting resource to figure out how to build an alternative present in dire times. Let us read this text so that we understand our past and present material conditions, as we envision ways beyond them.

NOTES

1. See the Human Rights Campaign's paid advertisement in the *New York Times* (April 19, 2021): A7.
2. Teresa J. Hornsby, "Capitalism, Masochism, and Biblical Interpretation," in *Bible Trouble: Queer Reading at the Boundaries of Biblical Scholarship*, ed. Teresa J. Hornsby and Ken Stone (Atlanta, GA: Society of Biblical Literature, 2011), 137.
3. Ibid.
4. Ibid., 141–142.
5. See, e.g., Steven Erlanger, "With Merkel Leaving, the Role of Germany's Green Party Is Expected to Grow," *New York Times* (April 18, 2021): A9. Emphasis added.
6. Helene Cooper, Eric Schmitt and David E. Sanger, "Debating Exit from Afghanistan, Biden Rejected General's Views," *New York Times* (April 18, 2021): A11. Emphasis added.
7. Aihwa Ong, *Neoliberalism as Exception: Mutations in Citizenship and Sovereignty* (Durham/London: Duke University Press, 2006).
8. Yanis Varoufakis, "Capitalism Has Become "Techno-Feudalism," *Al Jazeera* (February 19, 2021), https://www.youtube.com/watch?v=_jW0xUmUaUc.
9. For a historical review, see Susanne Scholz, "Discovering a Largely Unknown Past for a Vibrant Present: Feminist Hebrew Bible Studies in North America," in *The Bible as Political Artifact: On the Feminist Study of the Hebrew Bible* (Minneapolis, MN: Fortress Press, 2017), 193–222.
10. For a review of these economic developments, see, e.g., Yanis Varoufakis, *And the Weak Suffer What They Must? Europe's Crisis and America's Economic Future* (New York: Nations Books, 2016).
11. So articulated by Rita Gross, *Feminism and Religion: An Introduction* (Boston: Beacon, 1996), 46.
12. For an illustration of the global developments, see, e.g., the essays from African, Asian, and Australian scholars in Susanne Scholz, ed., *The Oxford Handbook of Feminist Approaches to the Hebrew Bible* (Oxford: Oxford University Press, 2021). For the breadth of perspectives, social locations, and geopolitical perspectives in feminist, womanist, queer, and gendered biblical studies, see, e.g., Susanne Scholz, ed., *Feminist Interpretation of the Hebrew Bible in Retrospect (Volume 2: Social Locations)* (Sheffield: Sheffield Academic Press, 2014); Gay L. Byron and Vanessa

Lovelace, eds., *Womanist Interpretations of the Bible: Expanding the Discourse* (Atlanta, GA: SBL Press, 2016); Deryn Guest, Robert Goss, Mona West, and Thomas Bohache, eds., *The Queer Bible Commentary* (London: SCM Press, 2006); Kyung Sook Lee and Kyung M. Park, eds., *Korean Feminists in Conversation with the Bible, Church and Society* (Bible in the Modern World; Sheffield: Sheffield Phoenix Press, 2011); Musa W. Dube Shomanah, ed., *Other Ways of Reading: African Women and the Bible* (Global Perspectives on Biblical Scholarship; Atlanta, GA: SBL Press, 2001).

13. See, e.g., the recollection of Carol Meyers in Helen Leneman, "Genealogies of Feminist Biblical Studies: An Interview Report from the 1970s Generation," in *Feminist Interpretation of the Hebrew Bible in Retrospect (Volume 1: Biblical Books)*, ed. Susanne Scholz (Sheffield: Sheffield Academic Press, 2013), 21–22.

14. For feminist, womanist, queer, or gender scholarship in Africa, Asia, or Latin America, see, e.g., Elisabeth Schüssler Fiorenza, ed., *Feminist Bible Studies in the Twentieth Century: Scholarship and Movement* (Bible and Women 9.1; Atlanta, GA: SBL Press, 2014); Dube, ed., *Other Ways of Reading*. For an international student exchange program, see, e.g, the World Council of Churches Scholarships Programme, available at http://www.wcc-coe.org/wcc/what/education/scholarships-leaflet-e.pdf.

15. See, e.g., David M. Carr, *The Hebrew Bible: A Contemporary Introduction to the Christian Old Testament and the Jewish Tanakh*, 2nd edition (Hoboken, NJ: Wiley-Blackwell, 2021); Watts, James W., *Understanding the Bible as a Scripture in History, Culture, and Religion* (Hoboken, NJ: Wiley-Blackwell, 2021).

16. See, e.g., Renita J. Weems, *Just a Sister Away: Understanding the Timeless Connection between Woman of Today and Women in the Bible* (San Diego, CA: LuraMedia, 1988); Marie-Theres Wacker, "Feministische Theologie und Antijudaismus: Diskussionsstand und Problemlage in der Bundesrepublik Deutschland," *Kirche und Israel* 5 (1990): 168–176; Gale A. Yee, ed., *Judges and Method: New Approaches in Biblical Studies* (Minneapolis, MN: Fortress Press, 1995); Musa W. Dube, *Postcolonial Feminist Interpretation of the Bible* (St. Louis, MI: Chalice, 2000); Gale A. Yee, ed., *The Hebrew Bible: Feminist and Intersectional Perspectives* (Minneapolis, MN: Fortress Press, 2018).

17. Brenner-Idan tells this story as part of an interview conducted by Leneman, "Genealogies of Feminist Biblical Studies, 23–24. Italics in the original.

18. See, e.g., the increasing number of sessions scheduled by the "Institute for Biblical Research" (IBR) during the annual meetings of the Society of Biblical Literature (SBL). This organization describes itself as "an organization of evangelical Christian scholars that fosters excellence in biblical studies within a faith environment" (https://ibr-bbr.org/). For a damning assessment of this situation, see, e.g., Hector Avalos, *The End of Biblical Studies* (Amherst, NY: Prometheus Books, 2007).

19. This situation is particularly puzzling since the humanities have been continuously threatened and de facto eliminated from many undergraduate colleges and universities; see, e.g., Frank Donoghue, *The Last Professors: The Corporate University and the Fate of the Humanities. With a New Introduction* (New York: Fordham University Press, 2018). For my attempt of making sense of this situation in biblical studies, see Susanne Scholz, "Occupy Academic Bible Teaching: The Architecture of Educational

Power and the Biblical Studies Curriculum," in *The Bible as Political Artifact: On the Feminist Study of the Hebrew Bible* (Minneapolis, MN: Fortress Press, 2017), 29–47.

20. See, e.g., Yee, *The Hebrew Bible: Feminist and Intersectional Perspectives*; Byron and Lovelace, eds., *Womanist Interpretations of the Bible*; Silvia Schroer and Sophia Bietenhard, eds., *Feminist Interpretation of the Bible and the Hermeneutics of Liberation* (London: T&T Clark International, 2004).

21. Katherine Doob Sakenfeld recalls this decisive moment of her life in an interview conducted by Leneman, "Genealogies of Feminist Biblical Studies," 14.

22. Esther Fuchs, "Biblical Feminisms: Knowledge, Theory, and Politics in the Study of Women in the Hebrew Bible," in *Feminist Theory and the Bible: Interrogating the Sources* (Lanham, MD: Lexington Books, 2016), 39.

23. Ibid., 41.

24. Hornsby, "Capitalism, Masochism, and Biblical Interpretation," 137.

25. Numerous feminist, womanist, queer, and gendered interpretations illustrate this tendency; see, e.g., Jaime Clark-Soles, *Women in the Bible* (Louisville, KY: Westminster John Knox Press, 2020); Alicia D. Myers, *Blessed among Women? Mothers and Motherhood in the New Testament* (New York: Oxford University Press, 2017); Wilda C. Gafney, *Womanist Midrash: A Reintroduction to the Women of the Torah and the Throne* (Louisville, KY: Westminster John Knox, 2017); Paul Heger, *Women in the Bible, Qumran, and Early Rabbinic Literature: Their Status and Roles* (Leiden, Netherlands, Brill, 2014); Irmtraud Fischer et al., eds., *Die Bible und die Frauen: Eine exegetisch-kulturgeschichtliche Enzyklopädie* (Stuttgart: Kohlhammer, 2010); Carol Meyers, Toni Craven, and R.S. Kraemer, eds., *A Dictionary of Named and Unnamed Women in the Hebrew Bible, the Apocryphal Deuterocanonical Books, and the New Testament* (Boston: Houghton Mifflin, 2000); Susan Ackerman, *Warrior, Dancer, Seductress, Queen: Women in Judges and Biblical Israel* (Anchor Bible Reference Library; New York: Doubleday, 1998).

26. Esther Fuchs, "Neoliberal Feminist Scholarship in Biblical Studies," in *Oxford Handbook of Feminist Approaches to the Hebrew Bible*, ed. Susanne Scholz (Oxford: Oxford University Press, 2021), 162–163.

27. Shawna Dolansky and Sarah Shectman, eds., "Gendered Historiography: Theoretical Considerations and Case Studies," *Journal of Hebrew Scriptures*, vol. 19, no. 4 (2019): 1–58.

28. Fuchs, "Neoliberal Feminist Scholarship," 170–171.

29. Dolansky and Shectman, eds., "Gendered Historiography," 5.

30. Elisabeth Schüssler Fiorenza, *The Power of the Word: Scripture and the Rhetoric of Empire* (Minneapolis, MN: Fortress Press, 2007), 49.

31. Ibid., 9. See also Guy M. Clicqué, "'Anything Goes?' Theology and Science in a Culture Marked by Postmodern Thinking," *European Journal of Science and Theology*, vol. 1, no. 2 (June 2005): 27–33.

32. Teresa J. Hornsby, "Neoliberalism and Queer Theory in Biblical Readings," in *The Oxford Handbook of Feminist Approaches to the Hebrew Bible*, ed. Susanne Scholz (Oxford: Oxford University Press, 2021), 219–228.

33. Alison L. Joseph, "'Is Dinah Raped?' Isn't' the Right Question: Genesis 34 and Feminist Historiography," *Journal of Hebrew Scriptures*, vol. 19, no. 4 (2019): 28.

34. Ibid., 32.

35. See W. K. Wimsatt Jr. and Monroe C. Beardsley, "The Intentional Fallacy," *The Sewanee Review*, vol. 54, no. 3 (July-September 1946): 468–488; Roland Barthes, "The Death of the Author," *Aspen*, vol. 5–6 (1967): http://www.ubu.com/aspen/aspen5and6/threeEssays.html#barthes. See also Michel Foucault, "What is an Author?" Lecture given at the Collège de France (February 22, 1969): https://www.open.edu/openlearn/ocw/pluginfile.php/624849/mod_resource/content/1/a840_1_michel_foucault.pdf.

36. Ibid., 33.

37. Joseph, "'Is Dinah Raped?'," 36.

38. Ibid., 37.

39. Ibid.

40. Caryn Tamber-Rosenau, *Women in Drag: Gender and Performance in the Hebrew Bible and Early Jewish Literature* (Picataway, NJ: Gorgias, 2018).

41. Ibid., 233.

42. Ibid.

43. Tamber-Rosenau, *Women in Drag*, 3.

44. Ibid., 11.

45. Ibid., 53.

46. Ibid., 129.

47. Ibid.

48. Marcella Maria Althaus Reid, "Searching for a Queer Sophia-Wisdom: The Post-Colonial Rahab," in *Patriarchs, Prophets and Other Villains*, ed. Lisa Isherwood (London/Oakville: Equinox, 2007), 132.

49. Vincent L. Wimbush, "It's Scripturalizations, Colleagues!" *Journal of Africana Religions*, vol. 3, no. 2 (2015): 194.

50. Tamber-Rosenau, *Women in Drag*, 12.

51. For the popularity of such an argument that "[i]f male protagonists can be sexy, merciless, bloodthirsty psychopaths, then women can be, too—and that's the morally questionable brand of feminism I'm sticking to," see, e.g., Jill Gutowitz, "In Defense of McG's Hypersexualized Female Protagonists in 'The Babysitter,' 'Charlie's Angels' and More," (October 31, 2027): https://decider.com/2017/10/31/the-babysitter-netflix-movie-samara-weaving-mcg/.

52. Mitchum Huehls and Rachel Greenwald Smith, "Four Phases of Neoliberalism and Literature: An Introduction," in *Neoliberalism and Contemporary Literary Culture*, ed. Mitchum Huehls and Rachel Greenwald Smith (Baltimore, MD: Johns Hopkins University Press, 2017), 10.

53. For this concept, see Yanis Varoufakis, *Another Now: Dispatches from an Alternative Present* (London: Bodley Head, 2020).

54. For his explanations of this shift, see, e.g., Yanis Varoufakis, "Capitalism Has Become 'Techno-Feudalism'," *Al Jazeera* (February 19, 2021): https://www.aljazeera.com/program/upfront/2021/2/19/yanis-varoufakis-capitalism-has-become-techno.

55. Alice Flanagan, "Techno-Feudalism and the End of Capitalism" (April 30, 2021): https://nowthenmagazine.com/articles/yanis-varoufakis-techno-feudalism-and-the-end-of-capitalism.

56. Mitchum Huehls, *After Critique: Twenty-First-Century Fiction in a Neoliberal Age* (Oxford: Oxford University Press, 2016), 12.
57. Ibid., 5.
58. Ibid., 19.
59. Ibid., 20.
60. Ibid., 29.
61. For a review, see, e.g., Kieran Smith, "An Ontological Turn," *Electronic Book Review* (April 17, 2017), https://electronicbookreview.com/essay/an-ontological-turn/.
62. Ursula McTaggert, "Literature of Resistance for a Neoliberal Era," *Contemporary Literature* (March 1, 2017): 154.
63. Ibid.
64. Huehls, *After Critique*, 28–33.
65. Stephen Best and Sharon Marcus, "Surface Reading: An Introduction," *Representations* 108.1 (2009): 1–21.
66. Rita Felski, *The Limits of Critique* (Chicago: University of Chicago Press, 2015), 11.
67. Huehls, *After Critique*, 3–4.
68. Ibid., 12.
69. Ibid.
70. Ibid., 12–13.
71. For this U.S.-American TV series (1987-1994), see https://www.imdb.com/title/tt0092455/.
72. Huehls, *After Critique*, 15.
73. Ibid.
74. Ibid., 17.
75. Ibid., 19.
76. Ibid..
77. See the excellent review on Huehls's *After Critique* by McTaggart, "Literature of Resistance for a Neoliberal Era," 153.
78. John Michael, "Tragedy and Translation: A Future for Critique in a Secular Age," in *Critique and Postcritique*, ed. Elizabeth S. Anker and Rita Felski (Durham/London: Duke University Press, 2017), 262.
79. Ibid., 254.
80. Felski, *The Limits of Critique*, 12.
81. Two early and well-known anthologies in biblical studies are Fernando F. Segovia and Mary Ann Tolbert, eds., *Reading from This Place* (vol. 1: Social Location and Biblical Interpretation in the United States; vol. 2: Social Location and Biblical Interpretation in Global Perspective; Minneapolis, MN: Fortress Press, 1995).
82. Kathryn Fleishman, "The Statue and the Veil: Postcritique in the Age of Trump," *Post45* (January 16, 20219): https://post45.org/2019/01/the-statue-and-the-veil-postcritique-in-the-age-of-trump/.
83. McTaggart, "Literature of Resistance," 155. For an excellent assessment of postcritique positions as "liberal" themselves, see Tim Lanzendörfer and Mathias

Nilges, "Literary Studies after Postcritique: An Introduction," *Amerikastudien/American Studies*, vol. 54, no. 4 (2019): 491–513, especially 500.

84. Huehls, *After Critique*, 19.
85. Fleischman, "The Statue and the Veil," [emphasis in the original].
86. Ibid.
87. See, e.g., Susanne Scholz, "Tell Me How You Read This Story and I Will Tell You Who You Are: Post-Postmodernity, Radicant Exegesis, and a Feminist Sociology of Biblical Hermeneutics," in *The Bible as Political Artifact: On the Feminist Study of the Hebrew Bible* (Minneapolis, MN: Fortress Press, 2017), 189.
88. Lanzendörfer and Nilges, "Literary Studies after Postcritique," 509.
89. Aaron Couch, "'Star Trek': The Story of the Most Daring Cliff Hanger in 'Next Generation' History," *The Hollywood Reporter* (June 20, 2015): https://www.hollywoodreporter.com/movies/movie-news/star-trek-story-daring-cliffhanger-803642/.

FURTHER READINGS

Eskenazi, Tamara, and Andrea L. Weiss, eds. *The Torah: A Women's Commentary*. New York: WRF/URJ Press, 2008.

Giroux, Henry A. *Race, Politics, and Pandemic Pedagogy: Education in a Time of Crisis*. London: Bloomsbury Academic, 2021.

Goundouriotis, Eleni, and Lauren M. E. Goodlad. "What Is and Isn't Changing? Introduction." *Modern Language Quarterly* 81, no. 4 (December 1, 2020): 399–418.

Guest, Deryn, Robert E. Goss, Mona West, and Thomas Bohache, eds. *The Queer Bible Commentary*. London: SCM, 2006.

Junior, Nyasha. *An Introduction to Womanist Biblical Interpretation*. Louisville, KY: Westminster John Knox Press, 2015.

Newsom, Carol A., Sharon H. Ringe, and Jacqueline E. Lapsley, eds. *Women's Bible Commentary*. Third Revision and Updated Edition. Louisville, KY: Westminster John Knox Press, 2012.

Scholz, Susanne. *Introducing the Women's Hebrew Bible: Feminism, Gender Justice, and the Study of the Old Testament*. London: Bloomsbury T&T Clark, 2017.

REFERENCES

Ackerman, Susan. *Warrior, Dancer, Seductress, Queen: Women in Judges and Biblical Israel*. Anchor Bible Reference Library. New York: Doubleday, 1998.

Althaus Reid, Marcella Maria. "Searching for a Queer Sophia-Wisdom: The Post-Colonial Rahab." In *Patriarchs, Prophets and Other Villains*, edited by Lisa Isherwood, 128–140. London/Oakville: Equinox, 2007.

Avalos, Hector. *The End of Biblical Studies*. Amherst, NY: Prometheus Books, 2007.

Barthes, Roland. "The Death of the Author." *Aspen* 5–6 (1967). http://www.ubu.com/aspen/aspen5and6/threeEssays.html#barthes.

Best, Stephen and Sharon Marcus. "Surface Reading: An Introduction." *Representations* 108, no. 1 (2009): 1–21.

Byron, Gay L. and Vanessa Lovelace, eds. *Womanist Interpretations of the Bible: Expanding the Discourse*. Atlanta, GA: SBL Press, 2016.

Carr, David M. *The Hebrew Bible: A Contemporary Introduction to the Christian Old Testament and the Jewish Tanakh*. Second Edition. Hoboken, NJ: Wiley-Blackwell, 2021.

Clark-Soles, Jaime. *Women in the Bible*. Louisville, KY: Westminster John Knox Press, 2020.

Clicqué, Guy M. "'Anything Goes?' Theology and Science in a Culture Marked by Postmodern Thinking." *European Journal of Science and Theology* 1, no. 2 (June 2005): 27–33.

Cooper, Helene, Eric Schmitt, and David E. Sanger. "Debating Exit From Afghanistan, Biden Rejected General's Views." *New York Times*, April 18, 2021: A11.

Dolansky, Shawna and Sarah Shectman, eds. "Gendered Historiography: Theoretical Considerations and Case Studies." *Journal of Hebrew Scriptures* 19, no. 4 (2019): 1–58.

Donoghue, Frank. *The Last Professors: The Corporate University and the Fate of the Humanities: With a New Introduction*. New York: Fordham University Press, 2018.

Dube, Musa W. *Postcolonial Feminist Interpretation of the Bible*. St. Louis, MI: Chalice, 2000.

Dube Shomanah, Musa W., ed. "Other Ways of Reading: African Women and the Bible." In *Global Perspectives on Biblical Scholarship*. Atlanta, GA: SBL Press, 2001.

Erlanger, Steven. "With Merkel Leaving, the Role of Germany's Green Party Is Expected to Grow." *New York Times*, April 18, 2021: A9.

Felski, Rita. *The Limits of Critique*. Chicago: University of Chicago Press, 2015.

Fischer, Irmtraud, ed. *Die Bible und die Frauen: Eine exegetisch-kulturgeschichtliche Enzyklopädie*. Stuttgart: Kohlhammer, 2010.

Flanagan, Alice. "Techno-Feudalism and the End of Capitalism." April 30, 2021. https://nowthenmagazine.com/articles/yanis-varoufakis-techno-feudalism-and-the-end-of-capitalism.

Fleishman, Kathryn. "The Statue and the Veil: Postcritique in the Age of Trump." *Post45*, January 16, 20219. https://post45.org/2019/01/the-statue-and-the-veil-postcritique-in-the-age-of-trump/.

Foucault, Michel. "What is an Author?" *Lecture Given at the Collège de France*, February 22, 1969. https://www.open.edu/openlearn/ocw/pluginfile.php/624849/mod_resource/content/1/a840_1_michel_foucault.pdf.

Fuchs, Esther. *Feminist Theory and the Bible: Interrogating the Sources*. Lanham, MD: Lexington Books, 2016.

―――. "Neoliberal Feminist Scholarship in Biblical Studies." In *Oxford Handbook of Feminist Approaches to the Hebrew Bible*, edited by Susanne Scholz, 159–179. Oxford: Oxford University Press, 2021.

Gafney, Wilda C. *Womanist Midrash: A Reintroduction to the Women of the Torah and the Throne*. Louisville, KY: Westminster John Knox, 2017.

Gross, Rita. *Feminism and Religion: An Introduction*. Boston: Beacon, 1996.
Guest, Deryn, Robert Goss, Mona West, and Thomas Bohache, eds. *The Queer Bible Commentary*. London: SCM Press, 2006.
Gutowitz, Jill. "In Defense of McG's Hypersexualized Female Protagonists in 'The Babysitter,' 'Charlie's Angels' and More." October 31, 2021. https://decider.com/2017/10/31/the-babysitter-netflix-movie-samara-weaving-mcg/.
Heger, Paul. *Women in the Bible, Qumran, and Early Rabbinic Literature: Their Status and Roles*. Leiden, Netherlands: Brill, 2014.
Hornsby, Teresa J. "Capitalism, Masochism, and Biblical Interpretation." In *Bible Trouble: Queer Reading at the Boundaries of Biblical Scholarship*, edited by Teresa J. Hornsby and Ken Stone, 137–155. Atlanta, GA: Society of Biblical Literature, 2011.
———. "Neoliberalism and Queer Theory in Biblical Readings." In *The Oxford Handbook of Feminist Approaches to the Hebrew Bible*, edited by Susanne Scholz, 213–229. Oxford: Oxford University Press, 2021.
Huehls, Mitchum. *After Critique: Twenty-First-Century Fiction in a Neoliberal Age*. Oxford: Oxford University Press, 2016.
Huehls, Mitchum and Rachel Greenwald Smith. "Four Phases of Neoliberalism and Literature: An Introduction." In *Neoliberalism and Contemporary Literary Culture*, edited by Mitchum Huehls and Rachel Greenwald Smith, 1–18. Baltimore, MD: Johns Hopkins University Press, 2017.
Joseph, Alison L. "'Is Dinah Raped?' Isn't' the Right Question: Genesis 34 and Feminist Historiography." *Journal of Hebrew Scriptures* 19, no. 4 (2019): 27–37.
Lanzendörfer, Tim, and Mathias Nilges. "Literary Studies After Postcritique: An Introduction." *Amerikastudien/American Studies* 54, no. 4 (2019): 491–513.
Lee, Kyung Sook and Kyung M. Park, eds. *Korean Feminists in Conversation With the Bible, Church and Society*. Bible in the Modern World. Sheffield: Sheffield Phoenix Press, 2011.
Leneman, Helen. "Genealogies of Feminist Biblical Studies: An Interview Report From the 1970s Generation." In *Feminist Interpretation of the Hebrew Bible in Retrospect. Volume 1: Biblical Books*, edited by Susanne Scholz, 11–32. Sheffield: Sheffield Academic Press, 2013.
McTaggart, Ursula. "Literature of Resistance for a Neoliberal Era." *Contemporary Literature* 58, no.1 (March 1, 2017): 149–156.
Meyers, Carol, Toni Craven, and R.S. Kraemer, eds. *A Dictionary of Named and Unnamed Women in the Hebrew Bible, the Apocryphal Deuterocanonical Books, and the New Testament*. Boston: Houghton Mifflin, 2000.
Michael, John. "Tragedy and Translation: A Future for Critique in a Secular Age." In *Critique and Postcritique*, edited by Elizabeth S. Anker and Rita Felski, 252–278. Durham/London: Duke University Press, 2017.
Myers, Alicia D. *Blessed Among Women? Mothers and Motherhood in the New Testament*. New York: Oxford University Press, 2017.
Ong, Aihwa. *Neoliberalism as Exception: Mutations in Citizenship and Sovereignty*. Durham/London: Duke University Press, 2006.

Scholz, Susanne. "Discovering a Largely Unknown Past for a Vibrant Present: Feminist Hebrew Bible Studies in North America." In *The Bible as Political Artifact: On the Feminist Study of the Hebrew Bible*. Minneapolis, MN: Fortress Press, 2017.

———, ed. *Feminist Interpretation of the Hebrew Bible in Retrospect. Volume 2: Social Locations*. Sheffield: Sheffield Academic Press, 2014.

———. *The Bible as Political Artifact: On the Feminist Study of the Hebrew Bible*. Minneapolis, MN: Fortress Press, 2017.

———, ed. *The Oxford Handbook of Feminist Approaches to the Hebrew Bible*. Oxford: Oxford University Press, 2021.

Schroer, Silvia and Sophia Bietenhard, eds. *Feminist Interpretation of the Bible and the Hermeneutics of Liberation*. London: T&T Clark International, 2004.

Schüssler Fiorenza, Elisabeth, ed. *Feminist Bible Studies in the Twentieth Century: Scholarship and Movement*. Bible and Women 9.1. Atlanta, GA: SBL Press, 2014.

———. *The Power of the Word: Scripture and the Rhetoric of Empire*. Minneapolis, MN: Fortress Press, 2007.

Segovia, Fernando F. and Mary Ann Tolbert, eds. *Reading From This Place*. Volume 1 and 2. Minneapolis, MN: Fortress Press, 1995.

Smith, Kieran. "An Ontological Turn." *Electronic Book Review*, April 17, 2017. https://electronicbookreview.com/essay/an-ontological-turn/.

Tamber-Rosenau, Caryn. *Women in Drag: Gender and Performance in the Hebrew Bible and Early Jewish Literature*. Picataway, NJ: Gorgias, 2018.

Varoufakis, Yanis. *And the Weak Suffer What They Must? Europe's Crisis and America's Economic Future*. New York: Nations Books, 2016.

———. *Another Now: Dispatches From an Alternative Present*. London: Bodley Head, 2020.

———. "Capitalism Has Become 'Techno-Feudalism'." *Al Jazeera*, February 19, 2021a. https://www.aljazeera.com/program/upfront/2021/2/19/yanis-varoufakis-capitalism-has-become-techno.

———. "Capitalism Has Become "Techno-Feudalism." *Al Jazeera*, February 19, 2021b. https://www.youtube.com/watch?v=_jW0xUmUaUc.

Wacker, Marie-Theres. "Feministische Theologie und Antijudaismus: Diskussionsstand und Problemlage in der Bundesrepublik Deutschland." *Kirche und Israel* 5 (1990): 168–176.

Watts, James, W. *Understanding the Bible as a Scripture in History, Culture, and Religion*. Hoboken, NJ: Wiley-Blackwell, 2021.

Weems, Renita J. *Just a Sister Away: Understanding the Timeless Connection Between Woman of Today and Women in the Bible*. San Diego, CA: LuraMedia, 1988.

Wimbush, Vincent L. "It's Scripturalizations, Colleagues!" *Journal of Africana Religions* 3, no. 2 (2015): 193–200.

Wimsatt, W. K., Jr., and Monroe C. Beardsley. "The Intentional Fallacy." *The Sewanee Review* 54, no. 3 (July–September 1946): 468–488.

Yee, Gale A., ed. *Judges and Method: New Approaches in Biblical Studies*. Minneapolis, MN: Fortress Press, 1995.

———, ed. *The Hebrew Bible: Feminist and Intersectional Perspectives*. Minneapolis, MN: Fortress Press, 2018.

Chapter 16

Slouching, together, after Pentecost

Toward a Post-traumatic Pedagogy of (De)formation, Discomfort, and Difference

Brandy Daniels

> Turning and turning in the widening gyre
> The falcon cannot hear the falconer;
> Things fall apart; the centre cannot hold;
> Mere anarchy is loosed upon the world,
> The blood-dimmed tide is loosed, and everywhere
> The ceremony of innocence is drowned;
> The best lack all conviction, while the worst
> Are full of passionate intensity.
> Surely some revelation is at hand;
> Surely the Second Coming is at hand.
> The Second Coming! Hardly are those words out
> When a vast image out of Spiritus Mundi
> Troubles my sight: somewhere in the sands of the desert
> A shape with lion body and the head of a man,
> A gaze blank and pitiless as the sun,
> Is moving its slow thighs, while all about it
> Reel shadows of the indignant desert birds.
> The darkness drops again; but now I know
> That twenty centuries of stony sleep
> Were vexed to nightmare by a rocking cradle,
> And what rough beast, its hour come round at last,
> Slouches towards Bethlehem to be born?
>
> —William Butler Yeats, "The Second Coming" (1919)

In the final season of *The Sopranos*, the immensely popular crime drama that aired on HBO in the early aughts, AJ Soprano, the troubled son of Mafia boss Tony and his wife Carmela, is battling a particularly severe bout of depression following a painful breakup. When his college English professor teaches Yeats' "The Second Coming," AJ is roused from his torpor, though not from depression.[1] AJ proceeds to ruminate on the seemingly never-ending violent conflict in the Middle East and the general horrors of the world. He lies awake one night, reading the poem aloud in bed in rapt attention. Shortly thereafter, he sits on the edge of his family's swimming pool, with a cinder block tied by a rope to his legs, pulls a plastic bag over his head, and jumps in, attempting to end his own life. Grappling with her son's suicide attempt, Carmela places at least some blame on "The Second Coming." In a family therapy session, she asks angrily: *"What kind of poem is that to teach college students?"*

This chapter uses Carmela Soprano's question as a starting point, turning to William Butler Yeats' poem as both an interlocutor and a kind of navigational guide, a compass, to explore teaching theology and religious studies and/at the intersections of gender, race, and sexuality (among other sites and forms of difference). In the contemporary sociopolitical context of the United States in the twenty-first century—one that bears notable resemblances to Yeats' early-twentieth-century Irish milieu—discomfort and (de)formation are imperative for liberative pedagogies that aim to address and affirm difference. This is particularly the case for those who teach religious studies and/or theology. This chapter explores why, and considers resources, toward these ends, placing "The Second Coming" in conversation with Megan Boler's pedagogical scholarship on discomfort and with *After Whiteness*, Willie Jennings' recent (ante-) treatise on theological education. A turn to our contemporary sociopolitical climate, and its relation to Yeats' context, is a helpful place to begin.

LIVING IN APOCALYPTIC TIMES

As the United States celebrates the centenary of (white) women's suffrage, persistent social and political problems continue to frustrate and thwart positive advances that have been made. Ever since women's rights and feminist movements began, there has been significant backlash from patriarchal, religious, and right-wing forces. The election and presidency of Donald Trump fueled and furthered antifeminist and misogynistic policies, attitudes, and practices. For instance, one might point to the stripping of hard-earned protections for sexual assault survivors and transgender women, or to eroding family economic security, or the range of attacks on reproductive rights, to offer just a few examples among many (not to mention the cultural impact of his own history of misogyny and sexual violence).[2] Alongside recent antiwomen agendas and achievements, the uptick in xenophobic and white supremacist violence and oppression has been even more devastating. Here, one might consider the "Muslim ban" and the efforts to build a bigger border wall, or the continued and increasing number of murders of black people at the hands of the police, or the rise of the alt-right and the racist violence on display at the "Unite the Right" rally in Charlottesville, Virginia.

The challenges to efforts at (and presumptions about) progress—in general, and particularly toward gender and racial justice and liberation—extend far beyond the United States. The effects of climate change and the rise in right-wing populism and totalitarianism have wreaked havoc globally, from democratic governments deteriorating in Haiti and Hungary to the mounting weapons programs of Iran and North Korea, and from the racial and religious oppression occurring in Australia and France, to the curbing of women's rights in Poland and Afghanistan. All of these realities, and then some, have led the Bulletin of Atomic Scientists to move the hands of the "Doomsday Clock" closer to midnight (read: Armageddon) than it has ever been in its seventy-three-year history.[3]

The political, social, and material devastation and division in the world today, and the feelings of doom and apocalypse it engenders for many, bear a great deal of similarity to Yeats' world. Yeats began composing "The Second Coming" in January 1919, in the aftermath of World War I and the Russian Revolution, and at the beginning of the Irish War of Independence.[4] The shared circumstances of intense geopolitical conflicts, cultural polarization and strife among ideological and factional lines, and social and political upheaval and fear led the Wall Street Journal to declare 2016 "the Year of Yeats."[5] Since 2016, the similarities have only multiplied, with the havoc wrecked globally by the coronavirus pandemic (Yeats penned "The Second Coming" while his pregnant wife was seriously ill with the Spanish flu, in the midst of the 1919 flu pandemic).[6]

The overlaps between Yeats' context and our own already offer an important answer to Carmela's question: *What kind of poem is this to teach college students?* A relevant one, one that will resonate with students' own contexts and feelings, and that will lead to critical reflection and constructive engagement. But what might it mean to teach this poem, to teach *with* this poem, for those of us who are not English professors, for those who are not teaching poetry? More specifically, what might thinking with this poem offer for those of us who teach gender, sexuality, and/or race?

LIVING, TEACHING, AND LEARNING IN APOCALYPTIC TIMES: ON DISCOMFORT, TRAUMA, AND DIFFERENCE

Carmela's emotional question to the family's therapist highlights a reality that college instructors are very familiar with, that they experience among their students, in the culture, and in themselves: a distaste, even a fear, of discomfort. From harsh critiques of "the plague of hypersensitivity" in the college classroom to impassioned defenses of trigger warnings, from debates about cancel culture to defenses of critical race theory, there is a great deal of literature—pedagogical, philosophical, and popular—that both speaks to and reflects this distaste of discomfort.[7] Within this broad corpus of literature grappling with discomfort is a pedagogical philosophy that embraces it. While this pedagogical approach has been around since Socrates, or at least since Diogenes, and has implicit manifestations in Paulo Freire and bell hooks (among others), it finds its most explicit and popular expression in Megan Boler's, *Feeling Power: Emotions and Education.* Drawing on poststructuralist and feminist thought to outline how "the politics of emotion" functions in public education to enforce social control (via a discursive analysis of the mental hygiene and character education movements and the notion of emotional intelligence), Boler illuminates how we are taught to internalize and enact emotional rules and roles that reinforce and reproduce society's stratifications of race, gender, and class.

While emotions have a pedagogical function of social control, Boler points out that they also serve as a site for political resistance and as a catalyst for social change. As an educator, Boler is concerned particularly about the "habituated numbness" observed among students and teachers alike, and rejects passive empathy "that produces no action towards justice."[8] Discomfort, Boler compellingly argues, is a key emotion that can be utilized in the classroom, particularly for liberative pedagogies, challenging social stratifications. Experiences of discomfort, she explains, can be used to "invite students and educators to examine how our modes of seeing have been shaped specifically by the dominant culture of the historical moment"—they can help students identify, and reassess, that which is taken for granted, the current order of things.[9] Importantly, this pedagogical discomfort is done with, by, and toward *difference*—it "develop[s] the capacity for critical inquiry regarding the production and construction of differences" and, and in part *because*, it "recognizes and problematizes the deeply embedded emotional dimensions that frame and shape daily habits, routines, and unconscious complicity with hegemony."[10] A pedagogy of discomfort engages *with* difference in that it focuses on the collective and the differences reflected therein. Pushing against Western conceptions of the liberal individual, a pedagogy of discomfort focuses on a relationally based, collective understanding rather than self-reflection. Building on the work of Shoshona Felman and Dori Laub on historical and cultural trauma—on testimony that attempts to communicate the unspeakable in, and of, history—Boler calls for "testimonial reading."[11] The testimonial process communicates trauma's excess, enabling the listener or reader to accept responsibility as a coproducer of truth. In our current sociopolitical climate of crisis, this bearing witness is needed on a collective level, as we grapple with difference and the impacts of hegemonies of power on difference. A pedagogy of discomfort pursues a (collective) witnessing of the broader collective(s) we are a part of and that we encounter and study, as "how we see ourselves and want to see ourselves, is inextricably intertwined with others."[12]

A pedagogy of discomfort also operates *by* difference—it is "flexible: leading to a willingness to reconsider and undergo possible transformation of our own self-identity in relation to others and to history."[13] To be discomforted by difference is not just affective, but it is (trans)formative, and, in fact, deformative, as one's own sense of self is undone by the difference of others. Finally, a pedagogy of discomfort works *toward* difference. It has difference in its aim. Because emotion, especially comfort, has been a pedagogical tool to reinforce social stratification through the enforcement of social norms, a central focus of a pedagogy of discomfort "is the recognition of the multiple, heterogeneous, and messy realities of power relations as they are enacted and resisted in localities, subverting the comfort offered by the endorsement of particular norms."[14] These entanglements—the ways in which pedagogical discomfort operates with, by, and toward difference—are not only significant for teaching at the intersections of gender, race, and sexuality, but are particularly valuable for, and resonant with, those who teach religion and particularly Christian theology.

LIVING, TEACHING, AND LEARNING (WITH) RELIGION AND THEOLOGY IN APOCALYPTIC TIMES: DEFORMING THE DISTORTED AND DOMINANT?

When Yeats wrote and published "The Second Coming," the abundant Christian imagery was not only undeniably recognizable to and resonant with his Irish audience, but with his U.S. audience. Since the Puritans and Pilgrims first came to the New England colonies in the seventeenth and eighteenth centuries to escape religious persecution, Christianity in the United States had been in a period of growth, fueled by the First and Second Great Awakenings, the birth of Mormonism, the Restorationist, Transcendentalist, and Holiness movements, the formation and growth of the Black church, and the influx of

Catholic immigrants from Ireland and Germany, amongst a range of other cultural and political trends. The Christian imagery in Yeats' poem is far less recognizable to students today. Just as a range of cultural and political trends and events led to the growth of Christianity in the United States, so too with its decline. As a report by the Pew Research Center puts it in 2019, "In U.S., Decline of Christianity Continues at Rapid Pace."[15] Given the declining influence of Christianity and of religion as a whole—reflected in the rapid rise of "none's," those who claim no religious affiliation—why even consider religion?[16] What is the point of studying it, of learning about it? This is a question familiar to many religious studies professors posed by students as well as colleagues.

To adequately address this question is far beyond the scope of this chapter, but to gesture toward an answer, one might turn to the news, to current events. One might consider how one of the demographics most hesitant to receive the Covid vaccine are evangelical Christians, and how some pastors have caused irreparable harm to their congregants and their communities by actively preaching disinformation and denying the harms of the novel coronavirus that, as of August 2020, has killed over four million people worldwide.[17] One might also consider how, between May and July of 2020, over a thousand unmarked graves of indigenous children have been uncovered in Canada on the former properties of boarding schools run by the Roman Catholic Church.[18] Alternately, or additionally, one might consider three recent rulings of the United States Supreme Court that have upheld religious liberty with significant impact on women and LGBTQ people. The court's ruling in *Little Sisters of the Poor v. Commonwealth of Pennsylvania* upholds the Trump administration's decision to allow private employers with religious or moral objections to deny women contraceptive coverage under the Affordable Care Act. In *Our Lady of Guadalupe School v. Morrise-Berru,* the Court ruled that certain employees of religious schools and hospitals cannot sue for employment discrimination.[19] Finally, in *Fulton v. City of Philadelphia*, the Court ruled unanimously in favor of a Catholic social services agency in Philadelphia to refuse to work with same-sex couples who apply to take in foster children, exempting them from the city's nondiscrimination policy.[20] Or, to offer just one more example, one might consider the Christianity on display during the attempted insurrection on January 6, 2020—from the insurrectionist's prayer inside the breached Senate chambers ("Thank you heavenly Father, for gracing us with this opportunity," they begin, going on to give thanks to God for things like "filling this chamber with patriots") to the Christian-themed signs (i.e., "God, Guns & Guts made America, let's keep all three"), to the Jericho march "to pray, march, fast, and rally for election integrity."[21] These examples are just a few of many, and only point to a small slice, of contemporary conservative-leaning Christianity in the United States, of a much broader—global, interreligious, historical—pie. While these examples may serve as evidence, or rather, a rationale, for the increasing uptick in religious disaffiliation and disavowal, they also point to how the decline of the prevalence of Christianity has not necessarily led to a correlating decline in its impact. As religious studies scholar, Megan Goodwin frequently puts it, "We may be done with religion, but religion is not done with us."[22] While the United States is becoming less and less Christian, Alexis de Tocqueville's insight on the stronghold Christianity holds on its citizens remains resoundingly relevant almost 200 years later.

Those who emphasize how Christianity is embroiled with—how it has led to and continues to lead to—some of the most heinous societal ills, and has been particularly harmful to those marginalized due to race, gender, and/or sexuality, do not only consist of Christianity's cultured despisers, but also find Christian theologians among their numbers. From its inception, feminist theology has not only considered resources within the Christian tradition that speak to a vision of women's equality and flourishing, but has also closely traced and challenged the deep-seated patriarchy within that same tradition. For instance, Mary Daly's *The Church and the Second Sex*, one of the founding texts in feminist theology, offers an indicting history of the sexism and antifeminism of the Catholic Church.[23] Queer theologians like Marcella Althaus Reid and Linn Marie Tonstad have explored at length the ways in which heterosexuality has functioned as an ideology, "as theology, as normative sociopolitical and, crucially, economic system" in Christian thought and practice in ways that have harmed and marginalized sexual minorities.[24] And Black theologians have spoken trenchantly on Christianity's, and, by extension, Western theology's, imbrication in white supremacy. James Cone, the father of Black theology, who critically examined and challenged White Christianity's role in slavery and racism in America throughout his career at one point put it bluntly: "American theology," he writes, "is racist."[25]

Following Cone, Black theologians like Jennings, J. Kameron Carter, and Kelly Brown Douglas have charted how theological discourse has not only functioned to uphold racism and White supremacy, but has been pivotal to its inception and ongoing operation—outlining and taking seriously how "colonial matrix of power, put in place in the sixteenth and seventeenth centuries, was framed in and by Christian theology."[26] In *The Christian Imagination: Theology and the Origin of Race*, Jennings argues that "Christianity in the Western world lives and moves within a diseased social imagination," and both traces and analyzes "the constellation of generative forces that have rendered people's social performances of the Christian life collectively anemic."[27] Through compelling narratives that both "show *and* tell," Jennings illuminates the hegemonic colonial logics entangled with Christian theologies and practices, tracing how they deformed the social imagination from that of the kindom of God rooted in God's covenantal relationship with Israel opened up to us all through Jesus and the Spirit to a distorted supersessionist and colonialist vision of mastery and control, a vision that severs people from one another and from the land, and that is bound up with what Jennings later identifies as "the racial paterfamilias."[28] After this critical examination of the range of ways in which the Christian social imagination has been "woven into processes of cultural domination," particularly in academic and political contexts, Jennings goes on to argue for a reimagination of sociality and intimacy across differences.[29]

Given the ways in which Christianity has been bound up with, has been a part of, the legacies of White supremacy, sexism, and cis/heterosexism in the United States, what does that mean for those of us who teach religion and theology who, at the same time, seek to critique and challenge, to even help dismantle, those legacies and their effects? This is precisely the topic Jennings speaks to in his recent book *After Whiteness: An Education in Belonging*. Following his analysis and critique of Christianity's diseased social imagination and call for a reimagined sociality and intimacy across differences, he then turns to what it might mean and look like to do theological education, to form students, toward this reimagined sociality. The central work of theological education, Jennings writes, is "to form us in the art of cultivating belonging," to form "erotic souls that are being cultivated in an art which joins to the bone and that announces a contrast life aimed at communion."[30]

This pedagogical formation that Jennings calls for also necessarily entails the work of *deformation* from the diseased and distorted imagination that we have inherited. Jennings likens theological education to "a spiraling wind that must be freed from the master's motions."[31] Acknowledging the ways in which "Western education was built to make us men," a reality that haunts but has also been subverted and used to emancipatory ends, Jennings asserts that we ultimately "must come to revolution," a word and notion that "has no natural confluence with education, the former an overturning, and the latter a building up," but that is a contradiction we embrace.[32] This overturning, this undoing, is toward and in the service of that radically reimagined sociality across difference, living into the Christian story of Pentecost, where the Spirit of God "beckon[s] people to want one another and envision lives woven together."[33]

For Jennings, Christianity has held a devastating grip on the soul of, and souls in, modern and contemporary America—fomenting and fueling a hegemonic order that leads to violence and oppression of difference across lines of race, gender, and sexuality (among others)—but it also offers a vision, and resources, to challenge that order, to, in effect, undo a version of itself. What might it look like to think Jennings' vision of theological education alongside Boler's pedagogy of discomfort? This is the final topic to which I now turn.

A SOMATIC ABOLITION? TOWARD A POST-TRAUMATIC, DISCOMFORTING, DEFORMATIONAL PEDAGOGY

The similarities and overlaps between Boler's pedagogy of discomfort and Jennings' vision of theological education, of erotic (de)formation, are abundant, and thus together are particularly rich resources for those who teach at the intersections of religion, race, gender, and sexuality. Both emphasize the value and role of emotions and desire within effective pedagogies.[34] Both seek to understand the influence of dominant culture, both socially and epistemologically, and to critically assess and challenge the ways it affirms and reproduces social stratifications and oppression. Both are attentive to the practices and processes of habituation/formation.[35]

Perhaps most notably, difference is central to both Boler's and Jennings' pedagogical visions—as both means and end. For instance, in discussing emotional literacy curricula, Boler offers an example of how differing emotions experienced in response to a particular example became a tool, enabling students to reflect on what accounted for those different responses—"the very different social situations faced by the different [students] and how their emotional responses reflected different hierarchies and the effects of racism in their culture."[36] Boler goes on to emphasize that such use of difference is not about individual emotional experiences, as that is how emotions are wielded for and by pastoral and disciplinary power. Rather, it is about critically examining precisely how those emotional responses are bound up with power to construct and delimit difference, and how emotional experiences across differences help us to see that. In a very different register, but nevertheless similar vein, Jennings demonstrates how "we inhabit a social world constricted through whiteness that has left us with limited options for imagining how we might be with each other."[37] Theological education, conversely, is—it should be—all about "a contrast life aimed at communion."[38] As he puts it elsewhere, theological education "must be formed to glory in the crowd, think the crowd, be the crowd."[39] For both Boler and Jennings, the diversity that comprises community is pivotal for the process of destabilizing and undoing harmful hierarchies and hegemonic structures—difference, in effect, begets difference.

Moreover, the kind of collective witnessing, the testimonial reading, that is at the center of Boler's pedagogy of discomfort is, in effect, precisely what Jennings performs and invites his readers into in his texts.[40] This way of reading the colonial legacy of Christianity's history—how it has been entangled with colonialist patterns of domination across lines of race, gender, and sexuality—resists and refuses a passive empathy, and instead implicates and entangles readers and students into history and difference. In ways that compel them to recognize "what it is one doesn't want to know," and from there, to "accept a responsibility founded on the discrepancy of our experiences."[41]

For those of us who teach theology or religious studies, to pursue discomfort and deformation in the classroom through testimonial reading, collectively witnessing ways in which Christianity is organized by and toward "white self-sufficient masculinity," may seem like a risky, not to mention fruitless, endeavor.[42] Given an increasing number of students have negative perceptions of religion and particularly Christianity, isn't it counterproductive to dwell on the negative? More significantly, given the ways many students, particularly those who are part of marginalized communities, have been and continue to be traumatized, especially by Christianity (its history, institutions, adherents, etc.), many professors of theology and religion might fear exacerbating that trauma. One might not only have serious concerns about the harm that would cause to students' mental health, but also about the compounding disruptive impact in the classroom and on course learning goals—not to mention the potential impact on educators themselves, given the ever-growing-surge in political attacks on faculty who address social injustices in the classroom and the additional emotional and material labor that is involved with this kind of pedagogical approach.[43] Concerns about the traumatic impact of such endeavors, however, are precisely the reason *why* such a pedagogical approach must be embraced. Boler and Jennings both point to how the processes of deformation and experiences of discomfort in the classroom are not themselves traumatic, but are in fact pivotal for addressing trauma—for avoiding and/or treating it, both individually and collectively.

In a recent review essay for *Modern Theology*, Shelly Rambo, a theologian who has done groundbreaking work at the intersections of theology and trauma studies, considers *After Whiteness* through the lens of trauma and recovery.[44] Focusing on the somatic turn in trauma theory and practice—the range of scholarship that has explored how our limbic systems (our fight/flight/freeze responses, the "alarm bell" of the brain) "remember" trauma, persisting in their response to threat long after the threat has disappeared—Rambo hones in on Resmaa Menakem's work interpreting historical and collective trauma through this somatic lens.[45] Given the way trauma works in the body, healing racialized trauma requires what Menakem calls somatic abolition—working through, in, and with our bodies, our limbic systems, and the memories that we hold on both an individual and collective level.

Rambo offers a compelling interpretation of *After Whiteness* through this lens, pointing out that "Jennings, similarly, is targeting the limbic system."[46] Just as the limbic system of the traumatized person (mal)adapts in light of their experience—such as when the impulse to fight or run, while useful in the war zone, is no longer useful but nevertheless persists back in civilian life, or when the freezing during an encounter of sexual violence becomes a pattern that persists in one's consensual romantic encounters—the institutional limbic system of whiteness, having adapted to function within a culture of White supremacy, fight to uphold that system even though it is maladaptive, and feels a sense of loss when it is challenged. "Jennings invites readers to become more attuned to what we—collectively—*do not want to feel*," Rambo writes. "He invites us to work with discomfort instead of escaping it" pointing out how, as is the case with somatic therapeutic approaches to trauma, "if we attune ourselves to stay with the difficult sensations—and breathe with them—over time, we may feel energy in the room begin to shift."[47] Rambo illuminates how Jennings' vision of education, and by extension Boler's pedagogy of discomfort, are *post*-traumatic—not post-traumatic in the sense of the painful repetition that occurs when the memories of our limbic systems persist far beyond the immediate threat in ways that cause us harm and suffering, but post-traumatic in the sense of recovering from, of working through, trauma: a somatic abolition.

SLOUCHING, TOGETHER, AFTER PENTECOST?

While an ever-increasing percentage of students may not be familiar with the Christian imagery of "The Second Coming," they nevertheless find it affectively resonant. This is particularly true of today's college-aged students, Gen Z, coming of age during a global pandemic and amidst a rise in political polarization and an uptick in authoritarianism and fascism not seen since World War II, though the crisis and chaos that "The Second Coming" evokes have been a poetic reservoir that has been tapped across generations and cultures (so much so that journalist Fintan O'Toole proposed the "Yeats Test," wherein the "more quotable Yeats seems to commentators and politicians, the worse things are").[48] College-aged adults in the United States today experience high levels of isolation and loneliness, report facing intense pressure in the midst of potential economic precarity and competition, and battle depression and anxiety at record numbers—realities that are admittedly faced by many adults today across generations.[49] Things seem to continue to fall apart, and when they start to feel glimmers of hope, that some revelation is at hand (a political regime shift, a growing economy, movements toward racial justice, or a Covid vaccine), yet another rough beast seems to emerge and encroach (political stagnancy, a global pandemic, another murder of an unarmed Black man by police, or the Delta variant).

While those of us who engage the intersections of religion, race, gender, and sexuality in our teaching may at times avoid discomfort out of fear of burdening or traumatizing students or distracting from our course goals, or at least tell ourselves as much, students are already experiencing it in their lives and worlds. The classroom can be a space for us to engage them where they are as well as offer resources for, and practice, somatic abolition.[50]

Rambo ends her review essay of *After Whiteness* by suggesting that a kind of pedagogical somatic abolition is enabled by and through changing postures and being curious about those changes. Instead of allowing the traumatic memories and the physical and emotional responses triggered by the limbic system "to burn and deplete energy," Rambo writes, you might "shift into different postures."[51] Rather than judging or trying to escape them, you might stay with the feelings, notice the sensations that come with the fear and desire to flee, being curious about your anger and impulse to fight, as the sensations are pointing to something being "off" in the system. Rather than fleeing or fighting or freezing, you instead shift postures, and begin to both see things differently, and to anticipate reactions, both your own and others, enabling change. Boler, similarly, talks about "the capacity to shift our positionality and modes of seeing," which is both important for and facilitated by a pedagogy of discomfort.[52]

Shifting postures might be painful or uncomfortable, certainly at first—embracing discomfort and the ways in which difference challenges and unforms us is certainly not easy. But "we, together, stand to gain."[53] As Rambo puts it, "curiosity needs its companion—courage. And it does best if it has companion bodies awakened with curiosity about what is going on. This," she concludes, "is the disruptive communing that might take place" in our classrooms.[54] It is through discomfort, through constructing a space where students might be discomfortably deformed by difference—through slouching, together, after Pentecost—that the aims of liberation, justice, and freedom, held by those of us who teach, learn, and reside at the intersections of religion, race, gender, and sexuality might be further enacted and realized.

NOTES

1. *The Sopranos*, Season 6, episode 19, "The Second Coming," May 20, 2007. This occasion is actually the *third* time the show references Yeats' "The Second Coming." Back in Season 5, episode 10 ("Cold Cuts," May 9, 2004), Dr. Melfi quotes a line from it to Tony Soprano. And in the very final episode, (Season 6, Episode 21," Made in America," June 10, 2007, AJ references it in a conversation with Paulie and others about the movie *Dreamgirls*.

2. See Sunny Frothingham and Shilpa Phadke, "100 Days, 100 Ways the Trump Administration is Harming Women and Families," *Center for American Progress,* April 25, 2017, https://www.americanprogress.org/issues/women/ reports/20 17/04/25/430969/100-days-100-ways-trump-administration-harming-women-famili

es/; Danielle Kurtzleben, "Feminists Weigh Their Wins and Losses After Nearly Four Years of Trump," *NPR*, October 16, 2020, https://www.npr.org/2020/10/16/924167976/feminists-weigh-their-wins-and-losses-after-nearly-four-years-of-trump. One might also consider here how the Women's March, likely the largest political march in recorded history, served as a response to the degree and scope of the concerns women had regarding their rights in light of Trump's presidency. See Sarah Frostenson, "The Women's Marches may have been the largest demonstration in US history," *Vox*, January 31, 2017, http://www.vox.com/2017/1/22/14350808/womens-marches-largest-demonstration-us-history-map.

3. See Bulletin of the Atomic Scientists, "Doomsday Clock," https://thebulletin.org/doomsday-clock/.

4. "The Second Coming" was first published in November 1920 (mere months after the ratification of the nineteenth amendment in August of that year—though the poem does not speak to or reference women's suffrage), in *The Dial* and *The Nation*. Yeats then included the poem in his 1921 collection of verses *Michael Robartes and the Dancer*.

5. Ed Ballard, "Terror, Brexit and U.S. Election Have Made 2016 the Year of Yeats," *The Wall Street Journal*, August 23, 2016. Utilizing the media database Factiva, the article notes that phrases and lines from "The Second Coming" appeared more times in the press in the first seven months of 2016 than during any period in the previous three decades.

6. The highest death rates of the 1918-1919 Spanish flu pandemic were among pregnant women—in some areas they had up to a seventy percent death rate. See Elizabeth Outka, *Viral Modernism: The Influenza Pandemic and Interwar Literature* (New York: Columbia University Press, 2019).

7. See, for instance, Kate Manne, "Why I Use Trigger Warnings," *The New York Times*, September 19, 2015, https://www.nytimes.com/2015/09/20/opinion/sunday/why-i-use-trigger-warnings.html; Todd Gitlin, "You Are Here to Be Disturbed," *The Chronicle of Higher Education*, May 11, 2015, https://www.chronicle.com/article/you-are-here-to-be-disturbed/; Kathryn D. Blanchard, "Trigger Warnings: Not the Greatest Threat to Higher Education," *The Chronicle of Higher Education*, January 8, 2016, https://www.chronicle.com/article/trigger-warnings-not-the-greatest-threat-to-higher-education/; John Warner, "I Want to Make Students Uncomfortable," *Inside Higher Ed*, August 21, 2016, https://www.insidehighered.com/blogs/just-visiting/i-want-make-students-uncomfortable.

8. Boler, *Feeling Power*, 161.

9. Ibid., 179.

10. Megan Boler and Michalinos Zembylas, "Discomforting Truths: The Emotional Terrain of Understanding Difference," in *Pedagogies of Difference: Rethinking Education for Social Change*, ed. Peter Pericles Trifonas (New York: RoutledgeFalmer, 2003), 108 [107–130].

11. Boler, *Feeling Power*, xxiii.

12. Ibid., 178.

13. Ibid.

14. Boler and Zembylas, "Discomforting Truths," 126.

15. Pew Research Center, "In U.S., Decline of Christianity Continues at Rapid Pace," October 17, 2019, https://www.pewforum.org/2019/10/17/in-u-s-decline-of-christianity-continues-at-rapid-pace/. The report draws on survey data from the Pew Research Center Religious Landscape Studies in 2007 and 2014, from aggregated Pew Research Center political surveys conducted via phone from 2009-June 2019, and from the long-running General Social Survey from NORC, an independent nonpartisan research institute at the University of Chicago. While in the 1970's, up to a whopping ninety percent of US adults identified as Christian, by 2019, that number has shrunk to sixty-five percent.

16. According to the Pew report, forty percent of Millennials (those born between 1981 and 1996) claim no religious affiliation. These religious "none's" have grown by nearly 30 million over the past decade. Among those none's, over half hold that "religion is not important" (whereas the others hold that religion is important but claim no particular affiliation—this sub-group is often identified as those who are "spiritual but not religious").

17. March 2021 poll by PRRI found that White evangelical Christians ranked highest among religious groups refusing to get vaccinated, with only 45% saying they would get it. https://www.prri.org/research/prri-ifyc-covid-vaccine-religion-report/; https://www.cnn.com/2021/04/14/us/covid-vaccine-evangelicals/index.html.

18. In May, 215 graves were found at the Kamloops Indian Residential School. On June 23rd, an astounding 751 graves were found at Marieval Indian Residential School. And one week later, on June 30th, 182 graves were found at St. Eugene's Mission School. Researchers anticipate more graves being uncovered in the months to come. See Kiara Alfonseca, "''As recently discovered unmarked Indigenous graves in Canada nears 1,000, activists demand justice," *ABC News*, July 3, 2021, https://abcnews.go.com/International/recently-discovered-unmarked-indigenous-graves-canada-nears-1000/story?id=78472829.

19. David Crary and Elana Schor, "Double win at Supreme Court elates religious conservatives," *The Washington Post*, July 11, 2020, https://www.washingtonpost.com/national/religion/correction-supreme-court-religious-exemption-story/2020/07/11/4bcff098-c37e-11ea-8908-68a2b9eae9e0_story.html.

20. Adam Liptak, "Supreme Court Backs Catholic Agency in Case on Gay Rights and Foster Care," *The New York Times*, June 17, 2021, https://www.nytimes.com/2021/06/17/us/supreme-court-gay-rights-foster-care.html. It is also perhaps relevant to note that all nine of the Supreme Court justices identify as religious—seven of them are Catholics, and two are Jewish.

21. Luke Mogelson, "A Reporter's Video from Inside the Capitol Siege," *The New Yorker*, January 16, 2021, https://www.newyorker.com/video/watch/a-reporters-footage-from-inside-the-capitol-siege (the prayer begins at the 07 minute:57 second mark); Emma Green, "A Christian Insurrection, *The Atlantic,* January 8, 2021, https://www.theatlantic.com/politics/archive/2021/01/evangelicals-catholics-jericho-march-capitol/617591/.

22. Megan Goodwin, in Megan Goodwin & Ilyse Morgenstein Fuerst, Episode 106: You may be done with religion, but religion isn't done with you, *Keeping it 101: A Killjoy's Introduction to Religion,* March 23, 2020, https://keepingit101.com/

e106; Megan Goodwin, "The University of Vermont might be done with religion, but religion isn't done with us," *Religion Dispatches,* December 7, 2020, https://religiondispatches.org/the-university-of-vermont-might-be-done-with-religion-but-religion-isnt-done-with-us/.

23. See Mary Daly, *The Church and the Second Sex* (Boston: Beacon Press, 1986 [1968]).

24. Linn Marie Tonstad, *Queer Theology: Beyond Apologetics* (Eugene, OR: Cascade Books, 2018), 76. See also Marcella Althaus-Reid, *Indecent Theology: Theological Perversions in Sex, Gender, and Politics* (New York: Routledge, 2000); and, Althaus-Reid, *The Queer God* (New York: Routledge, 2003).

25. James H. Cone, *A Black Theology of Liberation* (Maryknoll, NY: Orbis Books, 2010 [1970]), 46. This was not the only, or first, time Cone made such an assertion. Speaking to the *New York Times* in 1969, Cone remarked that "White theology is basically racist and non-Christian." See Harrison Smith, "James H. Cone, founder of black liberation theology, dies at 79," April 30, 2018, https://www.washingtonpost.com/local/obituaries/james-h-cone-founder-of-black-liberation-theology-dies-at-79/2018/04/30/94b5efc8-4c80-11e8-84a0-458a1aa9ac0a_story.html?noredirect=on.

26. Walter D. Mignolo, "Decolonizing Western Epistemology/Building Decolonial Epistemologies," in *Decolonizing Epistemologies: Latino/a Theology and Philosophy,* eds. Ada María Isasi-Díaz and Eduardo Mendieta (New York: Fordham University Press, 2011), 27 [19–43]. In *Race: A Theological Account* (New York: Oxford University Press, 2008), J. Kameron Carter outlines how modern and contemporary theological discourse has undergirded the production of the self-disciplining racialized subject, charting how Christian anti-Judaism biologized itself and thus racialized itself, and how this "pseudotheology" has been disseminated throughout Christian theology and practice, in effect making Christianity White. In a similar vein, in *Stand Your Ground: Black Bodies and the Justice of God* (Maryknoll, NY: Orbis Books, 2015), Kelly Brown Douglas carefully, and critically, charts the theological underpinnings of American exceptionalism, deftly demonstrating how "theo-ideologies" around natural law, providence, and sovereignty, were pivotal in the cultural formation of the black body as a guilty body and the development of stand your ground laws.

27. Willie James Jennings, *The Christian Imagination: Theology and the Origins of Race* (New Haven: Yale University Press, 2010), 6.

28. Willie James Jennings, *After Whiteness: An Education in Belonging* (Grand Rapids: Eerdmans, 2020), 79ff. The language of the *kin*dom of God stems from the work of Ada María Isasi-Díaz and has been taken up by a range of theologians who seek to emphasize a redemptive, eschatological vision that connotes family and relationship rather than sovereignty and rulership. See Ada Maria Isasi-Díaz, *La Lucha Continues: Mujerista Theology* (Maryknoll, NY: Orbis Books, 2004), 241–251.

29. Jennings, *The Christian Imagination,* 8. Similar to Goodwin's insight that "while we may be done with religion, religion is not done with us," Jennings challenges the notion that we are living in a post-Christian or post-religious world. These readings, Jennings argues, "are painfully superficial" and "bypass the deeper realities

of Western Christian sensibilities, identities, and habits of mind which continue to channel patterns of colonial dominance" (8).

30. Jennings, *After Whiteness*, 10, 13.

31. Ibid., 106

32. Ibid., 107; 123–124. For Jennings, we are to embrace this educational contradiction because it a microcosm of the contradiction of the Christian story of God's ongoing work in the world, the eschatological enactment and vision of the kindom of God. We "exist inside a revolution, the overturning that is the turning the world right side up by God," he explains. "It is an overturning that makes possible a beautifully strange kind of building up. It is a building up inside of crumbling…We are an overturning that facilitates a building up, but it is a building up that glories in the crumbling" (124).

33. Willie James Jennings, *Acts: A Theological Commentary* (Louisville: Westminster John Knox Press, 2017), 25.

34. Jennings emphasizes the passionate emotional energy of *eros*, the intoxicating and ecstatic desire bound up with erotic power (See the final chapter of *After Whiteness*, "Eros," 135–156). Boler, conversely, emphasizes our more *apophatic* desires, to avoid that which risks our sense of self and safety. "The first sign of the success of a pedagogy of discomfort," she writes, "is, quite simply, the ability to recognize what it is that one doesn't want to know and how one has developed emotional investments to protect oneself from this knowing" (*Feeling Power*, 199).

35. Jennings explains that his "use of the term 'whiteness' does not refer to people of European descent but to a way of being in the world and seeing the world that forms cognitive and affective structures able to seduce people into its habituation and its meaning making" (*After Whiteness*, 8–9). A few pages prior, he writes: "Formation. Formation. Formation. This is the most important word that I will consider in this book" (4). Drawing on both Aristotle and John Dewey, Boler considers the relationship between emotions, our sense of self, and habit, assessing and critiquing what she calls "inscribed habits of (in)attention" (*Feeling Power*, 180). A pedagogy of discomfort, she goes on to note, "invites students to leave the familiar shores of learned beliefs and habits, and swim further out into the 'foreign' and risky depths of the sea of ethical and moral differences" (181).

36. Boler, *Feeling Power*, 109.

37. Jennings, *After Whiteness*, 151.

38. Ibid., 14.

39. Ibid., 13.

40. As a previous student of Dr. Jennings, I can also say with confidence that this is also true of his pedagogy in his classrooms.

41. Boler, *Feeling Power*, 164, 199.

42. Jennings, *After Whiteness*, 8.

43. See Maria do Mar Pereira, "Uncomfortable classrooms: Rethinking the role of student discomfort in feminist teaching," *European Journal of Women's Studies*, vol. 19, no. 1 (2012): 128–135; Kyoko Kishimoto and Mumbi Mwangi, "Critiquing the Rhetoric of 'Safety' in Feminist Pedagogy: Women of Color Offering an Account of Ourselves," *Feminist Teacher*, vol. 19, no. 2 (2009): 87–102.

44. Shelly Rambo, Response to Willie James Jennings' *After Whiteness,*" *Modern Theology* vol. 37, no. 4 (2021): 1001 [997–1005].

45. See Resmaa Menakem, *My Grandmother's Hands: Racialized Trauma and the Pathway to Mending Our Hearts and Bodies* (Las Vegas: Central Recovery Press, 2017). Rambo explains how, while happening to read Menakem's and Jennings' texts alongside one another, she was struck by the connections between them. For more on the somatic turn in trauma theory and therapy, see especially Bessel van der Kolk, *The Body Keeps the Score: Brain, Mind, and the Body in the Healing of Trauma* (New York: Penguin Books, 2015) and Peter A. Levine, *In an Unspoken Voice: How the Body Releases Trauma and Restores Goodness* (Berkeley: North Atlantic Books, 2010).

46. Rambo, Response to Willie James Jennings' *After Whiteness,*" 999.

47. Ibid., 1001.

48. Fintan O'Toole, "'Yeats Test' criteria reveal we are doomed," *The Irish Times*, July 28, 2018, https://www.irishtimes.com/opinion/fintan-o-toole-yeats-test-criteria-reveal-we-are-doomed-1.3576078. See also Dorian Lynskey, "'Things fall apart': the apocalyptic appeal of WB Yeats's The Second Coming," *The Guardian*, May 30, 2020, https://www.theguardian.com/books/2020/may/30/things-fall-apart-the-apocalyptic-appeal-of-wb-yeats-the-second-coming.

49. See Jean M. Twenge, *iGen: Why Today's Super-Connected Kids Are Growing Up Less Rebellious, More Tolerant, Less Happy—and Completely Unprepared for Adulthood (and What That Means for the Rest of Us)* (New York: Atria Books, 2017); Juliana Menasce Horowitz and Nikki Graf, "Most U.S. Teens See Anxiety and Depression as a Major Problem Among Their Peers," Pew Research Center, February 2019, https://www.pewresearch.org/social-trends/2019/02/20/most-u-s-teens-see-anxiety-and-depression-as-a-major-problem-among-their-peers/; Kim Parker and Ruth Igielnik, "On the Cusp of Adulthood and Facing an Uncertain Future: What We Know About Gen Z So Far," Pew Research Center, May 14, 2020, https://www.pewresearch.org/social-trends/2020/05/14/on-the-cusp-of-adulthood-and-facing-an-uncertain-future-what-we-know-about-gen-z-so-far-2/.

50. Not to mention that it appears that many students actually *long for* the intellectual and collective space to wrestle with and move through the discomfort that comes when engaging emotionally difficult topics. When I began working on this chapter, I asked the undergraduate students who are working with me this summer on a research project, Jordan Ducree and Ryn Marcel, what they wished their professors knew or what they wished their professors would do differently—particularly those who both taught religion and had liberative pedagogical aims. They offered a number of suggestions (from wishing their female professors and professors of color would address issues of gender and race in the classroom more, to desiring more collaborative classroom activities, to balancing content and affect in class sessions) but the suggestion that drew the most energy and reflection from both was the desire for their professors to embrace conflict and discomfort. Both offered multiple examples of when professors would quickly move on after a class discussion even began to get emotionally heavy or heated, and they expressed frustration at how these experiences left them feeling unmoored and further isolated rather than relieved or "safe." The

"willingness to embrace conflicts and discomfort," they asserted, is an important part of being a good ally and teacher. Their insightful feedback is what led me to write on this topic, and I am deeply grateful for their time, honesty, and wisdom.

51. Rambo, Response to Willie James Jennings' *After Whiteness,*" 1005.
52. Boler, *Feeling Power*, 196.
53. Ibid.
54. Rambo, Response to Willie James Jennings' *After Whiteness,*" 1005.

FURTHER READINGS

Boler, Megan, ed. *Democratic Dialogue in Education: Troubling Speech, Disturbing Silence.* New York: Peter Lang, 2004.
Foucault, Michel. "For an Ethic of Discomfort." In *Power: Essential Works of Foucault, 1954–1984*, edited by James D. Faubion and translated by Robert Hurley, 443–448. New York: The New Press, 2000.
Goodwin, Megan, and Ilyse Morgenstein Fuerst. *Keeping It 101: A Killjoy's Introduction to Religion.* keepingit101.com.
Jennings, Willie James. *The Christian Imagination: Theology and the Origins of Race.* New Haven: Yale University Press, 2010.
Lorde, Audre. *Sister Outsider: Essays and Speeches.* New York: Crossing Press, 1984.
Rambo, Shelly. *Resurrecting Wounds: Living in the Afterlife of Trauma.* Waco, TX: Baylor University Press, 2017.
Trifonas, Peter Pericles, ed. *Pedagogies of Difference: Rethinking Education for Social Change.* New York: Routledge Falmer, 2003.

REFERENCES

Alfonseca, Kiara. "As Recently Discovered Unmarked Indigenous Graves in Canada Nears 1,000, Activists Demand Justice." *ABC News*, July 3, 2021. https://abcnews.go.com/International/ recently-discovered-unmarked-indigenous-graves-canada-nears-1000/story?id=78472829.
Althaus-Reid, Marcella. *Indecent Theology: Theological Perversions in Sex, Gender, and Politics.* New York: Routledge, 2000.
———. *The Queer God.* New York: Routledge, 2003.
Ballard, Ed. "Terror, Brexit and U.S. Election Have Made 2016 the Year of Yeats." *The Wall Street Journal*, August 23, 2016.
Blanchard, Kathryn D. "Trigger Warnings: Not the Greatest Threat to Higher Education." *The Chronicle of Higher Education*, January 8, 2016. https://www.chronicle.com/article/trigger-warnings-not-the-greatest-threat-to-higher-education/.
Boler, Megan. *Feeling Power: Emotions and Education.* New York: Routledge, 1999.
Boler, Megan, and Michalinos Zembylas. "Discomforting Truths: The Emotional Terrain of Understanding Difference." In *Pedagogies of Difference: Rethinking*

Education for Social Change, edited by Peter Pericles Trifonas, 107–130. New York: Routledge Falmer, 2003.

Bulletin of the Atomic Scientists. "Doomsday Clock." https://thebulletin.org/doomsday-clock/.

Carter, J. Kameron. *Race: A Theological Account.* New York: Oxford University Press, 2008.

Cone, James H. *A Black Theology of Liberation.* Maryknoll, NY: Orbis Books, 2010.

Crary, David, and Elana Schor. "Double Win at Supreme Court Elates Religious Conservatives." *The Washington Post*, July 11, 2020. https://www.washingtonpost.com/national/religion/correction-supreme-court-religious-exemption-story/2020/07/11/4bcff098-c37e-11ea-8908-68a2b9eae9e0_story.html.

Daly, Mary. *The Church and the Second Sex.* Boston: Beacon Press, 1986 [1968].

De Tocqueville, Alexis. *Democracy in America.* Chicago: University of Chicago Press, 2002.

Douglas, Kelly Brown. *Stand Your Ground: Black Bodies and the Justice of God.* Maryknoll, NY: Orbis Books, 2015.

Frostenson, Sarah. "The Women's Marches May Have Been the Largest Demonstration in US History." *Vox*, January 31, 2017. http://www.vox.com/2017/1/22/14350808/womens-marches-largest-demonstration-us-history-map.

Frothingham, Sunny, and Shilpa Phadke. "100 Days, 100 Ways the Trump Administration is Harming Women and Families." *Center for American Progress*, April 25, 2017. https://www.americanprogress.org/issues/women/ reports/2017/04/25/430969/100-days-100-ways-trump-administration-harming-women-families/.

Gitlin, Todd. "You Are Here to Be Disturbed." *The Chronicle of Higher Education*, May 11, 2015. https://www.chronicle.com/article/you-are-here-to-be-disturbed/.

Goodwin, Megan. "The University of Vermont Might Be Done With Religion, But Religion Isn't Done With Us." *Religion Dispatches*, December 7, 2020. https://religiondispatches.org/the-university-of-vermont-might-be-done-with-religion-but-religion-isnt-done-with-us/.

Goodwin, Megan, and Ilyse Morgenstein Fuerst. "Episode 106: You May Be Done With Religion, But Religion Isn't Done With You." *Keeping it 101: A Killjoy's Introduction to Religion*, March 23, 2020. https://keepingit101.com/e106.

Horowitz, Juliana Menasce, and Nikki Graf. "Most U.S. Teens See Anxiety and Depression as a Major Problem Among Their Peers." *Pew Research Center*, February 2019. https://www.pewresearch.org/social-trends/2019/02/20/most-u-s-teens-see-anxiety-and-depression-as-a-major-problem-among-their-peers/.

Isasi-Díaz, Ada Maria. *La Lucha Continues: Mujerista Theology.* Maryknoll, NY: Orbis Books, 2004.

Jennings, Willie James. *Acts: A Theological Commentary.* Louisville: Westminster John Knox Press, 2017.

———. *After Whiteness: An Education in Belonging.* Grand Rapids: Eerdmans, 2020.

———. *The Christian Imagination: Theology and the Origins of Race.* New Haven: Yale University Press, 2010.

Kishimoto, Kyoko, and Mumbi Mwangi. "Critiquing the Rhetoric of 'Safety' in Feminist Pedagogy: Women of Color Offering an Account of Ourselves." *Feminist Teacher* 19, no. 2 (2009): 87–102.

Kurtzleben, Danielle. "Feminists Weigh Their Wins and Losses After Nearly Four Years of Trump." *NPR*, October 16, 2020. https://www.npr.org/2020/10/16/924167976/feminists-weigh-their-wins-and-losses-after-nearly-four-years-of-trump.

Levine, Peter A. *In an Unspoken Voice: How the Body Releases Trauma and Restores Goodness*. Berkeley: North Atlantic Books, 2010.

Liptak, Adam. "Supreme Court Backs Catholic Agency in Case on Gay Rights and Foster Care." *The New York Times*, June 17, 2021. https://www.nytimes.com/2021/06/17/us/supreme-court-gay-rights-foster-care.html.

Lynskey, Dorian. "'Things Fall Apart': The Apocalyptic Appeal of WB Yeats's the Second Coming." *The Guardian*, May 30, 2020. https://www.theguardian.com/books/2020/may/30/ things-fall-apart-the-apocalyptic-appeal-of-wb-yeats-the-second-coming.

Manne, Kate. "Why I Use Trigger Warnings." *The New York Times*, September 19, 2015. https://www.nytimes.com/2015/09/20/opinion/sunday/why-i-use-trigger-warnings.html.

Menakem, Resmaa. *My Grandmother's Hands: Racialized Trauma and the Pathway to Mending Our Hearts and Bodies*. Las Vegas: Central Recovery Press, 2017.

Mignolo, Walter D. "Decolonizing Western Epistemology/Building Decolonial Epistemologies." In *Decolonizing Epistemologies: Latino/a Theology and Philosophy*, edited by Ada María Isasi-Díaz and Eduardo Mendieta, 19–43. New York: Fordham University Press, 2011.

Mogelson, Luke. "A Reporter's Video from Inside the Capitol Siege." *The New Yorker*, January 16, 2021. https://www.newyorker.com/video/watch/a-reporters-footage-from-inside-the-capitol-siege.

O'Toole, Fintan. "'Yeats Test' Criteria Reveal We Are Doomed." *The Irish Times*, July 28, 2018. https://www.irishtimes.com/opinion/fintan-o-toole-yeats-test-criteria-reveal-we-are-doomed-1.3576078.

Outka, Elizabeth. *Viral Modernism: The Influenza Pandemic and Interwar Literature*. New York: Columbia University Press, 2019.

Parker, Kim, and Ruth Igielnik. "On the Cusp of Adulthood and Facing an Uncertain Future: What We Know About Gen Z So Far." *Pew Research Center*, May 14, 2020. https://www.pewresearch.org/social-trends/2020/05/14/on-the-cusp-of-adulthood-and-facing-an-uncertain-future-what-we-know-about-gen-z-so-far-2/.

Pereira, Maria do Mar. "Uncomfortable Classrooms: Rethinking the Role of Student Discomfort in Feminist Teaching." *European Journal of Women's Studies* 19, no. 1 (2012): 128–135.

Pew Research Center. "In U.S., Decline of Christianity Continues at Rapid Pace." October 17, 2019. https://www.pewforum.org/2019/10/17/in-u-s-decline-of-christianity-continues-at-rapid-pace/.

Public Religion Research Institute. "Faith-Based Approaches Can Positively Impact COVID-19 Vaccination Efforts: Religious Identities and the Race Against the

Virus." *PRRI-IFYC*, April 22, 2021. www.prri.org/research/prri-ifyc-covid-vaccine-religion-report/.

Rambo, Shelly. "Response to Willie James Jennings' *After Whiteness.*" *Modern Theology* 37, no. 4 (2021): 997–1005.

Smith, Harrison. "James H. Cone, Founder of Black Liberation Theology, Dies at 79." *Washington Post*, April 30, 2018. https://www.washingtonpost.com/local/obituaries/james-h-cone-founder-of-black-liberation-theology-dies-at-79/2018/04/30/94b5efc8-4c80-11e8-84a0-458a1aa9ac0a_story.html?noredirect=on.

The Sopranos. "The Second Coming." *HBO*, May 20, 2007.

Tonstad, Linn Marie. *Queer Theology: Beyond Apologetics*. Eugene, OR: Cascade Books, 2018.

Twenge, Jean M. *iGen: Why Today's Super-Connected Kids Are Growing Up Less Rebellious, More Tolerant, Less Happy—And Completely Unprepared for Adulthood (And What That Means for the Rest of Us)*. New York: Atria Books, 2017.

Van der Kolk, Bessel. *The Body Keeps the Score: Brain, Mind, and the Body in the Healing of Trauma*. New York: Penguin Books, 2015.

Warner, John. "I Want to Make Students Uncomfortable." *Inside Higher Ed*, August 21, 2016. https://www.insidehighered.com/blogs/just-visiting/i-want-make-students-uncomfortable.

Index

African American, ix, xv, xvii, xx, xxi, 17–19; community, 22; life experiences, 201; philosophy, 23, 25, 200; political activist, 198; tradition, 181; worldview, 186
amendment, nineteenth, ix–xxi, 3, 9, 11, 107–8, 197–98, 205
anthropology, 87, 91, 95, 96, 98, 99, 130, 133–35, 156, 157; ecological, 158, 159; inclusive, 186–88; of independence, 137, 138; of surplus, 185; theological, 141–44, 162, 176, 184, 231, 233

church, 21, 61, 62, 64, 65, 67, 99, 107–12, 115, 131–33, 146, 239; African American, 25, 53; Black, 186, 201, 211, 216, 307; of Corinth, xii; documents, xv, 56; officials, 54, 55, 58, 60; Roman Catholic, ix, x–xii, xvi, xxi, 57, 68, 69, 73, 74, 308
constitution, 5, 237; constitutional right, xx; divine, 66; of the human person, 189; of the United States, ix, 3, 34, 202

discrimination, 7, 19–20, 22, 35, 45, 47, 59, 63, 64, 71, 72, 93, 132, 135, 138, 206, 239, 308; culture of, 94; forms of, 146; racial, 139, 140

family, xiii, 5, 25–27, 35, 64, 89, 93, 94, 96, 122, 131, 132, 135, 136, 138, 163, 164, 177, 205, 218, 220, 239, 256, 269, 304, 305
freedom, xviii, 7, 17, 21, 22, 86, 108, 118, 166, 179, 180, 182, 185, 186, 198, 201, 204, 205, 214, 218, 219, 224, 237–38, 240, 266, 314; political, 3, 4, 6, 11, 12; spirituality, 212

gender, xii, xiii, xvi, xvii, xviii, 7–11, 17, 20, 21, 26, 34–36, 38, 40, 41, 44, 46, 54, 55, 57–59, 61, 62, 66, 72, 74, 91–96, 98, 99, 108, 110–12, 119, 120, 123, 124, 129, 131, 133, 135–40, 144, 146, 166, 167, 178, 185, 186, 202–5, 207, 221, 223, 232, 239, 247, 252, 254, 265, 267, 268, 271, 279–89, 292, 304–7, 309–11, 313, 314
god, x, xvi, 17, 21, 22, 54–56, 58, 61, 63–65, 74, 92, 95, 96, 99, 107, 110, 115, 119, 120, 122, 124, 129–32, 134–37, 140, 141, 143–45, 155, 160, 162, 176, 185, 187, 201, 205, 207, 212, 214–19, 235, 308, 310; god-human, xi; image, 133, 142, 177, 189–91, 198, 233–34; likeness of, 97; word of, 66, 67, 188

325

intersectionality, x, 19–21, 36, 113, 185, 247

LGBTQIA+, ix, xiv, 180, 185, 251, 279, 308

patriarchy, x, xiv, xvi, xx, 42, 92–94, 117, 119, 135, 136, 138, 145, 166, 176, 177, 181–83, 238, 240, 254, 280, 283, 287, 309

power, 4, 6, 10, 18, 21, 22, 36, 37, 54, 55, 57, 59, 62, 67, 71, 72, 74, 86, 92, 94–96, 98, 116, 131, 135–38, 141, 143, 156, 165, 184, 188, 190, 199, 200, 203, 204, 206, 207, 211, 216–20, 223, 254, 255, 259, 263, 265, 268–70, 279, 280, 286, 289, 291, 293, 307, 309, 311; hegemonic, xv, 55, 67, 74

racism, 4, 5, 8, 9, 21–23, 111, 112, 115, 117, 130, 139–41, 156, 167, 219, 221, 249, 253, 309, 311; antiblack, xvii, 206; antimigrant, 39, 40; effects of, xvi; gender, 131–32; and sexism, 19, 145; systemic, 7, 254

rights, ix, xii, xvii, xviii, 7, 11, 18, 19, 23, 25, 34, 38, 42, 45, 107–9, 116, 139, 140, 146, 165, 179, 187, 197–99, 201–3, 206, 207, 211, 212, 218, 220, 231, 232, 236, 238, 240, 248, 266, 279, 305; civil, 3–5, 10, 205, 221–24; migrant, 35; political, 6; theology of women's, 233–38; voting, 5, 11, 23, 109, 197, 198, 203, 205, 207, 223, 224; women's, xiv–xv, xx, 8, 9, 33, 35, 37, 46, 204, 280, 304

sexism, 9, 19–21, 42, 62, 71, 115, 117, 138–44, 190, 199, 206, 247, 253, 283, 309

solidarity, xii, xiv, 34, 94, 198, 206

spirituality, xviii, 21, 22, 24, 115, 118, 166, 189, 191, 199, 212–20, 222–24, 247, 249, 251–52

struggle, ix, xiv, xviii, 6–7, 9, 11, 33–35, 37–39, 41, 43, 45–47, 74, 78, 92, 107, 168, 177, 180, 197, 199, 201–2, 206, 212–13, 217–18, 220, 223; for liberation, xii, xiii

United States of America, ix, xiv, xv, xvii, xx, 3; A brief critique of, xii

women, x–xii, 18, 53–57, 60, 92, 98–99, 107–11, 122, 129, 131–33, 135–40, 142–46, 155, 166; African, 177, 181–85, 187, 190; African American, 19, 178, 180, 199, 204; Asian American, 3; biblical, 285, 291–92; black, ix, xiii, xviii, 4–7, 11, 175, 205, 207, 213, 218–20, 238; catholic, 58, 64; club, 20, 22–27; of color, xv, 3; exclusion of, xx, 62; experiences of, xvii; importance of, 159; indigenous, 165; liberation, xiv; Muslim, 33–39, 41–42; National association of colored, 10, 17; Native American, xvi; ordained, 61, 67, 116; subordination of, 232; voices of, 188; voting rights of, 198; white, 8, 206, 284, 304

About the Contributors

Christin Lee Hancock, PhD, is a professor of history at the University of Portland in Portland, Oregon where she also serves as a member of the Gender, Women, and Sexuality Studies Advisory Board. She received her PhD in American Studies from Brown University in 2006. At the University of Portland, she teaches courses on the history of gender, race, mental illness, food, and social movements in the modern United States. Her scholarship explores the interconnections of health and health care with gender and race in the twentieth century. Her published work on women's and gender history has appeared in several journals including the *Journal of Women's History*. In 2016, she served as guest editor for a special issue of the *Oregon Historical Quarterly* titled "Regulating Birth." She is currently writing a book that uses a Disability Studies framework to explore constructions of gender and race through a social history of the experimental malaria treatment of neurosyphilis at a state mental institution in Indianapolis, Indiana 1924–1949.

Anita R. Gooding is a licensed clinical social worker who received a B.A. in women, gender, and sexuality from Trinity College, an M.S.W. from the University of Pennsylvania, and PhD in social work and social research from Portland State University. She also holds a certificate in gender, race, and nations from Portland State University. Dr. Gooding teaches social work practice courses including Human Behavior and the Social Environment, Introduction to Social Work and Social Justice, and Theory and Methods of Social Work Practice. Her own practice experience spans micro and macro levels of practice and includes community outreach and organizing, development, and marketing, treatment education for persons living with HIV/AIDS, outpatient therapy for LGBTQIA-identified persons, and service as a B.S.W. Field Director. Dr. Gooding's research centers on the subjugated knowledges of historically marginalized groups; race and social work practice, including use of self; and equity and inclusion within social work education. Some of her peer-reviewed pieces have been published in the *Journal of Social Work Education, Advances in Social Work Education*, and the *Encyclopedia of Social Work*.

Lara-Zuzan Golesorkhi, PhD, is an assistant professor of political science and global affairs, and the co-firector of the Gender, Women, and Sexuality Studies Program at the University of Portland (USA). Her work is concerned with issues that pertain to the intersection of migration and gender in a global context. Golesorkhi's scholarship examines how gender dynamics configure into migration experiences in origin-, transit-, and destination countries, and how these experiences are informed by structural factors. Her latest publications include: "Protection by whom, for whom? Muslim refugee women face a contested European identity" in *Studies in Ethnicity and Nationalism* and "Immobilities, Mental Health, and Livelihoods—Perspectives from the Field" in *Refugee Review*. Golesorkhi received the American Political Science Association Diversity and Inclusion Advanced Research Grant for Early Career Scholars for her book manuscript, *Integration and Anti-Discrimination at Crossroads*: *Muslim Refugee Women in the German Labor Market*. Golesorkhi is also the Founder, Executive Director, and Advocacy Director at the Center for Migration, Gender, and Justice (CMGJ). CMGJ is a nonprofit NGO that addresses migrant rights and gender justice through education, research, and advocacy. In her various capacities at CMGJ, Golesorkhi has contributed to the organization's vision of gender justice beyond borders by shrinking spaces between migrant communities and governing bodies across institutional levels, notably in directing the Migrant Youth Leadership Program. Based on her contributions as a migrant rights and gender justice advocate, Golesorkhi was nominated for the American Political Science Association Distinguished Award for Civic and Community Engagement.

Carol J. Dempsey, OP, PhD, is a professor of theology (biblical studies) at the University of Portland, OR, USA. Her research focuses on Prophets, biblical hermeneutics, especially feminist hermeneutics, literary and cultural methodologies, gender studies, ecofeminism, biblical ethics, and biblical theology. Author and editor of eighteen books, her latest works include "The Bible and Justice" and "Isaiah 56-66" for the *Jerome Biblical Commentary for the 21st Century* (2022); "Dominican Women Afire: Global Leaders and Trailblazers, Past and Present," *Religious Leadership of Women in Conflict and Crisis*; *Journal of the European Society of Women in Theological Research* (2021); "Understanding Hagar through the Eyes of Race and Ethnicity," *Journal of Feminist Studies in Religion* (2021); "Catholic Androcentric Bible Translations as Global Missionary Tools?" *The Oxford*

Handbook of Feminist Approaches to the Hebrew Bible (ed. Susanne Scholz; Oxford University Press, 2021); "Isaiah in Liberation Theology," *The Oxford Handbook on Isaiah* (ed. Lena Tiemeyer, Oxford University Press, 2021); and "Metaphor and the Minor Prophets," *The Oxford Handbook of Minor Prophets* (ed. Julia O'Brien, 2021). She is currently working on three contracted book manuscripts: *Isaiah* (Wisdom Commentary Series; Liturgical Press); *Beyond Christian Anthropocentrism: What It Means to Be Catholic in the New Diaspora*; under contract with Lexington Press for the New Diaspora Series); and *Responding to Climate Crisis: Hope at the Margins* with Norah Martin (Lexington Press for the New Diaspora Series). Carol serves on editorial boards for the Wisdom Commentary Series, the *Catholic Biblical Quarterly*, *Old Testament Abstracts*, and *The Paulist Biblical Commentary*.

Christina Astorga is professor and former chair of the Department of Theology, University of Portland. Prior to assuming this position, Astorga worked at other universities. She was the former chair of the Theology Department of the Ateneo de Manila—Loyola Schools (1994–2003) and was the Founding Director of the Center for the Study of Catholic Social Thought of Duquesne University (2007–2011). She has held fellowships at the Jesuit Institute, Boston College (2003–2004); Woodstock Theological Center, Georgetown University (2004–2005); and visiting scholarship at Fordham University (2011–2014) and (Fall, 2022). She was a Visiting Professor at Canisius College (2006–2007); University of San Diego (2005–2006); and Gonzaga University (2013–2014). She has taught in the areas of theological ethics (fundamental moral theology); theological bioethics; sexual ethics; feminist/gender ethics; and environmental/ecological justice. Astorga is well published. Her book, *Catholic Moral Theology and Social Ethics: A New Method*, won the Best Book Award by the College Theology Society (2014), and third place for the Book Award by the Catholic Press Association of America and Canada (2015). Her first book, *The Beast, the Harlot, and the Lamb: When Faith Confronts Systemic Evil*, won the National Book Award by the Manila Critics Circle in the Philippines. Astorga is working on a new book, *Postcolonial Feminism: Lifting the Veil of Asian Gender Resistance*. Her works have been published in prestigious publishing houses and high-impact journals like *Theological Studies*; *Horizons*; *Concilium*; *Journal of Society of Christian Ethics*; *Asian Horizons*; *Proceedings of the Catholic Theological Society of America*; and *College Theology Society*.

Valerie D. Lewis-Mosley, RN, DMin, MAPM, MSJ, is a professional registered nurse with a BSN (Boston College), and Graduate Studies in Nursing Leadership (New York University). She is retired from New York Hospital-Weill Cornell University Medical Center-Womens' and Children's Health. She has a Health Law Degree Master of Jurisprudence (Seton Hall University Law School—magna cum laude) and a Master of Arts Pastoral Ministry—Spiritual Direction—Christian Spirituality (Immaculate Conception Seminary School of Theology Seton Hall University—summa cum laude), and a D.Min. in Healing Mind Body Spirit (Drew University Theological School). Lewis-Mosley is a Master Catechist with certification from the Institute for Black Catholic Studies at the Xavier University of Louisiana and doctrinal certification from the Archdiocese of Newark. She is an evangelist that utilizes narrative storytelling to empower and lead others to conversion and a Lay Associate Order of Preachers—Caldwell Dominicans. Lewis-Mosley uses her Dominican Spirituality and Jesuit roots to facilitate her work as a Social Justice Advocate, to combat racism, and disparities in health care access, within society and the Church. She is an adjunct professor of theology at Caldwell University and Xavier University of Louisiana/Institute for Black Catholic Studies. She is also a member of the Black Catholic Theological Symposium and an Aquinas Institute of Theology Delaplane Preaching Scholar. Lewis-Mosley is on the Advisory Board for Black Catholic Ministries at the Archdiocese of Newark and the historian at Christ the King Church, Jersey City; a historically Black Catholic parish.

Anthonia Bolanle Ojo, SSMA, PhD, is a member of the Congregation of the Sisters of St. Michael the Archangel, a diocesan female religious Congregation in Nigeria. Ojo has a BA in theology from the Catholic Institute of West Africa (CIWA), Port Harcourt, Nigeria, (an affiliate of the University of Calabar), and MA and Ph.D. in moral theology with a focus in Social Ethics also from the same Institute. Ojo did a postdoc at Boston College, Massachusetts, USA. She is a member of the global network of Catholic Theological Ethics in the World Church (CTEWC). She was a formator and also served as the Academic Dean and lecturer of moral theology at Good Shepherd Major Seminary (Nigeria). She has engaged in many women and youth empowerment programs within the Church in Nigeria. She is currently the Vicar General of the Congregation of the Sisters of St. Michael the Archangel. Ojo's works have been published in high-impact scholarly journals nationally and internationally.

Lisa Ann Dellinger currently teaches as the Tinker Visiting Professor at Iliff School of Theology, Denver, Colorado. She is also the visiting assistant professor of constructive theologies as a Louisville Institute Postdoctoral Fellow at Phillips Theological Seminary, Tulsa, Oklahoma. She received her PhD in the Theology, Ethics, and History program from Garrett Evangelical Theological Seminary in 2020. Dr. Dellinger also obtained an MDiv from Phillips Theological Seminary in 2008. She served as a local pastor in the Oklahoma Indian Missionary Conference of the United Methodist Church. She is a citizen of the Chickasaw Nation and Mexican American.

SimonMary Asese A. Aihiokhai, PhD, is associate professor of systematic theology at the University of Portland (Portland, Oregon), and a fellow at the Westar Institute. He is on the editorial board of the journal, *Springer Nature* (*SN*): *Social* Sciences. He is the book editor of *Friday Focus*, a weekly book review initiative of the Pan-African Catholic Theology and Pastoral Network (PACTPAN); and the chair of the research unit on LGBTQIA+ realities in Africa for the Pan-African Catholic Theology and Pastoral Network (PACTPAN). He has worked extensively with communities at the margins in Nigeria and in the United States. As a product of multiple contexts, he is intentional at creating spaces for multiple perspectives in his research and teaching. His research focuses on religion, race, and identity constructions; African approaches to ethics; African philosophies, cultures, and theologies; religion and violence; comparative theology; themes in systematic theology; and interfaith studies. He is the co-editor of *Dimensions in Post-Secondary School Christian Religious Studies Curriculum in Nigeria* (2016). He has published over forty-five peer-reviewed essays. He has given over eighty scholarly papers at prestigious institutions and learned societies nationally and internationally on several topics ranging from social imaginations, decolonial approaches to identity construction, sociological approaches to understanding interfaith encounters and deconstruction of structures of marginalization, and many more. His recent work is *Fostering Interreligious Encounters in Pluralist Societies. Hospitality and Friendship* (2019). Dr. Aihiokhai's works have been published by Routledge, Palgrave Macmillan, Paulines Press (Africa), Oxford University Press, Cambridge Scholars Press, and several peer-reviewed national and international journals.

Kathleen Dorsey Bellow is a pastoral theologian who writes, consults, and presents on several aspects of Catholic ministry, including worship, evangelization, and faith formation. She currently serves as director of the Institute for Black Catholic Studies at Xavier University of Louisiana. She teaches in the Xavier Theology Department and holds the Drexel Society Endowed Professorship in Black Catholic Studies. Bellow earned the MBA from McNeese State University (Lake Charles), the ThM from Xavier University (New Orleans), and the Doctor of Ministry Degree in Liturgical Studies from Catholic Theological Union (Chicago).

C. Vanessa White, DMin, is an associate professor of Spirituality and Ministry at Catholic Theological Union in Chicago and associate director of the Master of Theology program at Xavier University of Louisiana's Summer Institute for Black Catholic Studies, the only historically Black and Catholic institution of higher education. Her articles and essays have appeared in *New Theology Review*, *U.S. Catho*lic, *The Bible Today*, *AMERICA*, *National Catholic*

Reporter, The Pastoral Musician, and CNN.org. She is co-editor of the book, *Songs of Our Hearts and Meditations of Our Souls: Prayers for Black Catholics* (St. Anthony Messenger Press, 2006); is a contributor to the Feminist Wisdom Bible Commentary (Liturgical Press, 2020); and has recently published a chapter on Black Spirituality entitled "GONNA MOVE WHEN THE SPIRIT SAY MOVE: A Black Spirituality of Resistance and Resilience" for the book the *Black Catholic Studies Reader* (Catholic University Press, 2021). She is an advisor for the Fetzer Institute's *Study of Spirituality in the Americas* published in 2020; a member of the American Academy of Religion; the Catholic Theological Society of America; the Society for the Study of Christian Spirituality; and the National Black Storytellers Association. Dr. White is the former convener/president of the Black Catholic Theological Symposium. She considers herself a womanist practical theologian whose research and teaching are focused on the intersections of spirituality and praxis/action and is attentive to issues pertinent to the life of Black Catholics.

Okechukwu Camillus Njoku received his PhD in systematic theology from Duquesne University, Pittsburgh, Pennsylvania where he also taught as an adjunct professor from 2017 to 2019. He is currently with Loyola University Chicago. He has published a number of articles in peer-reviewed journals, book chapters, and book reviews including "Translating the Divine in the Encounter of the Gospel and Cultures: A Pneumatological Perspective," in *Translating Religion*, ed. Mary Doak and Anita Houck (Orbis Books, 2013); co-authored "Widowhood Practices and Impacts on Women in Sub-Saharan Africa: An Empowerment Perspective," *International Social Work Sage Journal* (April 2017); and reviewed *Christianity, the Papacy, and Mission in Africa* (Orbis Books, 2012) by Richard Gray, ed. Lamin Sanneh, *Horizons* 40, 2 (December 2013). He has also presented at various conferences including "Sustainability: Recovering the Spirit in the Era of Ecoracism" (Annual Conference of Catholic Theology Society of America, CTSA 2019); "Ecofeminism and Dualism: Recovering the Spirit of Igbo Interconnectedness for Ecological Sustainability" (ISA 2019); and "Anti-Black Racism and Socio-Politics of Work: A Theologico-Decolonial Perspective" (CTSA 2021). Currently, he is working on an empirical study that explores the "Role of Religion in Illness Meaning and Coping among Sub-Saharan African Christian Immigrants (SSACIs) in the United States." He is equally working on another project that explores "Climate Change and Sustainability of Community Development Projects in Africa" (and in Nigeria in particular). His research interest areas include trinitarian theology, theological anthropology, decolonial/postcolonial theologies, inculturation, world theology, interreligious dialogue, race/ethnicity, gender, ecology, African philosophy, and sociology of knowledge.

Sarina Saturn (née Rodrigues) is an experienced neuroscientist, educator, researcher, mentor, and community builder devoted to equity, social justice, and belonging for those who belong to nondominant identities, including women and Queer, Transgender, Black, Indigenous, and People of Color (QTBIPOC). She is a bicultural (CHamoru and Indian) scholar-activist, grant recipient, and award winner whose expertise centers on the roots and development of compassion, intersectional advocacy, antiracism, and the neuropsychology and somatic manifestations underlying emotions, intergenerational and lifespan trauma, post-traumatic growth, resilience, coping, and healing. Sarina has served as faculty at both large state and small liberal arts universities, including Oregon State University and the University of Portland. Her post-academic career focuses on using trauma-informed practices, self-reflection, and cultural humility to improve the health and wellness of local QTBIPOC populations experiencing inequities and marginalization. Sarina also serves as editor for the ADVANCE Journal for Individual and Institutional Transformation for Social Justice. During time away from work, she enjoys spending time with family and friends, traveling, cooking, dining, dancing, and enjoying nature's beauty.

Dawn Michele Whitehead, PhD, is the vice president of the Office of Global Citizenship for Campus, Community, and Careers at the American Association of Colleges and Universities (AAC&U). Whitehead has written and presented nationally and internationally on global learning, community-based learning, experiential learning, and civic engagement. She is also the director of AAC&U's Institute on Engaged and Integrative Learning and co-director of the Institute on Interfaith Excellence. She is the co-editor of *Teaching Civic Engagement Globally* and *Interfaith Cooperation for Our Times*. Whitehead was named an inaugural member of the Institute for International Education's National Academy for International Education in 2021. She serves on the board of The Forum on Education Abroad and as a National Field Leader for the Bonner Foundation's Community-Engaged Learning and Pipeline Professional Development Initiatives. Whitehead earned her PhD from Indiana University, Bloomington in Education Policy Studies with a doctoral minor in International and Comparative Education and a concentration in African Studies.

Susanne Scholz, PhD, is a professor of Old Testament at Perkins School of Theology/Southern Methodist University (SMU) in Dallas, Texas, USA. Her research focuses on feminist biblical hermeneutics, the epistemologies, and sociologies of biblical interpretation, cultural and literary methodologies, biblical historiography and translation theories, interfaith and interreligious dialogue, as well as general issues related to women, gender, and sexuality studies in religion. She teaches regularly a graduate-level course on "Queer Bible Hermeneutics" with a student-driven blog site at https://blog.smu.edu/ot8317/. Among her fourteen books and over sixty essays and journal articles are, *The Oxford Handbook on Feminist Approaches to the Hebrew Bible* (editor; Oxford University Press, 2021); *The New Diaspora and the Global Prophetic: Engaging the Scholarship of Marc H. Ellis* (co-editor; Lexington Books/Fortress Academic, 2021); *The Bible as Political Artifact: On the Feminist Study of the Hebrew Bible* (Fortress Press, 2017); *Introducing the Women's Hebrew Bible: Feminism, Gender Justice, and the Study of the Old Testament* (second rev. and exp. edn; T&T Clark Bloomsbury, 2017); *Feminist Interpretation of the Hebrew Bible in Retrospect* (*Volumes 1- 3*) (editor; Sheffield Phoenix Press, 2013, 2014, 2016); *La Violencia and the Hebrew Bible: Politics and Histories of Biblical Hermeneutics on the American Continent* (co-editor; SBL Press, 2016); and *Hidden Truths from Eden: Esoteric Readings of Genesis 1-3* (Co-editor; SBL Press, 2014. She is the editor of the book series *Feminist Studies and Sacred Texts* (Lexington Books), and the co-editor of the book series *Dispatches from the New Diaspora* (Lexington Books Fortress Academic).

Brandy Daniels is an assistant professor of theology and of gender, women's, and sexuality studies at the University of Portland. Prior to coming to UP, Daniels served as a postdoctoral fellow in Religion and Its Publics at the University of Virginia. Her scholarship stands at the intersections of constructive and political theologies, social ethics, and feminist and queer theories. Brandy has published on topics ranging from Bonhoeffer and Foucault on racial identity, to poststructuralism and liberation theology, to Eastern Orthodox apophatic theology, and to Lacanian psychoanalytic theory. She is currently working on her first monograph, *How (Not) to Be Christian*, which explores the ways in which accounts and practices of formation in modern Christianity, particularly within feminist theologies, impact gender and sexual difference. Brandy serves as the co-chair of the Queer Studies in Religion unit of the American Academy of Religion, as co-chair of the LGBTQ working group and the Women's Caucus of the Society of Christian Ethics, and as a part of the executive committee of the Political Theology Network. She serves as the book reviews editor for *Theology and Sexuality* and on the editorial board of the *Journal of the Society of Christian Ethics*. Daniels is an ordained minister with the Christian Church (Disciples of Christ) and is a part of the Portland Interfaith Clergy Resistance. Daniels is an avid slow runner and a novice beer brewer and is the proud human companion to a delightful and especially tiny mutt, Karly Barx.

www.ingramcontent.com/pod-product-compliance
Lightning Source LLC
Chambersburg PA
CBHW021340300426
44114CB00012B/1024